The First Dance of Freedom

ALSO BY MARTIN MEREDITH

The Past is Another Country:
Rhodesia—UDI to Zimbabwe

The First Dance of Freedom

★

BLACK AFRICA IN THE POSTWAR ERA

★

MARTIN MEREDITH

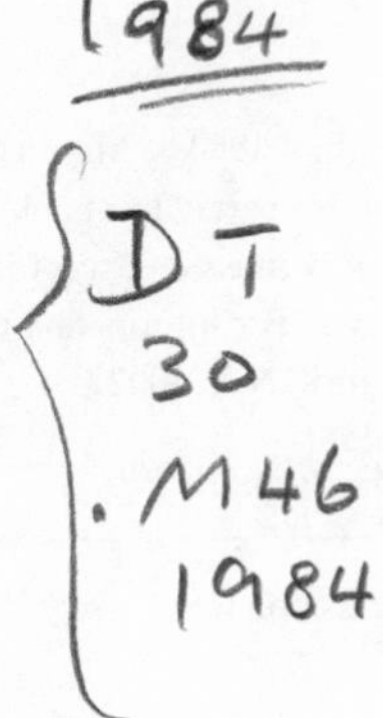

1817

HARPER & ROW, PUBLISHERS,
New York, Cambridge, Philadelphia, San Francisco
London, Mexico City, São Paulo, Singapore, Sydney

 For information address Harper & Row, Publishers, Inc., 10 East 53rd Street, New York, N.Y. 10022.

FIRST U.S. EDITION

Library of Congress Cataloging in Publication Data

Meredith, Martin.
The first dance of freedom.
Bibliography: p.
Includes index.
1. Africa—Politics and government—1945–1960.
2. Africa—Politics and government—1960–
3. Nationalism—Africa—History—20th century.
4. National liberation movements—Africa. I. Title.
DT30.M46 1984 960′.32 84-48181
ISBN 0-06-435658-2
ISBN 0-06-430150-8 (pbk.)

---

85 86 87 88 89 10 9 8 7 6 5 4 3 2 1

For J

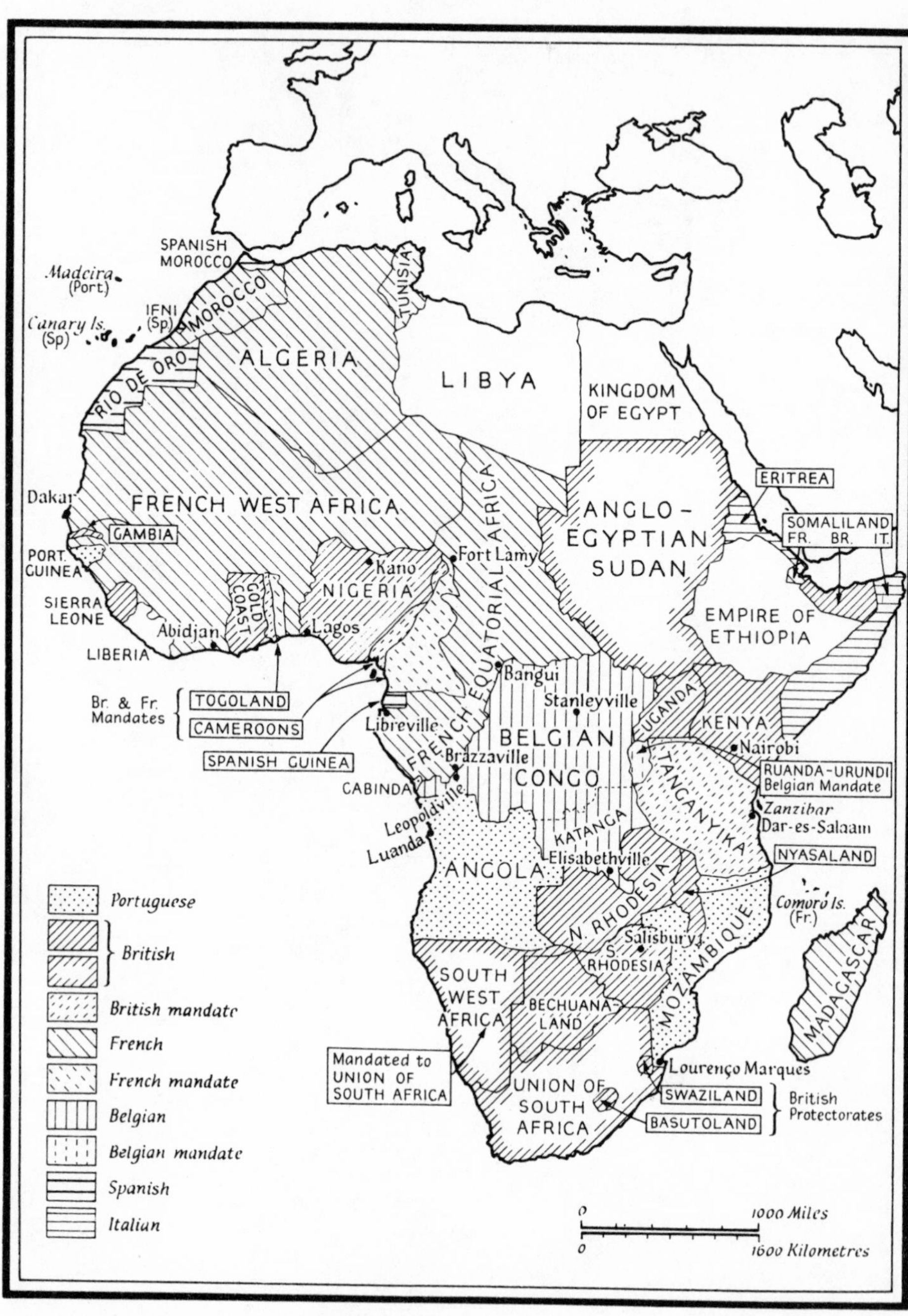

Colonial Africa, 1940s

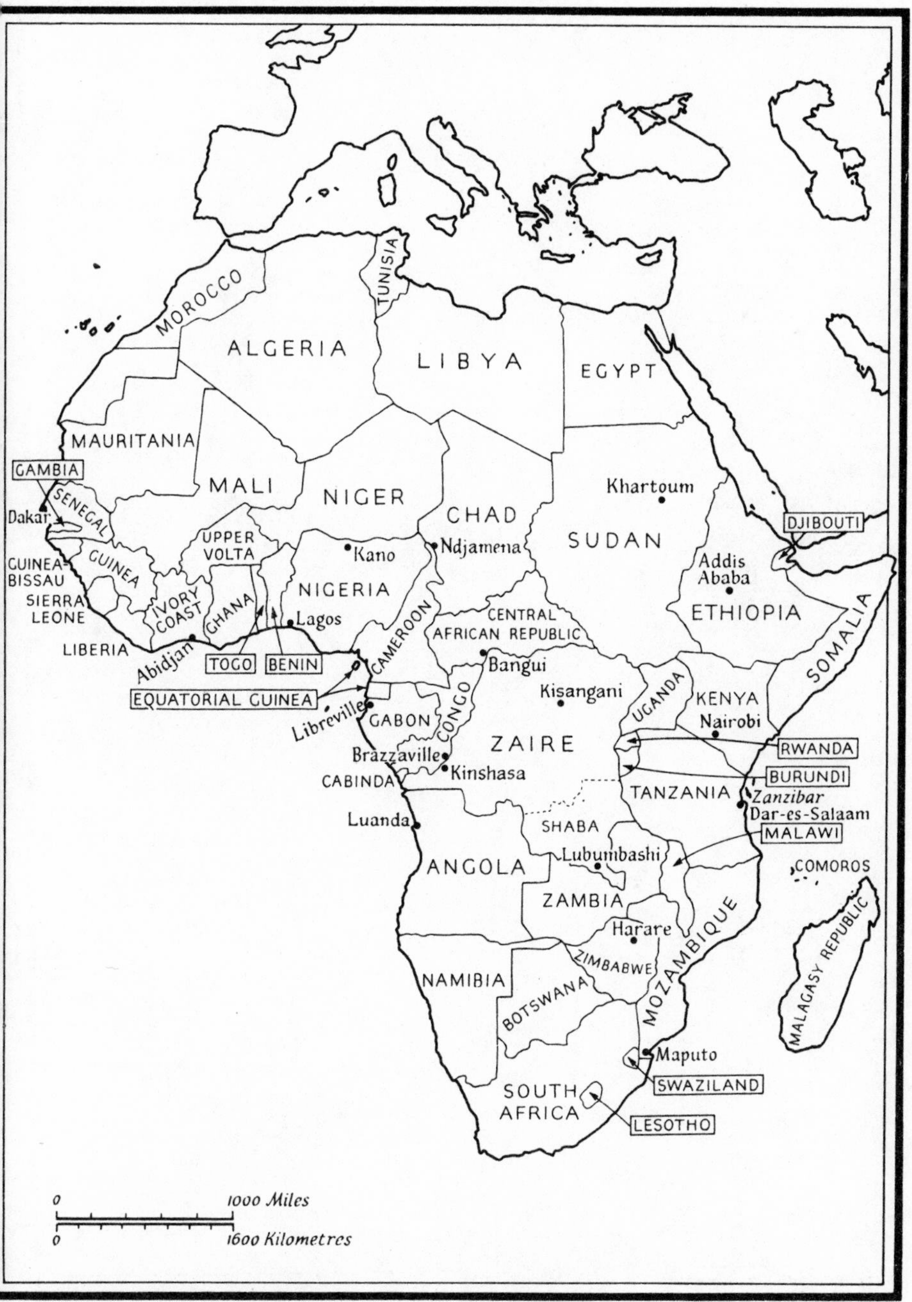

Independent Africa, 1980s

Contents

Acknowledgements

In the years that I spent living and working in Africa as a foreign correspondent, I met with much generosity and goodwill. Many people on many occasions gave me valued help and assistance. To list them here would cover too many pages. But for the innumerable acts of kindness, of hospitality and of friendship I received, I am profoundly grateful. In the writing of this book I owe some special debts of gratitude: to Piers Burnett, for his early encouragement of the project; to Raymond Carr, Warden of St. Antony's College, Oxford, and to other colleagues there; to Robert Townsend, librarian at the Institute of Commonwealth Studies, Oxford; and, above all, to Alistair Horne and to Renira Horne for their great generosity.

M. M.

I sometimes wish I was the Owner of Africa; to do at once, what Wilberforce will do in time, viz—sweep Slavery from her desarts, and look on upon the first dance of their Freedom

Lord Byron, *Detached Thoughts*, 1821–2

Author's Introduction

The fortunes of Africa in the past forty years have changed dramatically. At the end of the Second World War, Africa was largely the preserve of four European powers—Britain, France, Belgium and Portugal. No serious challenge to their rule then existed. It was generally assumed at the time that Africa would remain under European control for the foreseeable future. Britain, the only colonial power even to contemplate the possibility of self-government for its African territories, nevertheless expected to hold sway there at least until the end of the twentieth century.

In the event, the African empires that Britain, France and Belgium so proudly possessed vanished within the space of a few years less than two decades later; only the Portuguese held on, trying in vain to suppress by military force the tide of African nationalism before which other powers had decided to retreat. As colonial rule came to an end, a multitude of new African states was launched into independence, amid much jubilation and to the world's applause. African leaders stepped forward with energy and enthusiasm to tackle the problems of development and nation-building, boldly proclaiming their hopes of establishing new societies which might offer an inspiration to the world at large.

Inevitably the dreams soon faded. Africa was a continent too deeply affected by mass poverty, by meagre resources, by disease and illiteracy, to allow for easy solutions to its development. It was also a continent prone to civil strife and instability. In relentless succession, African states succumbed to military coups and brutal dictatorships, to periods of great violence and to economic decline and decay. By the 1980s, the future of Africa was spoken of only in pessimistic terms. No other area of the world aroused such a sense of foreboding.

This book sets out to trace the course that black Africa has taken during the past forty years, focusing on the major episodes that occurred and the personalities that helped to shape them. It is an overview of the period, not a history of it. It dwells more on the causes of crisis and change than on the narrative of events. In particular it concentrates on the role of certain individuals, men like Kwame Nkrumah, Jomo Kenyatta, Hastings Banda, Sékou Touré, Félix Houphouët-Boigny and Patrice Lumumba, whose activities had such a decisive impact on the destiny of their own countries and, indeed, on the wider African stage.

It endeavours, too, to draw some general conclusions. Though black Africa is a region of great diversity, it encompasses states which, by virtue of their colonial experience, shared much in common at the time of independence. In subsequent years, they were to suffer many similar misfortunes. Indeed, what is so striking about the current plight of African states is the extent to which they face the same predicament. When the sum of Africa's misfortunes is added up, the picture that emerges is truly daunting. The book ends, therefore, by examining the scale of adversity that confronts black Africa and the reasons why so much despair is felt about its future.

M.M.

CHAPTER ONE

London

Towards the end of the London 'Blitz' in 1941, a middle-aged West Indian moved into the shabby neighbourhood behind Euston Station. By outward appearances, the new tenant of Cranleigh Street was a quiet, scholarly figure. He lived in a small, second-floor flat with an English girl, smoked a pipe, enjoyed cricket and earned a living, precariously it seemed, as a journalist. Insofar as his Cockney neighbours were concerned, it was his cultivated English accent and rather haughty manner which caused most comment. Along the cobbled backstreets of Somers Town, he came to be known as 'The Major'.

But the past of George Padmore, as he called himself, was considerably more intriguing than the neighbourhood may have supposed. Since his student days in the United States, Padmore had been an active revolutionary. So remarkable were his talents as an organiser that Communist leaders in Moscow, seeking ways to promote revolution around the world, had provided him with an office in the Kremlin, supplied substantial funds for him to recruit agents and bestowed on him unique favours. Along with Stalin, he had been elected to the Moscow Soviet and for the May Day parade he had been invited to stand on the balcony of the Lenin Mausoleum—a lone black figure among the Russian hierarchy.

For four years, as a professional Comintern agent, Padmore pursued a footloose, clandestine lifestyle. In the ports and cities of Europe he searched among black student groups and seamen's clubs for possible recruits, despatching the more promising ones to Moscow; in Hamburg, he edited the Communist journal, the *Negro Worker*, spreading the message of anti-colonial revolt; in Moscow he taught at the University of the Toilers of the East, a training school set up in 1921 for colonial students; and secretly he made journeys through Africa, always on the lookout for new contacts. By the time he was thirty years old, Padmore had built up a personal network which could scarcely be rivalled.

In the turmoil that Europe faced in the 1930s, however, the Russians turned out to be less interested in pursuing revolutionary activities in the colonial world than George Padmore was. Alarmed by Hitler's rise to power in Germany in 1933, Stalin sought closer collaboration with Britain and France; in the process he abandoned nationalist movements in Asia and Africa which the Russians had previously sponsored. Among the victims was the front organisation that Padmore ran, the International Trade Union Committee of Negro Workers.

It was an experience that left Padmore with an abiding dislike of Stalin and deep distrust of Comintern. But he lost neither his revolutionary zeal nor his admiration for the Soviet system, nor, indeed, the cover name of George Padmore that, as a young student from Trinidad, he had adopted after joining the Communist Party in the United States eight years before. Imprisoned by the Nazis during the anti-Communist purge of 1933, spurned by the Communists elsewhere in Europe, he arrived penniless in London in 1935 as determined as ever to wage his anti-colonial campaign.

The task was not a particularly rewarding one. Among the small African and West Indian communities in England at the time, Padmore found few students willing to involve themselves in his radical schemes. Mostly, he complained, they were even more conservative than the English. Nor did he win many supporters within London's left-wing circles; socialists who took an interest in colonial affairs wanted reform of the Empire, not its overthrow.

Undaunted by such difficulties, Padmore persevered as an activist, writing prolifically for left-wing periodicals, lecturing at weekend summer schools, participating in protest groups, striving to build up a new organisation to replace the one that Moscow had shut down. Not even when war against Hitler was declared did his views change. Defiantly he argued that as the British Empire was 'the worst racket yet invented by man', colonial peoples would do better using the opportunity to revolt rather than to give Britain their support.

Set against the dramatic upheavals of the Second World

War, the activities of a largely unknown West Indian agitator were hardly of any significance. Certainly, when he arrived in Cranleigh Street in 1941, having lost a nearby home in German bombing, no-one thought it of much account. But with a single-minded determination, Padmore was soon to turn his tiny flat into a centre of anti-colonial intrigue. To Number 22 came a constant stream of visitors, old friends to discuss tactics, new arrivals seeking advice. Over many of them, Padmore, with his vigorous intellect and revolutionary background, exerted a profound influence. And over none more so than an African stranger who, as the war was ending, wrote a letter from New York asking Padmore to meet him at Euston Station.

*

As a young, ambitious primary school teacher in the British colony of the Gold Coast, Kwame Nkrumah had wanted to further his education by studying at the University of London. But he failed the entrance examination. Instead he gained admission to Lincoln University in Pennsylvania, arriving there in 1935. The ten years that Nkrumah then spent in the United States were at times harsh. To earn a living during student vacations, he worked as a labourer in a soap factory and as a steward aboard a ship plying between New York and Vera Cruz in Mexico and he even tried selling fish on street corners in Harlem. Along the way he acquired several degrees, including one in theology, preached in Negro churches and dabbled in left-wing politics. But the idea of a solid professional qualification, one that would place him in good standing in the Gold Coast, still appealed to him; and so at the end of the Second World War, he resolved to travel to London to study law. There was no-one in London, though, whom he knew; and rather than arrive friendless in a strange city, he wrote to Padmore, whose newspaper articles had impressed him, asking to be met. At Euston Station, Padmore was waiting for him.

At first, Nkrumah's intentions held firm. Shortly after he arrived in May 1945 he found comfortable lodgings in a house in Tufnell Park, where he was to stay for more than two years, and duly he enrolled as a law student. But it was not long before he was drawn into Padmore's orbit and included in the plans that were being made, as war-time conditions ended, to reactivate anti-colonial protest. Helped by a few West Indian and African friends, Padmore was busy trying to revive the old Pan African movement, founded after the First World War to campaign for the self-determination of coloured people, but dormant for fifteen years. As a start for this new venture, the Padmore group intended to convene a conference of as many representatives of black groups from Africa, the West Indies, the United States and Britain as could be assembled. Because extensive preparations had to be made, Nkrumah's help was welcomed.

After so many years as a student, Nkrumah found the work intoxicating. Night and day, he was fond of recalling, he and Padmore would labour over the paperwork on the kitchen table in Cranleigh Street. But while Nkrumah's energy and enthusiasm were useful to Padmore, politically, as Padmore soon realised, he was still unsophisticated. Beyond mere slogans, his grasp of revolutionary ideas was flimsy. Other acquaintances of Nkrumah had previously made the same judgement. After meeting him in Harlem, a left-wing writer, C. L. R. James thought that Nkrumah's talk about imperialism and Leninism was 'a lot of nonsense'. James had been willing to help Nkrumah by giving him a letter of introduction to Padmore in London, a close friend whom he had known since boyhood in Trinidad, in the days when Padmore used his real name, Malcolm Nurse. But James advised Padmore that though Nkrumah seemed determined to throw the Europeans out of Africa, he was not, in fact, very bright. What training Nkrumah lacked, however, Padmore was ready to give him. To his experienced eye, the drive and ambition that Nkrumah displayed held considerable potential. With other men whom he had recruited, he had searched for such qualities.

*

When Jomo Kenyatta first arrived in England from Kenya in 1929, carrying a petition on Kikuyu land grievances to the Colonial Office, he was looked on by the authorities as a raw political agitator with limited education, whose knowledge of English was poor and who showed an unwholesome taste for expensive clothes and loose women. The impression that he made on the missionary network in London which took an interest in his work was so unfavourable that after a while it was thought best that he should return to Kenya as soon as possible. But Padmore, who met him in that same year, saw him differently, as someone anxious to gain experience of a wider world, the sort of recruit that Moscow would welcome. Within a few months of reaching London, Kenyatta had been lured into Comintern activities, appointed a member of a committee to organise an international conference of black workers and taken on an extended trip through Europe and Russia. He returned to Russia in 1932, this time to study at Moscow's special revolutionary institute for colonial candidates, the University of the Toilers of the East, where Padmore taught. After completing his course in 1933, he seemed set for a career as a promising Comintern agent. In articles in Communist journals, his attacks on British rule, white settlers and missionaries had become virulent. Padmore, in that year, expressed high hopes about Kenyatta's usefulness in helping to exploit peasant discontent in Kenya.

But being a Moscow-trained revolutionary was only one of the roles that Kenyatta was adept at playing. In between his journeys to Russia he was equally at ease by then as a member of the 'Hampstead set', participating in drawing-room discussions, taking walks on the Heath and drafting letters to the newspapers. He attended left-wing summer schools, studied at a Quaker college and appeared before a British government commission investigating land issues in Kenya, all the time broadening his experience and range of contacts. After his return to London in 1933—when Moscow was losing interest in promoting colonial revolution—he joined Professor Malinowski's classes in anthropology at the London School of Economics and duly published a study of Kikuyu life and customs entitled *Facing Mount Kenya*. He also worked briefly as an extra in Alexander Korda's film of *Sanders of the River*, glad of the money that it brought him. For in those early years in London, he was often beset by poverty, lying cold and hungry in his bed-sitting room near Victoria Station, scrounging from his landlady, reduced to wearing cast-off clothes.

His friendship with Padmore, however, remained close. Together they collaborated in setting up in London the International African Service Bureau, a small, radical group intended by Padmore to coordinate anti-colonial activities in much the same way as his defunct International Trade Union Committee of Negro Workers. As war approached, Kenyatta, like Padmore, questioned whether colonial peoples should come to Britain's defence in time of war when their own plight, so he said, was little better than that of the Jews in Germany. But Kenyatta was never as obsessed as Padmore by politics. His interests, whether in women, music or flashy clothes, were much broader. While Padmore spent the war years writing a book extolling the virtues of the Soviet system, Kenyatta retreated to a village in Sussex, worked as an agricultural labourer, lectured to British troops and married an English girl. He even tried to join the Home Guard. For a while, a placid life suited him. But eventually it came as a relief when, with the rest of the Padmore group, he was able to throw himself energetically into the preparations for the Pan-African conference.

*

Hastings Banda spent the war working as a doctor in towns in northern England. He would have preferred to have returned to his home in Nyasaland as a medical missionary. It had been his ambition for nearly fifteen years while he had persevered with his studies in the United States and Scotland. But when in 1941 he applied to join the Church of Scotland mission at Livingstonia, a group of nurses there warned that they would not be prepared to serve under an African doctor; and subsequently, when the Nyasaland government offered him a job, he was told he would not be allowed to mix socially with white doctors. So he decided to stay in England.

By nature, he was an intensely conservative man, an Elder of the Church of Scotland, who sometimes carried his puritanical outlook on dancing and dress, for example, to an extreme. The route that he took into politics was gradual and cautious. After settling in London in 1945, he became a representative of the newly formed Nyasaland African Congress and thus was invited to the Pan-African conference. Invariably, the aspirations he expressed for his people were moderately phrased. In discussions with Padmore in the Soho basement club where they used to meet, he distrusted the Marxist arguments he heard. But his own convictions of the need for African advancement were held no less strongly. With both Nkrumah and Kenyatta he struck up close friendships. Over the years, all three would fight their separate battles with the British Government. All three would be branded as extremists. And all three would go to jail.

*

On 15 October 1945, the Fifth Pan African Congress, as it was called, opened in a draughty Victorian hall in Chorlton-on-Medlock, then a decaying suburb of Manchester. As a symbol of their hopes, the organisers had decorated the hall with the flags of Ethiopia, Liberia and Haiti, the only black-run states in the world. Nearly one hundred delegates turned up, most of them West Indians and West Africans, some having travelled on from a trade union conference in Paris. In the evenings, their hospitality was arranged by Ras Makonnen, a West Indian member of the Padmore group, who used his chain of restaurants along Oxford Road to finance many of the activities of the Pan African movement. One of the restaurants, The Cosmopolitan, famous for its black-market food, had been managed for a while by Kenyatta.

Apart from a sentimental attachment to the past, the Fifth Pan African Congress bore little resemblance to the previous four. In its earlier active phase in the 1920s, the Pan African movement had been dominated by black American intellectuals with the romantic notion of linking together the black world of the United States, the West Indies and Africa. At Manchester, the only survivor from that period present was an elderly American professor, W. E. B. Du Bois, who was invited there mainly to lend a mantle of respectability to the proceedings. The central figures now were hardened political activists of a different generation grouped around Padmore. As well as Kenyatta and Nkrumah, they included I. T. A. Wallace-Johnson, a former Comintern agent trained in

Moscow, renowned in Nigeria, the Gold-Coast and his native Sierra Leone, as a trade union organiser and outspoken journalist; the British authorities regarded him as 'an unscrupulous and dangerous agitator' and had interned him during the war. Also active at the conference was Peter Abrahams, a young coloured South African writer who had briefly worked in London for the communist *Daily Worker*.

The subjects under discussion were varied. Initially, the focus of attention was on the problems facing black communities in Britain: police harassment in the East End of London; the plight of illegitimate children left behind by black American troops stationed in England during the war; conditions in tough areas like Cardiff's Tiger Bay, Liverpool's South End and London's Stepney, where blacks congregated. But under the guidance of the Padmore group, the conference soon turned into a forthright attack on colonial rule. One speaker after another made the demand for political rights, for freedom, for independence. 'One thing we must do,' said Kenyatta, 'and that is to get political independence. If we achieve that we shall be free to achieve other things we want.' Because of the contribution that the colonies had made to the British war effort, in defence, as they had been told, of 'freedom and democracy', these demands were now put all the more vehemently. No longer were polite petitions of the kind that Kenyatta had once brought to London thought to be of much use; nor the help of liberal Europeans who cautioned against too much haste; nor even the support of the Communists always prepared, so it seemed to men like Padmore, to subordinate other interests to their own. What was required now, in the view of the Manchester activists, was mass political action by the colonial peoples themselves. Nkrumah, put in charge of drafting one of the conference's key resolutions, set the tone for this new mood of self-assertion:

> 'All colonies must be free from foreign imperialist control. The peoples of the Colonies must have the right to elect their own governments, without restrictions from foreign powers. We say to the peoples of the Colonies that they must fight for these ends by all means at their disposal. . . . The Fifth Pan African Congress therefore calls on the workers

and farmers of the Colonies to organise effectively. Colonial workers must be in the front of the battle against Imperialism. . . . Your weapons—the strike and the boycott—are invincible.'

The fiery words heard at Manchester would, in due course, become all too familiar to Britain's colonial governors in Africa. But for the time being they were spoken into a void, and raised no discernible echo throughout the vast, quiescent African empire. For the truth was that, in exile in Britain, Padmore's group had little idea of what was happening there: Nkrumah had not been home for ten years, Kenyatta for fourteen years. In Manchester, the plan for political action sounded exhilarating; but in Africa, there was no-one to carry it out. So too was it exhilarating to be able to raise the banner of revolution. 'There was nothing to stop you getting on your feet and denouncing the whole British Empire,' Nkrumah recalled. 'Nobody cared what you were doing.' But that merely emphasised the fact that, in the eyes of the British authorities, they seemed irrelevant and unimportant, without support in Britain and without influence in Africa.

*

Surveyed from the Colonial Office in Downing Street in 1945, Britain's African Empire was a quiet and orderly preserve. From the sleepy capitals of Africa, few issues ever emerged that required urgent attention. Through many years of experience, the African territories were efficiently administered and, insofar as the British exchequer was concerned, they were cheap to run. Strategically, as the war had shown, they were useful in providing bases, raw materials and large numbers of troops. In terms of their political future, there seemed little reason to doubt that they would remain under British rule for at least the rest of the twentieth century.

In keeping with a part of the Empire which felt so remote, British public interest rarely stirred. Between the pyramids of Egypt and the gold mines of the Transvaal, Africa remained, in the popular imagination, a dark continent, more the subject for romantic tales than for serious attention. Indeed, in only two periods, it was sometimes said, had public opinion ever been aroused: first, during the campaign against the slave trade and, later, when David Livingstone was lost somewhere in the interior. As for British politicians, colonial affairs in general were a backwater where few cared to venture. In Parliament, the annual debate on colonial finances tended to coincide with the Buckingham Palace Garden Party, an attraction which most members naturally preferred. Only a handful of conscientious MPs could be relied upon to participate. On the few occasions when colonial questions were at other times raised, the level of attendance in Parliament was usually just as poor. Not even within the Labour Party, proud of its humanitarian outlook, did the small group of colonial enthusiasts gain much of a following. In the Party's manifesto for the 1945 election, the colonies merited a single, brief reference. Insofar as events in the Empire did attract attention, it was centred on India, or on Palestine. But, in any case, in the bleak aftermath of the Second World War, as Britain struggled with food rationing, bomb damage, war debts and a desperate financial crisis, the new Labour Government was preoccupied more with problems of national recovery and its programme of domestic reform. In those circumstances, the colonies were looked on principally as useful assets.

Partly for reasons of self-interest, therefore, but also because a more enlightened mood about the conduct of colonial affairs prevailed in postwar years, Britain decided that its colonial properties should be properly developed. Whereas the guiding principle before the war had been that the colonies should pay their own way, afterwards large sums of British government money were allocated for their development. By gradual process, concentrating first on social and economic advancement, the colonies were to be transformed from poor and backward possessions into prosperous territories where, in due course, the local people could be introduced slowly to the business of government. For some time, the Colonial Office had been preparing for this change in policy. As a result of Lord Hailey's encyclopedic *African Survey*, first published in 1938, and the secret report he made of his journey through Africa in 1940 at the request of the Colonial Secretary, senior officials at Downing Street had long since accepted the need for a more constructive approach towards African affairs. Only the war had prevented earlier progress being made.

So, provided with a budget of £120 million and the encouragement of the Labour Government, the Colonial Office in the years after 1945 came alive with new schemes, new committees, a new sense of purpose. Technical experts and specialists on agriculture, education, health services were recruited by the score. New public corporations were set up. Hundreds of young men were despatched to the furthest corners of Africa with the assurance that a lifetime's work lay ahead of them. Not all these activities were successful. In Tanganyika, a scheme to grow groundnuts, from which margarine could be produced for 'the harassed housewives of Britain', ended in fiasco after £36 million had been spent. Battalions of bulldozers, including nearly six hundred converted Sherman tanks, were employed to clear the bush, a new town was built, experts swarmed about, but not one single groundnut was ever sold. Another idea to turn Gambia into an egg-producing country cost £5 million without a single egg being exported. Other plans were held up by postwar difficulties, shortages of capital equipment or money. But for all its failures, the postwar period of colonial development brought growth and prosperity to Africa on an unprecedented scale.

With plans for the political future of its African colonies, however, Britain was far more cautious. Between Labour and Conservative parties, and in the Colonial Office, there was broad agreement that, in principle, the ultimate goal of self-government should apply as much to backward African territories as to advanced nations within the Commonwealth. But for Africa that prospect seemed to be so far into the future—at least several generations ahead, far longer in some cases—that the matter hardly merited attention. In the first place, immense tasks of development and administration had to be undertaken. And while the Colonial Office was willing to concede some reforms—such as greater African representation on governing councils—generally Britain expected to see a higher level of economic and social development before granting more political rights. Much would also depend at a later stage on how adept African politicians proved to be in learning British traditions of government and democracy. The assumption underlying this policy was that Britain had unlimited time with which to work. No short cuts were envisaged. To give the colonies their independence, in the words of one senior Labour politician, Herbert Morrison, during the war, would be 'like giving a child of ten a latch-key, a bank account and a shot-gun'.

Even those Labour politicians sympathetic towards colonial aspirations tended to adopt a paternal outlook towards Africa. Among this group was Arthur Creech Jones, who, on appointment first as junior Minister in 1945 and then as Colonial Secretary in 1946, brought to office perhaps greater knowledge of colonial problems than that of any previous Minister. For ten years as a backbencher—sometimes referred to by his colleagues as 'the unofficial Member for the Kikuyu'—Creech Jones had acted as Parliament's conscience about the colonies. He had also been influential as founding chairman of the Fabian Colonial Bureau, established in 1940 to campaign for colonial reform. His arrival at the Colonial Office certainly helped to stimulate further the new spirit of progress there. But Creech Jones believed, no less firmly than his officials, that the main purpose of colonial policy was still to supervise the welfare of colonial peoples, to improve living standards, to provide education and social services. The essential problems facing the colonies, in his view, were 'their ignorance and poverty, their disease and widespread malnutrition, their primitive cultivation and harsh natural conditions, their hopelessly inadequate revenues and need of services of every kind'.

At the same time Creech Jones was in favour of giving Africans a greater role in the government and administration of their countries. Colonial rule, he believed, could only be justified if it included the tasks of 'nation-building' and brought closer the prospect of self-government. But the problem of devising a coherent long-term policy for Africa was complicated by the way in which Britain administered its Empire. Each of the fourteen territories in Africa was governed separately. Each one had its own budget, its own laws and public service. Each one was under the control of a Governor, powerful enough in his own domain to ensure that his views there prevailed. Each one was at a different stage of development. Some, like the miniature colony of The Gambia, consisting of little more than two river banks, or the desert wastelands of Somaliland, were thought to be too small or too poor ever to achieve self-government. As a general rule, the colonies adhered to the British tradition of governing through tribal institutions and chiefs. This system of indirect rule, as it was called, was still in favour at the Colonial Office at the end of the war. In a variety of ways it had been adapted to provide a political outlet for suitably educated Africans. But nowhere was the state of political progress the same.

Britain's West African territories were the most advanced. In the Gold Coast, Nigeria and Sierra Leone, the black professional elite—lawyers, doctors, teachers and merchants—had been given some role to play in ruling institutions since the end of the nineteenth century. In the Gold Coast, the first African to be nominated to the local legislature made his debut in 1888. In each of the three territories, the first direct elections had taken place in the 1920s, allowing a small minority of local representatives to sit alongside British officials and chiefs on legislative councils. During the war, Africans had been admitted to executive councils advising Governors and, in the case of the Gold Coast, a few had been introduced to that inner sanctum of the Colonial Service, the senior ranks of the administration. At the same time, constitutional reviews had been set in motion to see how Africans could be given greater representation. Since there were no settled British communities living in West Africa, the way ahead was relatively uncomplicated.

The result was that in 1946 the Gold Coast and, shortly afterwards, Nigeria were given new constitutions intended to set the pace for African political progress. In the Gold Coast, for the first time, Africans in the legislative council outnumbered colonial officials. Most of them were chosen by provincial councils largely controlled by chiefs or nominated by the colonial government; only five out of thirty-one members were elected directly. And, with customary prudence, the British ensured that the Governor kept real power; members were able to criticise policy rather than formulate it. But in the view of the Colonial Office, the new constitutions were a vital first step in the long process of training Africans for self-government, a sensible arrangement by which British officials, tribal chiefs and 'responsible', educated Africans could operate in tandem. Officials confidently expected the new constitutions to satisfy political aspirations for the next decade before more advances were made.

In Britain's colonies in east and central Africa, the centres of attention were white settlers intent on gaining more political power for themselves. In Southern Rhodesia, the whites had won internal self-government as far back as 1923. In Kenya, they had vigorously pursued the same aim. But Britain, having set the Rhodesian precedent, then stuck to the notion that the interests of the African natives should ultimately be paramount. In practice, this did not always amount to much. Because the African tribes of east and central Africa were considered to be so retarded, at least several generations behind West Africa in view of their more recent contact with Europe, the Colonial Office took the view that the future prosperity of this part of Africa depended largely on encouraging the white communities there, however troublesome and reactionary they may at times have been. Thus, in the White Highlands of Kenya after the war, more farming land was made available to former British soldiers, even though African land grievances were mounting. As Colonial Secretary, Creech Jones was fully in support of such schemes, and provided the money for them, on the grounds that European enterprise would benefit the country as a whole.

For many years after the war, the colonies of east and central Africa, offering a superb climate, lovely scenery and cheap labour, became the destination for thousands of emigrants escaping from the drabness and austerity of Britain and seeking to establish a grander, tropical version of an English way of life. In Southern Rhodesia and Kenya, the white populations doubled. And as their strength grew, as foreign investment poured in, as industry burgeoned, the whites sought even greater gains by spreading their influence to neighbouring British colonies. In Salisbury and Nairobi, great hopes were placed on building new white-led British Dominions in the heart of Africa. The British Government too thought that plans for inter-territorial cooperation should be encouraged.

As the number of schemes for Africa proliferated, the Colonial Office itself was transformed by new vigour. While other parts of the Empire were slipping away, Africa at least seemed set for an era of imperial renaissance. At Downing Street, the staff increased by such numbers that in 1947 the Colonial Office was obliged to move to larger premises. As a temporary measure, buildings in Great Smith Street, owned by the Church of England, were leased. But within a few years, the Colonial Office was expected to occupy new headquarters being designed for a spectacular site by Westminster Abbey.

It was never built.

*

For a short while after the Labour government took office in 1945, the African elite both in the colonies and in England expected dramatic change. At the offices of the Fabian Colonial Bureau in London, set up by Creech Jones five years before, letters and newspaper articles arrived from every corner of the Empire full of optimism about the new future the socialists would bring. Students in London too were enthusiastic. Even Padmore's group, acting in the name of the Pan African Federation, were moved to send an open letter to Prime Minister Attlee offering, as they saw it, the hand of friendship. 'The victory of the common man here is the victory of the common man in Africa, Asia and other colonial lands.'

The mood soon altered once it was realised that rapid political change was not part of the Labour Government's programme for the colonies and when Creech Jones, who previously had seemed such a firm ally, showed no sympathy for the slogans of freedom and independence voiced at meetings like the Manchester congress. So strong was the sense of distrust and resentment that the Fabian Colonial Bureau decided that a weekend of frank discussion and bracing sea breezes at Clacton-on-Sea might help clear the air. About one hundred and twenty people gathered at Oulton Hall on the seafront in April 1946, half of them from the colonies, among them Nkrumah, Kenyatta and Padmore. But the bitter speeches made there only served to show how little could be resolved in that way. Nkrumah, once again, took the lead in denouncing British policies, demanding nothing less than 'complete and absolute' independence for West Africans. 'Mr Creech Jones has changed quite a lot since he came into office,' said Nkrumah. 'He was an old Fabian. But more gratitude will be shown to the Fabians when they do more, when they put into practice their high-sounding principles.' Kenyatta too was disillusioned: 'While certain British people are willing to learn from colonials privately—over a cup of tea—they are unwilling to admit publicly that these people are ready for self-government.'

With so few gains to be made in England, the nationalists there faced a frustrating and arduous existence. Padmore, according to a black American journalist who met him after the war, had become an unhappy and forlorn exile, always impecunious, watched suspiciously by the British security services, complaining angrily in the left-wing press about Creech Jones's betrayal.

Amongst the others, Kenyatta was the most eager to return to Africa. He was by then nearly fifty years old. Outwardly he seemed as much at home whether gossiping with local villagers in the pub in Sussex or striding down Piccadilly dressed flamboyantly in a red sports jacket and carrying a silver-headed cane. He had an English family—a son now as well as a wife—and a wide circle of friends. But the years of experience that Kenyatta had gained in Europe had merely made him restless in wanting to put them to use in Kenya. 'I feel like a general separated by 5,000 miles from his troops,' he once exclaimed with exasperation to his wife, Edna. Kenya, as he had always made clear, was his real home and the centre of all his ambitions. There too he had a wife and two children whom he had not seen for fifteen years. Whereas in London Padmore and Nkrumah saw the struggle for colonial freedom on a wide and sweeping scale, Kenyatta's abiding concern was with Kenya alone. Already he sensed that any campaign against the British there would be difficult enough. 'Whatever we may think of their methods,' he wrote in a pamphlet on Kenya published in 1945, 'their foothold is secure, and it would be impossible to turn them out without a bloody insurrection.

Africans do not want this insurrection. What we do demand is a fundamental change in the present political, economic and social relationship between Europeans and Africans.' When Kenyatta set sail for Kenya in September 1946, cutting loose from his English family and friends, that insurrection was only six years away.

For Nkrumah, though life in London was often a struggle against impoverishment and the cold, it still offered for a time exciting possibilities. Soon after the Manchester conference, he befriended leading British Communists to see what could be gained from them. His 'double-dealings' with the Communists angered many of his old Manchester friends who wanted the Pan African movement to develop independently of foreign ideology. But Nkrumah's objective now was to get ahead as fast as possible. 'He was much less relaxed than most of us,' the South African author, Peter Abrahams, later wrote. 'His eyes mirrored a burning inner conflict and tension. He seemed consumed by a restlessness that led him to evolve the most fantastic schemes.'

One such scheme was the formation of a West African National Secretariat. Its aim was nothing less than to create a 'Union of West African Socialist Republics' free from all colonial links. Africans everywhere on the continent were called on to support it to hasten the day of their own freedom. Within the organisation Nkrumah intended to set up a secret society named The Circle, to act as a revolutionary vanguard. Members were required to take an oath of allegiance, accepting Nkrumah's leadership; they had their own sign of recognition—'ordinary handshake with thumb pressure'—and they were expected to prepare themselves for revolutionary work in any part of the African continent. For a start, Nkrumah approached Kenyatta and others in the Pan African movement, proposing that they should each take a blood oath of secrecy and dedication to the emancipation of Africa. But Kenyatta, for one, scorned the idea.

Nothing much came of Nkrumah's grandiose plans. A newspaper he launched, the *New African*, with a customary attack on Britain, soon folded; the West African National Secretariat became little more than a welfare organisation for West African seamen; and as for The Circle, it survived only on paper. His law studies he had long since abandoned and, short of money, he would spend hours discussing politics in cheap cafés in Camden Town, buying a cup of tea and a bread roll when he could afford them. In the winter months, he would later recall, the small office on Gray's Inn Road where he and friends in the West African National Secretariat worked was so cold that their breath fogged the electric light bulbs; and constantly they would trudge the streets looking for bits of coal that might have been left around coalholes.

Still, for all the hardships the nationalists faced, there were some compensations. Invariably, it seemed, they would find English girls ready to help. 'They would hear us addressing meetings at Trafalgar Square or in some of the London halls, and they'd come round and ask if there was anything to be done,' said Ras Makonnen. Nkrumah too remembered them warmly: 'These girls—most of them of good class families—used to come and type for hours on end in the evenings and they never asked a single penny for their work.' At his Cranleigh Street flat, Padmore lived with a North London girl, Dorothy Pizer, who remained a devoted companion, helping with typescripts and coping with a constant stream of visitors. And Kenyatta, as well as acquiring a wife, had numerous other liaisons, as the missionaries learned to their dismay soon after he first set foot in London.

'Looking back on this period,' said Makonnen, 'you certainly couldn't say we were living the sort of life that one heard the eighteenth century revolutionaries lived—morbid fellows who were distracted and had never a gay moment as they thought how they might destroy society.... It was a gay period, a period of purposefulness.'

And when Nkrumah finally decided to return to the Gold Coast in November 1947, he left England with a certain sadness: 'It was not a happy parting for me. I had thoroughly enjoyed my stay there and had become extraordinarily attached both to the country and the people.'

*

In contrast to most of his fellow Africans, Banda in London lived a prosperous, middle-class existence, becoming deeply attached to the English way of life. He owned a house in Brondesbury Park, drove a small car, dabbled on the stock market and took to wearing a black homburg hat and carrying a rolled umbrella. As a doctor, he was renowned for many acts of generosity and so highly respected that patients in the waiting room of his surgery would stand up when he entered. In politics, he tended not to venture beyond anything respectable. He joined the Fabian Colonial Bureau, befriended Creech Jones and, as the representative of the Nyasaland African Congress, was active in arranging for questions to be raised in the House of Commons. On Sunday afternoons, his house would be the meeting place for a host of people concerned with African affairs; Nkrumah was a frequent visitor in whom Banda, then aged fifty, took an avuncular interest.

But Banda, just as much as the other nationalists, was soon to be drawn into heated confrontation with the British government and to suffer eventually even more grievously from a sense of betrayal. In Northern and Southern Rhodesia, the white communities campaigned increasingly effectively for a semi-independent federation of the Rhodesias and Nyasaland, pointing out the huge economic advantages that could be gained. Against them Banda argued tirelessly that a federation would place the Africans of Nyasaland and Northern Rhodesia, then under the protection of the Colonial Office, at the mercy of reactionary whites, jeopardising all their hopes for political and social advancement. Britain's obligation in the circumstances, he said, was to safeguard African interests. His efforts were to no avail. After eight years of comfortable life in London, he left England, a sad and disappointed man, to work as a doctor in the Gold Coast, complaining bitterly of what he called Britain's 'cold, calculating, callous and cynical betrayal of a trusting, loyal people'.

CHAPTER TWO

Paris

When Paris fell to the Germans in 1940, France's African Empire acquired a dramatic importance. Responding to General de Gaulle's appeal for help in exile, French Equatorial Africa rallied to the cause of the Free French. For two and a half years Brazzaville, a small town on the north bank of the Congo river, became the temporary capital of what purported to be the government of France. From this base, an army was raised, equipped and sent across the Sahara to take part in the allied campaign in North Africa. In Africa, in de Gaulle's own words, France had found 'her refuge and the starting point for her liberation'.

Duly grateful, de Gaulle convened a conference of colonial administrators in Brazzaville in January 1944, even while the Germans were still occupying Paris, to discuss a new role for African colonies in the postwar era. Like most Frenchmen, whether Free French or pro-Vichy, de Gaulle was adamant that the links between metropolitan France and the colonies were *indissoluble*. Whatever setbacks had occurred during the war, the colonies would continue to be governed as part of *la plus grande France*. Indeed, de Gaulle looked on the Empire as the key to rebuilding France's power and prestige in the world. Accordingly, the Brazzaville conference declared that self-government was out of the question. But in recognition of their war effort, the colonies were promised a wide measure of political, administrative and economic reform. When the time came for drawing up a new constitution for the Fourth Republic, the African population, it was decided, should be properly represented.

Thus to Paris in 1945, as winter was setting in, came nine African deputies, a tiny band almost lost among nearly six hundred others who made up the Constituent Assembly. In outlook, they saw themselves, and were seen, as Frenchmen, brought up in a tradition of loyalty to France, willingly accepting its government and culture, and taking a certain pride in being citizens of a world power. As their main aim they hoped to secure for Africans the same rights and privileges enjoyed by metropolitan Frenchmen. No-one dreamed of independence. Not once was any voice raised in favour of breaking up the Empire. 'Our programme,' said the two deputies from Senegal, Léopold Senghor and Amadou Lamine-Guèye, 'can be summarised in a very simple formula: a single category of Frenchmen, having exactly the same rights since all are subject to the same duties, including dying for the same country.'

In conducting their 'civilising mission' in Africa, the French had been highly successful in absorbing the small black elite that emerged from their colonies. In Senegal, the most advanced of France's African colonies, black residents in four old coastal towns had exercised the right to elect a representative to the French Parliament since the nineteenth century. For a favoured few, education at the Ecole Normale William Ponty in Dakar, the capital of Senegal, or the Lycée Fairdherbe at St Louis was as good as any to be found in France, though only a handful ever gained a place at a French university. Officially, no public office was closed to the elite. The first African deputy elected to the French parliament from Senegal, Blaise Diagne, arrived in Paris in 1914 and rapidly rose to the rank of junior minister. In 1940, when de Gaulle desperately needed help, the first in Africa to respond was the Governor of Chad, Félix Eboué, a black Guyanese devoted to the Empire, who subsequently became the Governor-General of French Equatorial Africa.

For the most part, however, the French regime in black Africa was severe and autocratic. Outside Senegal, in the fourteen other French colonies, no organised political activity was permitted. Africans were subjected to forced labour and rigid laws such as the *indigénat* which enabled colonial administrators to impose arbitrary punishment on anyone whom they considered to be troublesome. Much of the terrain was harsh: vast expanses of desert, infertile bush and dense jungle, acquired during the scramble for Africa and since left largely untouched. *L'Afrique Noire* was a region of primitive agriculture, bad roads and rudimentary government services. When it came to economic development, France's African colonies, like Britain's, were expected to raise whatever funds they needed from their own meagre resources.

Arriving in Paris in 1945, the African deputies were determined to press for reforms as far reaching as possible. But the disadvantages they faced were considerable. Most of them had never before been to France. They had no experience of parliamentary life; and in the Palais Bourbon they found most of their colleagues uninterested in colonial issues, while on the right wing a powerful lobby fought to limit what reforms were passed. Their numbers were so small that only by attaching themselves to one or other of the rival political parties in Paris could they make their presence felt. Some at first chose the Socialists, some the Communists. Both parties were strongly represented in the Constituent Assembly.

The Communists were especially solicitous. They saw the Africans as natural allies in the struggle against capitalism and willingly provided help, in the bleak days after the war, with housing and transport and instruction on parliamentary procedures. But such alliances meant that the Africans were drawn fruitlessly into France's domestic political squabbles. In the Assembly they found their attention required for a wide range of issues, such as European defence or subsidies for French brewers, in which they had no real interest. Under French law, they were supposed to be representatives not of Africa alone, but of the entire French nation.

Nevertheless, the gains made initially were considerable. Under the Fourth Republic, all Africans received French citizenship and some—more than one million—the vote. In the Paris Chamber, black Africa was represented in all by twenty-four deputies. At home, local assemblies were established for each territory, and federal assemblies for the two main regions of French West Africa and French Equatorial Africa. For the first time political activity flourished throughout the African Empire. The social and economic reforms obtained were equally advantageous. As the Brazzaville conference had promised, old colonial practices like forced labour and the *indigénat* were abolished. Trade unions were now encouraged. Medical and educational services improved. Most important of all, France launched an economic development plan for the colonies, based on the *Fonds d'Investissement pour le Développement Economique et Social*, which ultimately was to lift them into the modern world.

However much these measures benefited French Africa, the central objective of the *'Union Française'*, as the postwar Empire was called, was still to bind the colonies tightly to metropolitan France. Whereas for British territories progress meant giving Africans greater control over their own affairs, for French Africa it was a matter of giving them a greater voice in the affairs of *la plus grande France*. But not, of course, too much. Among the French parties there was tacit agreement that too much power given to colonial subjects either in Paris or in the colonies might threaten the government or weaken the Empire. By virtue of their numbers, the colonies were ultimately in a position to swamp metropolitan France—if the principle of equal rights for all citizens embodied in the constitution of the Fourth Republic was followed through to its logical conclusion. The fear that France might eventually become a 'colony of her colonies' helped to ensure that only a cautious pace of political progress was pursued. In the dual system of voting adopted in black Africa, far greater weight was attached to the votes of metropolitan Frenchmen than to the votes of Africans—a practice that outraged African politicians. The territorial assemblies set up in Africa were given limited scope. In the search for a compromise which would give Africans enough local autonomy to keep them from asking for independence while enabling Paris to retain control of the colonies, metropolitan interests inevitably prevailed. Paris remained the centre of political activity. Real power still lay with officials at the Rue Oudinot, the Ministry of France d'Outre-Mer, and with the local French administrations in Africa. Most of the political parties which emerged in Africa at the beginning of the Fourth Republic were sponsored by French officials determined to ensure that their own approved candidates were elected to national and local assemblies. And, as the African *parlementaires* were to discover, French administrators were ready to break up any movement which challenged their own authority.

Among these *parlementaires* were two men whose influence on African affairs was to extend over the next four decades: Léopold Senghor and Félix Houphouët-Boigny. Senghor, the Senegalese deputy, had already gained a reputation as one of France's leading poets. Educated at lycées in Dakar and Paris, he had since spent most of his life in France. As a naturalised French citizen, he was mobilised in 1939 and spent the early part of the war in a German prisoner-of-war camp. On release he had gone back to teaching. Elected to the Constituent Assembly in October 1945, he had helped to draft the new constitution and later, as a member of the National Assembly re-elected in November 1946, he played an influential role within the Socialist party. Outside parliament, he was at the centre of Paris intellectual life, a passionate advocate of *négritude* and patron of the *Présence Africaine* group, established in Paris in 1947 by black intellectuals who shared hope for an African renaissance.

Like Senghor, Félix Houphouët-Boigny, a deputy from the Ivory Coast, was a member of the elite, an *évolué*, educated at the Ecole Normale William Ponty in Dakar, trained in medicine, a wealthy planter and traditional chief who held an official position as *chef de canton*. His entry into politics came in 1944 when he led a group of African planters, the *Syndicat Agricole Africain*, in opposition to the French policy of discriminating in favour of French planters in the Ivory Coast. As a deputy to the Constituent Assembly in 1945, he made it his special task to campaign for an end to forced labour. When in April 1946 he succeeded, by sponsoring a law which became known as the *Loi Houphouët-Boigny*, he established himself as a national leader, with a popular following in the Ivory Coast and beyond. In dances and songs, his achievement was celebrated throughout the colony. With this triumph, he was able to turn his *Parti Démocratique de la Côte d'Ivoire* (PDCI) into the first mass political party in black Africa.

For partners in the National Assembly in Paris, Houphouët chose the Communists. Initially, the alliance had its advantages. The Communists formed one of the largest groups in the Constituent Assembly and they were also represented in the coalition government. Like other French political parties, they valued the Empire. 'France is and ought to remain a great

African power,' a Communist deputy told the Constituent Assembly. They showed no enthusiasm for demands for autonomy from the colonies, but stressed the need for colonial peoples to unite with the French working class to bring about a Communist victory in France, through which they would gain their own emancipation. But in support of the African campaign for rapid reform, they were ready to offer any practical assistance, funds, training, personnel, both in Paris and in the colonies. With their help, Houphouët believed that African demands in parliament would be more easily realised.

To strengthen the African position, Houphouët forged an alliance of radical parties in 1946 under the banner of the *Rassemblement Démocratique Africain* (RDA), and threw its weight firmly behind the Communist cause. This policy worked well enough while the Communists remained in the government. By using the Communist network, particularly special study groups set up in African capitals by Free French Communists as early as 1943, the RDA spread rapidly throughout most of French Africa. But the penalty for this partnership was that the RDA was soon dragged into the politics of Europe's Cold War and into deadly conflict with the French administration. In 1947 the Communists abandoned the government in favour of a policy of 'revolutionary' action, urged the RDA to follow suit, and tightened their grip over RDA activities. By adhering slavishly to the Communist Party line, the RDA lost much of its support in French Africa. From Paris, 'tough' administrators were sent out to Africa with instructions to suppress it. Aided enthusiastically by local officials and *colons*, the French administration eventually brought the RDA to its knees. Government employees, village chiefs, teachers sympathetic to the RDA were dismissed; RDA meetings were banned; elections were blatantly rigged. The brunt of the repression, as it was frankly called, fell on the Ivory Coast, the RDA stronghold. Party officials were imprisoned en masse; pro-PDCI villages found their taxes raised; even pilgrims to Mecca known to be party members were prevented from leaving. The PDCI retaliated in 1949 with hunger strikes, boycotts, mass demonstrations, street fighting and sabotage. By the spring of 1950, at least fifty Africans had been killed, hundreds wounded and thousands imprisoned. In the end, Houphouët broke with the Communists, sued for peace and decided to collaborate with the government.

All through this turbulent period, Houphouët constantly affirmed his loyalty to France. In its policy, the RDA was neither anti-French nor did it at any time demand independence. It aimed at equality for Africans within the French Union and concentrated attacks on the dual system of voting and other forms of discrimination. Not for a decade after the Second World War, in fact, was any call for independence publicly heard from black Africa. Events in the rest of the French Empire—the war in Indo-China beginning in 1946, the revolt in Madagascar brutally suppressed in 1947, the independence movements in Morocco, Tunisia and Algeria—none of these seemed to affect the mood of black Africans. Black politicians remained deeply attached to France, proud of its political ideals and steeped in its culture and traditions. From an early age, through French education and, above all, through the use of the French language on which France insisted, they had aspired to become members of the civilisation that France offered. Now, playing an active role in the national institutions which France opened to its citizens from around the world, they felt a sense of common purpose.

Even so, at the Palais Bourbon, as France shifted from one government to the next, invariably preoccupied with its own crises, African deputies found it frustrating that such fleeting attention was given to their affairs. Since the initial burst of reforms in 1946, little else had been accomplished. Africa, for the most part, remained a neglected backwater, safely under the control of the French administration. 'Let us be frank,' complained one moderate African councillor in 1951, 'the coloured representatives obtained absolutely nothing during the five year term which is now ending. They did not even succeed in capturing for a few moments the attention of an Assembly indifferent to the point of insolence.'

CHAPTER THREE

Brussels

Much to the admiration of other colonial powers, the Belgians had devised a system for running the Congo which was efficient, profitable and, by the standards of the time, largely benevolent in its dealings with the African population. Through an alliance centred on Brussels between the government, the Catholic Church and the giant mining and business corporations, Belgium ensured more effective management of its African territories than any other European power. In essence, the government provided administration, the church looked after education and moral welfare, and the mining companies produced the revenue to support the whole enterprise. No other colony in Africa could boast of such advanced programmes in health or primary education or industrial training. Nor indeed were such riches of copper, diamonds and uranium to be found elsewhere in tropical Africa. The only interruption to this orderly state of affairs came in Belgium itself, when the Germans overran the country in 1940 and the government retreated to London. On its return to Brussels in 1944, the same colonial policies were employed. Government ministers saw no reason for change. The system, it seemed, was good enough to last indefinitely.

By convention, colonial matters were kept out of Belgian politics. In parliament, no-one gave them as much attention as politicians in England or France did, and debates were usually brief and perfunctory. Overall, the Belgian public were content to own the richest colony in Africa without being concerned about what happened there. Consequently, the affairs of the Congo were left to a small group of Belgians—officials, churchmen and businessmen—whose activities were virtually exempt from outside scrutiny. From the Congo itself, no views other than official ones were heard. Neither the Belgians living there nor the Congolese had a vote; no-one was consulted. Edicts and directives were simply passed down from Brussels.

The guiding principle of Belgian rule was that Brussels should retain control over every aspect of life in the Congo, thereby allowing the government to lead it slowly and methodically into the modern world. Even in the more remote areas of the Congo, the firm hand of Belgian authority was to be found dispensing law and order. Government officials were instructed to spend much of their time in the bush, making sure that villagers produced crops, maintained roads and provided labour for mines and plantations. Missionaries too were active building an impressive network of schools and clinics and carrying their evangelical work deep into rural areas. In the eastern Congo, the mining corporations provided housing, welfare schemes and technical training to keep the labour force stable and satisfied. Behind all this activity lay the belief that the African population, given strict upbringing, wise leadership and enough material benefits would be content with Belgian rule for the rest of their lives.

Beyond that, though, the Congolese were kept in a safe, subordinate role. They had no political voice, no rights to own land or travel freely. In urban areas, they were subject to curfews; in rural areas, to forced labour. Though primary schools abounded, there was no higher education available except in Catholic seminaries. Nor were students allowed to study in Belgium. Quite deliberately, the Belgians set out to isolate the Congo from any outside influence and to stifle the emergence of a black elite which might demand a change in the system. While Africans were encouraged to train as clerks, medical assistants or mechanics, they could not become doctors, lawyers or architects. Visits to Belgium were rarely permitted. One Colonial Minister explained in 1954: 'We have seen that those Natives who have been shown Europe, and given a very advanced education, do not always return to their homelands in a spirit favourable to civilisation and to the Mother Country in particular.'

The whites, too, though a privileged community, had their role clearly defined. White settlers were not encouraged. Except in the eastern Kivu region and in Katanga, few actually owned land. Nor were artisans wanted. To prevent their arrival, the government required emigrants to the Congo to post large financial bonds. Nor were government officials or Belgian employees on contract persuaded to regard the Congo as a permanent posting. Essentially, Belgium looked on the Congo as a valuable piece of real estate which just required good management.

Inevitably, in postwar years as the economy boomed, the black elite grew and their demands for more rights and a special status became more vociferous. Reluctant to concede any real change, Brussels devised half-hearted schemes which served mainly to harden black attitudes. Initially, in 1948, Africans who were literate, of good behaviour and free from such malpractices as polygamy and sorcery, were entitled to apply for a *Carte du Mérite Civique*. But since the *carte* brought no precise benefits, relatively few Congolese bothered to get one; after nearly five years, less than five hundred had been issued. Then, wanting a more permanent solution, the government appointed a commission in 1948 to study 'the problem of the status of the civilised Congolese population'—the *évolués*, as they were known. Some of the proposals put forward would have given the most sophisticated *évolués* equal status with Europeans. But this was too much for the whites. After years of debate and prevarication, the government established by decree a new status, *immatriculation*, which simply gave certain *évolués* the same juridical rights as whites: they could be tried in the same courts but social and economic barriers remained.

To reach this elevated status, an applicant had to satisfy Belgian officials that not only did he have the appropriate European education but that 'he is penetrated with European civilisation and conforms to it', a hurdle that many whites would undoubtedly have failed to pass. In the course of their inquiries, the officials would make the most detailed examination of a candidate's lifestyle, interrogating him about his relationship with his wife and friends and descending in a group on his house for inspection. A young postal clerk, Patrice Lumumba, later described the procedure in his book, *Le Congo, Terre d'Avenir*: 'Every room in the house, from the living room, bedroom and kitchen to the bathroom, are explored from top to bottom, in order to uncover anything which is incompatible with the requirements of civilised life.'

As an attempt to show Belgian goodwill, the *immatriculation* decree, introduced in 1952, was an unqualified failure. For the *évolués*, it brought them no nearer to the privileged lifestyle to which they so avidly aspired. After five years, only about two hundred had gained the rank of *immatriculé*. Lumumba, for one, was initially turned down on the grounds of 'immaturity'. Nor did the other reforms which Belgium so hesitantly implemented have much impact. In 1950, for the first time, Congolese children seeking higher education were permitted to enter white schools. But the numbers admitted were pitifully small—only twenty-one students in 1953—and, as with adults, they were required to pass tests to prove not only their educational ability, but also their standards of personal hygiene and propriety. In the higher realms of state, two Congolese were appointed in 1947 to represent African interests on the *Conseil de Gouvernement*; six more Africans were added in 1951. But the *Conseil de Gouvernement* was merely an advisory body with no power, called upon to examine proposals devised in Brussels.

For as long as the Congo could be kept in isolation from the rest of the world, the Belgians expected that their paternal system of government providing, as it did, mass primary education, industrial skills, economic opportunities and social services, would satisfy what thirst the Congolese had for advancement. Certainly, by reputation, the Congo was a stable and prosperous haven untroubled by any kind of political ferment. The main preoccupation within the *cercles des évolués* was that they should be freed from racial discrimination, to become more closely integrated with the white community. 'The essential wish of the Congolese elite,' wrote Patrice Lumumba in 1956, 'is to be "Belgians" and to have the right to the same freedom and the same rights.'

CHAPTER FOUR

Lisbon

As dictator of the poorest country in Europe, Antonio de Oliveira Salazar had long sought to restore Portugal's pride and prestige in the world by reviving its sense of imperial mission. Through colonial fairs, magazine articles, street names and postage stamps, the Portuguese public was constantly reminded of the golden age of Portuguese expansion, centuries before, and of how the flag still flew in distant lands where early explorers had planted Christianity and civilisation. In schools and universities, students were encouraged to take up the challenge awaiting them in the colonies; literary prizes were offered to writers on colonial affairs; journalists were despatched to Africa to describe Portugal's achievements there; and prospective emigrants were told of the bright future that could be found in lands like Angola and Mozambique. Through endeavours of this nature, Salazar told a conference of colonial governors in Lisbon in 1933, shortly after his regime began, Portugal would 'make clear to the rest of Europe our position as a great colonial power'.

Though Salazar never once set foot in his African territories during thirty-six years as Portugal's ruler, from a distance he remained passionately interested in their history and future. Convinced that Portugal had a unique responsibility to implant its culture and faith abroad, much as the great navigators had done in the sixteenth century, he insisted that Portugal's overseas possessions were not so much colonies as provinces, as inseparable a part of Portugal as, say, the suburbs of Lisbon. It was this vision of Portugal's imperial role which he believed made his country different from Europe's other colonial powers.

The result of all this nationalistic fervour was unimpressive. Portugal, beset by rural poverty, overpopulation and unemployment, was itself too destitute to expend much effort on developing its African empire. For the first decade of Salazar's rule, Angola and Mozambique remained stagnant backwaters; and those Portuguese seeking a new future abroad preferred to set sail for Brazil rather than risk the hazards of life in Africa. Nor did Salazar's grandiose concept of the Portuguese empire help to stave off international criticism of Portugal's colonial policies, especially the methods of forced labour adopted in Africa. A blunt editorial in the London *Daily Express* in 1937, for example, asserted that Portugal had learned nothing in four centuries of African rule and that it would be a blessing for the native population living in African territories if they were taken from Portugal and given to some other power. Salazar remained unapologetic. 'Contrary to what everyone may believe,' he declared in answer to his critics in 1937, 'we will not partition our colonies.... Our constitutional laws do not permit it, and, in the absence of these, our national conscience would not permit it.' Portugal's standing in the world was not improved by Salazar's open admiration for Hitler and Mussolini, nor by his support for the Franco rebellion in Spain. Only half way through the Second World War, when the outcome was becoming clear, did Salazar shift from his supposedly neutral stance in favour of a closer liaison with the Allies.

In postwar years, however, stories of prosperity in Angola and Mozambique persuaded thousands of Portuguese to seek their fortunes there. Most of the emigrants were poor, illiterate peasants and unskilled labourers desperate to escape from poverty at home and encouraged to go by the government's offer of assisted passages. The life they found was arduous. Many sought menial jobs as servants, waiters, shoe cleaners or farm labourers. Some drifted along with Africans to the urban slums—the crowded *muceques*—which grew up around the towns of Luanda and Lourenço Marques. According to one Portuguese writer who visited Angola in the early 1950s, three quarters of the white population there lived on the edge of poverty. For only a minority—successful coffee planters, merchants and senior government officials—were the stories of prosperity true.

As long as the flow of emigrants continued, the government

was well satisfied. Salazar's grand design for the African colonies was to populate them with Portuguese peasants, so transforming Africa slowly into a modern agrarian society which reflected Portugal's way of life. In time, over the centuries, the African population would be gradually absorbed into it. To support this aim, the funds at the government's disposal were necessarily limited. What money was released was spent on projects like railways and irrigation schemes to assist Portuguese settlement. Little could be spared for other programmes. When the first overall development plans for Angola and Mozambique were launched in 1953, they included nothing for education and social services. Nor was any provision made specifically for the African sector. As the model for future development, the government set up three *colonatos*, independent peasant colonies sited in remote areas of Angola and Mozambique. There Portuguese immigrants built small communities resembling as closely as possible life in Portugal. But most of those migrating to Africa preferred to remain in the towns, where life too blossomed increasingly in the Portuguese image.

Almost separate from the plans for developing the colonies were the vast mass of the African population. Despite Portugal's insistent claims to be engaged on a great 'civilising mission', the traditional role for Africans had been to provide labour and to pay taxes, and in the postwar era, officials at the *Ministrio das Colónias* in Lisbon saw no reason for any change. Above all, the Salazar regime believed in the virtues of work, even if it meant forced labour. As the Colonial Minister, Vieira Machado, wrote in 1943: 'It is necessary to inspire in the black the idea of work and of abandoning his laziness and depravity. . . . If we want to civilise the native we must make him adopt as an elementary moral precept the notion that he has no right to live without working.'

So for six months every year, African men were conscripted to work for the government or for private employers, on plantations, on roads, on mines, sometimes hundreds of miles from their homes, unless they could prove that they were otherwise gainfully employed. The conditions in which they were forced to live were often wretched, made worse at times by corrupt officials and employers who openly flouted the law.

Practices like the use of child labour, wage frauds, corporal punishment and bribery were well known in Lisbon, but little effort was made to rectify them. In 1947, a senior official in the colonial administration, Henrique Galvão, reported to the National Assembly in Lisbon on the damage caused by government policies. Whole areas of Angola and Mozambique, he warned, were being depopulated as African men crossed the borders to neighbouring territories in search of a better life. 'One sees only the pitiful, the old, the sick, and women and children.'

A fortunate minority escaped from this underworld—the *regime do indigenato* as it was called. Provided that an African was literate in Portuguese (only one per cent were), belonged to the Christian faith, had a sufficient income and was willing to give up native customs like polygamy, he could apply to the government tribunal for the status of *civilisado* or, as it was later called, *assimilado*. If he passed scrutiny, he then assumed full citizenship, alongside whites and *mestiços*. By 1950, the number of *civilisados* in Angola was about 30,000 and in Mozambique about 4,300, a pitifully small proportion of the black population perhaps, but for the Portuguese proof that their historic duty was being fulfilled. In race relations, too, the Portuguese tended to be more tolerant than other European settlers in Africa, accepting readily intermarriage and mixed living. And though the influx of 'poor white' immigrants competing for manual and semi-skilled jobs brought a hardening of racial attitudes, the Portuguese still believed that in their African empire they had found the answer to creating a multi-racial society.

In other ways, the colonies were ruled little differently than was metropolitan Portugal. Under Salazar's regime, political activity was tightly controlled; the press censored; dissidents ruthlessly dealt with. In Africa, anyone suspected of agitation was either jailed or sent to a penal colony or into exile. But the need seldom arose. To all outward appearances, Portugal's African empire was a sleepy outpost, cut off from the rest of the world, primitive perhaps, but seemingly free of political and racial tension.

CHAPTER FIVE

The Wider World

However secure the African colonies may have seemed in 1945, however confident governments in London, Paris, Brussels and Lisbon still were about the importance of their imperial mission, a tide of events had begun to flow, at times imperceptibly, that was to change the fortunes of Africa irrevocably. The war that had engulfed the world had been fought in the name of freedom and self-determination. To those who sought a new future in the colonial world, the Atlantic Charter, drawn up by Churchill and Roosevelt in Placentia Bay off Newfoundland in 1941, supporting the right of all peoples to choose their own government, seemed to constitute some form of official encouragement. Churchill later argued that he had in mind self-determination only for the conquered nations of Europe, not for British territories. 'We mean to hold our own,' he said stubbornly in 1942. 'I have not become the King's First Minister in order to preside over the liquidation of the British Empire.' But Roosevelt was adamant not only that postwar objectives should include self-determination for all colonial peoples, but that *timetables* for independence should be drawn up. As the leader of a nation bred in the tradition of anti-imperialism, he believed fervently that any endeavour to dismember the world's empires and end colonial exploitation was morally justified; furthermore, it also happened to suit American interests.

Roosevelt's views about British rule hardened considerably during the war when, on his way to the 1943 Casablanca conference, he stopped briefly in the tiny West African colony of The Gambia. Appalled by the poverty and disease he witnessed there, he wrote to Churchill describing the territory as a 'hell-hole'. About the French he was even more scathing and demanded that after the war all French colonies should be placed under international trusteeship. Above all, Roosevelt resented the barriers to free trade which the British and French erected around their colonies to keep them as captive markets and to protect their sources of raw materials from outsiders such as the Americans. In the critical middle years of the war, a wave of anti-colonial sentiment swept America. Though allies of Britain, Americans were anxious that their support should not be used to shore up the British Empire. The American press was foremost in attacking the colonial powers, stressing their sympathy for nationalist movements. In an open letter to the English people in 1942, the editors of *Life* magazine wrote: 'One thing we are sure we are *not* fighting for is to hold the British Empire together.'

By 1945, as the problems of postwar security came more sharply into focus, the Americans were less certain about the need for radical change, particularly when they required colonial bases of their own in the Pacific. If Britain's withdrawal from colonial regions was likely to create areas of instability, then American defence chiefs could see good reasons for the continued existence of the British Empire. When the cold war with the Soviet Union began in the postwar era, American concern about the strength of Western colonial powers became even more pronounced. Insofar as Africa mattered, the Americans anyway tended to agree with the British view that a long period of benevolent guardianship was the right policy. Even for the most advanced colonies, the Americans saw self-government at least half a century away. Asked in 1943 how long it might take dependent territories such as the Belgian Congo to achieve self-government, a senior American official replied, more than one hundred years. For parts of the Portuguese Empire, he thought a thousand years.

Nevertheless, by taking such a determined stand in support of the rights of colonial peoples, the United States had helped to sharpen the conscience of European powers about their handling of colonial affairs and encouraged British liberals, humanitarians and socialists to press for reform. Though the British, conservative and liberal alike, regarded American criticism of their colonial record as ill-founded, the case for colonial reform became far stronger when it could be shown that it helped to fortify the vital American alliance and secure American aid on which Britain so heavily depended. It was largely to placate American opinion that, in 1943, the British Colonial Secretary, Oliver Stanley, stated more clearly than ever before Britain's commitment to self-government as a goal of British policy. At the Brazzaville conference in 1944, de Gaulle insisted that the question of reforming the French Empire was exclusively 'the business of the French nation'. But he too had been sufficiently worried by Roosevelt's strictures about French rule to advocate change.

The war itself had thrown up decisive shifts in power, away from Europe and its colonial powers. In Asia, the defeat that Britain, France and Holland suffered at the hands of the Japanese dealt European influence a profound blow and provided great stimulus to opposition movements. After the fall of Singapore, the huge naval base that symbolised British might in the Far East, Britain never regained its standing. Though ultimately victorious, Britain emerged form the war with its power and prosperity greatly diminished. For France, the war brought the spectacle of a nation not only defeated but divided into opposing camps which fought each other for the loyalty of the Empire. At the war's end, de Gaulle strove to hold the Empire together. But the French in Indo-China were unable fully to restore their control against nationalist opposition. In Indonesia, the Dutch faced similar resistance. Leading the imperial retreat from Asia, Britain within three years granted independence to Burma, India and Ceylon. As European influence waned, the emerging superpowers, the United States and the Soviet Union, competed for ascendancy. For different reasons, both were anti-colonial powers. At the United Nations, with each new nation added to its ranks, the anti-colonial bloc became ever more vociferous. 'To possess colonies,' the British Colonial Secretary, Creech Jones, noted, 'was to acquire opprobrium.'

The impetus for change came too from the colonial powers themselves. In Britain and France a new generation of politicians and officials, influenced by the postwar mood of idealism, brought to bear a keener sense of responsibility towards the colonies. They saw themselves as planners and developers of Empire rather than its rulers as their predecessors had done. Under the United Nations Charter of 1945, colonial powers formally acknowledged that they had an obligation to ensure the political, social and economic advancement of their colonial subjects. Self-government—or, in the French text, 'self-administration'—officially became the goal of their policies. The reforms that they implemented, by increasing education, wealth and opportunities in the colonies, were bound in the long run to lead to heightened expectations and demands for greater freedom. In London, this prospect, however distant, was accepted more readily than in the other capitals of Europe. British colonies had always been regarded as separate states, existing in their own right and not, like French colonies, as part of a *République française, une et indivisible*. Political advancement, therefore, could be tailored to suit local circumstances in each colony, leading eventually to self-government. India and Ceylon had shown how, ultimately, parts of the British Empire other than the white Dominions could be launched as independent nations and still retain, through membership of the Commonwealth, the links that Britain, for reasons of national pride or commerce, desired.

The conventional view within the Colonial Office after the war was that the principal African territories would need another sixty or eighty years of British rule before self-government was merited. But at the end of 1946, Creech Jones, worried by Labour Party criticism that the government was making too little headway with colonial reform, asked his officials to 'chart a new approach to Africa'. Their brief was to consider ideas for political progress as well as ways of speeding up economic advancement. In Creech Jones's view, if the colonies were to be developed successfully, Britain needed to gain the cooperation of the educated African elite, by giving them some measure of political power. The result of this new approach was soon evident. In February 1947, Creech Jones sent to African Governors a despatch stressing the importance of developing, along British lines, a modern system of local government that would provide a training ground for democracy. With that move, Creech Jones signalled the end of the period of indirect rule. The chiefs, for so long the allies of Britain in running the colonies, were to make way in importance for the educated minority as the new collaborators.

Even bolder ideas were put forward. In May 1947, a high

level committee of officials completed a secret report attempting to forecast ten to twenty years ahead. One of its principal authors was the head of the African division, Andrew Cohen, a forceful personality whose radical views coincided with those of Creech Jones. Cohen's memorandum warned that unless Britain conceded to the African elite still faster political advancement and Africanisation of the civil service, the colonial authorities would find difficulties in implementing development plans and face serious violence and unrest. Though there was as yet little demand for self-government among the mass of the African population, the rise of nationalism as a major force was, in Cohen's view, inevitable. What the committee recommended, therefore, was an advance plan, a four-stage programme leading to internal self-government, ready to be introduced when the nationalist challenge was strong enough, so that the transfer of power could be carried out 'with the minimum of friction, the maximum of goodwill for this country and the greatest possible degree of efficiency'. The timescale suggested in this secret report, when compared to other predictions of the time, was startling: 'Perhaps within a generation many of the principal territories of the Colonial Empire will have attained or be within sight of the goal of full responsibility for local affairs.'

The 1947 memorandum was the first coherent plan ever devised for the transfer of power in Africa. Creech Jones thought that it was 'a fine job of work'. But within the colonial establishment the reaction at high levels was close to outrage. Many officials feared that in place of benign British rule, the outcome of bowing to a small minority of nationalist agitators would be a succession of dictatorships. The influential Governor of Kenya, Sir Philip Mitchell, wrote to the Secretary of State in May 1947: 'The Government of Kenya ... considers itself morally bound to resist processes which might be called "political progress" by the misinformed or opinionated but would, in fact, be no more than progress towards the abdication of its trust in favour of ... professional politicians.' The counter-attack against Cohen's ideas continued for several months. At a conference of Governors in London in November that year, the Governor of Nigeria, Sir Arthur Richards, scorned Cohen as 'the intellectual dreamer of

Whitehall'. Mitchell, at the same conference, noted sarcastically in his diary how the Colonial Office saw 'visions of grateful independent utopias beaming at them from all around the world'. He added: 'There is no understanding whatever of contemporary realities in the C.O.' Faced with stiff resistance, the Cohen report was put aside. But the thinking that lay behind it was to have considerable influence on Colonial Office strategy.

It was in Africa, though, that the most profound changes were being wrought. There, the Second World War left an indelible imprint. The Allies, showing a purpose and vigour never seen on the continent before, built airports, expanded harbours, constructed roads and supply depots, recruited thousands of African troops and demanded ever greater production of copper, tin, groundnuts, any commodity, in fact, useful in the war effort. Bases such as Freetown, Takoradi, Mombasa and Accra became a vital part of the Allied network. From British territories, some 374,000 Africans served in the British army. African units helped to defeat the Italians in Ethiopia and Somaliland and the Japanese in Burma, often fighting with distinction. The Royal West African Frontier Force, assembled to fight in Burma, was the largest colonial army to serve as an expeditionary force in the history of the British Empire. In India and Burma, African soldiers learnt how nationalist movements there had forced promises of self-government from the British government even though their populations were mainly poor and illiterate. Their views of the white man's world too began to change. Many fought alongside white men, met white soldiers who treated them as equals or who, like themselves, were hardly educated. They returned home to Africa with new ideas and skills, wider experiences and high expectations about the future, many believing that they had earned the right to have some share in the government of their own countries.

The aftermath of the war brought frustration and restlessness, in Africa as much as in other parts of the world. Ex-servicemen, no longer satisfied with village life, gravitated towards the towns. There, unemployment, high prices, poor housing, low wages, were already causing a groundswell of discontent. In the wartime boom, the towns had swollen.

Around cities such as Lagos, Accra, Dakar and Nairobi, shanty-towns and slums proliferated as a constant flow of migrants arrived from rural areas in search of work. Labour unrest was common. In many African towns, there was an air of tension. Tribal disciplines were weakening; old religions were losing ground; the spread of primary school education, particularly in West Africa, created new expectations. Newspapers and the radio, carrying news of the wider world, had an increasing impact. Events like the Atlantic Charter, promising the right of all peoples to choose their own form of government, had an electrifying effect on the West African elite. At the San Francisco conference in 1945 setting up the United Nations, the liberal sentiments expressed by the colonial powers there aroused their hopes anew. In India, the nationalists on the threshold of power set a potent example. For the most part, the African elite in countries such as the Gold Coast and Nigeria were conservative men, seeking no more than an enhanced political role for themselves. But more radical views were sometimes heard. In Accra and Lagos, 'youth' movements and African newspapers challenged the whole colonial system, vigorously attacking the limited concessions that Britain was willing to make and readily blaming the authorities for every social ill from high prices to low wages. Diatribes against imperialism were commonplace. But the radicals lacked popular support. The nationalist ideas they espoused reached only a tiny minority. The colonial authorities saw them as a handful of urban 'agitators' unlikely to cause much trouble so long as local chiefs and notables, hence the bulk of the population, remained loyal.

CHAPTER SIX

The Rise of Nkrumah

After twelve years abroad, Nkrumah returned to the Gold Coast in December 1947, penniless and virtually unknown. He had decided in London to accept an offer from a group of Gold Coast lawyers and businessmen who had set up a new political movement and wanted a full-time secretary to run it on their behalf. About Nkrumah the lawyers knew little, but his name had been recommended to them by a young graduate recently returned from London. On receiving the invitation, Nkrumah's first thought, according to his autobiography published ten years later, was that it would be 'quite useless to associate myself with a movement backed almost entirely by reactionaries, middle-class lawyers and merchants, for my revolutionary background and ideas would make it impossible for me to work with them'. But, after some further prompting, he changed his mind, accepted £100 for passage money and presented himself to the working committee of the United Gold Coast Convention on 28 December at the small coastal town of Saltpond. 'I am happy to be here with you at last,' Nkrumah told the lawyers.

The Convention had been formed in August 1947 as a result of growing disenchantment among middle-class Africans—the intelligentsia, as they were called locally—about the benefits of the 1946 constitution. Although the Legislative Council now had an African majority, the chiefs retained a powerful role and the middle-class felt that their own influence was too restricted. As its long term aim, the Convention wanted self-government 'in the shortest possible time'. But its leaders were conservative men with a high regard for constitutional methods and from the outset they were hopeful merely that self-government might be achieved in their lifetime. Their more immediate interest was to build up a national movement to press their case for greater representation on the Legislative

Council.

Seeking support for the Convention, Nkrumah and the lawyer J. B. Danquah, its most prominent member, spent much of January and February 1948 touring central and southern Gold Coast. The response they found, particularly from local youth societies, was enthusiastic. In the main towns, Convention meetings drew large crowds. Across much of the country serious grievances against the government were mounting and each one Convention leaders took up as part of their own campaign. In rural areas, cocoa farmers, ordered by the government to destroy diseased trees, were openly hostile to the authorities; for several months, protest meetings had been held, and in some areas clashes had occurred between individual farmers and gangs of labourers sent by the government to enforce the order. In the towns, a campaign protesting against high prices and consumer shortages, organised by an Accra businessman, received strong support. When no action was taken to bring prices down and the government remained aloof from the dispute, a national boycott, aimed mainly at European and Lebanese firms, was launched on 24 January. The boycott continued for a month, whereupon the firms promised to reduce their profit margins and introduce new prices for a trial period. The date set for the price changes and the end of the boycott was 28 February. On that day too, ex-servicemen arranged to march with a petition to the Governor about their own grievances.

The events of 28 February 1948, bringing violence so unexpectedly to a colony that the British had long regarded as a model of progress and good sense, had an impact which was to set the Gold Coast and indeed British West Africa on an entirely new course. By themselves, when compared to other tumultuous episodes in Britain's colonial history, the incidents were of a minor order. But British officials were astonished that they had happened at all. First, the procession of ex-servicemen, once their leaders had delivered their petition at the Secretariat, began to march towards the Governor's residence at Christiansborg Castle, a few miles from the centre of Accra. At a road junction on the way, they were stopped by a small police detachment. In a growing commotion, stones were hurled and a British officer, snatching a rifle from one of his men, opened fire killing two men and wounding several others. Starting quite separately, angry crowds in the centre of Accra, dissatisfied with new shop prices and incited by agitators, set fire to European-owned stores. When news of the shooting near Christiansborg Castle spread, riots developed. Looting continued into the night; and the following morning the gates of Ussher Fort prison were battered down and some prisoners released. The disturbances then spread to other towns. By the time they were finally brought under control two weeks later, twenty-nine people had been killed and more than two hundred injured.

Meeting in Accra on the first night of the riots, Convention leaders discussed how best to profit from the situation. In the end they decided that telegrams sent to the Secretary of State and the world press would help publicise their demands for self-government. Danquah's telegram was long and rambling. 'Civil government ... broken down ... disorder and lawlessness ... unprovoked massacre of civilians and unarmed ex-servicemen ...' He warned of worse violence unless a new government was installed, declared the Convention to be ready to take over an interim government and ended with the words: 'God Save the King and Floreat United Gold Coast.' Nkrumah's much briefer telegram, sent to the United Nations and newspapers in New York, London and Moscow, claimed that the civil authorities had lost control, asked for the recall of the Governor and stated: 'People demand Self-Government Immediately.'

The Governor, Sir Gerald Creasy, who had recently arrived from London, could find no other explanation for the violence than that it had been fomented deliberately by the Convention. In his own telegram to the Secretary of State on 29 February, he reported: 'Convention is certainly behind, and almost wholly responsible for, the bitterness and violence ... the present riots ... appear to have been thoroughly planned ...' In the following days, he became increasingly convinced that he was dealing with a Communist-inspired conspiracy to overthrow the government in which the Convention's working committee was involved, and he ordered the arrest of its six principal members. Nkrumah was the centre of suspicion. His activities in London, monitored by the police, were well known to the authorities. In the view of the Colonial Office at that time he was 'a thorough-going Communist'. Other evidence accumulated. In Nkrumah's possession at the time of his arrest was a membership card of the British Communist Party and a document relating to the secret society, The Circle, that Nkrumah in London had wanted to form. There came to light too a memorandum he had produced for the working committee, shortly before the riots, advocating the use of 'organised demonstration, boycott and strike' in the campaign for self-government. In radio broadcasts, Creasy referred to the danger of Communists seizing power and of new forms of terrorism.

A Commission of Enquiry, sent out from London in April, found more profound causes behind the riots. The most serious problem facing the Gold Coast, its chairman, Aiken Watson, Recorder of Norwich, reported, was the general suspicion which surrounded government activity of any sort. In particular, the chiefs had come to be regarded as mere tools of the government used to suppress political aspirations. The intelligentsia felt especially frustrated at their lack of influence over government policy and wanted the chiefs confined to an 'ornamental' role in society. While the constitutional advances introduced in 1946 had been regarded at the time as appropriate, because of the quickening pace of social and economic change since the war, they were 'outmoded at birth'. In their place, the Watson Commission recommended sweeping constitutional changes giving Africans not only increased legislative responsibilities but executive power.

As for the immediate circumstances of the riots, no convincing evidence implicating the Convention was ever produced. The telegrams sent to the Secretary of State by Danquah and Nkrumah, implying a measure of coordination, were dismissed by George Padmore in London as 'a piece of comic-opera politics'. Indeed, many of the Convention's leaders, respectable pillars of African society as they saw themselves, were appalled to be caught up in such ugly events and blamed Nkrumah for their misfortune. In his report, Watson paid due attention to Nkrumah's position, suggesting that he had become 'imbued with a Communist ideology' and referring to his avowed aim to set up 'a Union of West African

Soviet Socialist Republics'. But Nkrumah himself, never slow to push forward his own revolutionary credentials, disclaimed any involvement. His arrival in the Gold Coast at such a time, he said, was simply a coincidence. When the riots began, he was sixty miles away in Saltpond.

In retrospect, more lay behind the riots than the particular grievances of ex-servicemen or cocoa farmers, or discontent over high prices, or the complacency of a colonial government and its ill-informed governor, or indeed the activities of a group of ambitious lawyers and the man with revolutionary ideas they had inadvertently hired, though each no doubt contributed in some way. For the protests on the streets marked the coming of a new generation, disgruntled and restless, thrusting for their own place in society, ready to challenge not just colonial rule but the authority of the Gold Coast chiefdoms on which the British had relied for so long. To the chiefs, these men, drawn mainly from the ranks of primary school leavers, were known as 'malcontents' and 'agitators'. For a time, they proved useful to the intelligentsia in their own campaign to wrest power from the chiefs. But they were eager too for more radical leadership, for action that would bring them a new future, for a taste of power. And it was all these things which Nkrumah in time would offer them.

The detention of Nkrumah, Danquah and other Convention leaders raised them to national fame. Everywhere 'the Big Six' were acclaimed as popular heroes. New branches of the party proliferated. But though gratified by the response, Danquah and his associates, having glimpsed what one British newspaper, *The Daily Herald*, referred to at the time as 'the Frankenstein monster in African nationalism' were anxious on their release to return to the more familiar path of moderate reform. So, of course, were the British. In London, the Colonial Office had at first feared that the kind of political violence predicted by Andrew Cohen in his secret memorandum was already upon them. For some time afterwards, officials in London believed the danger remained acute. Despatching a new Governor to the Gold Coast in 1949, Creech Jones warned him that 'the country is on the edge of revolution'. All the more reason was seen, therefore, to press ahead with the political changes that the Watson Commission, and indeed Cohen earlier, had recommended. In what now seemed like a race against time, Creech Jones was anxious to find moderate nationalists who would cooperate with Britain's plans for orderly progress towards self-government. Conveniently, Danquah and his colleagues were ready to respond. When the British government proposed that an all-African committee on constitutional reform should examine the whole field of government and invited Convention leaders to participate, Danquah welcomed the opportunity. In due course, the intelligentsia and the chiefs, assisted by British officials, were sitting down together, amicably working out a new programme.

Of 'the Big Six', only Nkrumah was not invited to take part. Distrusted by the British and, by now, Convention leaders alike, he went his own way, remaining at first within the Convention, but assiduously building up his own personal following among youth societies. Assured of their support, he finally broke with Danquah's Convention—'the men of property and standing'—and in June 1949, only eighteen months after returning to the Gold Coast, launched the Convention People's Party. Master at last of his own organisation, he threw himself tirelessly into the task of turning it into a modern political machine. The message he carried was simple and uncompromising: 'Self-Government NOW.' As a party slogan, it was far more potent than the rival 'Self-Government in the shortest possible time'. With audiences eager to hear of political change, Nkrumah promised that self-government would solve the grievances and hardships inflicted by colonial rule. It would bring a new world of opportunity, of prosperity and progress across the country. The heady propaganda was spread at rallies, by party workers and through roughly produced newspapers that Nkrumah established in Accra, Sekondi and Cape Coast. In the party press, no occasion was lost to vilify the colonial government or political opponents like Danquah or the Constitutional Committee, to blame them all for holding back the march to freedom.

To the campaign, Nkrumah brought to bear formidable talents as a political activist. Possessing a restless energy and great ability as an organiser, he pursued power with obsessive determination. His fiery speeches, his flamboyant manner, his winning smile made him the most famous politician in the country, the 'Showboy' who could generate a sense of excitement, of hope, of expectation. Unerringly he used the popular touch. Every grievance was exploited, every aspiration aroused. To the youth, to the homeless 'verandah boys' who slept on the verandahs of the rich, he was already an idol. His radical appeal now spread among trade unionists, ex-servicemen and farmers; it reached clerks and storekeepers, petty traders and primary school teachers, 'youngmen' as they were known, seeking a better way of life. To those without money, without position, without property, 'Free-Dom' was an offer of salvation. 'Seek ye first the political kingdom,' Nkrumah told them, 'and all else will follow.'

By the end of 1949, Nkrumah felt strong enough to challenge the government outright. When the Constitutional Committee, headed by Sir Henley Coussey, a 55-year-old African judge, recommended a form of 'semi-responsible' government, with a nationally elected assembly and eight African ministers represented in the Executive Council, Nkrumah denounced the plan as 'bogus and fraudulent' and threatened to start a campaign of 'Positive Action'—strikes, boycotts, agitation and propaganda—unless Britain agreed to immediate self-government. Defying warnings from the new Governor, Sir Charles Arden-Clarke, the CPP declared a nation-wide strike and boycott in January. Well prepared this time, the government declared a state of emergency, imposed curfews and arrested Nkrumah and other party leaders. Brought before the courts, they were convicted, some of promoting an illegal strike and attempting to coerce the government, others of sedition; Nkrumah was sentenced separately on three counts to a total of three years imprisonment. In Danquah's words, the 'wolf had been driven away'.

Far from hindering the campaign, the arrest of Nkrumah and his lieutenants turned them into martyrs. The 'prison graduate cap' became a possession admired and respected. Those who completed their sentences were welcomed back rapturously and returned to the fray with renewed enthusiasm. Though Nkrumah remained in James Fort prison in Accra, his aides carried party activity into every corner of the country. As the election scheduled for February 1951 drew near, the CPP brought into play the whole paraphernalia of modern politics: flags, banners, slogans, loudspeaker vans, processions, dances, rallies, bands. Its manifesto made sweeping promises: free education, free health service, piped water supply, new railways, roads, industrialisation. At every turn, Danquah's Convention was outmatched, as the election result eventually showed. Of the thirty-eight popularly contested seats, the CPP won thirty-four, the Convention three.

Well before the election took place, the government was in no doubt about what the result would be, or about the reaction that would follow unless Nkrumah was released. 'It was obvious that the CPP would refuse to cooperate in working the Constitution without their leader,' recalled the Governor, Arden-Clarke. 'Nkrumah and his party had the mass of the people behind them and there was no other party with appreciable public support to which one could turn. Without Nkrumah, the Constitution would be stillborn and if nothing came of all the hopes, aspirations and concrete proposals for a greater measure of self-government, there would no longer be any faith in the good intentions of the British Government and the Gold Coast would be plunged into disorders, violence and bloodshed.'

So Nkrumah was released, invited by the Governor the next day to Christiansborg Castle and asked to form a government. 'That meeting was redolent of mutual suspicion and mistrust,' said Arden-Clarke. 'We were like two dogs meeting for the first time, sniffing around each other with hackles half raised, trying to decide whether to bite or to wag our tails.'

But a second meeting was more relaxed. 'This time the hackles were down, and before the end the tails were wagging.'

The transformation that had occurred was remarkable—for Nkrumah, for the Gold Coast and for the British government alike. Four years before, Nkrumah had been an undistinguished student, hanging about cheap cafés in London, dreaming of absurd schemes but accomplishing nothing. He had arrived in the Gold Coast, his fare paid for, to take up the life of an itinerant political organiser and found himself after a few months under arrest, unjustly accused of being at the centre of a Communist-inspired plot to overthrow the government. By the next year, he had acquired a large enough following to launch his own political party and within six months was sufficiently bold or reckless to try to force the government's hand by inciting a general strike. While he was in jail, his party nevertheless won a famous election victory and he himself was chosen by a massive vote to represent an Accra constituency. Released from prison, he was within twenty-four hours shaking the Governor's hand and ready to preside as Chief Minister over the government.

The Gold Coast, after the war, was a 'model' colony, much admired in Annual Reports, administered in what seemed to be reasonable harmony between British officials and chiefs representing the people, with a minor role played by the intelligentsia. A new constitution in 1946, the most advanced yet devised by Britain for its African colonies, gave the intelligentsia a greater say in government affairs and was generally welcomed at the time. The Governor, Sir Alan Burns, was able to express in 1946 'great confidence in these extremely sensible people' and report that they 'are really satisfied with the new Constitution'. His assessment was supported by other knowledgeable men. A highly reputed British expert, Martin Wight, writing in 1947, calculated that the new constitution would 'for several decades satisfy legitimate aspirations of the political class'. The following year, Accra was beset by the worst riots that the capital had ever seen and a new Governor was alerting the Colonial Office to the dangers of a Communist takeover. A commission of enquiry found little evidence of Communist involvement but was strongly critical of the colonial government and suggested an entirely new constitution. It advised, in particular, that 'the star of rule through the chiefs was on the wane'. The African view, as expressed by the Coussey Constitutional Committee, confirmed that the Gold Coast was ready for a period of 'semi-responsible' government, complete with a national parliamentary system and national elections. When the British government accepted these recommendations, the assumption was that the group of lawyers, businessmen and other professional figures who led the Convention, would make admirable partners in this new venture. In what was the country's first national election, they were upstaged by men at the head of a People's Party proclaiming themselves, as Nkrumah did after his release from prison, to be implacably opposed to imperialism. The verandah boys had come to power.

The British government started out after the war accustomed to taking a long term view of Africa and stressing the need for economic and social progress before political advancement. In the Colonial Office, the last battles over indirect rule were still being fought between an old guard, led by Lord Hailey, who favoured the chiefs, and a more 'modern' group who saw the African middle class as the heirs to British power. A pioneer of colonial reform, Creech Jones, the Colonial Secretary, issued firm directives in 1947 that in future local government would provide the main thrust of British policy, enabling democracy to grow from 'the bottom', while at 'the centre' the middle class would be rewarded with a more substantial role. All too clearly at the time, the Colonial Office was sensitive to the dangers of allowing a small elite group—'professional politicians'—to acquire too much power on their own behalf. More radical suggestions, like those put forward the same year by Andrew Cohen, urging a much faster pace of development to keep ahead of the challenge that African nationalists would inevitably pose in the future, were met with stout resistance by the colonial establishment. Shaken a few months later by relatively minor riots, the Colonial Office was suddenly prepared to leapfrog several stages, agreeing to establish a mainly African cabinet and a national parliamentary system. Fully expecting that the groomed middle class would step forward, the British found themselves in 1951 dealing instead with a man who described himself as a 'Marxian Socialist'. With customary aplomb, they settled down, in Arden-Clarke's words, to 'a close, friendly and if I may say so, not unfruitful partnership'.

In British eyes, though, the Gold Coast had always been an exception. It had advantages of wealth and attainment unrivalled in tropical Africa. Its educational system was the most advanced, offering more schooling by the 1940s, for example, than in the whole of French black Africa. For several decades, thriving middle class families—successful merchants and cocoa farmers—had been able to send their sons to long established secondary schools and many subsequently went for further education to the universities, medical schools and Inns of Court in Britain. Returning home as doctors, lawyers and teachers they eventually formed the largest reservoir of trained men to be found in any tropical African country. The level of political sophistication was unusually high even for West Africa. The Gold Coast was small and relatively homogenous, seemingly free of tribal and religious tension; half of the population was of Akan origin and spoke related dialects. By almost every standard, therefore, and because of its great potential, the Gold Coast was marked out in Africa as a special case.

The new system of government too was thought by many British officials as being in the nature of 'an experiment', one that would be carefully controlled and monitored; if something went wrong, it could be delayed or halted; certainly it was not to be repeated on a larger scale until careful studies had been made. But from the outset, the reality was different. Once the nationalist urge had taken hold, the British role in the Gold Coast was no more than 'a holding exercise'. In office, Nkrumah became the sober administrator, but all the time he pressed Arden-Clarke for more power. In 1954 he obtained a new constitution granting full self-government, won new elections, and began to demand independence. It was an example that was watched closely, with awe or with a certain trepidation, elsewhere in Africa.

CHAPTER SEVEN

The Mau Mau Rebellion

By the time that Jomo Kenyatta returned to Kenya in 1946, he had become to many Africans a legendary figure. In the years of his absence, much had been heard of the battles for African rights that he had fought in London, of his book extolling the Kikuyu people, and of his travels in Europe. His life abroad, the knowledge and experience he had gained of British politics, had earned him great prestige; and his return now aroused a sense of expectation that the nationalist campaigns he had waged abroad he was bringing to Kenya. On the quayside of Mombasa harbour, African porters crowded around him; during his rail journey to Nairobi, groups of tribesmen waited at wayside halts to catch a glimpse of him; and at Nairobi station he was carried shoulder high through an excited African throng. With equal enthusiasm, the African press acclaimed him a hero.

Kenyatta lost no time in seeking a political role for himself. Shortly after his return, he went to see the Governor, Sir Philip Mitchell, to discuss the matter. Within the Colonial Office, Mitchell was highly regarded. His career in east and central Africa, stretching back for more than thirty years, had made him the most experienced and trusted British proconsul in the region. He had arrived in Kenya as Governor in 1944 with a liberal reputation, determined to build a new kind of partnership between the European, African and Asian communities. In line with Colonial Office thinking at the time, he believed the key to African progress lay in economic development. In his memoirs, written in 1953 at his farm in Kenya to which he retired when his term as Governor ended, he noted that 'the great mass of the people of this region (east and central Africa) are still in a state of ignorance and backwardness, uncivilised, superstitious, economically weak to the point of near helplessness and quite unable to construct a civilised future for themselves.' The priority for Africans, therefore, was to transform the subsistence society in which they lived. Towards the views of African nationalists he gave little attention; their nationalism, he said in 1950, was 'an emotional movement rather than a rational policy'. With Kenyatta he was complimentary about 'his undoubted talents and considerable influence'. But his advice to him in 1946 was that if he wanted to take an active role in politics, he should start by seeking election to a local Native Council rather than try immediately for anything more ambitious. Kenyatta had been given similar advice by a previous British governor in 1930. He chose not to heed it.

Throughout his term of office, Mitchell was preoccupied more with the truculent white community than with any sign of African discontent. Their numbers were few: at the end of the Second World War, less than 30,000. But successive British governors had always been wary of losing their cooperation. In the past, to get their way, the whites had resorted to threats of 'direct action' and rebellion; on one occasion they had actively plotted to kidnap the Governor. While some still hoped to obtain the form of self-government given to white Rhodesians twenty years before, others, more realistically, set their sights on gaining as much control over the government as possible. Their distrust of the British government was intense. Frequently, they demanded to be rid of Colonial Office ties. Above all, they insisted that the leadership of Kenya remain in European hands.

Foremost among the whites were the farming communities. They had endured hardship, depression and often disaster in taming the land; some, like Lord Delamere, had spent their fortunes on it. By nature they tended to be stubborn, resourceful and headstrong, scornful of colonial authority and determined to keep the White Highlands for their exclusive use. In their view, Kenya had been transformed from a primitive wilderness into a modern state solely through the enterprise and skill of white farmers; and its prosperity was still dependent on their efforts. Towards their African servants and employees they often showed paternal affection; but for the African mass, little but contempt. Any suggestion that Africans should share in the political future of the country was greeted with derision. When the editor of the local newspaper remarked in 1944 that self-government for Kenya could only be achieved 'on the basis of all races cooperating', rather than by Europeans alone, his words provoked a storm of outrage and cost him all hope of a successful political career.

Mitchell's plans for introducing a multi-racial society were soon caught in the same snare. He had arrived in Kenya bearing the outline of a scheme for an inter-territorial organisation linking common services between Kenya and the two neighbouring British territories of Uganda and Tanganyika. The idea appealed to most whites as a first step towards the creation of an East African federation in which they believed they would play a commanding role. But when Mitchell's proposals were published for public perusal in December 1945, the whites discovered to their horror that in drawing up the composition of the inter-territorial assembly, he had provided for equal representation between Europeans, Africans and Asians. In the ensuing uproar, Creech Jones flew out from the Colonial Office in London, made his own consultations and ordered revised proposals. When these appeared in 1947, the whites had won their way and were given more seats than anyone else.

At any sign that Africans or Asians might advance at the expense of the white community, the white reaction was invariably hostile. Constantly they pressed their own claim for greater political power. In the Legislative Council, the whites constituted the largest elected group; in the government they controlled two portfolios; and these leads they were determined to maintain. To erase any doubt about their position, the white Electors' Union published in 1949 a blunt affirmation of white power called the *Kenya Plan*, in which they demanded that European leadership be recognised as 'paramount'. They also called for the creation of a new 'British East African Dominion' and cooperation with Rhodesia and South Africa. 'Any attempt to hand over power to an immature race must be resisted,' said an Electors' Union spokesman. 'To the Africans we offer sympathetic tutelage which will lead them to full participation in the government of the country. But we have made our position clear. We are here to stay and the other races must accept that premise with all it implies.'

With reckless abandon at times, the whites were prepared to oppose any change not to their advantage. After the Legislative Council passed an ordinance requiring men of all races to carry an identity card with fingerprints, many whites erupted in fury. Until that time, only Africans had been required to carry identity cards, a measure which they intensely resented. Across the White Highlands, angry meetings were held at which the more zealous whites advocated open defiance of the new law. Fingerprinting, it was said, was a method employed only by totalitarian regimes; it was the mark of a criminal. At one stormy meeting in Nakuru, a member of the Legislative Council who supported the ordinance was faced with an opponent who strode up and down the gangway of the hall with two large pistols hanging from his belt, fixing a threatening eye on anyone voting against him. In the end, the administration retreated. A compromise was reached by which those who could complete a form in English and provide two photographs were not required to be fingerprinted.

The way in which the whites sought to block any African advancement aggravated the sense of grievance building up amongst the African population. In the aftermath of the Second World War, Kenya was affected, like other African colonies, by the flood of returning servicemen and the unrest that demobilisation caused. Some 75,000 Africans had joined the armed forces from Kenya, many serving abroad and expecting a new life on their return. But, as Kenyatta noted, while British ex-servicemen were encouraged by the government to take up farming, African soldiers were confronted by the colour bar and pass laws and offered meagre gratuities. In Nairobi, unemployment, poor housing, low wages and the high cost of living, produced a groundswell of discontent and worsening crime; the government estimated that 4,000 Africans there were 'completely homeless' while thousands more endured appalling conditions. The African reserves, too, suffered from overcrowding.

The most potent grievance was over land. Amongst the Kikuyu tribe, living directly north of Nairobi on the lower slopes of the Aberdare mountains, a deep conviction had taken hold that much of their land had been 'stolen' during the white occupation of Kenya and incorporated in the White

Highlands. For years, the Kikuyu had campaigned for the recovery of these 'lost lands'; protests and petitions of the kind that Kenyatta took to London in 1929 were frequently made to the British government. To settle the issue, the British government set up a land commission in 1932 to examine the evidence. Its report, published two years later, concluded that some injustice had occurred. Because of drought, famine and a smallpox epidemic in 1898, the Kikuyu population in southern Kiambu had been drastically reduced just as the first white settlers arrived, and an area amounting to 110 square miles in the vicinity of Nairobi, normally used by the Kikuyu, had been lying vacant and was taken by white owners. As compensation, the Kikuyu were awarded by the commission an appropriate area of land elsewhere, and the British government then considered the matter closed. The Kikuyu, however, continued their agitation. And as their numbers in the Kikuyu reserves grew and overcrowding developed, the cry for more land became insistent. For most Kikuyu, the land was the only form of security they had. Yet around them lay the frontiers of the White Highlands, an area where they were debarred by law from owning land and which the whites were determined to protect for themselves.

The whites pointed out that when they occupied the Kenya Highlands, an area covering in all about 12,000 square miles, the land was largely uninhabited. Out of the virgin bush they had carved coffee plantations, tea estates, dairy farms and cattle ranches, and though vast stretches of land remained undeveloped, they saw no reason to give any of it up. Indeed, they looked with contempt at the poor use to which Africans, and notably the Kikuyu, put their own land. In their determination to hold fast, they were supported by both the colonial government in Nairobi and the British government in London. As Governor, Mitchell refused any re-examination of the land dispute. To replace European farmers with Kikuyu peasants, he maintained, would destroy the country's economy which depended heavily on the prosperity of the agricultural industry. In the House of Commons, Creech Jones used similar arguments, warning that if the White Highlands were opened to African settlement, it would undermine white confidence: 'The government would have the greatest difficulty in persuading the European farmer to adopt long-sighted and efficient farming practices.' Thus, after the war, a quarter of a million acres in the White Highlands were set aside for use by British ex-servicemen, with the assurance that no change in land policy would be made during their lifetime.

The resentment that the Kikuyu felt over land was made worse by the government's restrictions on their growing coffee. In southern Kikuyu areas, coffee planting was banned. As late as 1950, the Director of Agriculture advised that the ban should continue. Through such rigid measures the government lost the support of one of the most influential Kikuyu chiefs, Senior Chief Koinange. Once he had been a staunch defender of the government. In 1937, the district commissioner in Kiambu described him as an 'outstanding personality' who had exerted 'a sober and moderating influence over the Kikuyu in times of potential trouble'. Since part of his own land had been taken for a European coffee farm, Koinange had asked the land commission for its return. In 1937 he received about one-tenth of what he claimed and he was ordered by the authorities to root out the coffee bushes growing there. Koinange took the case to court, but lost. From then on, he became increasingly alienated from the government. 'When someone steals your land,' he told a visitor in 1950, 'especially if nearby, one can never forget. It is always there. Its trees which were dear friends, its little streams. It is a bitter presence.'

For the myriad pressures building up, there was no outlet. In the Legislative Council, the first African representative was not appointed until 1944; by 1948 the number had grown to four, but all were still nominated by the government. Because most of the African population was illiterate, the government considered the idea of elections at a national level to be far too premature. Only after several generations had passed was it thought that Africans would be competent to assume more serious government responsibilities. What efforts the four African representatives made to draw attention to African grievances were largely ignored. Indeed, to many Africans it seemed that the government, by protecting the White Highlands and deferring on major issues to white opinion, had become identified solely with the interests of the white community.

In this troubled atmosphere, Kenyatta found a ready response to his plans for political action. Welcomed back as the dominant political figure in the country, he was soon able to assume command of the Kenya African Union, formed in 1944 to campaign for African rights. His intention was to turn the KAU into a national movement. Constantly he appealed to Africans to think in national rather than in tribal terms. But the mass support that KAU won and its leadership came largely from the Kikuyu tribe. It was the Kikuyu whose sense of grievance against the government and against the whites was strongest. And it was among the Kikuyu that thoughts of rebellion were already beginning to stir.

They were an industrious, able and acquisitive people, deeply religious, secretive, with a mystical attachment to the land. Their language was complex and understood by few Europeans. In numbers, they were the largest tribe in Kenya, more than one million, and constituted about one fifth of the African population. Living close to Nairobi and almost surrounded by the White Highlands, they were brought more abruptly into contact with white settlers and became the most politically conscious tribe. They were often divided amongst themselves. From the 1920s, the more militant Kikuyu had tended to support the Kikuyu Central Association, whose main battle cry was 'to get back the land'. At the outbreak of the Second World War, the KCA's opposition to government policies was deemed subversive, the movement was banned and its leaders detained. But in secret, its members kept in touch and clandestine branches were soon revived.

In Kenyatta, the Kikuyu had a leader whose knowledge and understanding of tribal traditions enabled him to articulate with passionate conviction the aspirations they felt and yet whose experience of the modern world gave him a practical insight into the wider dimensions of the confrontation that was gathering. His involvement in Kikuyu politics had begun twenty-five years before when, after a mission education and sundry jobs, he joined the KCA, becoming its full-time general secretary. On behalf of the KCA he had first travelled to London to petition the British government. In exile there he had continued to act as their spokesman; and it was as the

KCA delegate that he had attended the Manchester conference in 1945. Often arrogant, vain and autocratic, he saw himself destined to become a nationalist leader not just of the Kikuyu, but of Kenya. His forceful personality, his powers of oratory, his flamboyant manner soon captivated the crowds that flocked to listen to him. Within months of his return, the white-run *East African Standard* was reporting 'scenes of enthusiasm, probably without parallel in Kenya' during his appearance at a meeting in Nyeri. On Sundays, if he was in the neighbourhood, churches normally packed were deserted. In the vernacular press, he was hailed as a 'Saviour'.

His speeches at first were moderate enough to win the grudging approval of the white establishment. At KAU meetings, he castigated Africans for idleness, for dishonesty, for bad farming practices, for taking to crime. On occasion he was willing to lend his authority to help settle minor problems for the authorities. But all along there was no mistaking his determination to unite the Kikuyu behind the campaign for African rights. And the demands he made for political reform, for land, for an end to racial discrimination soon echoed across the ridges and ravines of Kikuyuland and far beyond.

As his headquarters, he chose Githunguri, in northern Kiambu, where he was invited to become the principal of an independent Kikuyu teachers training school. There he built a spacious house, filling it with books, pictures and mementoes from Europe. From Githunguri, Kenyatta formed an intricate network which kept him at the centre of political activity. To this retreat in the hills above Nairobi came old colleagues from the banned KCA, visitors from KAU, the ex-servicemen's association, trades unions and Kikuyu age-group organisations. His influence spread too through the independent Kikuyu schools, set up in the 1930s after a clash with missionaries over female circumcision. And he developed a close friendship with Senior Chief Koinange, taking one of his daughters as a wife.

But it was in Nairobi, among the thousands of unemployed and homeless, that the most militant elements were emerging. Mixing politics and crime, the 'Forty Group', consisting largely of former soldiers of the 1940 age group who had seen service during the war in India, Burma and Ethiopia, were ready to employ strong-arm tactics in opposing government policies and in dealing with government supporters. Young 'Forty' men played an active role in stirring up Kikuyu resistance to the government's conservation measures in the reserve. The trades unions, gathering strength in Nairobi, carried the agitation further, conducting a virulent campaign against the granting of a Royal Charter to Nairobi. In the African press, too, the tone was becoming increasingly strident.

The rising temper of the Kikuyu made little impression on the government. Nor was much attention paid to other warnings. In July 1947, the African representative in the Legislative Council, Eliud Mathu, sent a memorandum to the government in which he referred to meetings at night behind locked doors, in caves, and in the depths of banana groves, where men gathered, whispering and cursing the Europeans and their own headmen. Receiving no reply to this memorandum, he read passages from it to the Legislative Council in January 1948. That same month, a moderate white member of the Legislative Council presented a motion expressing grave concern about the unrest in African areas. The motion was soundly defeated. From rural outposts, district officials sent reports of mounting anti-government and anti-European feeling, noticeable particularly among Kikuyu farm labourers living on white farms—squatters as they were known. The officials referred too to an upsurge in oath-taking among the Kikuyu. And in 1948 the District Commissioner of Nakuru in the Rift Valley, in his annual report, made the first official mention of what was then thought to be a clandestine movement called *Mau Mau*.

It was a name which in the Kikuyu language was meaningless. It had evolved out of the activities of the banned KCA sowing seeds of rebellion among a disaffected people. But the origin of the name was lost in the Kikuyu passion for riddles. The authorities, convinced that it was a sinister secret society, outlawed the '*Mau Mau* Association' in August 1950. But what they were really facing was an incipient revolt among the Kikuyu for which *Mau Mau* became, by common usage, the fearsome expression.

As a way of mobilising the Kikuyu and binding them

together in their resistance to the government, secret oaths were employed on an ever widening scale. By tradition, the Kikuyu used oaths openly for a variety of social purposes. At the end of the Second World War, however, KCA leaders, released from detention, devised a political oath. Gradually the oath-taking spread and came to the government's attention. In April 1950, the police decided to take action and arrested two leading KCA figures. One of them, Dedan Mugo, was a prominent oath administrator in Kiambu, whose career exemplified the multiple strands of the Kikuyu network: he was a former army warrant officer, a member of the Forty Group, president of the ex-servicemen's association, leader of the Kikuyu Age Groups, a member of the Kiambu Local Native Council, a KAU organiser and one of Kenyetta's colleagues at Githunguri. Mugo was convicted of administering an illegal KCA oath. After a second court case, in which the name *Mau Mau* was mentioned, the government issued its ban. By then, however, the campaign was gaining momentum. Kikuyu leaders had been strongly impressed by the solidarity shown by a colony of Kikuyu squatters at Olenguruone who had devised their own oath to bind them together in defiance against the government over a land dispute, and they recognised the potential for the use of oathing on a greater scale. Meeting at Koinange's house at Banana Hill, north of Nairobi, in February 1950, they decided on a campaign of mass oathing. The oaths kept to a traditional form and thus helped to ensure secrecy. By the end of those years, perhaps ninety per cent of the Kikuyu tribe, certainly several hundred thousand, had taken some form of oath. In the Kikuyu press, open invitations were made to 'tea parties' at the Kikuyu Club in Nairobi which usually included secret oathing ceremonies. Simultaneously, KAU spread its activities. At fervent gatherings, Kikuyu songs, adapted from church hymns, would be sung in praise of Kenyatta, and prayers recited to glorify him. Not all Kikuyu took the oath voluntarily or approved of the religious parodies. Many Christian Kikuyu resisted; a large number of government employees remained loyal; and Kikuyu traditionalists opposed the new oaths because women and children were encouraged to participate, contrary to Kikuyu custom. In such cases, intimidation and violence were often used.

The signs of African unrest only made the whites hold more adamantly to their own position. Many were worried by Britain's policy in the Gold Coast, which had led to the introduction of an African-led government, and feared the impact that it might have among Africans in Kenya. When constitutional discussions were under way in 1951, the whites vehemently opposed any increase in African representation in the Legislative Assembly that threatened their own numbers and demanded parity with other races. For the African side, KAU sought twelve elected members to equal white representation. KAU also drew up a land petition which complained of severe overcrowding in the reserves, of 'ghetto-like conditions' in urban areas, and of 'the increase of poverty, malnutrition, crime and moral degradation among the Africans'. When the new Colonial Secretary, James Griffiths, visited Kenya in May 1951 to discuss constitutional measures, Kenyatta gave him a list of African political demands and included a version of the land petition. Later that month, in the House of Commons, Griffiths announced his decision. There was to be no major change. African representatives would be increased from four to six, but all would still be nominated by the government; white representation would be increased to fourteen. To the white Electors' Union, it seemed to be for them a considerable victory. From Nyeri, however, the District Commissioner reported in a confidential despatch to the central government in Nairobi: 'The district is hot with rumours of "deeds not words".'

From mid-1951, militant Kikuyu set the pace. In Nairobi, a hardened group including two prominent trade unionists, Fred Kubai and Bildad Kaggia, took control of the local KAU branch, ousting all former office bearers. They were tough, uncompromising men, willing to use violence. Within a few months, the young militants in Nairobi had gained virtual control over the national executive committee of KAU and formed their own secret Central Committee, with plans for an armed uprising. Throughout Kikuyuland, they built up a network of secret cells, sent out mobile oathing groups and slowly started to organise supplies of arms and ammunition.

With only limited evidence at hand to indicate what was

happening, the authorities in Nairobi considered the *Mau Mau* scare to be greatly exaggerated. The Governor, Sir Philip Mitchell, nearing the end of a long and distinguished career in the Colonial Service, saw nothing serious amiss. Race relations were good, he believed, and, visiting London briefly in February 1952, he reported that the general political feeling in Kenya was better than he had known it for years. On his fishing trips in Kikuyu country, he recalled in his memoirs, he met only 'smiling faces and happy, cheerful people'. Writing to his successor, Sir Evelyn Baring, in June, he dwelt on the social difficulty of how a Governor should deal with divorced people in the colony, like the Delameres, but gave no hint of graver developments. As for *Mau Mau* itself, he believed, according to his memoirs, that it was little more than a religious cult of the kind which periodically sprang up in Kenya then vanished. On 21 June, Mitchell went on holiday before retiring, leaving a gap of several months before his successor was due to arrive.

But in the field, district administrators were far more worried. At the beginning of 1952, there had been an outbreak of arson, suggesting that an 'action group' was at work; pro-government headmen found their huts burned down in the night; a sudden increase in grass fires was recorded; and several incidents were reported from European farms. From their outposts, officials noted down scores of rumours warning that whites would soon be driven out and their land taken by the Kikuyu. Passing the information on to Nairobi, they recommended that decisive action should be taken. Then in June, police in Kiambu and Nyeri reported that a new 'killing oath' against Europeans was being administered in their districts.

Suddenly, the leaders of the white community, who hitherto had given little thought to African problems, became alarmed by the signs of growing disorder. In July, the first public debate on the extent of Kikuyu subversion opened in the Legislative Council. At a meeting with senior government officials the following month, white representatives pressed for the introduction of emergency powers and the detention of KAU leaders; unless the government acted, they warned, the whites might take matters into their own hands. All there were convinced that Kenyatta was the mastermind of the disturbances. Everywhere his name was mentioned: in the oaths, the hymns, the propaganda; every path seemed to lead to his door. But the government remained doubtful about the legal consequences of arresting him. Though all Kenyatta's movements had been watched by the police, though informers had reported at every opportunity his words, the government still had no evidence to link him with *Mau Mau* or any subversive activity. At a meeting of government officials on 17 August, the Member for Law and Order advised that if Kenyatta was arrested, he would be released as soon as he appeared before a judge.

Another ploy was tried. Because of Kenyatta's enormous influence over the Kikuyu, the government allowed him and other Kikuyu leaders to hold a meeting at Kiambu on 24 August for the express purpose of denouncing *Mau Mau*. In the past, Kenyatta's references to *Mau Mau* had always seemed to the authorities to be ambiguous, wrapped up in the riddles in which the Kikuyu so delighted. But in their growing concern, the authorities now believed that if Kenyatta was asked to make an outright attack on *Mau Mau* in public, it might turn the tide of subversion. To capture the moment, film cameras and tape recorders were laid on.

Before a crowd of some 25,000 Kikuyu, Kenyatta came to the microphone, wearing around his waist a beaded *kinyata* belt, from which his name was derived, and in one hand carrying a carved stick. 'This meeting,' he began, 'is one of the Kikuyu elders and leaders who have decided to address a public meeting and see what the disease in Kikuyuland is, and how this disease can be cured. We are being harmed by a thing called *Mau Mau*. Who wants to curse *Mau Mau*?' Immediately every hand went up. Kenyatta then used a traditional Kikuyu curse to condemn *Mau Mau*, casting it into 'oblivion'. He went on: '*Mau Mau* has spoiled the country. Let *Mau Mau* perish for ever. All people should search for *Mau Mau* and kill it.' One by one, other leaders came forward to denounce *Mau Mau*.

Some whites believed that Kenyatta meant what he said; others distrusted him too deeply. Within the government, there were mixed views. But among the African militants in

Nairobi, there was immediate concern. Kenyatta, they thought, had gone too far. Shortly after the Kiambu rally, Kenyatta was asked to meet the Central Committee. The meeting took place at KAU headquarters in Nairobi. According to one of its members present, Bildad Kaggia, Kenyatta had never before met the committee and was clearly surprised to discover who some of its representatives were. 'We knew Kenyatta did not mean what he said,' said Kaggia. 'But his terms were too strong, and there was always the possibility that some weaker members of "Mau Mau" might take him seriously.' Kenyatta argued with them at length, but in the end agreed that no more meetings of the kind would be held.

The violence grew worse. By the time that Baring arrived in Kenya on 29 September, daily incidents of murder, forced oathing and intimidation of government witnesses were occurring; chiefs and headmen were threatened; and on five white farms, buildings were set on fire and cattle maimed. On a tour of the troubled Kikuyu areas shortly after his arrival, Baring was told by everyone whom he met—missionaries, local chiefs, government officials—that law and order had broken down, the blame for which they attributed to Kenyatta and his KAU associates. As if in confirmation, towards the end of Baring's tour, a senior Kikuyu chief, one of the government's staunchest supporters, was assassinated in broad daylight seven miles from Nairobi. With mounting rage at the disorders, the white community insisted on government action. The hurried advice that Baring took from his own officials was that if Kenyatta and other leaders were arrested, the rebellion would rapidly die out. In a message to London on 9 October, Baring warned that the government was facing a planned revolutionary movement which, if not stopped, would lead to administrative breakdown and bloodshed. He recommended the use of emergency powers. On the night of 20 October, as British troop reinforcements were flown in from the Middle East, Kenyatta was arrested at Githunguri; and army and police units started rounding up 180 suspected ringleaders. The next day Baring announced a state of emergency.

The rebellion continued for four years before the army was able to withdraw. From small-scale, random and brutal episodes, it grew into a grinding guerrilla war. At the height of the Emergency, as it was commonly called, the government employed eleven infantry battalions, some 21,000 police, air force heavy bombers and thousands of African auxiliaries. The rebel *Mau Mau* forces, built up from small groups of young men sent to the heavily wooded regions of the Aberdares and Mount Kenya from August 1952 and reinforced by thousands more recruits during a mass exodus of Kikuyu squatters from white farms the following year, eventually totalled about 13,000. Armed mainly with *simis*, flat, double-edged swords, they were formed into loosely controlled fighting groups which raided white farms and neighbouring Kikuyu territory. At one time, they had the tacit support of most of the Kikuyu tribe and were backed up by a 'passive' wing of some 30,000 men, women and children in the reserve and an underground central committee in Nairobi which kept them supplied with weapons, ammunition, recruits, money and medicines. Not until 1954 did the security forces succeed in breaking up the Nairobi base and regaining control in the reserves. For another two years, small *Mau Mau* groups, their support cut off, their morale deteriorating, their leaders resorting to ever more obscene oaths to hold them together, held out in the thick mountain forests of the Aberdare range and around Mount Kenya, pursued by special tracker units and pseudo-gangs. Only when the last remaining *Mau Mau* leader, Dedan Kimathi, was captured in October 1956, after a manhunt lasting nearly a year, were operations officially ended.

In the course of the campaign, the government established a Kikuyu Home Guard; built protected villages; employed loyal medicine men to administer counter-oaths; used captured *Mau Mau* guerrillas as informants, guides and in pseudo-gangs; and detained up to 80,000 Kikuyu. But as much as the government's own measures, what defeated *Mau Mau* were the divisions among the Kikuyu themselves. Enough Kikuyu remained loyal for the government to build an effective defence. In the *Mau Mau* war, the Kikuyu loyalists, not the whites, bore the brunt of it. From the start, they were the target of *Mau Mau* leaders, who wanted first to enforce complete unity among the Kikuyu before turning on the whites. It was the massacre of Kikuyu loyalists at Lari in 1953, in scenes of appalling brutality, that convinced many Kikuyu to turn against *Mau Mau*. Units like the Home Guard, eventually some 25,000 strong, were able to provide them with protection. As the tide turned against *Mau Mau*, gang leaders tried to keep control by employing perverted oaths and by intimidation, methods which only succeeded in alienating more Kikuyu. By the end of the war, nearly 2,000 loyalist Africans had died. The death toll of rebels and their supporters was listed as 11,500. By comparison, the white community escaped lightly. Though white families in isolated farmsteads often lived in fear of attack, horrified by the savage murders that occurred in the White Highlands, after four years only thirty-two white civilians had been killed, less than the number who died in traffic accidents in Nairobi during the same period.

When seeking an explanation for *Mau Mau*, the white settlers, the missionaries, the administration and the British government were unanimous. They saw it as a secret tribal cult, inspired by ambitious men who, for their own power and profit, stirred up a largely primitive and superstitious people, confused and bewildered by their contact with the civilised world. The repugnant oaths, the crude witchcraft, the blasphemous prayers and songs, all were taken as examples of a tribe rejecting the ways of modern European society and Christian values and reverting to a primitive, barbaric mentality. In the words of the official Colonial Office report published in 1960, *Mau Mau* was a subversive movement 'based on the lethal mixture of pseudo-religion, nationalism and the evil forms of black magic'.

All the fear, anger and hatred that the white community felt facing this threat focused intensely on the person of Kenyatta. No other figure in colonial Africa was so reviled. Everything about him—his Russian connections, his left-wing friends in London, the grip he exerted over the Kikuyu, the hypnotic effect of his eyes—aroused in them a sense of loathing. From the moment of his return, they had seen him as a danger. As early as 1947, the more extreme whites had called for his deportation. Tracing the signs of African unrest back to the time of his arrival in Kenya in 1946, they became increasingly convinced that he had brought with him an evil scheme to subvert the Kikuyu and drive out the whites. The oathings, the violence, the demented murders intensified their revulsion. For everything, they held Kenyatta responsible. What they felt, moreover, was vindicated by a British court of law.

The trial of Jomo Kenyatta opened on 24 November 1952 in the cramped schoolroom of an agricultural training college in the remote administrative outpost at Kapenguria nearly three hundred miles from Nairobi. He was charged with the management of *Mau Mau*, an unlawful society. In presenting its case, the government was hampered by a lack of direct evidence. Being a secret society, so the government asserted, *Mau Mau* kept no records nor any list of members nor any insignia. The government therefore had to rely on witnesses. But potential witnesses were fearful of giving evidence. In a private letter to the Colonial Secretary in November, the Governor, Sir Evelyn Baring, explained that 'every possible effort has been made to offer them rewards and to protect them', but even so he was still uncertain about the outcome of the trial. The main prosecution witness was a man named Rawson Macharia, who claimed to be on friendly terms with Kenyatta and who described how Kenyatta had administered oaths to several people in 1950 while he was present. Kenyatta denied the story and so did nine defence witnesses. But the magistrate chose to accept Macharia's evidence as the truth. Two other statements of lesser importance were made by witnesses directly implicating Kenyatta in oathing ceremonies. The prosecution also attempted to show that Kenyatta, because of his enormous influence over the Kikuyu, had the power to stop *Mau Mau* if he so wished, but that he had failed to denounce *Mau Mau* effectively or, alternatively, that when he had appeared to do so, his words always had a double meaning. After a long argument on these points, Kenyatta retorted: 'I have done my best and if all other people had done as I have done *Mau Mau* would not be as it is now. You (the government) made it what it is.' He argued that, instead of arresting the leaders of *Mau Mau*, the government had made matters worse by picking up those leaders of KAU who by their stature and moderation might have been able to control the movement and prevent its worst excesses.

The trial continued for five months. While in the courtroom lawyers laboriously contested the meaning of Kikuyu words, the significance of oaths and the reliability of police informers, and the prosecution dwelt on the links which existed between the KCA, KAU, *Mau Mau* and Kenyatta, in the outside world the *Mau Mau* attacks reached a peak of horror. In March, as the trial drew to a close, the Lari massacre occurred.

In a climate of mounting public hysteria, the magistrate, a retired High Court judge, Mr Justice Thacker, gave his verdict on 8 April 1953. Kenyatta, he said, was the mastermind behind the *Mau Mau* society, the objective of which was to drive out from Kenya all Europeans, killing them if necessary. Using his influence over the Kikuyu, Kenyatta had persuaded them in secret to murder, to burn, to commit evil atrocities. 'You have let loose upon this land a flood of misery and unhappiness affecting the daily lives of all the races in it, including your own people.'

He gave Kenyatta the maximum sentence of seven years' imprisonment with hard labour, to be followed by an indefinite period of restriction. Five KAU officials tried with him were given similar sentences. Two of them, Fred Kubai and Bildad Kaggia were, in fact, members of the secret Nairobi Central Committee responsible for organising much of the violence.

As an attempt to prove that Kenyatta was a common criminal, as the prosecution asserted, his trial was hardly convincing. The evidence was flimsy. In an English setting it would almost certainly not have produced a conviction. Later, several curious aspects of the affair emerged, arousing even greater doubt. In 1958, the key witness, Rawson Macharia, signed an affidavit swearing that he had given false evidence against Kenyatta and that he had been paid by the government of Kenya to do so. He was able to produce a letter purporting to come from the Attorney-General's office in which were set out the terms of a government offer enabling him to study for two years at an English university, with all expenses paid, and, on his return, to obtain government employment. Macharia was prosecuted for perjury, not for what he had said during Kenyatta's trial, but for making a perjured affidavit. He was convicted and sentenced to two years' imprisonment. During his trial, government officials admitted that Macharia had received the rewards which he said the government had offered. Another curious aspect was the payment of £20,000 made to the magistrate on the instructions of Sir Evelyn Baring to compensate him for having to leave Kenya after giving his verdict, to avoid reprisal. The negotiations on this matter were conducted during the course of the trial.

On a wider scale, however, there could be no doubt of how inextricably involved with the rebellion Kenyatta was. He had returned to Kenya with the aim of achieving what amounted to revolution in a colonial society, knowing full well that a violent upheaval might be unavoidable. When constitutional methods failed to make any headway, like many others he was carried along by the more militant mood and at various times in speeches openly encouraged the idea of revolt: 'The land is ours. When Europeans came they kept us back and took our land . . . Don't be afraid to spill your blood to get the land,' he told a KAU meeting in Thika in 1951. Quite deliberately, he distanced himself from the militant activists, preferring not to know too much about their plans, so that while some of his closest colleagues were plotting violence in his name and using his party's headquarters to do so, Kenyatta himself remained uninvolved. Yet, as their accepted leader, he stood to bear the consequences of their actions, as he well knew. At his home in August 1952, talking to a group of young Kikuyu about to head for the forests, he told them of the sacrifices that had to be made in the cause of freedom. 'I shall go to prison, and perhaps I shall die,' one of them, Waruhiu Itote, remembered him saying. 'Everything in this world has to be paid for.'

After the trial, Kenyatta was imprisoned at an inaccessible spot in the barren north-west corner of Kenya called Lokitaung, and the government did its best to erase memory of him. Githunguri was turned into an administrative centre; Kenyatta's house at Gatundu was pulled down and his small farm there was made into an agricultural station. Baring publicly promised that never again would Kenyatta and other convicted leaders be allowed to return to Kikuyuland, not even when their sentences were finished.

To the whites, it seemed that the victory over *Mau Mau* had ensured their future. By way of an admonition, the British government suggested that they could no longer expect to hold all political power, excluding Africans from government; a gradually developing multi-racial partnership was now to be the goal. But otherwise, assurances about their role were given unhesitatingly and white emigrants were still encouraged to settle in Kenya. 'Her Majesty's Government,' said the Colonial Secretary, Alan Lennox-Boyd, in Nairobi in 1954, 'are not likely to lend themselves to encouraging people to come if they intend to betray them or their predecessors. They will be entitled to feel confidence in the possession of the homes they have built or will build for themselves and their children.'

The reality, however, was different. By employing British troops to help suppress the rebellion the British government wrested back from the whites political control in Kenya. Never again were the whites able to bully a British governor in Nairobi or even to take a political initiative. So long as Britain believed in its imperial mission, that change of circumstance held no threat for the white community. But within only a few years, it was to make all the difference to their fortunes.

CHAPTER EIGHT

The Battle for Central Africa

In their vision of the future of Central Africa, the white leaders of Northern Rhodesia, Southern Rhodesia and Nyasaland had often talked of forming a powerful and prosperous British dominion stretching across the Zambezi. Periodically they had demanded from Britain the amalgamation of their three territories. In response, the British government had despatched commissions to Africa to investigate the matter, the first in 1929 and again in 1938. On each occasion the commissioners had reported from the two northern territories, Northern Rhodesia and Nyasaland, strong opposition to the idea from the African population which feared that, in place of the relatively benign rule of the Colonial Office, they would come under the control of white Rhodesians and be subjected to the restrictive racial policies prevalent in Southern Rhodesia. Consequently, the British government had stood firmly against the idea of amalgamation, but nevertheless pronounced itself in favour of closer cooperation between the three territories.

In postwar years, as an economic boom and the arrival of thousands of white immigrants bolstered their confidence, the leaders of Northern Rhodesia and Southern Rhodesia renewed the campaign for amalgamation with greater vigour. In their favour, they stressed the considerable economic advantages that would accrue from linking the territories: Southern Rhodesia had agricultural and manufacturing potential but required larger markets; Northern Rhodesia depended almost entirely on copper, of which it was among the world's major producers, and it needed a more diverse economy; Nyasaland, if it was included, was poor, heavily in debt, but offered a large surplus of labour. Combined together in a central African state, they would constitute a more attractive proposition for foreign investors and produce a much faster rate of economic development.

These were arguments which carried considerable weight in Britain, as much with the Labour government as with Conservative politicians. Though neither Labour nor Conservative was willing to agree to amalgamation, the possibility of a looser, federal arrangement, which bound together three otherwise unevenly balanced economies, seemed a promising alternative. The drawback was that the three territories were at very different stages of constitutional and political development, and pursued divergent policies towards the African population.

Southern Rhodesia was internally self-governing. The white electorate there over the years had constructed a system of separate development which consigned the African population strictly to a subordinate role. Land, jobs and housing were apportioned according to race. No African was allowed to own land in any town or to take up skilled work. Only the franchise remained non-racial, but the qualifications were so high that by 1948 the total number of Africans with the vote amounted to 258. In theory, the British government retained certain reserve powers, including the right to veto legislation which discriminated against the African population. But not once, since Southern Rhodesia became a self-governing colony in 1923, had Britain exercised its veto; and, as a result, the whites came to resent any suggestion that they were not entitled to complete control over their own affairs. Like the whites in Kenya, they had built up a modern economy, the richest in central Africa, founded on a thriving agricultural industry. By extending their influence northwards, they looked for even greater gains. Among the advantages of federation for Southern Rhodesian whites was the access they would get to the revenues of the giant copper mines, as well as the opportunity of wider markets. Their prime minister, Sir Godfrey Huggins, an elderly surgeon born in Britain, was a determined advocate of closer union, a politician of considerable skill and an outspoken champion of white rule. He had been schooled in the old imperial tradition: 'I wanted Africa to be a nice bright British pink, just as (Cecil) Rhodes did, all the way to Egypt.'

For their part, the whites of Northern Rhodesia looked

enviously at the semi-independent status of Southern Rhodesia and hoped that by joining with the south they would rid themselves of Colonial Office rule. In 1945, they had won the right to administer several government departments. They also formed the largest group in the Legislative Council. Constantly they demanded greater autonomy. But on their own they numbered only 40,000. Linked together with Southern Rhodesia's 135,000 whites, they would strengthen their position not only with the Colonial Office but also in relation to the country's two million Africans. With relentless energy, the Northern Rhodesian leader, Roy Welensky, pursued this goal. He was a tough, resourceful campaigner, born in Salisbury, the son of a poor immigrant family, who had left school at the age of fourteen and become a heavyweight boxing champion at nineteen. Working as an engine driver, he had taken up trade union activity, rising eventually to lead the white railwaymen's union in Northern Rhodesia and then the white representatives in the Legislative Council. He was a large, affable man with great charm, but also volatile and emotional. His record included vigorous support for the colour bar. He made no secret of his views that Africans would not be ready for some responsibility for government affairs for a hundred or two hundred years.

In Nyasaland, the whites were too few to lay any claim to self-government. Only 4,000 lived there, many of them missionaries and administrators with a paternal interest in the welfare of the African population, which totalled two and a half million. In the Legislative Council, nominated whites sat in equal numbers with government officials, but they had no serious political ambitions of their own. Nyasaland was often referred to as the 'Cinderella colony', a land of spectacular beauty but so poor that it depended on British funds to balance its budget, and so densely populated that thousands of Africans emigrated every year to the Rhodesias or South Africa in search of work. Indeed, the only real asset that Nyasaland had to offer was its supply of labour. Neither Huggins in Southern Rhodesia nor Welensky in Northern Rhodesia was keen that it should be included. But in the British view, Nyasaland formed a natural part of any Central African scheme.

While Creech Jones was Colonial Secretary, the federal campaigners failed to overcome the concern still expressed in London about the extent of African opposition to federation. During a visit to Central Africa in 1949, Creech Jones was so struck by the vehement African views he heard in the two northern territories that he gave public assurances that no moves would be made on federation without taking them into account.

But other factors were soon to make themselves felt. In South Africa, the 1948 election victory of the Nationalist Party, led by Afrikaners hostile to Britain and determined to impose the *apartheid* system in South Africa, aroused fears in London that the racial and political policies favoured by the Afrikaners might spread northwards, engulfing the Rhodesias. Soon after taking office, the new Nationalist government forcefully pressed demands to incorporate into South Africa the three neighbouring British territories of Basutoland, Swaziland and Bechuanaland, making clear its dislike of Britain's native policies there. When the young chief elect to the Bamangwato tribe, Seretse Khama, after studying law at Oxford University returned to Bechuanaland with a white English wife, the outrage in South Africa and the threats made by the South African government were so strong that the British authorities were obliged to send him into exile. Because they feared that Southern Rhodesia and possibly Northern Rhodesia, with their substantial Afrikaner populations, might be drawn more closely into South Africa's orbit, British officials now saw clear advantages in setting up a British-run Central African state, governed according to more liberal principles, to act as a counterweight to the thrust of Afrikaner nationalism.

The staunchest advocate in the Colonial Office of this strategy was Andrew Cohen, the head of the African division, well known for his ardent support for African aspirations. It was largely as a result of Cohen's advice that the new Labour Colonial Secretary, James Griffiths, a trade unionist with little experience of colonial affairs, agreed to convene a conference of government officials from Britain, the Rhodesias and Nyasaland to examine the feasibility of a federation. In March 1951, the conference met in England and completed its findings by the end of the month. On every ground—economic, strategic and administrative—the officials supported the case for federation. African objections, they believed, could be taken into account by allowing Northern Rhodesia and Nyasaland to remain under the auspices of the Colonial Office, retaining their own constitutions and control over local African affairs. Additional safeguards could be written into the federal constitution.

The publication of the officials' report in June 1951 was just the opportunity that Huggins and Welensky needed to push their campaign to the brink of victory. Though the Labour Government was in no way committed to follow their recommendations, such a positive verdict amounted to British endorsement of the Federal scheme. Support was already forthcoming from the giant copper mining companies and other business interests. Huggins and Welensky spoke enthusiastically of how federation would bring about a new partnership between European and African, though invariably they explained partnership in terms of senior and junior partners or, as Huggins put it more memorably, 'the partnership between the horse and its rider'. Few listeners were left in any doubt that in view of the backward status of Africans, their apprenticeship could be expected to stretch on indefinitely.

For many whites in Central Africa, especially those still deeply attached to Britain, the idea of partnership in a multiracial federation seemed to offer a sensible middle course between South Africa, where Afrikaner nationalism with its anti-British bias was becoming increasingly assertive, and West Africa where Britain was seen to be involved in the premature surrender to African nationalists. Like white settlers throughout Africa, the Rhodesians looked aghast at the Gold Coast experiment which in 1951 had produced a radical African-led government. 'The feeling is growing among the European community,' complained Welensky, 'that the (British) government is not going to judge the question of self-government for the colonies on the ability of the people to govern themselves; it will all be a matter of political expediency. In the eyes of the British Socialist government, the ills of the colonies are dispelled by the provision of the ballot box and a trade union. This is a travesty of development.' With similar bluntness, Huggins spoke of the dangers of turning democracy into mob rule. Faced with the Gold Coast precedent, Huggins and Welensky saw all the more reason to conclude a deal over federation while the opportunity still existed. The only alternative for Southern Rhodesia, Huggins frequently warned the British, skilfully exploiting their own fears, was to link up with South Africa.

Whatever arguments were used to explain federation to Africans in Northern Rhodesia and Nyasaland, their opposition never wavered. The consensus of African opinion there was that federation was nothing more than a device to strengthen white supremacy throughout Central Africa. No explanation of the economic advantages that would follow or of the safeguards that would be written into the constitution made any difference. At every opportunity, through chiefs, welfare societies, provincial councils, at meetings of the African Congresses of the two territories, they voiced their fears and objections. At Dr. Banda's house in London, a memorandum, drawn up by a group of Africans from Northern Rhodesia and Nyasaland, listed one point after another in condemnation of federation. Instead of Colonial Office rule, they warned, Africans would be subject to a government, dominated by Southern Rhodesian whites, determined to extend northwards their race laws and block African progress. 'In all their dealings with the Africans they always assume the attitude of conquerors. . . . It is these Europeans . . . who will rule and govern the federation.'

On a tour of Northern Rhodesia and Nyasaland in August 1951, Griffiths, the Colonial Secretary, was left in no doubt about the strength of African feeling. At a conference on federation at the Victoria Falls the following month, the five Africans permitted to attend—three from Nyasaland, two from Northern Rhodesia—all expressed their dissent. The British delegation there was so preoccupied with African objections that Huggins in anger later described the conference as 'a Native Benefit Society led by the Secretary of State for the Colonies'. No Africans from Southern Rhodesia were present. The conference still ended with a general pronouncement in favour of federation, but in a mood of frustration and uncertainty.

As it happened, the British general election in October 1951 removed the Labour government from office and ushered in a Conservative administration more impressed by the economic potential of federation and far less sensitive about African views, which it judged to be largely misguided. Whereas Labour had given public assurances that African opinion would be fully consulted, the new Conservative government was quite prepared, if necessary, to override African objections. As the federal campaign moved rapidly ahead, African opposition reached its peak. From Northern Rhodesia and Nyasaland, pleas and petitions denouncing federation were sent to Britain; African delegates invited to further talks in London in April 1952 boycotted the official proceedings; missionaries, Labour politicians and liberal academics in Britain added their own protest. It was to no avail. After a final conference in London in January 1953, a motion in the House of Commons in March setting up the Central African Federation was carried by 304 votes to 260. All that remained was for the electorate in Southern Rhodesia to give their verdict in a referendum, in accordance with an undertaking that Huggins had given. When they voted in April, federation was approved by 25,570 to 14,729; of the total electorate, some 429 Africans were eligible to vote.

In its final form, the Federation was an undoubted triumph for Huggins and Welensky. Through a skilful combination of bargaining, bluff and promises of partnership, they managed to obtain a strong central government with considerable autonomy, which ensured white control of Central Africa for the foreseeable future—on Huggins's reckoning, for at least sixty years. In the federal government, in the federal parliament, in the civil service, white authority prevailed. Huggins himself became the Federal prime minister and Salisbury was chosen as the federal capital. Among thirty-five members of the federal parliament, six were Africans, but their views were usually ignored. When a black MP from Northern Rhodesia introduced a motion in 1954 asking for legislation to end the colour bar, Huggins mocked and derided him. Further attempts by black MPs to deal with discrimination were no more successful. No effort was ever made by the government to implement partnership once Federation was achieved. In the complex way that the three territories of the federation were governed, the Colonial Office retained responsibility for Northern Rhodesia and Nyasaland, enabling Africans there to increase their representation on local legislative councils. African rights, in theory, were further protected by an African Affairs Board, a principal safeguard in the constitution, which had the right to appeal to the British government. But on the first occasion that the African Affairs Board protested at the passage of legislation—a revision of the Federal constitution in 1957 which, by enlarging the membership of the Federal Assembly, had the effect of diminishing African influence there—it was overruled by the British government. One of its leading white members consequently resigned: 'In my opinion,' he said, 'further service on the Board is useless. I feel we have got past the "point of no return" as far as an approach to real partnership is concerned.'

No sooner had Federation been established than Huggins and Welensky turned their attention to obtaining independent Dominion status. Their relationship with the Conservative government remained cordial. In both Salisbury and London the common view in government circles was that until the African population achieved higher standards, political power should remain in European hands. In the meantime, the Conservative government saw no reason to hold back the Federation from moving along the road to independence. In 1957, new bargains were struck. Henceforth the federal government was allowed to establish its own diplomatic and consular links and to acquire membership of international organisations. Of even greater importance, Britain agreed to refrain from touching any legislation in connection with the federation, except at the request of the Federal government, thus leaving federal ministers free to conduct their affairs without the threat of interference from London. Furthermore, Britain promised that eventually all civil services, federal and territorial, should be locally based, thus severing another tie with Colonial Office administration. Finally, in a move which clearly implied the advent of independence, Britain consented to hold a review conference in 1960 to discuss further constitutional advancement and to consider a programme under which the Federation might join the Commonwealth as a full member. Once more, it seemed, the federal campaign was close to victory. 'Almost nothing can stop the Federation ... moving on to independence,' Welensky told the Federal parliament.

Yet in the battle for Federation, the spirit of African nationalism had been born. With each successive move by the whites to gain their own independence, the nationalist movement gathered momentum. To the distrust and suspicion felt about the Federation was now added ill-feeling towards Britain as it withdrew the protection it had promised. The outcome was that demands for African self-government, free of both federal and British rule, grew apace.

CHAPTER NINE

On the Threshold

The map of Africa, as it stood in 1955, was still drawn largely in imperial colours. Only five countries were independent: Egypt and Libya in the Arab North; the old feudal empire of Ethiopia in the east; the decaying republic of Liberia, founded on the west coast in 1847 for freed American slaves; and in the south, the Union of South Africa. The rest were the preserve of European powers. Though the winds of nationalism were sweeping across North Africa, bringing independence to Morocco and Tunisia in 1956 and enflaming a protracted guerrilla war against the French in Algeria, south of the Sahara they had begun only to stir. Of the four major colonial powers—Britain, France, Belgium and Portugal—only Britain in West Africa had devised plans for the transfer of power, a policy thought by the other three to be ill-considered.

The French, though losing Indo-China and parts of North Africa, were still committed to preserving the French Union, with its vast African hinterland. France's relationship with black Africa remained as firm as ever. The Senegalese politician, Léopold Senghor, remarked in 1953 that French Africans were not tempted by the prospect of independence: 'We consider ourselves better off than our comrades in Gold Coast, in Liberia, or in British Gambia,' he said. In 1956, the number of deputies that black Africa sent to Paris increased to thirty-three, and the number of voters in the elections that year rose to six million, almost one third of the metropolitan electorate. In 1957, the French government included four Africans as ministers or secretaries of state. The financial benefits for black Africa in belonging to the French Union were considerable. The French government paid a substantial part of administrative costs and provided subsidies for export crops. Between 1946 and 1958, more than seventy per cent of total public investment and more than thirty per cent of annual running costs were financed by France. Vast sums were spent on roads, bridges, schools, hospitals and agriculture. The scale of development—greater than that attempted by any other colonial power—made French Africa inextricably dependent on Paris. French influence was paramount throughout the region—in the administration, in the economy and in political life. Frenchmen held a wide variety of posts, many on a far lower level in the administration than was ever permitted in British West Africa. As well as managers and technicians posted from France, there came a host of *petits-blancs*, bakers, barmaids, taxi drivers, shop assistants, hairdressers, dressmakers. Political debate too tended to reflect metropolitan tastes. The writer, Thomas Hodgkin, noted in 1954: 'In British West Africa, everyone who is politically conscious is a nationalist of some kind. In French West Africa there are Catholics and anti-clericals, Communists and Gaullists, Socialists, Syndicalists and Existentialists.'

Belgium and Portugal, too, adhered to the same postwar strategy, still firmly believing that they could isolate their African territories from whatever changes were occurring elsewhere on the continent. In 1955, a Belgian professor of colonial law, A. A. J. Van Bilsen, criticised the absence of any clear direction in Belgium's colonial policy and proposed a thirty-year plan leading to self-government. But the idea was greeted with scorn and abuse in many quarters and with indifference by the government. The Minister of the Congo spoke contemptuously of 'irresponsible strategists who fix dates'. He continued: 'Such an attitude shows that they either know nothing or that they understand nothing of Africa.' So the Congo remained 'an empire of silence'. Portuguese Africa, too, was as much a closed world as ever.

The British view of such policies was that ultimately they were destined to fail. 'No country can expect to isolate itself indefinitely,' Lord Hailey observed in 1956. 'There is a wind blowing through Africa, and it will be felt in the Congo and Mozambique as surely as it is being felt in French North Africa today.'

The British, though, acknowledged that in their own policies there were dangers and difficulties at every stage. Britain's objective was clear enough: as defined by Creech

Jones in 1948, it was to guide the colonial territories to responsible government within the Commonwealth in conditions that ensured to the people concerned both a fair standard of living and freedom from oppression from any quarter. But whereas, immediately after the war, the British seemed to have virtually unlimited time in which to accomplish this objective, by the mid-1950s they had been obliged to adjust to a much quicker tempo. Once Britain had granted 'responsible' government to the Gold Coast in 1951, it could not hold back rapid advancement for Nigeria, its more populous neighbour, or, consequently, for its other main West African territory, Sierra Leone, even though the difficulties involved were far more complex. The only alternative was to risk a rising tide of bitterness and tension. Elsewhere in British Africa, on the other side of the continent, a different, much longer timescale still applied. There Britain was concentrating its efforts for the most part on establishing multi-racial governments to secure a long-term role for both white and black populations. Whenever the voice of African nationalism was heard, the demands made were comparatively modest. In Tanganyika, for example, where each race—European, African and Asian—was represented equally in the Legislative Assembly, the young nationalist leader, Julius Nyerere, who had begun his campaign virtually single-handed on his return from Edinburgh University, asked in 1955 for no more than a guarantee of independence in twenty to twenty-five years ahead.

In judging the pace at which each African colony should move along the road to self-government, Britain still set rigorous conditions. Each colony was required to undergo a prolonged period of apprenticeship to enable Africans to gain experience of running a parliamentary democracy along Westminster lines and to prove their ability to manage public finances competently; in addition each colony needed an adequate reservoir of trained personnel to staff the new state. In the case of the Gold Coast, with its many advantages, the apprenticeship was to last six years. For most other colonies, British administrators believed that a much longer period of benevolent colonial rule, lasting in some cases several more generations, was needed before new states could be launched confidently with stable and efficient administrations and a thorough grounding in democracy. But the gradual progress envisaged in the past was no longer possible. The timescale, through force of circumstance, was being reduced. The danger was that in the quickening pace of colonial emancipation, as Britain withdrew its framework of control, internal strains and stresses held in check during British rule would break to surface. In several cases this had happened already.

Almost all countries in Africa were created by European powers during the scramble for territory at the end of the nineteenth century. The boundaries they marked on their maps in the Chancelleries of Europe, to demarcate their separate spheres of influence, were often drawn in straight lines. One third, in fact, when measured according to length, were geometrical. Rarely were ethnic or tribal divisions taken into account. African states therefore enclosed sometimes hundreds of diverse and independent tribes, with no comman history, culture, language or religion. In numerous cases, tribes historically antagonistic to one another were linked together, whilst homogenous groups were rent apart. For a period of only fifty or sixty years, imperial rule had boarded over the divisions. During that time, no real sense of national identity had emerged. Britain, by treating each colony separately, enabled a spirit of nationalism to develop more fully than did any other European power. But the will for unity was weak. Temporarily, nationalist leaders were able to arouse united opposition to British rule. But once the British had made plain their intention of disengaging, older loyalties reasserted themselves.

*

Nigeria, the most populous country in Africa and the most important African colony that Britain possessed, was already caught in a web of regional and tribal rivalry. In many ways Nigeria, at the end of the war, resembled the Gold Coast. The same wave of disaffection over low wages, rising prices, unemployment swept the towns, resulting in a general strike in 1945. Ex-servicemen returning home grumbled bitterly about gratuities and the lack of opportunities offered them. The educated elite too were resentful over discrimination and about proposals for constitutional advancement which the authorities put forward in 1945 without consultation. In the Nigerian press, the British administration came under constant attack. Its most notable opponent was Nnamdi Azikiwe, a versatile nationalist leader who, after returning to Nigeria from American universities in 1937, established a string of newspapers and vigorously campaigned for an end to colonial rule. The British Colonial Secretary in 1943 described Azikiwe as 'the biggest danger of the lot'. In 1944, Azikiwe formed the first modern political organisation, the National Council of Nigeria and the Cameroons, a confederation of tribal unions, professional associations, social clubs and a few trade unions, with the objective of seeking self-government. He hoped to build the NCNC into a powerful national movement capable of challenging the British authorities. Initially, he achieved some success, championing the right of workers and attracting a youthful following. But within a few years the Nigerian nationalists had fallen into disarray, irreconcilably divided into rival camps.

The difficulties that Nigeria faced were magnified by its great size and diversity. In the north, powerful Muslim emirs still ruled from their crenellated palaces of red clay, in accordance with Islamic traditions of law and discipline which stretched back for centuries. In these feudal societies, few traces of the modern world—in education or economic life—had been allowed to intrude. In 1955 there was not yet one qualified northern doctor, and little interest was shown in gaining Western skills. The British, though amalgamating northern and southern Nigeria in 1914, treated the North as a distinct and separate entity, preserving most of its traditional ways. Indeed, some British administrators regarded city-states such as Bornu and Sokoto virtually as semi-independent territories. In all, the North comprised two-thirds of Nigeria's territory and contained more than half of the population. The predominant tribal groups there, the Hausa and Fulani, looked disdainfully on the peoples of the South. The principal Northern leader, the Sardauna of Sokoto, never even travelled to Lagos, the capital, until 1949. He recalled in his memoirs: 'The whole place was alien to our ideas and we found the members for the other regions might well belong to another world as far as we were concerned.'

The South was divided into two regions, each with its own dominant tribal group. In the Western region, the Yoruba, because of their early contact with Europe and long experience of city life, had progressed far in education, commerce and administration and absorbed a high degree of Western skills. In the Eastern region, on the other side of the Niger river, the Ibo, occupying the poorest, most densely populated region of Nigeria, initially lagged behind but, ambitious and industrious, they had swarmed out of their homeland to find work in neighbouring areas. By the end of the Second World War, Ibo clerks, artisans, traders and labourers, formed a sizeable minority group in every town in Nigeria. Thousands of southerners, notably Ibo, migrated to the North to take up clerical and technical jobs, but their presence there provided a constant source of tension. They were treated with hostility by most northerners and obliged to live outside the walls of northern cities in strangers' quarters known as *sabon garis*. In 1953, tribal riots and murders broke out in the ancient city of Kano.

Nigerian politicians themselves did not attempt to minimise the differences that divided them. In 1948, a prominent northern leader, Abubakar Tafawa Balewa, who was destined to become the first federal prime minister, told the Legislative Council: 'Since 1914 the British Government has been trying to make Nigeria into one country, but the Nigerian people themselves are historically different in their backgrounds, in their religious beliefs and customs and do not show themselves any signs of willingness to unite. . . . Nigerian unity is only a British invention.' In a book published in 1947, the Yoruba leader, Obafemi Awolowo, who dominated Western Nigerian politics for more than thirty years, wrote: 'Nigeria is not a nation. It is a mere geographical expression. There are no "Nigerians" in the same sense as there are "English", "Welsh", or "French". The word "Nigerian" is merely a distinctive appellation to distinguish those who live within the boundaries of Nigeria and those who do not.'

Finding a constitutional arrangement which satisfied so many diverse interests proved difficult. In addition to the three major groups, the Hausa, the Yoruba and the Ibo, there were a host of 'minority' tribes, more than one hundred separate 'Native Administrations' and, in all, some 248 languages. The constitution that the British devised in 1946 brought northern representatives into the central legislature for the first time, created regional councils for the North, the West and the East, and established for Nigeria the basis of a Federation in which one region, the North, was twice the size in area and population of the other two regions. This constitution, introduced in January 1947, was expected to last for nine years, but after the Gold Coast riots in 1948, the British government decided to hasten constitutional progress for Nigeria as well as for the Gold Coast. The announcement in 1948 that a new constitution would be forthcoming, this time in full consultation with Nigerians throughout the country, started a struggle for power between rival groups which sharpened all past animosities. Each region produced, in effect, its own political party. Azikiwe's NCNC controlled the East; Awolowo's Action Group held the West; and the Northern People's Congress, led by the Sardauna of Sokoto, Ahmadu Bello, dominated the North. The 1951 constitution, which gave considerable powers to the regions but kept a strong central legislature and executive, lasted for only a few years. When southerners in 1953 pressed in the federal assembly for a resolution demanding self-government in 1956, northern members held back, fearing that the North would be swamped by better educated, more sophisticated southerners. In the crisis that followed, the British government realised the need for a different constitution. The 1954 constitution gave to the three regions much greater power: each had its own government, assembly and civil service. Under this arrangement, the East and the West were able to move on separately to self-government, while the North was given more time to prepare. In effect, there were now three separate parts of Nigeria. And the bitter contest that had divided them provided an ill omen for the future.

*

A similar crisis occurred in Uganda. There, Britain was bound by treaty to four ancient kingdoms, each of which retained substantial powers. At the heart of the country was the kingdom of Buganda, the most prosperous and developed part of Uganda, with a history stretching back for centuries that was unique in East Africa. The Baganda were a wealthy and self-sufficient people, taking great pride in their monarchy and its established traditions. Their king, the Kabaka, Edward Mutesa II, ruled through an elaborate system of government which included its own parliament, the Lukiiko, ministers and a separate administration. He had inherited the throne in 1939 at the age of fifteen, the thirty-fifth member of his line. His education had been completed at Cambridge University; and he had also received an honorary commission in the Grenadier Guards. To the British he was popularly known as King Freddie.

The road to self-government was expected to be relatively uncomplicated. Uganda had always been regarded in official circles as primarily an African country. The white resident population was small and few white settlers had been allowed to acquire land. But in the process of trying to unite the country under a single government and introduce democratic reforms, the British authorities encountered stubborn resistance from Baganda traditionalists who looked on the Baganda as a separate nation, linked to Britain not as a colonial people, but as the result of a treaty negotiated originally by Mutesa's grandfather, Mwanga, in 1893. The issue was made worse by a clash of wills between a strong-minded Governor, Sir Andrew Cohen, on secondment from the Colonial Office, who was impatient with the feudal practices of the Baganda ruling class, and the young Kabaka determined to preserve his royal heritage.

What precipitated the crisis was nothing more than a chance remark made in London. In a dinner speech in June 1953, the Colonial Secretary, Oliver Lyttelton, who had recently pushed through the Central African Federation against African protests in Nyasaland and Northern Rhodesia, mentioned in passing the possibility one day of establishing an East African Federation. In Kenya, the Nairobi press seized enthusiastically on the remark as new hope that Britain still intended to create a 'white Dominion' along the lines of the Central African Federation. The result in Uganda was to send a gust of fear through the Baganda that, against their will, they were to be placed under the control of Kenya's white settlers. Using the opportunity to attack British plans for democratic reform, Baganda traditionalists in the Lukiiko demanded that responsibility for Buganda's affairs should be transferred to the Foreign Office, in recognition of Buganda's separate status, and that a timetable should be drawn up for Buganda's separate path to independence. The British government gave an undertaking that no form of federation would be allowed without the assent of Ugandans, but flatly rejected the idea that Buganda could achieve a separate independence. The campaign, however, continued and gained the support of the Kabaka. As a means of protest, the Kabaka refused to nominate Baganda members to the Legislative Council. A series of meetings between the Kabaka and the Governor failed to find a way through the impasse. Cohen insisted that the Kabaka withdraw the Baganda demands; the Kabaka refused. Finally, in November 1953, Cohen summoned the Kabaka to Government House and told him that as his refusal to cooperate with the government was in breach of the 1900 agreement with Britain, under which the Uganda protectorate was established, he had been deposed. In a matter of hours, without even being permitted to return to his palace and pack his clothes, the Kabaka was put on a military aircraft and sent to exile in England.

The shock for the Baganda was profound. On hearing the news, the Kabaka's sister collapsed and died. Deeply demoralised and dismayed, the Baganda concentrated all their efforts on securing his return. When the British authorities failed to obtain support for the election of a new Kabaka, they were obliged to work out an agreement which allowed Mutesa to return in October 1955. In theory, he went back to Uganda as a constitutional monarch stripped of political power. But the reality was that among the Baganda his influence was greater than ever before. Still the Baganda refused to take their seats in the Legislative Council. And still they demanded a separate independence. Over Uganda too the shadow of tribal dissension had fallen.

*

Even the Gold Coast was afflicted by a sudden upsurge of

tribal sentiment. In 1954, just when Nkrumah was planning to move rapidly on to independence, a serious challenge came unexpectedly from Ashanti, the central region of the Gold Coast. With the blessing of the Ashanti king, the Asantehene, and the paramount chiefs of the Asanteman Council, and backed by fervent support from the Ashanti heartland, a new political party, the National Liberation Movement (NLM) demanded a federal constitution before Britain withdrew, giving Ashanti and other areas that wanted it a substantial measure of local autonomy. The NLM found allies for its federal proposals in the Northern Territories and Togoland. As the NLM and Nkrumah's CPP struggled for control, violent disturbances broke out. The British government, alarmed by the disorders, refused to set a date for independence and eventually insisted on resolving the issue by calling another general election. At the polls in July 1956, Nkrumah's CPP won 72 of 104 seats, though only 57 per cent of the votes cast. Satisfied with the result, Britain finally pronounced a date for independence: 6 March 1957.

It was a date which marked the beginning of an era for black Africa as much as for Ghana, as the new state was to be called. The chain reaction of independence that followed was in part due to the spirit of the times. Decolonisation was an idea whose moment had come. What was remarkable, though, was the speed at which it happened. Within a few years, the African empires that France, Belgium and Britain once so proudly possessed had all but vanished. Only the Portuguese remained, impervious to the wind that Lord Hailey had noted was blowing through the continent and utterly convinced that, alone among Europe's powers, their imperial role would never change. In those hectic years, independent Ghana stood out as a symbol of freedom that other colonies wished to attain and Nkrumah, seeing new heights to conquer, threw himself tirelessly into the wider cause of African liberation and unity. As leader of the Gold Coast, he had set the pace for the emancipation of Britain's African colonies. Now he sought to shape Africa's destiny. It was a time of great optimism, when new ambitions abounded, when new worlds seemed possible. Certainly, in the heady days of March 1957, Ghana was seen as a portent, watched and admired from many quarters of the globe. No other African state was launched with so much promise for the future. Nor was there an occasion when the feeling of euphoria was so strong.

CHAPTER TEN

A Time of Triumph

Accra, according to the description in one British newspaper, looked the happiest place on earth. To the celebrations came delegations from fifty-six countries, exuding warmth and goodwill. Messages of congratulations arrived from world leaders—from Eisenhower, Bulganin, Nehru, Chou en Lai and Harold Macmillan. Among the personal guests whom Nkrumah invited were colonial servants, educationists and missionaries whose years of service he effusively praised. Even his former London landlady, for whom he had washed dishes, was remembered. From Britain, representing Queen Elizabeth, came her aunt, the Duchess of Kent; the Chinese sent a general; the Russians, a junior minister with a fistful of invitations to Moscow; the South Africans, an all-white delegation. But the limelight was held by Richard Nixon, then the United States Vice-President. From the moment he touched down in Accra, he rushed about shaking hands, hugging paramount chiefs, fondling black babies and posing for photographs, full of compliments about 'the kind of colonialism that can produce a Ghana'.

At midnight on 6 March, as the Union Jack in Parliament Square was lowered and the new flag of Ghana, red, green and gold, was hoisted in its place, the crowds roared and danced and sang. Through their midst, borne from Parliament on the shoulders of his colleagues, came Kwame Nkrumah, wearing a convict's white skull cap embroidered on the front with the letters 'PG'—the 'prison graduate' badge for those nationalists who, like Nkrumah, had once been jailed by the British. Under the glare of floodlights, Nkrumah performed an impromptu dance on a wooden platform erected on the old polo ground opposite Parliament and then, as he spoke of the moment of freedom that had arrived, tears began to stream down his face.

But if it was a time of triumph for Nkrumah, the British felt entitled to share in it. Ghana embarked on independence as one of the richest tropical countries in the world, with an efficient civil service, an impartial judiciary and a prosperous middle class. Its system of government was rooted firmly in the British democratic tradition. Parliament functioned along familiar Westminster lines; the Speaker wore a wig; the record of debate was called after Hansard; and, on both sides of the House, able politicians were to be found. The prime minister himself, then only forty-seven years old, was regarded as a leader of outstanding ability, popularly elected, who, during a six-year apprenticeship under British auspices, had proved his aptitude for handling the business of government. The country's economic prospects were equally propitious. Ghana was the world's leading producer of cocoa, a crop grown by myriads of small farmers who shared in its wealth. Other economic resources included gold, timber and bauxite. Foreign currency reserves, built up during the 1950s cocoa boom, stood at nearly £170 million. With a population of five million, per capita income at £70 was high, when compared, for example, to Tanganyika at £17, or Nyasaland at £7. (Britain's at the time was £300.) From the British, Ghana had inherited a continuing sense of orderly progress and awaited, in the words that Queen Elizabeth used in her independence message, 'a bright and happy future'.

At the birth of Ghana, consequently, the British press considered that a measure of self-congratulation was in order. Newspaper comment from as far apart as Washington and Delhi was also favourable. Nkrumah, too, paid tribute to the British record: 'We part from Great Britain with the warmest feelings of friendship and goodwill,' he said. 'Instead of that feeling of bitterness which is often born of a colonial struggle, we enter our independence in association with Britain and with good relations unimpaired.'

Even while the celebrations were underway, Nkrumah was busy preparing for his next move. He was determined to turn Accra into the centre of African liberation, to provide a base from which nationalist leaders from colonial Africa could draw support and encouragement. 'Our independence is meaningless unless it is linked with the total liberation of the

African continent,' he proclaimed before the vast crowds assembled at the Polo ground on Independence Day. He also canvassed the idea of holding a Pan African conference of representatives from eight African states that were already independent. To assist with these endeavours, Nkrumah invited his old mentor from London, George Padmore, to take up a post as his advisor on African Affairs. For Padmore, it was the climax of his life's work. 'Once more,' his friend C. L. R. James wrote, 'George sat in an office with adequate resources, doing the work he had done in the Kremlin and in his little London flat.' Soon, Accra became a place of pilgrimage for aspiring nationalists, political refugees from Africa and left-wing intellectuals from Europe attracted by the aura of a brave new world.

One success followed another. In April 1958, Nkrumah was the host to a conference of eight independent African states, at which delegates pledged their support for African liberation and spoke confidently about the prospects for African unity. The delegates also announced with assurance that Africa was to become a powerful force in a third world of non-aligned countries. An African voice was thus added to the rising clamour against colonial rule coming from newly independent Asian and Arab nations. In international forums like the United Nations, Europe's colonial powers found themselves constantly placed on the defensive.

In December 1958, Nkrumah and Padmore brought together an array of political parties, trades unions and student bodies from across the continent with the aim of coordinating 'the African non-violent revolution'. Under the banner of the All-African People's Conference, some three hundred African representatives gathered in an atmosphere of radical fervour. Many were later to achieve prominence. Hastings Banda was present; so too was Kenneth Kaunda from Northern Rhodesia, Joshua Nkomo from Southern Rhodesia, Patrice Lumumba from the Belgian Congo, Holden Roberto from Angola, Amilcar Cabral from Portuguese Guinea and the young Kenya trade unionist, Tom Mboya, who was chosen as the conference chairman. To such men, Nkrumah stressed the need for disciplined mass movements, along the lines of his CPP, committed to 'positive action' and determined to oust the colonial powers. For a week, nationalist leaders drew in the intoxicating draught of revolutionary rhetoric, and departed eager for the fray. Tom Mboya, in his concluding speech to the conference, reflected their belligerent mood. The colonial powers, he said, should now reverse the scramble for Africa. 'Your time is past,' he told them. 'Africa must be free. Scram from Africa.'

CHAPTER ELEVEN

The French Solution

The lead that Britain had given in West Africa, together with the growing momentum in the world towards colonial emancipation, drew France along in its wake. A new French government in 1956 brought to office as Minister of France d'Outre-Mer, Gaston Defferre, a Socialist strongly convinced of the need for colonial reform in black Africa. 'It is not a question for us of plagiarizing the British,' he said, 'but the fact that they have transformed the political and administrative regime of their territories has certainly contributed to the growth of impatience among the peoples of French West and French Equatorial Africa.'

Concerned that the kind of violence afflicting Algeria might surface elsewhere in Africa, Defferre moved swiftly. He pushed through the French Assembly a *loi-cadre*—a 'framework law'—enabling the government to take action by decree, thus avoiding the delays that resulted from protracted parliamentary wrangling. Some reforms which the government now conceded had been demanded of France ten years before in the Constituent Assembly; they included universal franchise and a single college for elections. But the most important effect of the Loi-Cadre was to give the African colonies a considerable measure of internal autonomy. Each territory acquired its own prime minister, cabinet and assembly with control over matters such as budgets, the civil service, public works and primary education. No longer was Paris solely the centre of political gravity. Now local politics assumed a crucial importance. Yet all this was achieved without altering the concept of the French Union or , as it was becoming known, the Franco-African Community. Indeed, Defferre argued that the Loi-Cadre reforms were designed 'to maintain and reinforce the necessary Union between Metropolitan France and the peoples of the overseas territories'.

The Loi-Cadre became law in June 1956 and was implemented in the elections to the Territorial Assemblies in March 1957, the same month that Ghana became independent. In the debate which followed its introduction, no African voice was heard demanding independence. Every leading African politician accepted that France should retain major powers. Given the extent to which the African colonies depended on France for their survival, there seemed to be no realistic alternative. Where the Africans differed was over the kind of association that they wanted with France. The Loi-Cadre had broken up the two great regions of French West Africa and French Equatorial Africa into twelve separate states. Some African leaders, notably Senegal's Léopold Senghor, saw this move as an attempt by France to 'balkanise' Africa, to maintain its control there by keeping African states small, divided and therefore dependent. What Senghor proposed instead was a federation of African states within the French Union. But though Senghor bitterly attacked provisions of the Loi-Cadre, his commitment to the idea of a Franco-African Community never wavered. 'Independence has no positive content,' he said. 'It is not a solution.'

Other African politicians, though a minority, favoured the plan for individual association with France. The leader of this group was Houphouët-Boigny of the Ivory Coast. By 1956, Houphouët had emerged as the most influential black politician in France. Recovering from his 1951 setback, he had rebuilt the RDA into the strongest political movement in *Afrique Noire*. In the 1956 election, the RDA became the largest African party in the Paris Assembly and Houphouët, as its leader, was awarded a full Cabinet post in the French government. In that role he was able to exert considerable influence over the final form of the Loi-Cadre. He became an ardent advocate of the Franco-African Community, arguing that Africa's future lay not in complete independence but in partnership with the metropolitan powers. In answer to the ideas that Nkrumah propounded—the 'mystique of independence', as Houphouët put it—he proposed the 'idea of fraternity'.

The two men had first met in Paris in 1947, when

Houphouët was a deputy in the French parliament and Nkrumah, an itinerant student from London, was canvassing support for his plans for African unity. Ten years later, in April 1957 in Abidjan, the capital of the Ivory Coast, they met again: Nkrumah, prime minister of newly independent Ghana and champion of African liberation and unity, paying his first official visit abroad, and Houphouët, minister in the Government of France and pillar of the Franco-African Community. Neither was impressed with the other's plans for the future. Houphouët feigned indifference to Ghana's independence, predicting that in ten years the Ivory Coast, with the assistance of France, would have surpassed its neighbour Ghana in economic and social progress. Between them a wager was made to see who turned out to be right. 'You are witnessing the start of two experiments,' Houphouët told his compatriots. 'A wager has been made between two territories, one having chosen independence, the other preferring the difficult road to the construction, with the metropole, of a community of men equal in rights and duties.... Let each of us undertake his experiment, in absolute respect for the experiment of his neighbour, and in ten years we shall compare the results.'

Where Nkrumah's views received greater attention was in French Guinea. The young Guinean leader, Sékou Touré, belonged to a more radical generation. His route to power had not been through the closeted world of the African elite but through the rough and tumble of union politics. Expelled from school for leading a food strike, he had formed Guinea's first trade union in 1945, then built up the *Parti Démocratique de Guinée* into a powerful mass movement. In 1957 the PDG won 56 out of 60 seats in the territorial assembly elections and Touré, at the age of thirty-five, became Guinea's prime minister. Ensured of solid support, he adopted a militant role. He was more interested in the idea of Pan-African unity than the Franco-African Community, and greatly admired Nkrumah. When the two men first met in Conakry in 1957, they were said to have taken to each other immediately. By 1957 Touré, with his radical ideas and revolutionary rhetoric, was not alone. Other voices, from student groups and labour unions, were being raised in favour of independence from

France.

The independence issue was finally brought out into the open in the middle of 1958. Amid the chaos of the Algerian war, France's Fourth Republic collapsed and General de Gaulle assumed power. De Gaulle began work on a new constitutional settlement for France principally to enable him to deal with Algeria, but at the same time he took the opportunity to head off any colonial distractions elsewhere in Africa by offering French colonies a large degree of self-government. He proposed that the new constitution should be ratified by referendum on 28 September. De Gaulle's intention was to turn the Franco-African Community into a tight federation, giving each territory local autonomy but leaving France effectively in control of foreign affairs, defence and overall economic policy. He abruptly dismissed African requests for a looser confederation: 'I, de Gaulle, say "Federation" and there we stop.' In his draft constitutional proposals, moreover, he made no mention of any territory's right to independence. That issue, he said, would be settled once and for all in the referendum. By voting 'Yes', Africans would bind themselves permanently to the Community; by voting 'No', they could take their independence shorn of any French assistance. 'Of course I understand the attractions of independence and the lure of secession,' he said in August. 'The referendum will tell us whether secession carries the day. But what is inconceivable is an independent state which France continues to help. If the choice is for independence, the government will draw, with regret, the conclusions that follow from the expression of that choice.'

Expressed in that way, de Gaulle's offer appalled most African politicians: By voting 'Yes', they might renounce irrevocably the right to independence; by voting 'No', they faced economic ruin and administrative chaos. They urged de Gaulle to be more flexible. On a tour of African capitals in August, de Gaulle, as a war hero and the architect of the 1944 Brazzaville conference, was generally given an enthusiastic welcome, but the weight of African concern about the right to independence impressed him. In Brazzaville, he was warned that at least five territories would be obliged to vote 'No' if a 'Yes' vote was taken to mean that they were willing to renounce independence altogether. Accordingly, de Gaulle promised that in the future if any member of the Community wished to seek independence, France would raise 'no obstacles'. For most African leaders, his assurance, later written into the constitution, was enough to obtain their approval.

In Conakry, however, the mood was different. Lining the streets from the airport, when de Gaulle arrived, were well marshalled crowds shouting independence slogans. Sékou Touré had made plain long beforehand his irritation with de Gaulle's plans for the Community—'a French Union rebaptized—old merchandise with a new label'; and he intensely resented the threat that de Gaulle had made about the consequences for any territory voting 'No'. In the old white Assembly Hall, as de Gaulle listened, his face furrowed and lined with fatigue, Touré spoke harshly of France's colonial record. He insisted on the need for complete decolonisation before Guinea joined the Franco-African Community and he declared: 'We prefer poverty in freedom to riches in slavery.' From the assembled audience there was enthusiastic applause. Deeply affronted, de Gaulle rose in reply to defend France's record and repeated his offer: 'I say it here, even louder than elsewhere: independence is at Guinea's disposal. She can take it by saying "No" to the proposal which is made to her, and in that case I guarantee that metropolitan France will raise no obstacles. . . .' He already felt sure of what the result in Guinea would be. Turning to his entourage, he is said to have remarked: 'Well, gentlemen, there is a man we shall never get on with. Come now, the thing is clear: we shall leave on 29 September, in the morning (the morning after the referendum).' On the way back to the airport in the same car, the two men sat tightlipped, in silence. They shook hands for the last time and de Gaulle departed with the words: 'Adieu la Guinée!'

In the referendum on 28 September, the vote in eleven territories was overwhelmingly in favour of de Gaulle's proposals for a French Community; in Ivory Coast, 99.9 per cent; in Senegal, 97.6 per cent; in Upper Volta, 99.1 per cent. Only in Guinea was the result different, but no less overwhelming: 95 per cent said 'Non'. Touré's popularity and prestige had carried the country. Soon after de Gaulle had left

Conakry, Touré had summed up the reasons for his uncompromising stand: 'Between voting "Yes" to a constitution which infringes the dignity, unity and freedom of Africa, and accepting, as General de Gaulle says, immediate independence, Guinea will choose that independence without hesitating. We do not have to be blackmailed by France. We cannot yield on behalf of our countries to those who threaten and put pressure on us to make us choose, against heart and reason, the conditions of marriage which could keep us within the complex of the colonial regime.... We say "No" unanimously and categorically, to any project which does not cater for our aspirations.'

De Gaulle's reaction to Guinea's vote was swift and vindictive. Even though Touré, after proclaiming Guinea's independence on 2 October, made overtures to de Gaulle, clearly preferring to retain links with France, de Gaulle ignored him. From Paris a note was sent to the Guinea government simply advising that all French aid had been stopped and that French civil servants would be withdrawn within two months. French army units, including army doctors largely responsible for providing health services to the civilian population, would also leave. There followed a mass exodus of some three thousand French administrators, teachers, engineers, doctors and businessmen. They took with them any French government property they could carry and destroyed what had to be left behind. Government files and records were burned; offices were stripped of their furniture and telephones, even of their electric light bulbs. Army doctors took away medical supplies; police officers smashed windows in their barracks. When Touré moved into the former French Governor's house at the end of November, he found that the furniture and pictures had been removed and the crockery smashed. Only 150 French government employees, mostly volunteers, stayed behind.

As a demonstration to other members of the Community of the advantages of continuing an association with France, de Gaulle's ruthless treatment of Guinea was only temporarily effective. Guinea certainly suffered grievous disruption. But offers of aid were immediately forthcoming from Russia and the Eastern bloc. Nkrumah too was ready with a large loan and proposals for a union between Ghana and Guinea. Britain and the United States accorded Guinea recognition. And much interest was shown by Western mining groups in Guinea's mineral resources. In the anti-colonial world at large, Sékou Touré was acclaimed a hero and for a brief spell Guinea enjoyed international fame. When Touré attended the United Nations General Assembly in 1959, he received a triumphant welcome as head of a new sovereign state. Far from being repentant, he recovered his confidence sufficiently to start urging other members of the Community to demand their independence.

Within a few months, de Gaulle's Community was showing signs of strain. France expected to run the Community as it had done in the past, whilst the Africans wanted greater control. Several African leaders who had all along preferred a looser confederal association with France, demanded changes. In July, Senegal and Soudan (later renamed Mali) pressed for independence within the Community. At first, de Gaulle resisted the demands, but he came to recognise that independence was, as he said, 'a sort of elementary psychological disposition'. By the end of 1959, little more than a year after the Community had been formed, de Gaulle accepted the inevitability of African independence. In 1960, the eleven members of the Community, along with Cameroun and Togo, two trust territories administered by France for the United Nations, were launched as independent states.

Formally, France's hegemony in Africa came to an end. Yet so swiftly did the transition take place and so dependent did the new states remain on French aid, that the changes which occurred were largely ceremonial. Countries like Chad, Niger and Mali were land-locked, mostly desert, thinly populated and desperately poor. Even Senegal, the second wealthiest French colony in Africa, relied heavily on French subsidies. Only the Ivory Coast was thought to be economically viable and there, ironically, Houphouët-Boigny was the most reluctant of all African leaders to leave the French Community and seek independence. Indeed, he scorned the idea. The independence granted to African states in such parlous conditions, he said in 1959, would be purely 'nominal'. 'It is not the shell of independence which counts, it is the contents: the economic contents, the social contents and the human contents.' Yet Houphouët too was swept along on the same tide. Towards these new protégés de Gaulle adopted a benevolent stance. The 'Man of Brazzaville' became the 'Man of Cooperation'. At every level of aid—financial, technical, cultural and military—generous agreements were made. France supplied presidential aides, military advisors and civil servants to staff government ministries. The French treasury supported a monetary union with the new African states, providing them with a stable and convertible currency. French troops were permanently stationed in several African capitals under defence agreements designed to provide a guarantee of internal security. France continued to dominate industry, banking and trade as consistently as before. The French also operated an extensive intelligence network in Africa controlled from the Elysée Palace by de Gaulle's African adviser, Jacques Foccart. For their part, most African leaders remained profusely grateful for France's help and particularly devoted to de Gaulle. 'General de Gaulle,' Senghor wrote some years later, 'is the great African of our time.'

CHAPTER TWELVE

A Fire in Nyasaland

In the years that Hastings Banda spent in the Gold Coast practising as a doctor, he shut himself away from all political activity, living quietly in Kumasi, the capital of Ashanti, with an Englishwoman who had worked for him as a secretary in London. He took little interest in the events leading to the Gold Coast's independence and refused to answer letters from Africans in Nyasaland asking for his advice and assistance. When Nkrumah invited him to the independence celebrations in Accra in March 1957, Banda declined to go.

But as the Federal Government in Salisbury, now led by Sir Roy Welensky, insistently pressed demands for Dominion status from 1960, Banda paid more attention to appeals for help coming from Nyasaland. In March 1957, he received a letter from Henry Chipembere, a young radical graduate recently elected to the Legislative Assembly, pointing out the need for an experienced leader to take command of the Nyasaland African National Congress, which had fallen into disarray. What was required, Chipembere wrote, was a kind of saviour. 'Human nature is such that it needs a kind of hero to be hero-worshipped if a political struggle is to succeed.' Banda, he said, had all the right qualifications.

Banda, approaching the age of sixty, was still reluctant to commit himself. Only after further approaches had been made during 1957 did he indicate that he would be willing to return. Chipembere responded warmly to the news. He wanted to build up Banda, he said, into a 'political messiah'. His return to Nyasaland, if handled well, would cause great excitement and should precipitate 'almost a revolution in political thought'. Back in London in 1958, after an absence of five years, Banda renewed his campaign against the Federation, addressing public meetings and appearing on television. On 13 June he led a Nyasaland delegation to see Alan Lennox-Boyd, the Colonial

Secretary, who was an enthusiastic supporter of Welensky and the Federation. Privately Lennox-Boyd urged Welensky to prohibit Banda from entering the Federation. Of his meeting with Banda, Lennox-Boyd recalled: 'Banda said to me "I go back to break up your bloody Federation." I said: "This may well end in your detention." We got on very well.'

On 6 July 1958, Banda returned home to Nyasaland to be acclaimed the saviour of his people. Like Kenyatta, in his time, he had become a legend. For forty-two years he had not set foot in Nyasaland; indeed his knowledge of his own language, chiNyanja, had long since faded. But his fame as a doctor and as a defender of African rights was widespread; and, in the words of one young nationalist that day, he had become 'the symbol of Nyasa independence'. The tone he adopted initially was sufficiently moderate to impress both the Governor, Sir Robert Armitage, and the small white community. His aim, he said, was to obtain universal suffrage, African majorities in the Legislative and Executive Councils and secession from the Federation. But he stressed that his campaign would be non-violent, and that he would work towards self-government through negotiation.

In the first few months of his campaign, he concentrated his energies on building Congress into a nationally-based movement, and set out on tour to gain support. In almost every district, the figure of the elderly doctor, invariably dressed in a dark three-piece suit and black homburg hat even under the hot, midday sun, soon became a familiar sight. To his surprise, Banda found he had a talent for mob oratory—'I didn't know I had it in me', he confided to a friend. Wherever he went there were excited, cheering crowds, relishing his attacks on the 'stupid' Federation and on Welensky as the arch-villain. In early November, Banda was able to write to a Congress official, '. . . things are hot here. I have the whole of Blantyre and Zomba on fire. Very soon I hope to have the whole of Nyasaland on fire.' In his dealings with the government, though, over Congress demands for constitutional progress, Banda made no headway. The white community remained solidly in support of Welensky and some whites, disturbed by the defiant mood of the African population, talked of the need to have 'a showdown' with

Congress. Throughout the country, an air of tension was growing.

In December, Banda travelled to Accra to attend the All-African People's Conference. He played only a minor role but, like other delegates from colonial Africa, he was inspired by the call for 'positive action'. Only one full year was now left before the Federal review conference, promised to Welensky, was due to be held. On his way home, Banda stopped in Salisbury and, to his indignation, he was questioned for an hour and his baggage was searched. He discovered, moreover, that the Nyasaland government had cancelled his weekend flight to Blantyre to deprive him of the opportunity of receiving a large welcome there. Using the extra time he now had to spend in Salisbury, he addressed a meeting in the black suburb of Highfield, venting his anger and urging militant action. Africans, he said, should be prepared to go to prison in their millions to gain freedom. 'I am prepared for anything, even death. I am not afraid of anything. I will fight Federation from prison. Even from the grave my ghost will return to fight Federation.' The idea of moderation he now spurned: 'Throughout the history of the world there is no incident where a so-called moderate has achieved anything.' On arrival in Blantyre, his mood was just as aggressive. 'In Nyasaland we mean to be masters, and if that is treason, make the most of it.'

An open confrontation with the government now seemed unavoidable. Banda constantly referred to his willingness to go to jail; indeed at times he appeared to welcome the idea. Certainly his young lieutenants were eager for action. At an emergency conference in Blantyre starting on 24 January, some two hundred Congress delegates met to discuss what tactics to adopt in their campaign against the government. On the following day, the delegates moved outside Blantyre to an open place in the bush where conditions of great secrecy were observed. What occurred there was later the subject of prolonged controversy. Banda himself, quite deliberately, was absent. In charge were officials such as Chipembere who wanted 'real' action. According to a subsequent inquiry, there was 'a great deal of talk about beating and killing'. Extremists advocated the murder of government officials, but many delegates still favoured a non-violent campaign. The outcome was in favour of a campaign of civil disobedience and resistance, including acts of sabotage.

The version that eventually reached the government through accounts supplied by police informers was a good deal more lurid. These suggested that, in the event of Banda's arrest, a date would be set for the mass slaughter of Europeans and Asians, including women and children, and the murder of the Governor and all senior officials. While this information was being assessed, the authorities were confronted by a sudden increase in demonstrations, illegal meetings and violent incidents, all of which tended to confirm the police view that the government was facing a widespread conspiracy. On 18 February, the police commissioner told the Governor, Sir Robert Armitage, that, in the light of new evidence, he thought that the original information about the murder plot was accurate; and he urged the government to act. During the next few days, the disorders spread. Turning for help to Welensky, Armitage requested reinforcements from other parts of the Federation. In the middle of a deteriorating security situation, white Rhodesian troops were flown to Nyasaland, compounding the tension. To Banda, their arrival was proof that the government was no more than 'a puppet in the hands of European settlers' intent on a showdown. And in Blantyre, Chipembere declared: 'We are no longer playing. . . . We mean to die for this country or win liberation.'

A state of emergency was finally proclaimed on 3 March 1959. Banda was arrested and taken to a Federal prison in Southern Rhodesia; Congress was banned; and police began to round up its officials, detaining eventually more than 1,300 Africans. But far from restoring order, the government's measures provoked even greater violence. In the following weeks, arson, sabotage, demonstrations and riots ensued. The death toll rose from five, as it had stood before the emergency, to fifty-three. Noticeably though, not a single European was killed, and none was seriously injured.

In Britain, the Nyasaland emergency reopened old wounds over the Federation between the Conservative government and Labour opposition. Before the House of Commons on 3 March, Lennox-Boyd, announcing the arrest of Banda, declared that a massacre had been planned; his junior minister, Julian Amery, talked even more wildly of *Mau Mau* and a bloodbath. But Labour politicians remained sceptical and pointed accusing fingers at the Federal government. Those who knew Banda were incredulous. In North Shields, where Banda had worked as a doctor during the war, residents who had met him wrote letters on his behalf to the local press; and former patients from his London surgery presented a petition to Lennox-Boyd, demanding the release of their 'beloved doctor'. Three weeks later, the government bowed to Labour demands for an independent commission of inquiry and appointed a four-man team led by Sir Patrick Devlin, a High Court judge, to investigate the circumstances surrounding the emergency in Nyasaland. 'I do not doubt,' said Lord Perth, a Colonial Office minister, 'that, with such eminent men of such wide experience, we will get to the heart of things.'

The Devlin Report, published in July, had a devastating impact. The commissioners made it quite clear that in their view Armitage, as Governor, was fully justified in declaring a state of emergency. 'The Government had either to act or to abdicate.' Though they dismissed claims about a murder plot, they were in no doubt that Congress was bent on a policy of violence. But along with these conclusions came some damaging observations. Much of the commission's evidence had to be heard in secret. This, as the commissioners explained, was because in Nyasaland 'it is not safe for anyone to express approval of the policies of the Congress party . . . and . . . it is unwise to express any but the most restrained criticism of government policy'. The effect of the emergency measures, said the commissioners, had produced 'a police state', though no doubt, they added, only a temporary one. They pointed to numerous examples of brutality and rough treatment by the security forces and harsh punitive action taken by government authorities to suppress the disorders.

But their most trenchant remarks related to the controversy over the Federation. The commissioners noted that in the government's opinion nationalist agitation over the Federation was confined to 'a small minority of political Africans, mainly of self-seekers who think that their prospects of office will be worse under Federation', while the great majority were indifferent to the issue. The commissioners, however, did not accept this view. Opposition to the Federation, they said, 'was deeply rooted and almost universally held'. They continued: 'Even amongst the chiefs, many of whom are loyal to the Government and dislike Congress methods, we have not heard of a single one who is in favour of Federation. Witness after witness appeared before us for the sole purpose of stating that the cause of all the troubles we were investigating was Federation.'

British ministers were stunned by the implications of the Devlin Report. They had portrayed the Federation as a bold multi-racial experiment, whose success was vital to the interests of the Western world. When previously explaining signs of unrest, they had been content to follow Welensky's lead in dismissing them as the work of a few, unrepresentative agitators. But the evidence of the Devlin Report undermined the entire British approach in central Africa and, worse still, opened Britain's colonial policy to more general attack. Whatever Devlin may have meant, his description of Nyasaland as 'a police state' reverberated around the world. For tactical reasons, the Conservative government closed ranks and formally rejected the Report's main conclusions, provoking scenes of uproar in the Commons not witnessed since the Suez crisis of 1956. But privately, the British prime minister, Harold Macmillan, began to doubt that the Federation in its existing form could survive.

CHAPTER THIRTEEN

The Winds of Change

As late as 1959, the Colonial Office strategy for dealing with territories in east and central Africa was based on the assumption that, although the amount of time now left to Britain in Africa was diminishing, long-term plans could still be laid. When the Colonial Secretary, Lennox-Boyd, and the British Governors of East Africa, gathered for a conference at Chequers in the English countryside in January 1959, they considered some likely dates for independence. Tanganyika, they agreed, would come first, but not before 1970; Uganda and Kenya would follow by about 1975. In Parliament in April 1959, Lennox-Boyd measured British policy in even more distant terms: 'I am unable to envisage a time when it will be possible for any British Government to surrender their ultimate responsibilities for the destinies and well-being of Kenya,' he said. Touring the White Highlands of Kenya in May, the Governor, Sir Evelyn Baring, in one speech after another, calmed fears that white farmers had about their future. British support, he told them, was assured; Kenya would become a 'fortress colony', providing a vital link in Britain's global defence network. When referring to the future of the Central African Federation, British ministers readily offered the same kind of assurance.

There were sound reasons for encouraging white confidence. The white populations were the economic mainstay of each colony; they constituted the only reservoir of professional skills; on them depended the future prosperity of the whole region. Little progress had been made in training the African populations. Only a handful of qualified Africans were available. Whereas, for example, the Gold Coast could boast of some sixty lawyers by the late 1920s, Kenya's first African lawyer did not begin to practice his profession until 1956. In northern Rhodesia in 1959, only thirty-five Africans had received higher education; in Nyasaland the figure was twenty-eight. Using the old Colonial Office criteria for self-government, British officials estimated at the time that a minimum period of between ten and fifteen years of intensive training was needed to prepare reasonably efficient and stable modern administrations.

However ill-prepared for self-government these colonies may have seemed, other considerations began to press their attention on the British government. The Nyasaland emergency had come as a disagreeable surprise; even worse was the damaging criticism contained in the Devlin Report. But the most profound shock came from Kenya. On 3 March 1959, at a camp for hardcore *Mau Mau* supporters near Hola, eleven prisoners died. The first explanation issued by the Kenya government was that the men had died after drinking contaminated water. But subsequent inquiries revealed that they had been beaten to death by their African warders, that several scores more prisoners had been injured at the same time, and that, as a matter of policy, force was used in detention camps if necessary to compel recalcitrant prisoners to work. The Hola incident shook the British Cabinet and many Conservative politicians and led once again to heated debates on African policy in Parliament during the summer.

The future of the east and central African territories thus came under more careful scrutiny. In Parliament and in the press, the cause of colonialism no longer attracted much support. The fateful Suez adventure of 1956, causing division at home and isolation abroad, had finally laid to rest Britain's imperial ambitions. Except for a dwindling, though vociferous, group of empire loyalists, the idea that the Union Jack could be kept flying in distant lands, coloured red on the map, where Britain once held sway, now seemed outdated. In the world-wide withdrawal from Empire, Africa represented the last stage. Initially, Britain had led the way in West Africa. But in east and central Africa, the presence of white communities, blocking the way to African advancement, complicated the process, leaving Britain vulnerable to constant attack from the anti-colonial world. During 1959 Britain's position became more exposed. Not only did de Gaulle concede the right to independence for France's black African colonies, but the Belgians, having resisted Congolese demands for basic political rights for so long, suddenly decided to set independence as the goal for the Congo. Britain therefore, once considered the most progressive colonial power in Africa, now found itself trailing behind. From the United States came further pressure. The Americans, anxious that Africa should be kept out of the hands of the Communist bloc, believed that the best way to preserve Western influence there was for Britain and other colonial powers to hasten the advance of independence and thereby gain the goodwill of African leaders. As for Britain's existing plans for establishing multiracial states in east and central Africa, such limited progress had been made since the idea flourished in the early 1950s that they seemed of increasingly dubious value. As Roy Welensky ruefully noted, even within the Conservative party, younger politicians in 1959 tended to look on the Federation more as an attempt to maintain white settler control than as a brave experiment in racial partnership.

Among the issues that faced Prime Minister Harold Macmillan in 1959, therefore, the problems of Africa assumed a growing importance. Hitherto. Macmillan's acquaintanceship with black Africa had been brief: for just under a year during the Second World War, he had held a position as junior minister in the Colonial Office. But during that time he had demonstrated an inclination for radical thinking on African problems. Turning his attention to Kenya, he had warned in a confidential paper in 1942 that where a small white land-owning population was surrounded by increasing numbers of crowded and land-hungry Africans, the outcome would be violence. As a solution, he proposed that the government should buy up white farms and encourage white farmers to stay on as managers. In this way, the whites would get security of their money and employment, the land would be farmed in the most productive way and the government would be free to allocate land to Africans when the need arose. The idea was not pursued.

In the same dispassionate manner, Macmillan began to weigh up the wider issues that Africa now posed. Sooner or later Britain would have to come to terms with African nationalism in east and central Africa, just as it had done in

West Africa or, before that, with the nationalists in Asia. The tide of African nationalism, as it reached eastern Africa, could no more be halted there than in the west. To try to hold it back, Macmillan was told by one experienced colonial administrator, would be to invite rebellion. Since Britain, with a huge army at its disposal, had recently failed to hold the small island of Cyprus, and France, using half a million troops, could not contain Algeria, the prospect of colonial unrest was viewed with some alarm. The emergency in Nyasaland served as a warning of how a seemingly peaceful colony could erupt unexpectedly into violence. Moreover, any attempt to drive back nationalism was likely to provide opportunities for the Communist block to exploit.

Macmillan's concern was shared by another member of the Cabinet, Iain Macleod, who, in the summer of 1959, joined a small government committee set up to examine the problems of multi-racial societies in Africa. At the age of forty-five, Macleod was the youngest member of the Cabinet and well known as a Tory radical. He had previously shown no great interest in colonial affairs but, like other members of the government, he had been shaken by the Hola incident. Macleod's view, coinciding with Macmillan's, was that Britain, for both practical and moral reasons, could not withold the transfer of power in east and central Africa once it had been conceded in West Africa. Nor could African political progress be delayed merely because of the objections of white settlers. The result would be massive unrest and bloodshed. Neither Macmillan nor Macleod believed that African states were in fact ready for independence. They recognised that there were some powerful arguments in favour of delay. Some states faced tribal dissension; most were economically weak; all were inadequately prepared. But though the risks of moving rapidly in Africa were considerable, the dangers of moving too slowly were, they believed, even greater.

The opportunity to press ahead resolutely came in October 1959. In the British general election that month Macmillan won a resounding victory. A new generation came to prominence in the Conservative party, an older school retired. And Macmillan, his leadership assured, was determined to keep the Conservative party 'modern and progressive'. For the

Colonial Office the change was signalled by the appointment of Macleod as Colonial Secretary. Taking stock of the problems he now faced, Macleod was all the more convinced that urgent action was required. In Kenya, a state of emergency had been in force for seven years. Nyasaland too was in a state of emergency, with hundreds in detention. In Northern Rhodesia, the authorities, fearing disorders in the 1959 election there, had banned one militant African group which had advocated a boycott of the polls and placed its leaders in detention. In these circumstances, the idea of orderly and gradual progress in accordance with the exacting standards which the Colonial Office had previously laid down no longer seemed feasible. Nor were the old guidelines about economic viability and parliamentary experience thought to be quite so relevant. France, after all, had conceded independence for its string of African colonies, virtually none of which was viable on its own. What mattered more now, in Macleod's view, was the speed at which African political progress could be introduced. Little time was left, he believed, to devise solutions. In east and central Africa, therefore, change would have to be radical and swift.

Conscious of 'dangers and storms' ahead, Macmillan decided to see for himself the nature of the difficulties on the ground and to warn of the new direction of British policy. No previous British prime minister in office had set foot in Africa. Thus his six-week journey beginning in January 1960—to Ghana, Nigeria, the Central African Federation and South Africa—was a mildly historic occasion. What it was to be remembered for, however, was the time when Britain sounded the retreat from Africa.

In Accra, Macmillan found Nkrumah, characteristically, not so much interested in the problems of Ghana as in the liberation of Africa, and outspoken in his attacks on colonialism. But Macmillan liked him—'an engaging character', he wrote in his memoirs, 'with much charm of manner and courtesy when he cared to display these qualities.' Macmillan was also impressed by the economic progress that Ghana had made since independence. At a state banquet in Accra on 9 January, Macmillan spoke in glowing terms about the prospects for more British investment. It was there too that he first referred to the 'winds of change blowing through Africa'. Throughout his travels, in fact, he continued to draw attention to the immense changes taking place in Africa. But only at the end of his journey, when he spoke in Cape Town, was the full import of his words recognised.

In Lagos, Macmillan was able to witness Nigeria in its final stage before independence, due on 1 October. The transition had been slow and painful. It had taken nearly ten years in all to complete constitutional negotiations. After holding back independence, the northern region had finally reached self-government in 1959. Since then federal elections had again aroused tribal antagonism. But Nigeria now seemed destined for a quieter experience. The three regions were committed to the Federation; a coalition government had been arranged; and the federal prime minister, Abubaka Tafawa Balewa, a Muslim teacher from the North, was a leader who was highly respected and capable. Macmillan noted the sense of fun and merriment for which West Africans were renowned.

In Central Africa, by contrast, he was struck by the prevailing mood of uncertainty and unease among both white and black. On a visit to Nyasaland he found 'extreme hostility' to the Federation. 'The cause of Federation was almost desperate,' he wrote in his memoirs, 'because of the strength of African opinion against it. The only grounds for hope seemed to lie in so rapid an advance to self-government in all matters of territorial interests as to reconcile Dr Banda and his supporters to continue to work within the Federal framework.' In a private dispatch to Queen Elizabeth on 31 January, he mentioned his concern about Nyasaland. 'There the white population is small and anxious, and the Administration struck me as tired—from the Governor downwards.'

In Salisbury, Macmillan was given the opportunity to explain British policy before a public audience. The audience had assembled in a large cinema normally restricted to Europeans but opened to all races especially for the occasion of his visit. Macmillan reiterated British support for the Federation, but warned that independence would not be forthcoming without the prior agreement of the two northern territories of Northern Rhodesia and Nyasaland. In a further signal, he provided some of the background to current British thinking on Africa. 'In all parts of the continent the tide of nationalism is flowing fast,' he said. 'This is one of the facts of the African situation today. We must accept it as a fact, and take it into account in forming our policies.'

His speech in Cape Town, made to the two Houses of Parliament in the Chamber of the old Cape Colony Parliament on 3 February, combined the broad sweep of history, on which Macmillan enjoyed dwelling, with a political message that the South Africans found discomfiting. He praised their achievements but made clear British disapproval of apartheid. What was most noted, however, was his exposition on the rise of nationalism in Africa:

> 'In the twentieth century, and especially since the end of the war, the processes which gave birth to all the nation states of Europe have been repeated all over the world. We have seen the awakening of national consciousness in peoples who have for centuries lived in dependence upon some other power. Fifteen years ago this movement spread through Asia. Many countries there of different races and civilisations pressed their claim to an independent national life. Today the same thing is happening in Africa, and the most striking of all the impressions I have formed since I left London a month ago is of the strength of this African national consciousness. In different places it takes different forms, but it is happening everywhere. The wind of change is blowing through this continent, and whether we like it or not, this growth of national consciousness is a political fact. We must all accept it as a fact and our national policies must take account of it.'

CHAPTER FOURTEEN

The Release of Kenyatta

The first territory to feel the wind of change was Kenya. While Macmillan was making his tour of Africa, Macleod in London presided over a constitutional conference on Kenya at which he was determined to break white resistance to the idea of African rule. Since the end of the *Mau Mau* war in 1956, notable progress had been made with agrarian reform, and in October 1959 the White Highlands were formally opened to all races. Politically, however, African advancement was still held up by white objections. The first African elections in 1957 had brought eight elected Africans to the Legislative Council. The following year their number increased to fourteen, giving them parity with white representatives. This racial balance, according to the Colonial Secretary, Lennox-Boyd, was expected to remain unaltered for the next ten years. But in the meanwhile African demands for a majority of parliamentary seats had grown louder. Even more disconcerting for the white community, African politicians were also insisting on the release of Kenyatta.

The conference at Lancaster House, which opened on 18 January 1960, was marked by interminable wrangling, acrimonious exchanges and walk-outs. It was nearly a month before Macleod was able to put his final proposals to the delegates. From the start he had made clear his view that Kenya was destined to become an 'African' country. The claims of a small white minority, however important it was, could no longer stand in the way of African rule. With a population of 60,000 whites and six million Africans, there was no possible alternative. What he proposed, as a means of transition, was a multi-racial government, tipped slightly in favour of the African majority, but allowing whites a major political role. The offer made to the African delegates was for thirty-three of the sixty-five seats in the Legislative Assembly, for four government ministries compared with the three given to whites, and for a wide franchise that would put more than one million Africans on the voters' roll. Eventually, the African delegates accepted the deal. But the main white political group, the United Party, representing most white opinion in Kenya, did not.

Macleod's hopes for an agreement, therefore, rested on white delegates from the New Kenya Group, a political party formed in 1959 by liberal European politicians, with the support of business interests, which appealed to membership from all races. By Kenyan standards the New Kenya Group, advocating a multi-racial approach to politics, was a radical innovation. Even so, its leader, Michael Blundell, a prominent farmer and former government minister, thought that Macleod's proposals were far too advanced. By setting Kenya on the road to African majority rule, they clearly meant the demise of the multi-racial ideas that the New Kenya Group had been founded to represent. Blundell also realised, however, that if liberal whites rejected the deal, they would quickly be written off by African opinion and Kenya would again plunge into a period of dangerous tension. Macleod pressed him hard to accept. Though he had strong misgivings, Blundell agreed to the deal, thereby providing Macleod with the breakthrough he so desperately needed.

The prospect of black rule appalled most of the white community. Shocked and dismayed, white politicians spoke of the 'cynical abandonment of the Europeans in Kenya' and described the new constitution as a 'victory for *Mau Mau*'. The leader of the United Party, Group Captain Briggs, commented: 'I regard the outcome of this conference as a death blow to the European community in Kenya.' The Speaker of the Legislative Assembly resigned, accusing the British government of breaking its many previous pledges to the whites. The stock market in Nairobi slumped, there was a massive outflow of capital, the building industry came to a standstill and white confidence collapsed. When Blundell returned to Nairobi from the conference, he was met by angry white demonstrators shouting abuse at him. One of them threw a bag of thirty pieces of silver at his feet. Friends ostracised him and his family. At an election meeting he was pelted with eggs and tomatoes. Once when an African crowd cheered him, a white women pushed her way through them to the front, spat in his face and snarled: 'Why don't you let them kiss you, Judas Iscariot?' Rather than risk life under an African government, thousands of whites decided to leave, many heading for the white-ruled territories of southern Africa, deeply embittered by what they saw as a British betrayal.

The African campaign to obtain the release of Kenyatta now gathered momentum. Kenyatta had completed his prison sentence at Lokitaung in April 1959 but, in accordance with government policy, he was now held in restriction at the administrative centre at Lodwar, still in the far north. His living conditions had improved. He was allowed the company of his young wife, Ngina, and their two children, and approved visitors occasionally arrived from Nairobi. But the authorities were adamant that he would not be released. In answer to African demands for his release in May 1960, the new Governor, Sir Patrick Renison, condemned Kenyatta as 'the African leader to darkness and death'. His release, said Renison, would be a danger to security.

Though Renison's decision was of some relief to the white community, the continued detention of Kenyatta proved politically embarrassing. The elections of February 1961, the first to be held under the new constitution, were won by a convincing majority by the newly formed Kenya African National Union (Kanu), which acclaimed Kenyatta as its leader. Without the release of Kenyatta, Kanu refused to form a government. Unwilling to relent, Renison was obliged to turn to the minority Kenya African Democratic Union (Kadu) to fill government posts. In the Legislative Assembly, official nominees had to be used to help secure a majority for the government.

Only reluctantly did Renison come to accept the necessity for Kenyatta's release. Like other senior members of the Kenya administrations, Renison found great difficulty in coming to terms with a man officially held to be responsible for the *Mau Mau* rebellion and its many outrages. Renison's view was that Kenyatta was 'an implacable opponent' of any cooperation with people from tribes and races other than the Kikuyu, though African politicians allowed to visit Kenyatta assured him that this was not the case, nor ever had been. Yet without Kenyatta constitutional progress seemed impossible. Still fearing that his release would incite disorders, Renison made plans for his 'phased' return. In April 1961, after spending two years in Lodwar, Kenyatta was moved to Maralal, a pleasant hill station only 180 miles from Nairobi. There he received a constant stream of visitors—diplomats, politicians, priests and friends—and, at a specially arranged press conference, he gave his views to the world's press. He spoke of his belief in non-violence; denied any Communist affiliations; stressed the need for reconciliation; and explained how an independent Kenya would protect the rights of all citizens. But there were many who were sceptical about his performance. Among the visitors to Maralal at this time was Michael Blundell, then a government minister, who reached the conclusion that Kenyatta, though one of the most intelligent Africans he had ever met, was nevertheless 'an extreme nationalist', thinking only in terms of Africa for the Africans. As Blundell was leaving, Kenyatta asked him why the Europeans hated him so much. Blundell thought it best to tell him the truth. The Europeans, he said, thought that it was he who hated them and that he had planned *Mau Mau*, with all its horrors and murders, to be rid of them.

Kenyatta was finally allowed to go home to Gatundu in the green hills above Nairobi on 14 August 1961, nearly nine years after his arrest. He swiftly re-established his position in Kenyan politics. In October he formally accepted the Kanu presidency; in January 1962 he was elected to parliament unopposed; in April he became a minister in the Kanu-Kadu coalition government. But to many of his colleagues he seemed past his prime, his mental and physical energy dwindling, his influence no longer so strongly felt. By then he was nearly seventy years old. The harsh years he had spent at Lokitaung and Lodwar had taken their toll. Neither in Kanu nor in parliament did he display the authority he once had. Younger men, like Tom Mboya and James Gichuru, were often left to take the initiative. To the new governor, Malcolm MacDonald, a former politician and diplomat brought in to pilot Kenya to independence, Kenyatta sometimes appeared indecisive and unsure of himself.

The victory that Kenyatta won at the polls in May 1963, six months before independence, gave him renewed spirit. As prime minister, his leadership was at once firm and effective. All doubts about his abilities were soon forgotten. Finally in control, he set out to overcome the tribal rivalries that had flared up during the struggle for power and to make his peace with the white community. Soon after the election he travelled to Nakuru, a farming centre in the heart of the old White Highlands, to address a meeting of some three hundred white farmers and their wives. Many in the audience had come reluctantly. On their faces were sketched all the resentment, fear and suspicion they still felt about Kenyatta.

Kenyatta began by pleading for reconciliation. He urged that both whites and blacks should forgive the 'wrongs' they had done to each other. In the past, the whites had made a valuable contribution to Kenya and he hoped that they would continue to do so. 'Continue to farm your land well and you will get all the encouragement and protection of the government.' He referred to his imprisonment: 'This has been worrying many of you. But let me tell you Jomo Kenyatta has no intention of retaliating or looking backwards. We are going to forget the past, and look to the future. I have suffered imprisonment and detention; but that is gone, and I am not going to remember it. Let us join hands and work for the benefit of Kenya. . . .'

At the end of his speech the whites gave him a standing ovation.

CHAPTER FIFTEEN

The Fate of the Federation

With the Central African Federation, the way ahead was far more complex to resolve. After Macmillan had visited the Rhodesias and Nyasaland in January 1960, he wrote privately to the Queen: 'I find myself with a great deal of evidence but still a long way from disentangling the plot.'

Both Macmillan and Macleod thought that the Federation was worth preserving. Macmillan's view was that to break up a multi-racial experiment begun with such promise only seven years before was too drastic a course of action. The economic advantages, he considered, were particularly strong. In the case of Nyasaland, half of its income came from Federal subsidies. The only way though that the Federation could survive was if it gained African support. African support for the Federation would not be forthcoming without their obtaining a greater share in its affairs. Hence there was an urgent need to give Africans more power and responsibility in the two northern territories of Nyasaland and Northern Rhodesia and within the federal structure. The difficulty with this policy lay with the white reaction it provoked. As Macmillan had learned during his stay in Salisbury, the whites in Southern Rhodesia were already becoming restive and impatient about the idea of remaining in the Federation if this jeopardised their own chances of achieving full independence. Indeed, they were hostile to remaining in the Federation at all if there was a possibility that the two northern territories might come under African control. If British policy appeared to threaten white interests, there was a risk that the Southern Rhodesian authorities or even the Federal government might resort to unilateral action. Several previous warnings had been dropped. In a speech to the Federal Assembly in 1956, Huggins, then prime minister, noted the advantage of the Federation having control of its own defence force. 'I only hope we will not have to use it, as the North American colonies had to use theirs, because we are dealing with a stupid government in the United Kingdom.' Welensky made similar hints. When asked about possible British intervention in federal matters, he referred pointedly to 'a certain historical tea party'. Privately, and unknown to Macmillan, he enquired from close advisors as to what the consequences might be. Their replies were not encouraging.

The battle over the Federation raged across central Africa and along the corridors of Westminster, Whitehall and the City for three years before it was finally over. On all sides it was fought with bitter intensity, and at times against a background of violence. In defence of the Federation, Welensky concentrated his energies not so much on trying to win African support, as on attempting to influence British opinion. With considerable success, he enlisted the help of right-wing Tories and industrialists, hired a posse of public relations consultants and loudly raised a storm of protest at every adverse turn of events. The air was often thick with acrimonious exchanges. To many Rhodesian whites it seemed that Britain, in coming to terms with African nationalism, was prepared, solely for reasons of expediency, to sacrifice the interests of whites. British ministers dealing with Central Africa invariably came to be regarded with distrust and, in some cases, with loathing. Welensky was convinced of British treachery. Almost every British move he saw as an example of duplicity and betrayal. One pledge after another, he later claimed, had been broken. By the end of the battle, there existed a legacy of distrust and bitterness towards the British government that was to have a marked effect on the events leading to the fateful Rhodesian rebellion in 1965.

The first skirmish came over the release of Dr Banda. Welensky and the Federal authorities were adamantly opposed. One Federal minister, reputed to be an expert on Nyasaland, predicted that it would lead to a massive breakdown of law and order and to thousands of deaths. The Governor, Sir Robert Armitage, thought it inadvisable on security grounds, and so did several members of the British Cabinet. Even Macmillan was doubtful. Macleod, however, insisted that the only way forward in Nyasaland was to bring

Banda into negotiation, and he pressed his determination to have Banda released to the point of resignation. Macmillan eventually concurred. On 1 April 1960, thirteen months after his arrest, Banda was released from Gwelo prison in Southern Rhodesia, flown to Blantyre and taken straight to Government House in Zomba, then the capital. There, in the Governor's study, he talked for an hour with Macleod, who was paying his first visit to Central Africa. They agreed that Banda should make a broadcast, in tandem with the Governor, announcing his release and appealing for calm. To almost everyone's surprise there was no disorder.

Macleod now moved swiftly. In June he lifted the state of emergency. In July, six months after resolving Kenya's fate, he convened a constitutional conference of Nyasaland delegates in London. By August he had won their agreement on the introduction of African majority rule for Nyasaland the following year. The white delegates, led by Welensky's supporters, accepted the outcome. And since they knew that Banda was committed to breaking up the Federation, their agreement implied that Welensky himself was not averse to the idea of letting Nyasaland leave the Federation. With its large black population and weak economy, it had always been regarded as a liability for the more prosperous Rhodesias.

The major clashes over the Federation soon followed. In October, a British commission set up by Macmillan to advise on the future of the Federation, in preparation for the Federal review conference due to meet in 1960, published its report. The commission, led by a distinguished lawyer, Sir Walter Monckton, had toured the Federation earlier in the year to collect evidence. Their overall conclusion was that the Federation was worth preserving, particularly on economic grounds. But because of the weight of African opinion in the two northern territories—their 'almost pathological' dislike of the Federation—its form would have to be substantially changed. The commission recommended 'prompt and far-reaching' reforms. They suggested, among other things, that Africans should be given equal representation in the Federal Assembly; that racial discrimination should be made illegal; and that the name of the Federation, so deeply reviled by Africans as a symbol of white domination, should be changed.

In sum, their observations amounted to an indictment of the way that the Federation was being run. All this was bad enough. But what infuriated Welensky was the commission's suggestion that the British government should acknowledge the right of any territory to secede from the Federation. The commission had included this suggestion in the belief that it might provide a safety-valve for African fears and help secure 'a fair trial' for the new association. Welensky charged that not only had the commission, by proposing the secession clause, breached the terms of reference to which he had originally agreed, but that he had been given a categorical assurance by the British government that secession would not be included as part of the commission's business. The British response to such accusations was to maintain that whatever assurances had been given, the question of secession could no longer be sensibly ignored. Welensky, railing against British duplicity, asserted that Britain, by officially opening up the issue of secession, had in effect passed sentence of death on the Federation.

He did not intend to give up without fighting every inch of the way. The battleground that he chose was over the Northern Rhodesian constitution. To Welensky's dismay, Macleod, having dealt with Kenya and Nyasaland, had then turned his attention to Northern Rhodesia. There the 1958 constitution had provided some African political progress but otherwise left white control virtually unimpaired. As he had done with the Kenya constitution, Macleod now wanted to tip the balance in favour of the African nationalist parties. In strictly legal terms, the British government alone was responsible for political advancement in Northern Rhodesia. But since the political status of Northern Rhodesia also affected the nature of the Federation, Welensky was entitled to be consulted. Using every available poinι of pressure, Welensky set out to thwart Macleod's plan. The issue for Welensky was no longer a matter of political gain, as it had been in the past. What hopes he had retained of obtaining independence for the Federation had vanished during an abortive Federal review conference in London in 1960. Now the Federation's very survival was at stake. For the advent of a black nationalist government in Northern Rhodesia as well as

Nyasaland, both of them determined to secede, meant that the Federation was doomed. Southern Rhodesia certainly would not remain a part of it.

The uproar that Welensky managed to raise after Macleod put forward his proposals in February 1961 was remarkably effective. In Northern Rhodesia, his colleagues in the government resigned and dark warnings were made about resistance among the 75,000 whites in the country. In the British parliament, Macleod faced a back-bench revolt of some ninety Conservative members and came under sharp attack from Tory peers. So intense was the pressure that Macleod was forced to retreat, his political career fatally damaged. By June he had devised constitutional proposals more favourable to Welensky. The reaction from the nationalists, however, was severe. In August and September, supporters of Kenneth Kaunda's United National Independence. Party, the leading nationalist group, resorted to violence and sabotage. By February 1962, after a year of intense infighting, the British Cabinet finally agreed to a constitution which gave Africans a narrow majority. For some months more, as Welensky fought on, British ministers endeavoured to salvage parts of the Federation. But in Nyasaland, Banda, who had become chief minister in the government in August 1961 after sweeping the polls, remained as adamant against it as before. So too in Nothern Rhodesia was Kaunda. In December 1962 Nyasaland was given the right to secede. In April 1963 Northern Rhodesia was given the same right. By the end of 1963, ten years after it was launched, the Federation was dead.

With bitterness and anger, Welensky heaped the blame for the demise of the Federation on Britain. 'The British Government have ratted on us,' he thundered in December 1962, after Nyasaland had been given the right to secede. 'They have gone back on the most solemn understandings and intentions. They have wrecked the foundation upon which they themselves built the Federation and on which they were determined at that time to construct a lasting edifice. They have been guilty of an act of treachery . . . I say that Britain has lost the will to govern in Africa and that Britain is utterly reckless of the fate of the inhabitants of the present Federation, including those of our kith and kin. By contrast we in the

Federation have neither lost faith in ourselves nor in our will to be governed decently and fairly.'

Certainly, British ministers were guilty of dealing evasively and at times dishonourably with Welensky. The British objective, nevertheless, was to devise some form of association between the Central African territories that would be politically acceptable to both black and white. Right to the end they persevere in the hope that such a solution could be found. Welensky's attacks, in fact, merely exasperated them and helped to harden white opinion against the kind of compromise that Britain thought might be possible. Macmillan, in his diary in March 1961, wearily wondered why it was that Welensky continually insulted the British government, quarrelled with ministers, incited his party to revolt and stirred up the right wing when the British government were the *only* friends he had. Indeed, Welensky himself did little to improve whatever chances of success the Federation ever had. In terms of reaching out to gain African support, at the end of the day the Federation had seen one African, Jasper Savanhu, brought to office as a junior minister in the government and nine Africans out of a complement of 1,900 given posts in the top ranks of the civil service. Even this record was blighted when Savanhu resigned in 1962. In a letter to Welensky he wrote: 'Your government, in spite of strong representations from the African party members and other quarters, has failed or has no intention of implementing a policy of partnership.' Savanhu described later how he had been used by the government merely as 'window-dressing' to impress the Tory government in Britain. In the Rhodesian context, the appointment of an African minister and African senior civil servants represented a major advance. Similarly the relaxation of the colour bar in hotels, restaurants and cinemas was seen as a considerable concession. As offerings to the rising clamour of African nationalism, such measures were of no account. In the dying stages of the Federation Welensky could muster hardly a single ally. No-one in the three territories was much concerned by its death.

CHAPTER SIXTEEN

The Transfer of Power

One by one, in swift succession, the new African states emerged, amid much jubilation and to the world's applause. In 1960, Nigeria, the giant of Africa with a population of 35 million, was duly launched as a 'showpiece of democracy', with greater optimism than had once seemed possible. In 1961 came Sierra Leone and Tanganyika; in 1962, Uganda; in 1963, Kenya and Zanzibar. In 1964, Nyasaland gained independence as Malawi and Northern Rhodesia became Zambia. In 1965, even the Gambia, a 300-mile strip of land lying along the banks of the Gambia river, was set up as an independent state. The southern African territories of Bechuanaland (Botswana) and Basutoland (Lesotho) followed in 1966 and Swaziland in 1968. In all, during the independence era, thirty-two new states appeared.

So rapid was the pace that in some cases British officials dealing with arrangements for the transfer of power were hard pressed to complete them in time. For Uganda, the decisive constitutional conference paving the way for independence took place as late as September 1961. There for the first time Baganda delegates were ready to take part in negotiations with other Ugandan representatives. The negotiations, under Macleod's auspices, were drawn out and difficult, but ended with agreement for independence one year later. In the intervening period, the Colonial Office had to fit new elections, a new interim constitution, further negotiations over the future of the four kingdoms, an independence constitution and parliamentary legislation at Westminster. The drafting of the Independence Order in Council for Uganda was completed only one week before the independence date. In Nyasaland, where only a handful of trained Africans were available to fill even key posts in the administration, officials set up crash courses in government. In the case of Northern Rhodesia, negotiations over the transfer of mineral rights owned by the British South Africa Company were still going on behind a tea-tent at a garden party in the grounds of Government House a few hours before independence.

Yet for all the unseemly haste, the transfer of power was accomplished efficiently and with a remarkable amount of goodwill. In the setting stages of Britain's African empire, the Governors appointed to wind up its affairs were recognised as men of foresight and skill whose preoccupation was to effect a transition as orderly as possible. In Ghana, Arden-Clarke had set a tradition which earned Nkrumah's profound gratitude. Other proconsuls, the last of their line, were to gain similar recognition—among them, Sir James Robertson in Nigeria, Malcolm MacDonald in Kenya, Sir Richard Turnbull in Tanganyika and Sir Maurice Dorman in Sierra Leone. Nationalist leaders recently denounced as dangerous extremists were now found to possess previously unrecognised qualities. For their part, the nationalists, whatever their experience of British rule, responded warmly. When the Sierra Leone leader, Sir Milton Margai, was asked by Macleod at a conference in London in 1960 on what date he would like his country to become independent, he burst into tears and said he never expected to live long enough to be asked that question. Dr Banda, commenting on his year's detention by Britain, remarked: 'It was the best turn the British ever did for me.' Seretse Khama, once banished from Bechuanaland because of his marriage to an English girl, duly became president of Botswana, still deeply attached to the British. In Independence messages, the tributes paid were as fulsome as those given first by Nkruma. Sir Abubakar Tafawa Balewa in Nigeria spoke positively of Britain's colonial contribution 'first as masters, then as leaders, finally as partners, but always as friends'. Kaunda, twice jailed by the British authorities, referred proudly to the fact that independence had been achieved in Northern Rhodesia without bitterness. But perhaps the most poignant speech, in the circumstances, was made by Kenyatta: 'We do not forget the assistance and guidance we have received through the years from people of British stock: administrators, businessmen, farmers, missionaries and many others. Our law, our system of government and many other aspects of our daily lives are founded on British principles and justice.'

For the white communities facing life under black rule there were many uncertainties, doubts and fears. Thousands decided to leave. In Zambia more than half of the colonial civil servants left the administration. Kenya by independence had lost about one third of its white farmers. Those whites who stayed, however, found the adjustment to be not nearly so painful as they had once imagined. Street names changed, old statues were removed. In Nairobi, the majestic Delamere Avenue named after the wild, eccentric pioneer leader of the whites, became Kenyatta Avenue, and Delamere's statue was taken away. Some streets were renamed after *Mau Mau* leaders. In Lusaka, an equestrian statue in front of the High Court commonly known as 'the Rider and the Horse' and bearing the words 'In memory of Cecil Rhodes' was dismantled, transported across the Zambezi river to Salisbury and there set up again. But otherwise life in the tropics seemed to go on much as before. Within a short time, white settlers became reconciled to the habits of African government. Indeed, in Kenya Kenyatta's rule appeared to be so stable and benign that many whites there who had only recently thought of Kenyatta with nothing but revulsion now began to worry about his passing.

Other whites, though, saw Britain's withdrawal from Africa as an act of surrender to the forces of black extremism. Nowhere was this view held with such conviction as in Southern Rhodesia and nowhere was the determination greater to bring a halt to Macmillan's winds of change. Most whites there shared Welensky's opinion that Britain had 'lost the will to govern in Africa' and they believed that Britain's decline as a world power held acute dangers for their own position. Welensky himself, as a result of a notorious luncheon in Salisbury in February 1962, was convinced he knew the truth of the matter. In conversation with Duncan Sandys, Britain's Commonwealth Secretary, Welensky had insisted that it would not be difficult to keep Nyasaland in the Federation with the firm exercise of authority. 'No, Roy,' replied Sandys, 'you see, we British have lost the will to govern.' Welensky's colleague, Julian Greenfield, snapped back, 'But we haven't.' According to Lord Alport, who was also present as Britain's High Commissioner in Salisbury, Sandys had meant that Britain was no longer prepared to govern by force. Indeed, Macmillan tried to make the same point to Welensky on one of his numerous visits to London. 'It is too simple a reading of history,' Macmillan told him, 'to think that you can exercise control simply by the use of power.' The Rhodesians, however, thought differently.

Macmillan was sufficiently incensed by the suggestion that Britain had lost the will to govern its Empire to refer to the charge in his memoirs. 'It is a vulgar but false jibe,' he wrote, 'that the British people by a series of gestures unique in history abandoned their Empire in a fit of frivolity or impatience. They had not lost the will or even the power to rule. But they did not conceive of themselves as having the right to govern in perpetuity.' Macleod too, who wrought so much change in Africa, rebutted the view that Britain, in transforming the Empire into the Commonwealth, was fighting a series of bitter rearguard actions. 'We did not "lose" an Empire,' he wrote in 1965, 'We followed to its logical end what has always been British colonial policy.'

For much of black Africa, the advent of independence produced a wave of optimism and exhilaration. As the British and French withdrew, leaders of talent and integrity stepped forward, brought to power by popular election. With energy and enthusiasm, new governments set out to tackle the tasks of development and nation-building; bright young men went quickly to the top; ambitious projects were launched. Africa, so it was thought, once freed from colonial rule, was destined for an era of unprecedented progress. African leaders spoke of building new societies which might offer the world at large an inspiration. The promises they made of combating disease and illiteracy, of providing education, housing, medical care, employment and land for all, though absurdly extravagant, were at least exciting goals for which to strive and which the departing colonial powers found commendable. On the world stage, too, African states were now accorded due attention. With both the West and the Soviet bloc vying for their support, African politicians became adept at playing one side off against the other. The more idealistic leaders, however, preferred that Africa should stand aloof from the sterile quarrels of the Cold War. In 1963, representatives from thirty-one African governments met in Addis Ababa, the capital of Ethiopia, to establish the Organisation of African Unity which, it was hoped, would provide Africa with a powerful independent voice in world affairs. The more fervent leaders, like Nkrumah, even proposed that Africa should be run by a single Union government.

The dreams, inevitably, were soon to fade. Too many expectations had been aroused for them ever to have been fulfilled. The relative ease with which black Africa attained its independence gave the new states a false idea of their own potential. When the vast dimensions of Africa's poverty, its backwardness, disease and harsh climate were examined in the cold light of day, these alone provided monumental obstacles which had to be faced. But at least the launching of the independence era inspired a real sense of new hope and new purpose, which made such problems seem less daunting. And as the old colonial order passed away in comparative peace, a new kind of partnership with the world's powers was made possible.

There was, however, one notable exception.

CHAPTER SEVENTEEN

Chaos in the Congo

The demise of Belgian rule in the Congo came in a climate of suspicion, fear and foreboding. The Belgians never devised any coherent policy for bringing independence to the Congo. When faced suddenly with an outbreak of violence, they reacted with surprise and alarm, uncertain of what course of action to take. As the demands of the Congolese nationalists became more insistent, they improvised with reforms, hoping to stem the tide. Finally, fearing the possibility of a colonial war, they simply handed over power as rapidly as they could. In the final months of Belgian rule, the colonial administration, once so vigorous and forceful, was gripped by inertia; while in the political arena, rival African factions competed recklessly for support. The stark reality facing the Congo on Independence Day in 1960 was that this vast and complex country was under the control of a collection of ill-assorted politicians, none of whom had any experience of government or parliamentary life or administration. The result, perhaps inevitably, was disaster. But the disaster was compounded by one fatal event after another until the Congo, within weeks of its independence, had become a byword for chaos and disorder.

In a period of only eighteen months, Belgian rule crumbled from a position of rigid certainty about the Congo's future to a confused and demoralised transfer of power. Until January 1959, the Belgian authorities had seemed successful in their attempt to insulate the Congolese from politics. What protests there were against Belgian rule came mainly from groups of *évolués* seeking greater status for themselves. Some nationalist ideas had taken root in Léopoldville, the capital, and other major towns, but for the most part they were expressed only timidly. Officially, no political parties were permitted to exist; nor was press freedom allowed. For advice on the future of the Congo, the Belgian government in 1958 set up a special study group, consisting entirely of Belgians. Their recommendations, presented in Brussels in December that year, were thought to represent a major advance. They proposed local government elections, to be followed at a later stage by the creation of provincial and national assemblies.

Ten days later, starting on 4 January 1959, Léopoldville was torn by vicious rioting. By the end of three days, at least fifty Africans had been killed and two hundred and fifty injured; some fifty whites were also injured. The immediate cause was a decision by the local authorities to refuse permission for a scheduled Sunday afternoon meeting of the tribal organisation, Abako—the *Alliance des Ba-Kongo*—which had widespread support in Léopoldville province. Belgian investigations subsequently showed that unemployment, overcrowding and discrimination had produced a groundswell of frustration and discontent. They also pointed out that events outside the country, such as de Gaulle's visit to the neighbouring town of Brazzaville in August 1958, during which he offered self-government to the French Congo, had greatly impressed the Léopoldville population and inflamed opinion against Belgian rule. Coming so unexpectedly, the riots shook Belgium to the core. For the first time the Belgian public was alerted to the difficulties and dangers that the Congo might present. In the Belgian Cabinet intense argument ensued about what response to make. Finally, one week after the riots, the Belgian government went ahead as planned with an announcement of government reforms based on the recommendations of the special study group but, hoping to mollify African opinion further, it added a vague promise about independence as being the eventual goal of Belgian policy. No target date was mentioned; no programme was laid out; no effort was made to change the pattern of government. The Belgian government, having taken that momentous decision, then fell into protracted debate about the wisdom of the move.

Across the Congo, however, political activity now burst out in wild and hectic profusion. By November 1959, as many as fifty-three political groups were officially registered; a few months later the number had increased to one hundred and twenty. Almost every party sprang from tribal origins. Some were based on major tribes like the Bakongo, the Baluba, the Balunda and the Bamongo; others were only of local importance. The vast distances in the interior of the Congo hampered the formation of nationally based movements. From Léopoldville to Stanleyville, for example, involved a journey upriver of 1,100 miles. Indeed, more important to many Congolese politicians than the idea of national independence was the hope that, with the departure of the Belgians, they might revive ancient African empires which had existed before the days of Belgian rule.

Nowhere was this tribal sentiment more pronounced than among the Bakongo of the Lower Congo region around Léopoldville. Under the leadership of Joseph Kasavubu, a conservative *évolué* who had once trained as a priest, Abako was transformed from a cultural and social group into a militant political organisation championing the Bakongo cause. Kasavubu's dream was to reunite the Bakongo people divided by the boundaries of the French Congo, the Belgian Congo and Angola and rebuild the old Kongo empire which had last flourished in the sixteenth century. In pursuit of this goal, Kasavubu became the most outspoken Congolese critic of Belgian rule. After the Léopoldville riots in January 1959, Abako was banned, its leaders including Kasavubu were arrested, but its popularity spread. In June, Abako leaders sent the Belgian government a detailed plan for an independent state called the Republic of Central Kongo and threatened to declare independence at the end of the year. As a further warning of Bakongo intentions, Abako in October embarked on a resistance campaign in the Lower Congo region to undermine the Belgian administration.

In the province of Katanga, a thousand miles to the southeast, similar tribal associations burgeoned into political parties. Two main rival parties emerged. One, the *Confédération des Associations Tribales du Katanga*, otherwise known as Conakat, was dominated by the Lunda tribe and drew its strength from southern Katanga, where the giant copper industry was located. Conakat's leader, Moise Tshombe, a shrewd, clever man, was the son of a wealthy Katanga merchant who had unsuccessfully taken up a business career before turning to politics; he was related by marriage to the Lunda royal family. Conakat favoured provincial autonomy for Katanga, the Congo's richest province, worked closely with local Belgian groups pursuing the same interest, and advocated continuing ties with Belgium. The other group, the *Association des Baluba du Katanga*, Balubakat, was strongest in northern Katanga, and declared itself in favour of Congolese unity.

In the proliferation of political groups which occurred in 1959, one organisation stood out as the champion of Congolese nationalism. The *Mouvement National Congolais* (MNC) was founded in Léopoldville in October 1959 by a group of young educated Congolese intending to rally support on a national basis. Its leader, Patrice Lumumba, was an outstanding organiser whose articles in various journals and newspapers had made him well-known. A tall, thin, intense man, born a member of the small Batatela tribe in Kasai province in 1925, he received only a primary school education but displayed high intelligence and remarkable energy. His application to enter the new university at Louvanium, near Léopoldville, was turned down only because married men were not admitted there. In 1956 while employed as a postal clerk in Stanleyville, he was charged with embezzlement and spent one year in jail. He used the time to write a book—*Le Congo, terre d'avenir*—setting out his views on colonial rule. On his release he moved to Léopoldville where he worked as a salesman for a local brewery, and there he became a prominent political activist. As leader of the MNC, Lumumba initially found favour with the Belgian authorities, who were disturbed by the trend towards secession that Kasavubu advocated. While Kasavubu was prevented from leaving the Congo, Lumumba and two companions were allowed to travel to Accra to attend the All-African People's Conference in December 1958. Like other African delegates present at the conference, he returned home burning with enthusiasm for the struggle against colonial rule and determined to build the MNC into a mass political movement, along the lines of Nkrumah's CPP. Lumumba travelled around the Congo stirring crowds with his impassioned speeches. He was a powerful orator, capable of winning over audiences even under the most difficult circumstances. As he sought to keep the MNC ahead of other political parties, his demands became increasingly extreme. At a congress in Stanleyville in October 1959, delegates agreed to launch a campaign of positive action for the immediate liberation of the Congo. Following Lumumba's speech, riots broke out in the town, twenty-six Africans were killed and Lumumba was arrested.

By the end of 1959, growing disorder in the Congo had produced a state of alarm in Belgium. In Bakongo areas, law and order was breaking down; in the Kasai province, tribal war between the Lulua and the Baluba had erupted; disturbances continued in Stanleyville and when King Baudouin visited the town in December, the mob of demonstrators which greeted him at the airport had to be dispersed with tear gas. Local elections which took place in December, in accordance with the Belgian announcement the previous January, were boycotted in many parts of the country. In Brussels, public opinion was aghast at the possibility that Belgium might be drawn into an Algerian type of war. Strong opposition to the use of troops was mounted by socialist politicians and trade unions. 'Not one soldier for the Congo,' became a familiar slogan heard throughout the country.

Hoping to break out of the spiral of violence, the Belgian government reluctantly decided to convene a conference with Congolese delegations in Brussels in January 1960. The Round Table conference, as it was called, was the first occasion on which the Belgian authorities had consulted Congolese opinion about the future. Invited to attend were some ninety-six Congolese including Kasavubu, Tshombe and Lumumba, who was released from jail especially so that he could be present; in all, thirteen political groups were represented. The Belgian negotiators had been hoping for an agreement which would lead to a phased transfer of power over a period of about four years. But unexpectedly at the beginning of the conference they were faced with a united front of Congolese delegates claiming independence for 1 June 1960. The choice for the Belgians then was either to reject the demand and prepare for a possible uprising in the Congo or to urge a longer period of transition. Yet they could neither envisage holding the Congo by force nor could they get the

Congolese to agree to any delay. The Congolese delegates, distrustful of Belgian intentions and excited by the prospect of power and position, were in no mood to give way. The most they were willing to concede was an extra thirty days of Belgian rule. Thus on 27 January 1960, with virtually no preparation possible, Belgium agreed to the independence of the Congo on 30 June.

The Belgians were comforted in part by the thought that so swift a transfer of power would leave the Congolese as dependent as before on Belgium to run the country for them. Yet the risks involved were enormous. At that point, the Congo, a country of fourteen million people, was controlled entirely from Brussels. Except at a local level, no Congolese had acquired any experience of government. No national or even provincial elections had ever been held. In the top ranks of the civil service no more than three Congolese out of an establishment of 1,400 held posts and two of those were recent appointments. By the time of independence, there were only sixteen university graduates in any field. Indeed, the largest complement of trained personnel in the country were priests: of those there were more than six hundred. At the end of the 1959–60 academic year, only a hundred and thirty-six children completed full secondary education. There were no Congolese doctors, no secondary school teachers, no army officers.

Politically the country was fragmented by rival factions competing for support with reckless abandon. Tribal tensions, held in check during Belgian rule, broke violently to the surface. In several areas the administration was close to collapse. In Katanga, secessionist activity was growing. Fearing greater unrest during the elections scheduled for May, the Belgian government sent troop reinforcements to the Congo, thereby arousing suspicion that Belgium intended to hold the Congo by force. In the event, the elections passed in relative calm, but they failed to produce a decisive result. The Belgians had hoped that moderate, pro-Belgian parties would gain the upper hand, allowing them to continue to run the country without fuss. But the moderates fared badly. Instead, Lumumba's MNC, which had become increasingly hostile towards Belgium, gained a leading position. Of the one hundred and thirty-seven national seats, the MNC took thirty-three, the largest single total; it could also count on the backing of several allied groups. In two crucial areas, however, in Léopoldville and southern Katanga, the MNC could claim no effective support. In the wheeling and dealing that followed, the Belgian authorities showed themselves unduly reluctant to allow Lumumba to form a government, turning instead to Kasavubu. But when Lumumba managed to obtain majority support in the Chamber of Deputies, they were obliged to call on him. The final result achieved five days before independence was a cumbersome coalition of twelve different parties, which included bitter rivals. Kasavubu was chosen as a non-executive president; and Lumumba, then only thirty-five years old, a volatile personality, ill-prepared for office and harbouring deep resentment about Belgian intrigues during the election, became the Congo's first prime minister.

Even the first day of independence was inauspicious. In the morning, dignitaries and guests gathered for a special ceremony in Léopoldville at the new Palais de la Nation, a building started the previous year as a residence for the Belgian Governor-General but hastily converted into a national assembly. In the great rotunda, King Baudouin made the first address. He spoke at length in praise of Belgium's colonial record and offered some patronising advice on how the Congo should manage its affairs. His Congolese audience was not impressed. As President, Kasavubu replied in suitably moderate tones with his prepared text, but he decided to leave out the final passage which paid personal tribute to the King. Then came Lumumba's turn. Since early in the morning, he had been working on his speech, chopping and changing parts until the last minute. Aides had tried to soften the language. But while Baudouin was listing Belgium's many achievements in the Congo, Lumumba could be seen furiously making more notes in the script. Quite deliberately, his speech was rude and vindictive. In terms more attuned to an election rally, he spoke bitterly of the 'appalling suffering' and exploitation of Belgian rule, throwing in gratuitous warnings to Europeans living in the Congo. His remarks were warmly applauded by the Congolese present. But the Belgians were infuriated. The official lunch which followed the ceremony was delayed for two hours while the King and Belgian ministers debated whether to boycott it and fly back at once to Belgium. When the lunch eventually took place, it was cold and disorganised. In the Belgian press subsequently Lumumba was portrayed as a dangerous extremist. Lumumba himself felt pleased enough with the result to have copies of his speech sent all over the Congo.

Only a weekend of celebrations intervened before the new government was faced with its first crisis. In the ranks of the Force Publique, the Congo's 25,000-man army, unrest over low pay and the lack of promotion had been simmering for some months. While the government was now run by Congolese, the army remained under the control of the same 1,100-strong Belgian officer corps. Only in May had the first group of Congolese officer cadets been sent for training in Belgium and they were not due to return until 1963. The Force Publique commander, General Emile Janssens, a tough, right-wing career officer, was adamant that there would be no acceleration in the Africanisation programme. After an incident of indiscipline at the army base in Léopoldville on 4 June, Janssens summoned officers and men on duty at army headquarters and lectured them on the need for absolute obedience. To make his point clear, he wrote on a blackboard the words: 'Before independence = after independence'. A protest meeting of soldiers held in the army camp that night demanded the dismissal of Janssens and ended in a riot. Troops at the garrison at Thysville, 95 miles away, were ordered to intervene, but mutinied and the next day roamed about arresting Europeans, beating them up and raping several women. In a radio broadcast, Lumumba caused widespread alarm and rumour by accusing European officers of fomenting rebellion. Janssens and senior officers were dismissed. In subsequent negotiations with the army, Lumumba agreed that the entire officer corps should be replaced by Congolese. The new army commander he appointed was Victor Lundula, a former sergeant who had last served during the Second World War; at the time of his appointment he was a mayor in Jadotville, a Katanga mining town. His chief of staff, Joseph Mobutu, had served for seven years in the Force Publique as a clerk, but he had left in 1956 to work as a journalist. At the time of independence, he was acting as Lumumba's private secretary. Despite these changes, the mutiny spread to other towns across the Congo.

In Léopoldville, the white population, seized by panic, fled in thousands across the Congo river to Brazzaville, convinced that the army would turn against them next, spreading as they went tales of violence, rape and disorder. From other towns, too, the white exodus began. Within ten days some 25,000 Belgians had left. The Belgian government at first tried to persuade the Léopoldville authorities to permit Belgian troops stationed at two bases in the Congo to restore order. But Lumumba and his ministers refused to sanction the use of Belgian troops. Under strong pressure to intervene to protect the lives and property of the 80,000 strong Belgian community, the Belgian government then authorised the deployment of some 3,800 Belgian troops stationed in the Congo and arranged to fly in reinforcements. On 10 July, Belgian troops took action, rescuing Europeans under siege in Luluabourg, the capital of Kasai province, and moving into Elisabethville, the capital of Katanga, where mutineers had shot dead five whites including the Italian vice-consul.

The crisis then suddenly grew worse. On 11 July Belgian forces arriving in the port of Matadi, which had already been evacuated by almost its entire white population, were caught in a battle with Congolese troops. Accounts of the fighting and of Congolese casualties, no doubt greatly exaggerated, were swiftly relayed on the army's radio network to other units, setting off a new wave of mutinies and reprisals against European residents. In scores of incidents, whites were humiliated, beaten and raped; priests and nuns were singled out for special insults. As Belgian troops, numbering eventually nearly 10,000, spread out across the Congo to restore order, taking control of key points like Léopoldville airport, Lumumba became convinced that Belgium was trying to reimpose its rule.

With even more profound consequences, on 11 July the Katanga leader, Moise Tshombe, seized the opportunity of the chaos in the Congo to declare Katanga an independent state. Appealing for Western support, he accused the Congolese government of falling under communist influence and suggested that the disorder in the Congo was designed to drive the Belgians out.

In launching Katanga as a separate state, Tshombe had widespread support from the African population in the south of the province and from most of the European community, numbering about 32,000. He had complete control of the provincial government, the backing of the local press, and access to the huge tax revenues of the copper industry. But his success at that point depended entirely on the reaction of Belgium. Without the support of the Belgian troops which had moved into Katanga, Tshombe's regime could not survive. Two days before independence, the Belgian authorities had thwarted a previous attempt by Conakat ministers and a group of local Europeans to set up a separate state. At that time, both the Belgian government and most business interests favoured a unified Congo. Since the mutiny, however, Belgian opinion had drastically changed. The secession of Katanga was now seen as a way for Belgium to insulate the province from the disorder and militant nationalism sweeping the rest of the Congo and to safeguard Western investment there. The Belgian government stopped short of giving Katanga official recognition as an independent state; to have done so would have jeopardised Belgian interests elsewhere in the Congo; but otherwise Brussels was ready to offer whatever assistance was needed. Belgian troops were thus used to disarm and expel Congolese army units from the province; Belgian regular officers, formerly attached to the Force Publique, began training a new Katangese *gendarmerie*; and a Belgian technical assistance mission was sent to Elisabethville.

The plight of the Congo was now critical. Internal security had collapsed. The Congolese army, regarded only a week or so before as the most reliable organisation in the country, had degenerated into a disorganised rabble. The white population, on whom government services depended, was fleeing in thousands. Léopoldville was in turmoil. And the secession of Katanga threatened to break the country apart.

Amid this calamity, the feud between Lumumba and the Belgian government grew worse. Lumumba became obsessed by the idea that Belgian troops were planning to take control of the Congo. He accused Belgium of assisting the secession of Katanga, then severed diplomatic relations. All his efforts he now directed towards ending Belgian intervention and crushing the rebellion in Katanga. In telegrams to the United Nations he asked for military aid to help prevent Belgian 'aggression'. In response, Belgium said that its troops would only withdraw when the Congolese authorities were capable of maintaining law and order. On 14 July, the United Nations Security Council agreed to provide UN military assistance and asked Belgium to withdraw its troops, fixing no particular date; a technical assistance programme for the Congo was also set in motion. Acting swiftly, the UN organised a major airlift of troops from four other African countries; within three days, 3,500 UN troops arrived in the Congo, the advance contingents of a force which at its highest level reached some 19,000 men from twenty-six different countries. But Lumumba, in an increasingly irascible and impatient mood, was not satisfied. On 16 July, he warned that unless Belgian troops evacuated the Congo within twenty-four hours, he would appeal to the Soviet Union for help. A few days later he repeated his threat. To the Congo's misery and confusion was now added the possibility of a Cold War imbroglio.

By the end of July, the UN force had been deployed in five of the Congo's six provinces, allowing Belgian troops to be withdrawn. But the problem of Katanga remained unresolved. Lumumba's aim was to use the United Nations to end the secession of Katanga, if necessary by force. Tshombe, however, insisted on retaining Belgian troops to keep order and warned that the entry of the UN force would be resisted. Caught in the middle, the UN Secretary General, Dag Hammarskjöld, sought a negotiated settlement. His objective was to secure an agreed withdrawal of Belgian troops, in accordance with UN resolutions, but as for the matter of Katanga's secession, he saw it as an internal dispute for the Congolese to resolve. Angered by the delay in dispatching the UN force to Katanga, Lumumba now turned to attack the United Nations operation. His relationship with Hammarskjöld steadily deteriorated. Though by mid-August Hammarskjöld had managed to negotiate the entry of the UN force into Katanga and the withdrawal of regular Belgian troops, Lumumba's criticisms became increasingly wild and intemperate. He complained that the UN had not done enough to end Katanga's secession, asserted that the Congolese had lost all confidence in Hammarskjöld, whom he described as a Belgian 'puppet', and demanded that UN forces should be put at the disposal of the Congolese government. As a result of Lumumba's attacks on the UN, UN personnel in Léopoldville were harassed by Congolese soldiers; in a major incident in Stanleyville, American and Canadian airmen were severely beaten. The dispute also flared up at the UN Security Council where the Soviet Union, supporting Lumumba's position, claimed that Hammarskjöld, by failing to take action in Katanga, was acting as a Western stooge, while the United States accused the Russians of manipulating Lumumba.

Frustrated by the impasse in Katanga, Lumumba then turned to the Soviet Union for help. The Russians had already proved willing to give Lumumba direct aid, rather than channel it through the United Nations. In early August, Soviet planes began flying in food supplies to the Congo and a consignment of one hundred trucks was dispatched by sea. Without consulting his colleagues, Lumumba on 15 August asked the Soviet government immediately to send transport aircraft, crews, technicians and military equipment. His position was becoming increasingly desperate. Another separate state had been proclaimed in South Kasai, the source of the Congo's diamond riches, by Albert Kalonji, one of his most bitter opponents. With the support of Russian aircraft, trucks and technicians, Lumumba planned to send a military force first to regain control in south Kasai and then to march on Elisabethville to overthrow Tshombe. By the end of August, a fleet of fifteen Ilyushin aircraft based on Stanleyville and more than three hundred Soviet bloc technicians, including some Czech military advisers, had been put at Lumumba's disposal. Using Russian planes and commandeered Air Congo airliners, one thousand Congolese troops were flown to Kasai. The ensuing action turned into a tribal massacre in which hundreds of Baluba tribesmen supporting Kalonji were killed.

Lumumba's arbitrary decision to accept direct military aid from the Russians finally precipitated a political upheaval in Léopoldville. In the sixty days that he had led the government, his position had become increasingly insecure. His incessant quarrelling, his erratic temperament, the impetuous decisions he frequently took, all had propelled the Congo into further turmoil and turned many politicians against him. Often he listened neither to argument nor advice, driving colleagues and UN representatives alike to despair and causing concern about his dictatorial methods. His attacks on Hammarskjöld also alienated African leaders who had contributed troops to the UN force. While the Congo slid deeper into muddle and chaos, Lumumba had become obsessed by the need for a military victory against his opponents in Katanga and Kasai, ignoring the possibilities of a negotiated settlement. When the United Nations refused to subdue Tshombe, Lumumba reacted in frenzy. Hammarskjöld feared then that Lumumba's actions might wreck not only the Congo but the United Nations as well. By subsequently accepting Russian military aid to do the job, Lumumba pitched the Congo's struggle for power to the level of a Cold War confrontation. The alarm that this caused in Western circles, among Congolese politicians in Léopoldville and among UN officials at the Secretariat in New York and in the Congo, contributed directly to his downfall.

American officials had already decided that Lumumba represented a serious threat to Western interests. The view of the Central Intelligence Agency Director, Allen Dulles, expressed at a meeting of the National Security Council in Washington on 22 July, according to minutes later cited by the Senate Select Committee on Intelligence Activities, was that Lumumba was 'a person who was a Castro or worse'. After meeting Lumumba in Washington during a visit he made there later in July, US officials were all the more convinced of how dangerous he really was. The US Under Secretary of State, Douglas Dillon, concluded that Lumumba was 'an irrational, almost "psychotic" personality'. He told the Senate Intelligence Committee in 1975: 'The impression that was left was . . . very bad, that this was an individual whom it was impossible to deal with.' Lumumba's subsequent attacks on Hammarskjöld and on the UN operation, together with his willingness to deal directly with the Russians, led American officials to fear that by then he wanted the UN operation in the Congo to collapse, thus opening the way for Russian intervention. At a meeting of the National Security Council on

18 August, according to the minutes, President Eisenhower expressed acute concern that 'one man supported by the Soviets' could endanger the UN operation. Dillon's opinion given at that meeting was that 'the situation that would be created by a UN withdrawal was altogether too ghastly to contemplate'. On that same day in Léopoldville, after a group of Canadian UN technicians had been brutally beaten by Congolese troops on arrival at the airport, the CIA station chief, Lawrence Devlin, reported his view that the Congo was experiencing a 'classic Communist effort' to take over the government. Uppermost in everyone's mind was the need to remove Lumumba as rapidly as possible. From Léopoldville, the US ambassador, Clare Timberlake, recommended that Lumumba's opponents should be encouraged to oust him. The CIA, however, as a result of the National Security Council meeting on 18 August, began to think more in terms of his assassination. One week later, as reports of the Soviet airlift started reaching Washington, the problem of Lumumba assumed a new urgency.

At a meeting on 25 August of the National Security Council's Special Group, a committee responsible for supervising CIA covert operations, officials agreed at Eisenhower's behest that 'planning for the Congo would not necessarily rule out consideration of any particular kind of activity which might contribute to getting rid of Lumumba'. The following day, CIA Director Dulles sent a message to his station chief in Léopoldville, Lawrence Devlin, stressing the need for swift action. 'In high quarters here it is the clear-cut conclusion that if (Lumumba) continues to hold high office, the inevitable result will at best be chaos and at worst pave the way to Communist takeover of the Congo with disastrous consequences. . . . Consequently we concluded that his removal must be an urgent and prime objective. . . .' A major difficulty facing the Americans was the lack of a credible alternative leader to Lumumba. The most likely candidate was President Kasavubu. But Ambassador Timberlake found him an unimpressive figure. 'In my opinion,' he told the State Department, 'he is naive, not very bright, lazy, enjoying his new found plush living and content to appear occasionally in his new general's uniform.'

Amid the commotion over Lumumba's decision to use Soviet military aid, Kasavubu, urged on by American diplomats, his Belgian political advisers and Congolese supporters, finally roused himself. In a radio broadcast on 5 September, he announced that he had dismissed Lumumba as prime minister. He accused him of governing arbitrarily and plunging the Congo into civil war. In his place, he appointed Joseph Ileo, a widely respected moderate politician. He then returned to his residence and went to bed. The UN force commander, General van Horn, recalled in his memoirs how, after the broadcast, the atmosphere changed to one of 'relief, almost of satisfaction'. But then Lumumba in turn rushed to the radio station to announce that he had dismised Kasavubu as president. In the stalemate that followed, some parts of the Congo declared for Lumumba, others for Kasavubu and Ileo; parliament voted to annul both decisions. As Lumumba and Ileo competed for support from the army and the populace, arrests and counter-arrests began. The outcome was decided on 14 September. With American encouragement and the connivance of UN officials, Colonel Joseph Mobutu, the twenty-nine year old army chief of staff, a relatively unknown figure who controlled the Léopoldville troops, stepped forward and declared that he was neutralising all politicians until the end of the year and assuming power himself. At the same time he ordered the expulsion of all Russian and Czech personnel.

Mobutu's coup caused uproar at the United Nations in New York. The Soviet premier, Nikita Khrushchev, attending a session of the General Assembly, launched a ferocious attack on Hammarskjöld's handling of the Congo crisis and proposed that the post of Secretary-General should be abolished altogether. The coup also led to further division in the Congo.

Mobutu formed an interim civilian government, retaining Kasavubu as president but excluding all Lumumba's supporters. Lumumba himself, after seeking UN protection, continued to live at the prime minister's residence in Léopoldville, guarded by an inner ring of UN troops in the garden to prevent his arrest and surrounded by an outer ring of Mobutu's soldiers on the perimeter to prevent his escape. US officials, fearing that he might return to power, sought ways to have him arrested and also continued with their assassination schemes. On 26 September, a senior CIA scientist, Dr Sidney Gottlieb, arrived in Léopoldville, with instructions to help with the assassination and bearing a specially prepared poison for the purpose. He left, however, before any method had been found of penetrating Lumumba's entourage. Other endeavours proved no more successful. Lumumba's supporters, meanwhile, regrouped in Stanleyville, his main base, with plans to set up a rival government there. When Kasavubu's delegation, helped by some hard lobbying by the United States, managed to secure a seat at the United Nations Assembly at the end of November, Lumumba decided to risk leaving the protection of his UN guard in Léopoldville and escape to Stanleyville to join his supporters. 'If I die, *tant pis*,' he told a friend, Anicet Kashamura, 'The Congo needs martyrs.' But for his insistence on stopping on the way to harangue local villagers whenever the opportunity arose, he might have reached Stanleyville safely. On 1 December, however, he was arrested in Kasai province, taken back to Léopoldville and after several heavy beatings by soldiers handed into the army's custody.

While Lumumba languished in an army jail at Thysville, in Léopoldville province, his supporters in Stanleyville led by Antoine Gizenga formally established their own government—the 'Free Republic of the Congo'—and raised an army under General Lundula. The Congo, six months after independence, was now divided into four regimes, each with its own army and each with its foreign sponsors. Mobutu and Kasavubu in Léopoldville were supported by Western nations; Gizenga in Stanleyville received help from the Soviet bloc and radical leaders like Nasser in Cairo; Tshombe, though still unrecognised, relied on Belgian assistance; and the ramshackle 'Diamond State' of Albert Kalonji in south Kasai also received help from Belgian interests. Only the presence of United Nations troops and civilian personnel provided some semblance of national order. But the United Nations operation itself was constantly buffeted by rows and disputes among rival delegations in New York and by fierce tensions in the Congo.

The fate of Lumumba was central to the Congo crisis. Even in prison, he remained a potent force—a rallying symbol to his supporters, a persistent danger to his enemies. While in Léopoldville Kasavubu and Mobutu failed to provide an effective lead, the new Stanleyville regime formed in Lumumba's name grew from strength to strength. In late December, the provincial government of Kivu, in the eastern Congo, fell into Stanleyville's hands. Mobutu dispatched troops to regain control but the expedition ended in disarray. A week later, Stanleyville troops drove into North Katanga, where Tshombe's Baluba opponents were already in open revolt against his Elisabethville regime. They took control of the town of Manono and attempted to set up a separate 'Province of Lualaba'. These advances in the eastern Congo produced a wave of alarm in Léopoldville. In the army and police there was mounting unrest. Rumours abounded about the possibility of a coup in favour of Lumumba. Then on 13 January, at the Thysville army camp where Lumumba was imprisoned, troops mutinied demanding higher pay. Kasavubu and Mobutu rushed to the barracks and with offers of more pay and privileges they managed to restore order. But the effect that Lumumba had on the troops guarding him was clearly unsettling. Kasavubu tried to persuade Lumumba to join his government, but Lumumba refused. Back in Léopoldville, Kasavubu and his advisers decided that Lumumba would have to be removed. As a suitable destination, they chose Elisabethville, Tshombe's capital.

On 17 January 1961, Lumumba and two colleagues were taken to Katanga. On the five-hour flight there they were savagely beaten by their guards. Tshombe, who met them after their arrival in Elisabethville, admitted later that they were then 'in a sad state'. That night, in a farmhouse on the outskirts of Elisabethville, Lumumba was killed. His death, at the hands of Katangese officials and Belgian mercenaries, established him as one of the most famous political martyrs of modern times.

For some weeks after the event, the murder of Lumumba was kept secret. Though rumours of his fate began to circulate, the Katanga authorities remained silent. Then on 13 February, Katanga's Interior Minister, Godefroid Munongo, claimed that Lumumba, having escaped from custody, had been killed by villagers in the bush. The admission of

Lumumba's death caused shock in much of the Congo and was followed by worldwide protest. In Cairo, the Belgian embassy was sacked and there were demonstrations in more than thirty cities including Washington, New York and London. Many protesters saw the murder as the work of Western powers. At the United Nations, Hammarskjöld came under ferocious attack, notably from the Soviet Union, for failing to prevent Lumumba's death. The Russians demanded his dismissal, proposed the withdrawal of the UN force from the Congo and promised full support for the Stanleyville regime.

The circle of violence, meanwhile, steadily widened. Following Katanga's example, Kalonji in south Kasai ordered the execution of six Lumumbist prisoners, including a prominent Stanleyville politician. In reprisal, fifteen political prisoners in Stanleyville were shot by firing squad. Into North Katanga, Tshombe sent an expeditionary force of Katangese *gendarmerie*, supported by groups of newly-hired white mercenaries, with orders to crush Baluba opposition. In that separate war thousands died; atrocities were common on both sides.

In an endeavour to prevent the Congo sliding irretrievably into civil war, the Security Council in New York agreed to give the United Nations force there wider powers. A new UN resolution passed in February, shortly after the announcement of Lumumba's death had stunned UN delegates, insisted on the immediate withdrawal of all foreign military personnel, political advisers and mercenaries; it also proposed the reorganisation and retraining of the Congolese army. The immediate result of the new UN policy was to unite Tshombe and Kasavubu in a makeshift alliance against the UN. Both feared that the UN would act against them and disarm their respective forces. In Elisabethville, Tshombe warned that the UN resolution was tantamount to a declaration of war against Katanga and the whole Congo and he called for a 'total mobilisation' to resist the UN. In Léopoldville, Mobutu's headquarters decried the danger of the army falling under 'foreign domination' and Kasavubu made an impassioned appeal to Tshombe to join forces. In the tense conditions that followed, UN troops in Léopoldville were harassed and clashes between UN units and the Congolese army broke out in Banana and Matadi, forcing the UN to withdraw. At a summit meeting in March in Tananarive, the capital of the Malagasy Republic, Tshombe, Kasavubu and Kalonji agreed on military cooperation to combat the threats posed by the UN and the Stanleyville regime. They also resolved, much to Tshombe's advantage, that the Congo should become a confederation of states with each region virtually autonomous. Further negotiations were planned. But by the time they took place in April in Coquilhatville, the capital of Equateur province, Kasavubu had had second thoughts about the idea and had reached an accord with the UN. He and Tshombe quarrelled; Tshombe walked out of the conference; but he was then arrested and subsequently taken to Léopoldville. The conference at Coquilhatville, meanwhile, agreed to reconvene parliament for the purpose of choosing a new government. On promising that Katanga would send a deputation to parliament, Tshombe was released. But once back in Elisabethville, he withdrew his consent and reasserted the independence of Katanga.

As a means of reconciling the Congo's warring factions, the meeting of parliament in July 1961, held under the protection of the UN at the University of Louvanium, was crucially important. Among those who agreed to attend were representatives from Stanleyville, South Kasai, Léopoldville and North Katanga. Strenuous efforts were made to persuade Tshombe to change his mind and send delegates. The United States, now in the hands of the Kennedy administration, favoured a strong central government in the Congo and wanted Katanga to participate both to ensure the reunification of the Congo and to increase the chances of a moderate, pro-Western administration controlling the country. American officials applied every available pressure on Tshombe, warning of the dangers for Katanga of allowing the new government to be formed without him. But Tshombe was confident of Katanga's ability to survive and stayed away. On 2 August, a new coalition government was formed, bringing together all the Congo's rival regimes except Katanga. It was led by Cyrille Adoula, a moderate politician favoured by the Americans. The government's aim, said Adoula, was to break 'the vicious circle of vengeance, hatred, recrimination and insecurity'. But he made equally clear his determination to bring Katanga back under the central government's control. Indeed this became his overriding objective.

Tshombe's Katanga, one year after he declared its independence, appeared as a prosperous and secure corner of the Congo. Supported by huge tax revenues from the copper mining giant, Union Minière du Haut Katanga, and its associate companies, Katanga had retained the services of a large contingent of European advisers and civil servants; it boasted an efficient administration and it had established its own army. Katanga's *gendarmerie* by mid-1961 was a well-equipped force of some 13,000 men under the command of Belgian regular officers seconded for duty in Katanga, and reinforced by groups of white mercenaries usually known, for their rough behaviour and wild appearance, as *les affreux*. Though Tshombe's rule in North Katanga was only partially and brutally enforced, the south for the most part was an orderly preserve. As a solution to the Congo's problems Tshombe favoured a loose confederation, along the lines that he had proposed at the Tananarive conference, which would permit Katanga to continue its life as a prosperous, pro-Western mining state. In this objective he was supported by a vociferous Katanga lobby in Western capitals, by friends in government circles in Belgium, France and Britain, and by Welensky's Federation of Rhodesia and Nyasaland.

For the central government in Léopoldville, however, the defeat of Katanga was important for reasons of prestige and economic recovery. Without the reintegration of Katanga, the Congo was not thought in the long run to be viable. Previously, the Katanga copper industry had provided the central government with forty per cent of its revenue. As Léopoldville's principal supporter, the United States, drawn ever deeper into the Congo's affairs with the aim of preventing Soviet intervention there, feared that if the Adoula regime failed to deal with Tshombe successfully, then either more militant groups would bid to take control or a rival, pro-Communist regime would be set up again in Stanleyville. The United Nations, for their part, had no authority either to intervene in the secession dispute or to impose a political solution. But Hammarskjöld, seeking a peaceful settlement, took the view that if Tshombe could be detached from his white advisers and the foreign military officers on whom the Katanga *gendarmerie* depended, then he would be more inclined to reach agreement with Adoula. Under the terms of the Security Council resolution passed in February 1961, Hammarskjöld was empowered to insist on the withdrawal of all foreign military personnel, political advisers and mercenaries. Since then little action had been taken. Some Belgian advisers had been expelled, but nearly five hundred white officers and mercenaries remained with the Katanga *gendarmerie*. In June, Hammarskjöld posted to Katanga as UN representative there an ambitious Irish diplomat, Conor Cruise O'Brien, with instructions to implement more forcefully the new UN policy. And in August, O'Brien, together with the Tunisian head of the UN civilian operation in the Congo, Mahmoud Khiary, agreed on a plan to expel all foreign military personnel from Katanga.

The plan was given the codename 'Rumpunch'. In a swift, sharp action, in the early hours of 28 August, UN troops in Elisabethville took control of the radio station and the post office, put out of action the telephone exchange, posted a guard at the *gendarmerie* headquarters and began to arrest white officers and personnel. Similar action was taken by UN troops at other *gendarmerie* posts in Katanga. Taken by surprise, the officers gave no resistance. In discussion with O'Brien that day, Tshombe agreed to dispense with the services of all foreign officers; and, on condition that they all left Katanga by 9 September, O'Brien stopped the arrests. By 8 September, some three hundred and thirty Belgian officers and other personnel had either been repatriated or were waiting to leave. But a hardcore of mercenaries remained at large, among them a group of French OAS officers who had left Algeria after the failure of the April putsch. This mercenary group now began to exert control over the *gendarmerie*.

Flushed with the success of 'Rumpunch', Khiary and O'Brien decided that with another quick coup it would be possible to end Katanga's secession altogether. The plan they devised this time was given the codename 'Morthor', a Hindu word meaning 'smash'. On September 13, UN troops were given orders to re-establish control over the radio station and the post office, to blockade Tshombe in his villa and to arrest his ministers. But from the beginning the plan went wrong. This time the element of surprise was lost. At the radio station and the post office, when UN troops tried to take over, Katangese paratroops put up fierce resistance before being overrun; because of a muddle in the UN command, Tshombe was allowed to escape from Elisabethville; and by the end of the day only one of his ministers had been arrested. Despite these setbacks, O'Brien boldly announced that Katanga's secession had been ended and that it was now a Congolese province run by the central government.

It was, of course, not quite so simple. Hammarskjöld, when informed of the day's events, on his arrival in Léopoldville from New York, was appalled by the fighting and furious about O'Brien's statements. He now had to deal with an international uproar over an action for which he had given no approval and which clearly went beyond the UN's mandate. But even worse, UN troops in Katanga—contingents from Ireland, Sweden and India—came under counter-attack from Tshombe's forces and found themselves outmanoevred and at risk. With mastery of the air, a single Fouga Magister jet fighter piloted by a Belgian mercenary was able to bomb and strafe UN positions at will. In Jadotville, a mining town fifty miles from Elisabethville, an Irish UN company was surrounded and eventually forced to surrender. Determined to end the fighting rather than bring up UN reinforcements, Hammarskjöld arranged to meet Tshombe for ceasefire negotiations in Ndola, a town on the Northern Rhodesian Copperbelt close to the Katanga border. On 17 September, Hammarskjöld left Léopoldville in a UN aircraft for Ndola, taking a circuitous route to avoid crossing Katanga and in conditions of strict secrecy. As the aircraft prepared to land at Ndola that night, it crashed in the bush ten miles from the airfield. Hammerskjöld and all others on board were killed. Though pilot error was the probable cause, no final answer as to the cause of the crash was established.

The outcome of Operation 'Morthor' left the Katangese triumphant and the UN force humiliated. A ceasefire was swiftly arranged and under a more permanent settlement in

October, the UN agreed to give up the public buildings it occupied in Elisabethville, including the radio station and the post office. Tshombe remained confidently in power; and the *gendarmerie* was soon reinforced with new mercenary recruits and more arms supplies. When Congolese troops tried to invade from the neighbouring Kasai province in November, they were beaten back and went on the rampage. Worried about the repercussions of Katanga's success on the Adoula government, the United States advocated more decisive pressure. On 24 November the Security Council authorised UN contingents in the Congo to take action to arrest and deport all foreign military personnel, political advisers and mercenaries—using force if necessary. The threat of force, the Americans hoped, would make Tshombe more amenable to the idea of negotiations.

Tshombe, however, chose the opposite course. In radio speeches, he warned of war with the UN and his ministers threatened a 'scorched earth' campaign. In the *gendarmerie*, mercenary officers were eager for another round of fighting, confident that they could again beat the UN. In early December, the *gendarmerie* began a series of raids; road blocks were set up; UN personnel were assaulted and kidnapped. As a result of these incidents, UN troops were authorised to take action in self-defence. What occurred was a massive military operation designed to bring Tshombe to heel.

Moving cautiously, UN troops took positions on the edge of Elisabethville, while a huge airlift organised by the Americans brought in reinforcements. Jet fighters, flown to the Congo after Operation 'Morthor', soon established the UN's control of the air. After a week of skirmishing, the UN force began to advance to the centre of Elisabethville. In the fighting, schools, hospitals and churches were damaged; the headquarters of Union Minière was attacked; trainloads of white refugees were evacuated to Northern Rhodesia; some thirty-two white civilians were killed; and the Katanga government fled. From Northern Rhodesia, where he had taken refuge, Tshombe called for a ceasefire and agreed to negotiate with Adoula. Under the auspices of the UN and the United States, he was flown to a military base at Kitona in the Lower Congo region and there, on 21 December, he signed a declaration renouncing Katanga's secession.

This, however, was not the end of Katanga. Once back in Elisabethville, Tshombe claimed that the accord with Adoula had been imposed on him. For a whole year longer, while Adoula's government steadily grew weaker and Tshombe's own position deteriorated, negotiations dragged on. To break the deadlock, the United Nations threatened to impose economic sanctions against Katanga, but with little effect. By December 1962, the United States, despairing of a negotiated settlement and worried that the Adoula government might fall, giving way to a pro-Soviet government that would invite the Russians to the Congo, decided to provide the UN with whatever military equipment was needed to bring down Tshombe's regime. Even Belgium by this time concurred with the use of force to end Katanga's secession. In the final trial of strength at the end of December, the UN took control of key points in Elisabethville—the radio station, the post office, the presidential palace—this time without difficulty, and then cautiously moved against other towns, encountering little resistance. On 14 January 1963, after two and a half years, Katanga's secession formally came to an end.

The struggle which had engulfed the Congo since its independence left the country in a state of exhaustion. Yet the climax of its long ordeal was still to come. Adoula's regime in Léopoldville proved to be weak, incompetent and corrupt, torn by factional rivalry and surviving mainly on American aid and bribes. Its support within the Congo steadily dwindled. In 1962, former Lumumba ministers who had joined Adoula's coalition government either left or were driven out and from exile began to organise resistance. Parliament was shut down. The country's economic plight was desperate: inflation soared, unemployment was rife. In vast areas of the Congo, administration had come to a standstill; teachers, civil servants and soldiers often went unpaid for months; marauding youth bands and armed groups of disbanded soldiers roamed the countryside unchecked. The Congolese army—*Armée Nationale Congolaise* (ANC)—existed as a brutal, undisciplined and often lawless force, whose officers were mostly incapable of enforcing order. Little progress had been made in retraining it. By the end of 1963, the United Nations military operation in the Congo, virtually bankrupt, was being phased out.

Out of the misery and disorder came revolt and rebellion on a scale which surpassed anything that the Congo had experienced before. In the eastern Congo, Lumumba's former stronghold, one uprising followed another until, in the space of three months in 1964, the government lost control of half of the entire country. Faced with rebel forces poorly armed but professing magical powers, the ANC simply fled or capitulated without a fight. From the Maniema area, Simba rebels, gathering recruits as they sped from town to town, swept on towards Stanleyville and, with little effective resistance from the ANC, captured the town on 4 August. Once occupied, Stanleyville became the capital of the 'People's Republic of the Congo', set up under the control of a former Lumumba minister, Christopher Gbenye. In the wake of the rebellion, mass executions were ordered. In Stanleyville and other towns in the eastern Congo, thousands died—clerks, teachers, civil servants, merchants, men deemed to be 'counter-revolutionaries' or 'intellectuals'. Often the executions were performed with appalling cruelty in public at the foot of monuments to Lumumba. In the west of the Congo, closer to Léopoldville, another former Lumumba minister, Pierre Mulele, gained control of much of Kwilu province and sought to establish a revolutionary regime there.

In desperate straits, the Léopoldville regime turned to Moise Tshombe, then living in self-imposed exile in Spain, for help in forming a new government. Once in office as prime minister, Tshombe installed his former advisers from Katanga days and, with American and Belgian assistance, undertook a massive rescue operation. For a second time the Congo became an international battlefield. To help defeat the Stanleyville rebels, the United States supplied transport planes, trucks, combat aircraft and counter-insurgency experts. Under the auspices of the Central Intelligence Agency, Cuban refugee pilots and European mechanics were hired to staff a new combat air force. The Belgians provided army officers for key command posts together with several hundred technicians. As well as ANC units, Tshombe added a contingent of the Katangese *gendarmerie* which had been hiding in exile in Angola, awaiting his orders. And to spearhead the ground attack, he asked a South African mercenary leader, Major Mike Hoare, to assemble a mercenary force as rapidly as possible. In short order, a rough assortment of adventurers, desperados and misfits, together with some professional soldiers, were recruited, mainly in Rhodesia and South Africa.

The Stanleyville rebels, too, had their friends. Initially, China, through its embassies in Burundi and Congo-Brazzaville, provided some assistance—money, instruction manuals and some weapons—though in limited amounts. Once the rebels had taken control of Stanleyville, Algeria and the United Arab Republic dispatched substantial quantities of Soviet-made arms. But the arms supplies made little difference. Under attack from mercenary columns advancing towards Stanleyville and constant bombardment from the air force, rebel resistance swiftly collapsed. Facing defeat, Gbenye's regime in Stanleyville seized three hundred Belgian and American hostages and threatened to kill them and other whites trapped in rebel-held areas unless the government's forces were halted. In a joint rescue mission organised by the Belgian and American governments, 550 Belgian paratroops were dropped on Stanleyville on 24 November. As the paratroops dashed through the streets of the town, rebels guarding the hostages opened fire, killing twenty-seven and wounding some sixty others. While sporadic fighting continued, Belgian troops began to organise the evacuation of Stanleyville's 1,600 whites. Two days later a second paratroop drop was made on Paulis, 220 miles to the northeast of Stanleyville, but it came too late to save the lives of another twenty-three hostages. In all, some 2,000 whites were rescued from the eastern Congo. Three hundred others, some of them missionaries living in remote outposts, were executed. When the Belgian force departed, mercenary groups and the ANC continued with the rescue operation. As they beat back rebel opposition, they left behind a trail of terrible repression and plunder.

Back in Léopoldville, the politicians fell once more to squabbling and intrigue. Tshombe survived as prime minister for fifteen months until, in October 1965, President Kasavubu dismissed him. The following month, in scenes reminiscent of the 1960 struggle for power, General Mobutu, the ANC commander, stepped forward for a second time, suspended all political activity and assumed the presidency for himself. The regime that Mobutu instituted was harsh, repressive and corrupt. But it nevertheless provided the Congo with a degree of stability; and it endured longer than any previous administration.

CHAPTER EIGHTEEN

Rhodesia's Rebellion

The tide of African nationalism, so powerful a force in challenging colonial rule, came abruptly to a halt on the banks of the Zambezi river. In Southern Rhodesia, the affluent white community, as they watched with foreboding the spectacle of African independence to the north, while their own claims for independence were ensnared in difficulties with the British government, grew ever more embittered and recalcitrant until, fearing that their own survival was in danger, they determined to stamp out the nationalist menace inside Rhodesia and to seize independence for themselves. To the entire white population, the notion of black rule spelt disaster. African nationalism, in their view, was an extremist doctrine of benefit only to a few power-hungry demagogues. Once the guiding hand of Europeans was removed from Africa, the inevitable result, they asserted, was the kind of chaos and disorder which had descended on the Congo. The threat to Rhodesia, as they saw it, came not just from the activities of African nationalist parties inside the country demanding political power; it derived too from the policies of a Conservative government in Britain willing to bow to African demands. Ever since Macmillan in 1960 had warned of a change in British policy in Africa, their distrust of British intentions had grown. White Rhodesians, once so proud of the links which bound them to Britain, its Empire and its traditions, were appalled at the way in which the British government, for reasons they construed to be of misguided liberalism or commercial interest or simply weariness, was ready to abandon the white communities it had encouraged to settle in Africa and leave them to the mercy of African rulers. In one country after another, Britain was seen to be handing over power to men whom they regarded as extremists: in Kenya to Kenyatta, a man condemned by a British Governor as a 'leader to darkness and death'; in

Nyasaland to Banda, whose name was associated with a plot to murder Europeans; in Northern Rhodesia to Kaunda, who had once threatened that if he did not get his way, he would make *Mau Mau* look like a picnic. In such cases, British policy seemed to white Rhodesians to amount to nothing less than appeasement, to a betrayal of white interests which held dangerous implications for their own position. All the while the nationalist challenge inside Rhodesia grew stronger and more violent. Reacting against this tide of events, the whites rallied behind diehard politicians who promised them that as long as they remained united, the white community could withstand indefinitely any threat that either the British government or African nationalists could mount.

When the nationalists launched their first mass political party, the African National Congress, in 1957, their aims and objectives were notably modest. There was much talk of non-racialism and economic progress, but little was heard about political power. The nationalists suggested a wider franchise; they attacked discriminatory laws; and they wanted reform of land legislation which gave white farmers exclusive use of half of Rhodesia's land area. The image that the ANC set out to create was one of moderation and quiet purpose. The man chosen as leader, Joshua Nkomo, was an affable and easy-going politician, with a record of multi-racial and church activities, who had gained popularity as a skilful union organiser. On Sundays he performed as a lay preacher in the British Methodist Church and at one time he had flirted with Moral Rearmament. When negotiations for the proposed Federation of Rhodesia and Nyasaland were underway, he had accepted an invitation from the Rhodesian prime minister, Huggins, to attend a conference in London as one of two African representatives. Like other leading Africans in Southern Rhodesia at that time, he hoped that a Federation which promised 'partnership' would offer greater opportunities for African advancement than the existing white regime. At the London conference, Nkomo's final speech was conspicuous for its moderation.

In both urban and rural areas, the ANC found a ready response. Poverty and frustration in the towns, land hunger and overcrowding in the African reserves were causes of long-standing discontent. In the thirty years since the government had introduced the Land Apportionment Act, more than half a million Africans had been uprooted from their homes on land designated as European land. By organising opposition to government measures in rural areas, the ANC shattered the complacency with which native commissioners had administered them since white rule began. The government's response was to deal ruthlessly with the nationalists. In February 1959, the ANC was banned and three hundred Africans were detained. The Rhodesian prime minister, Sir Edgar Whitehead, justified the move by referring to the growing tendency of the nationalists to incite the African population to defy the law and ridicule government officials and chiefs. To control any future African opposition, Whitehead then devised a series of laws so sweeping and severe in their extent that the Chief Justice, Sir Robert Tredgold, felt obliged to resign in protest. In subsequent years, whenever the government saw fit, further draconian measures were added.

Though Whitehead acted unhesitatingly to suppress nationalist activity, he recognised the need to encourage moderate African support for the government, particularly among the rising black middle class. Accordingly, a series of reforms was introduced to relax some of the discriminatory laws which kept the African population in a subordinate position. Africans, for example, were now allowed entry into cinemas and the larger hotels and permitted to buy lottery tickets and bet at horse races; separate queues at post offices and banks were abolished; municipal swimming pools and parks were integrated. Of greater importance, the higher ranks of the civil service were opened to Africans; pass laws were modified; and restrictions which excluded Africans from competing directly with whites in skilled occupations were removed.

But such reforms, though marking a major change in Rhodesian society, were no longer sufficient to impress African opinion. In January 1960 a new nationalist organisation, the National Democratic Party, was launched. It demanded not simply the redress of grievances over land and discrimination but political power as well. And to Whitehead's dismay, this militant platform attracted the very middle class whom he had hoped to lure into partnership with the government. In the heady atmosphere which existed in the early 1960s, it seemed to the Rhodesian nationalists that the tide of events elsewhere in Africa, bringing independence to a host of African countries, would carry them too to power.

The opportunity for the nationalists to advance their cause came in 1961 when the British government convened a constitutional conference on Rhodesia to which they were invited. The purpose of the conference was to settle on a new constitution which reconciled white demands for independence with African demands for political progress. Until then, Africans in Southern Rhodesia were unrepresented in parliament, though a few were entitled to vote. What the British government wanted was a compromise under which the Rhodesian government accepted substantial African advancement in exchange for Britain's agreement to give up its reserve powers in Rhodesia, as the final step before full independence. The deal which was eventually worked out was remarkably favourable to the Rhodesian government. Under the 1961 constitution, Britain withdrew its reserve powers including the right to veto discriminatory legislation; it could no longer interfere in Rhodesia's constitutional affairs or have dealings with the African population. The remaining safeguards which Britain retained were described by the Commonwealth Secretary, Duncan Sandys, as trifling. In return, the Rhodesian government conceded to the nationalists fifteen out of sixty-five parliamentary seats, based on a complex franchise which would have delayed majority rule for several decades; a justiciable Declaration of Rights which did not affect any of the discriminatory legislation in force at the time; and a multi-racial Constitutional Council with limited powers. In effect, the new constitution guaranteed white rule for the foreseeable future. It was a miracle, said Sandys, that the nationalists had accepted it.

No sooner were the results known than a storm of African protest broke out. Joshua Nkomo, who had negotiated the terms of the 1961 constitution on behalf of the National Democratic Party, faced severe criticism from his own officials and after ten days he was obliged to repudiate the agreement. Since it was then too late for the nationalists to stop the passage of the 1961 constitution, they refused instead to participate in any activity related to the new constitution and resorted to reckless violence to prevent African voters from registering for the 1962 elections. African homes, schools, beer halls and shops were looted and burned; gangs of youths roamed the black suburbs seeking out victims who were identified with the government or who were not Party members. In December 1961, Whitehead banned the NDP. One week later, a new nationalist organisation, the Zimbabwe African People's Union, was formed, with identical aims and tactics. The violence increased. White targets were now included; forests and crops were burned, cattle maimed, sabotage attempts made on railway lines and attacks carried out on schools and churches. In September 1962, Zapu was banned. Other than violence the nationalists offered no coherent political plan. Nkomo's strategy was based on the notion that eventually the scale of violence would force Britain to intervene, as it had done after similar agitation in Nyasaland and Northern Rhodesia. Most of the time he spent touring the world seeking international support for the nationalist cause, leaving the party organisation inside Rhodesia in disarray. But the support that he gained abroad had little bearing on the conflict in Rhodesia, and all that the violence achieved was to strengthen the growing reaction among Rhodesia's white electorate.

The election in December 1962, which was to set Rhodesia on a perilous course, was a contest between the old Rhodesian establishment which had run the country uninterrupted for thirty years and a collection of little known right-wing politicians who had banded together only nine months before under the name of the Rhodesian Front. As prime minister, Whitehead was confident of victory. His ruling United Federal Party was backed by a formidable network of business, mining and financial interests and it also had the support of the local press. In his election campaign, Whitehead tried to steer a middle course between the extremities of Rhodesian politics. He sought to convince whites that some African progress was necessary both to satisfy British requirements for full independence and to attract moderate African support for the government; and to reassure them that, provided that the pace of African advancement was properly controlled and gradual, they had nothing to fear. As evidence that he was in no mood to tolerate the extremist demands made by the nationalists, Whitehead pointed to the government's record in banning three nationalist parties—the ANC, NDP and Zapu. Simultaneously, Whitehead needed to overcome the opposition that the nationalists had mounted to the 1961 constitution and their campaign to boycott the election, and convince moderate, middle class Africans that the government had their interests in mind too. Without clear African support, he might have forfeited Britain's willingness to grant independence. Accordingly he promised to repeal more discriminatory measures, including the Land Apportionment Act, the cornerstone of Rhodesian society which divided the country into separate white and black areas.

The Rhodesian Front's strategy was decidedly more straightforward. In answer to the seemingly irrepressible nationalist threat and the growing uncertainty about Rhodesia's future, the Rhodesian Front called for a firm stand in favour of continued white rule. The argument that the RF used was that the liberal, multi-racial approach advocated by Whitehead would lead to white abdication. Any concessions to the nationalists or the British government would be taken as a sign of weakness. Already the 1961 constitution, by implying the possibility of majority rule, had gone too far. Further concessions like the abolition of the Land Apportionment Act would be tantamount to surrender. But there was simply no need for such appeasement, to use the words of Ian Smith, for 'this mad idea of a handover, a sellout of the European and his civilisation'. The nationalists, in the RF's view, were only a group of unrepresentative fanatics who had to resort to violence and intimidation to gain support. The mass of simple Africans were better off under white rule and wanted nothing else. In time, given white tuition and discipline, they would slowly learn the lessons of Western democracy. But in the meantime what was required was strong law and order and a stable government, and the election was the last chance the whites would ever have to vote for one.

The RF programme seemed eminently sensible to an increasing number of white Rhodesians. Traditionally, about one third of the electorate had favoured a tough and uncompromising policy in dealing with the African population, and their ranks were now swelled by thousands more whites alarmed by the threat that African advancement posed. Many feared, as indeed they were told by the RF, that Whitehead's policy would open the African floodgates and lead to 'forced' integration in schools, hospitals and residential areas and a decline in the high living standards which they enjoyed. For farmers there were worries about the rights to their land; for artisans the prospect of job competition. Liberal whites, too, those who had once welcomed the idea of partnership, were disillusioned with the nationalists, with the way in which they had rejected the concessions offered under the 1961 constitution, with their insistent demand for nothing less than 'one man, one vote', and with the violent campaign they had mounted to enforce an election boycott. When it came to the vote, the Rhodesian Front won a major victory. Of the fifty white seats, the RF gained thirty-five; Whitehead was left with fifteen white seats and the support of fourteen African MPs who collectively amassed 1,870 votes.

Once in power, the Rhodesian Front government became obsessed with the need for independence from Britain. Without independence, the government argued, neither the whites nor foreign investors would have confidence in the country's future. Hundreds of whites were already emigrating. Rhodesia, after forty years of self-government and loyal service during wartime, had earned the right, far more so than had other African states with less experience of self-government which were already independent. Rhodesia, moreover, was a country with high standards of justice, order and good government which could be relied on to defend Western interests. For three fruitless years, the Rhodesians pressed these arguments on the British government. The dispute during this time was never over the question of Britain's granting independence to a white minority government; for neither the Conservative government nor Harold Wilson's Labour government which came to office in 1964 raised any objection to that prospect. It centred on whether the Rhodesian government should make constitutional concessions that Britain demanded before granting independence. The Rhodesian government wanted independence on the basis of the 1961 constitution, without substantial alteration. The British government, concerned about the Rhodesian Front's commitment to indefinite white rule, insisted on changes which involved the gradual repeal of discriminatory legislation, a wider franchise and a constitutional blocking device to ensure that no independent government could thwart African progress once it was set free from British control. The Rhodesian Front saw no reason to pay such a price.

The first prime minister that the RF installed to wrest independence from Britain was clearly the wrong choice. Winston Field was a conservative gentleman farmer, born in the English counties, who had a reputation for being cautious and fair-minded. When, after sixteen months in office, he failed to make any headway in negotiations with Britain and balked at the idea of seizing independence unilaterally, he was removed.

His successor, Ian Smith, was at the time a relatively unknown right-wing politician, with no obvious talent or flair, whose career both in politics and farming had so far met with little success. As a member of parliament for sixteen years, his contribution had been insignificant. His brief record as Minister of Finance in Winston Field's government was equally colourless. He was a dull speaker with a limited, repetitive vocabulary and narrow interests. His parochial nature, however, concealed an astute tactical mind, a flair for political infighting and a remarkable tenacity. Smith was a man of simple and fixed beliefs. White rule, in his view, was essential not only for the benefit of the white population but for the welfare of the blacks. The whites, through their own endeavour and expertise, had built a sophisticated modern economy from a wilderness, and they expected the rewards. Unless they were offered high standards of living, they would not remain. Without their leadership, Rhodesia would fall into ruin. Smith was incredulous that any well-meaning person should fail to understand these arguments. The views of the nationalists, and those who supported them, he dismissed with contempt, insisting that men like Nkomo represented only a small clique motivated by their own desire for self-aggrandisement. The true leaders of the African people, he asserted, were the tribal chiefs, and they invariably gave their support to the government.

Smith's immediate concern, on assuming office as prime minister in April 1964, a few days after his forty-fifth birthday, was to restore white confidence about Rhodesia's future. Coming from a rural Rhodesian background, born and brought up in the small mining town of Selukwe, the son of an immigrant Scottish butcher and cattle dealer, he had an instinctive understanding of the fears which beset the white community. What he offered them was permanent control and he convinced the disillusioned that it was possible. There was never any doubt about what he stood for. 'I cannot see in my lifetime that the Africans will be sufficiently mature and reasonable to take over,' he declared after becoming prime minister. From then on, the slogan of 'no majority rule in my lifetime' became a guarantee for those who had any doubts. In pursuing this goal, Smith was ready to deal forcefully with any opponents who stood in the way, whether they were liberal white critics or African nationalists or ultimately the British government.

The nationalists, in the end, sealed their own fate. Nkomo's faltering leadership eventually produced a split in the nationalist movement, which divided it into two irreconcilable camps. Nkomo's group was relaunched in 1963 under the name of the People's Caretaker Council. His principal critics, Ndabaningi Sithole and Robert Mugabe, set up their own Zimbabwe African National Union. The differences between the two groups were at first negligible. Both advocated the same goal of majority rule; both continued to seek foreign support and to lobby the British government; both established external bases in Africa to coordinate their foreign activities, and recruited members for guerrilla training outside the country. Initially, tribal loyalties were not affected. What differences there were lay largely in rhetoric. But as each group tried to assert itself, their rivalry developed into uncontrolled violence. Gang warfare, petrol bombing, arson, stoning and assaults became commonplace. Little attention was paid to whites. The spectacle of nationalist strife caused disenchantment among nationalist sympathisers abroad, provided evidence for Rhodesian whites who maintained that black rule would inevitably end in turmoil and eventually gave the government sufficient pretext to crush the nationalist movement in the name of law and order. In 1964, Smith banned both groups. Nkomo, Sithole and Mugabe and hundreds of others were sent to prison or detention camps and many remained there for ten years.

In his dealings with the British government, however, Smith proved no more successful than his predecessor. As a negotiator he was intransigent and inflexible, unwilling to make any concession towards the British position. For Smith's benefit, the British government drew up a set of principles which represented their terms for granting independence. The most important was the principle of 'unimpeded progress to majority rule'. The British also stressed that the final step towards independence would depend on the consent of all Rhodesians. Smith, believing that he could demonstrate that he had popular support for independence under the 1961 constitution, seized on this point; the white electorate, he assumed, would overwhelmingly approve of the idea and he relied on the chiefs, the 'true' representatives of the African people, to deliver their consent. Duly, in a referendum, the white electorate gave their overwhelming support; and at a secret meeting outside Salisbury, some six hundred chiefs and headmen gave their unanimous consent. The British government, however, refused to accept the outcome of the referendum and the view of the chiefs as a legitimate test of opinion—a point they had made clear to Smith all along.

At every twist and turn in the negotiations, white distrust of Britain increased. Every new failure was taken as evidence of British duplicity. To many whites it seemed that Britain was pressing for majority rule merely to satisfy the opinion of the United Nations and the Commonwealth, disregarding the consequences for Rhodesia. And Smith lost no opportunity to assure them this was of course the case. Britain, he told Rhodesians, was seeking to impose conditions which in the end would lead to black dictatorship. Therefore, the Rhodesian government, to protect its own interests, might be forced to take matters into its own hands. In the emotional climate of the time, when the only choice seemed to be between black rule and a unilateral declaration of independence, more and more whites came to believe that their only hope lay in UDI. In Smith they were ready to place implicit trust. Many saw him as a man of unwavering determination who would firmly stand against the British government and save Rhodesia from the perils of black rule. When in May 1965, Smith called a general election asking for a decisive vote of confidence to strengthen his hand in negotiations with Britain, the result was a resounding success. All fifty white seats went to the Rhodesian Front; the opposition was obliterated.

The warnings against UDI came from many quarters. Harold Wilson, soon after taking office as prime minister in 1964, threatened to impose economic sanctions. An illegal declaration of independence, he said, 'would inflict disastrous economic damage and would leave (Rhodesia) isolated and virtually friendless in a largely hostile continent.' Rhodesian commerce and industry predicted a host of financial and trade difficulties. Opposition politicians like Welensky and Whitehead cautioned against such precipitate action; and similar advice was given by the South African government, on whose goodwill Rhodesia, in the event of a UDI, would largely depend.

But Smith felt his position was secure enough. He had the overwhelming support of a large and resourceful white population, some 220,000 strong, largely united in their determination to keep Rhodesia in white hands and confident of their ability to overcome whatever challenge was thrown at them. Though as many as two thirds of the white community were post-war immigrants from varying backgrounds, most had quickly adapted to the idea of being loyal Rhodesians. The government was backed by an efficient administration and well-equipped defence forces. It also had control of radio and television, which were used with considerable effect for propaganda purposes. Since the detention of African nationalist leaders and the banning of the nationalist parties, virtually all disorders among the four million African population had ceased, and the security apparatus at the government's disposal was capable of dealing with any new threat. The greatest concern, in fact, that troubled Smith and his colleagues about a UDI was the possibility of armed British intervention. But that threat diminished with Wilson's repeated pledges that force against Rhodesia would never be used.

So it was that on 11 November 1965 Smith and his ministers signed their Proclamation of Independence. It was a curious document, drawn up in archaic language intended to resemble the American Declaration of 1776 and embellished with red, green and gold scrolls. In his independence message, Smith portrayed his act of defiance in grandiose terms. 'I believe that we are a courageous people and history has cast us in a heroic role,' he said. 'To us has been given the privilege of being the first Western nation in the last two decades to have the determination and fortitude to say "So far and no further".... We Rhodesians have rejected the doctrinaire philosophy of appeasement and surrender.... We have struck a blow for the preservation of justice, civilisation and Christianity.'

*

Thus across Africa a frontier was drawn, dividing the black north from the white-ruled countries of southern Africa. The white south—Rhodesia, the Portuguese territories of Angola and Mozambique, and South Africa—were thought to possess sufficient economic and military strength to withstand any challenge that was likely to arise. Yet there, too, the winds of change were eventually to be felt. And within a decade, the frontier had to be redrawn.

CHAPTER NINETEEN

The Early Years

The honeymoon period of African independence was memorable but brief. The mood of euphoria aroused by the advent of African rule and raised to ever greater heights by the lavish promises of nationalist politicians campaigning for power soon died away, leaving behind a sense of expectation unfulfilled. Africa was a continent too deeply affected by mass poverty, by meagre resources, by disease and illiteracy, to allow for easy solutions to its development. And once the momentum that nationalist leaders had achieved in their drive for independence began to subside, so old tribal rivalries and ambitions came thrusting to the surface. Almost no African country was immune from such tensions. 'We have all inherited from our former masters not nations but states,' remarked the Ivory Coast's president, Félix Houphouët-Boigny, 'states that have within them extremely fragile links between ethnic groups.'

African leaders thus became as preoccupied with the problems of political control, of holding the state together, of simply staying in power, as with the policies of development. In their quest for political stability, many governments were attracted to the idea of establishing one-party systems. In some cases, one-party systems were achieved by popular verdict. In pre-independence elections in French West Africa in 1959, Houphouët-Boigny's *Parti Démocratique de la Côte d'Ivoire* won all seats in the Legislative Assembly; so too did Léopold Senghor's *Union Progressiste Sénégalaise*, and Modibo Keita's *Union Soudanaise* in Mali. In East Africa, Nyerere's Tanganyika African National Union won all open seats in parliament in 1960; and in the 1964 elections in Nyasaland, Hastings Banda's Malawi Congress Party also swept the board. In other cases, one-party systems were arranged through negotiation, whereby opposition parties accepted a merger with the government. Sékou Touré's *Parti Démocratique de Guinée* won fifty-six out of sixty seats in the Legislative Assembly elections in 1957, and the following year he arranged for opposition politicians to join the PDG. In Kenya in 1964, Kenyatta persuaded opposition politicians from the Kenya African Democratic Union to cross the floor and take up prominent posts in the government.

Many arguments were used in favour of one-party systems. New states, it was said, needed strong governments which were best served by concentrating authority within a single, nationwide party. Only a disciplined mass party, centrally directed, was an effective means to overcome tribal divisions, to inspire a sense of nationhood and to mobilise the population for economic development. Multi-party politics usually deteriorated into a competition between tribal blocs and alliances. Since opposition parties tended to rely on tribal groups for support, they undermined the cause of national unity and weakened the efficiency of the state. They were thus a luxury which new states with limited resources could ill afford. Some African leaders argued that opposition parties were in fact alien to African practice and that a one-party system, if properly managed, provided a democratic outlet just as adequate as did a multi-party system. Julius Nyerere, one of the staunchest advocates of a one-party system, went further, asserting that it offered a better framework for democracy than a multi-party system which resulted in endless bouts of political warfare. 'Where there is *one* party—provided it is identified with the nation as a whole—the foundations of democracy can be firmer, and the people can have more opportunity to exercise a real choice, than where you have two or more parties.' Houphouët-Boigny, in his defence of a one-party system, offered a different explanation: 'Democracy is a system of government for virtuous people. In young countries such as our own, we need a chief who is all-powerful for a specified period of time. If he makes mistakes, we shall replace him later on. . . .'

In practice, one-party systems were used by politicians in power mostly to suppress any sign of opposition to their regimes and to keep themselves in office. Mass parties, once founded upon popular support, simply withered away, leaving, as Frantz Fanon remarked, nothing but the shell, the name, the emblem and the motto; they served only as the stronghold of a privileged few. With similar consequences, one-party regimes took control of the press, trade unions, farmers' organisations, subordinating them all to the interests of the government. Political debate became a matter of platitudes, no longer taken seriously. The press existed merely as an outlet for government propaganda. Rarely was criticism of any kind tolerated. When political opponents grew too troublesome, they were either harassed or detained. With few exceptions, one-party rule came to mean no more than government by a ruling elite with a monopoly of political power. It was Houphouët-Boigny's version rather than Nyerere's version that prevailed.

African politics, in time, were reduced mostly to a matter of personal and factional struggles for power. Indeed, the fate of many a country was determined largely by the personality of the man who held power. For most African leaders sought to acquire vast personal power and ruled not through constitutions or through state institutions, such as parliament, that the departing colonial authorities had bequeathed, but by wielding power in a personal and authoritarian manner. Constitutions were either amended or rewritten or simply ignored to suit the purposes of whoever was in power. Parliaments, where they survived, were packed with supporters of the government, chosen for their known obedience. The system of personal rule that eventually prevailed in many African states relied on no more than small, select groups of officials and political associates to make it work.

The new African elite, whatever the circumstances, used their position to great personal advantage. The very first legislative act of the Congo's parliament in Léopoldville in July 1960, for example, was to raise fivefold the annual salary of parliamentary deputies. No opportunity was lost by politicians, most notably in West Africa, to accumulate wealth, privilege and power. Government budgets soon became burdened with the huge cost of salaries, allowances and presidential expenses. Writing in 1962, the respected French agronomist, René Dumont, noted that a deputy in Gabon was paid more than a British member of parliament. He went on: 'As for the cost of the Gabonese presidency, parliament and ministers, with all their supposedly useful trips, it probably represents, in relation to the national income of the country, more than the cost to France of the court of Louis XVI in 1788.' From a position of political power or public office, the opportunities for personal gain were enormous and were seized on unashamedly. In numerous cases, ministers and officials became more preoccupied with their own business deals, with contracts, commissions and quick profits, than with government affairs. Indeed, political activity was seen by ambitious Africans as the most direct way to securing wealth and social standing. The wealth that they acquired was ostentatiously displayed in luxury cars, grand houses and lavish lifestyles. In East Africa a new tribe appeared, cynically known as the WaBenzi, in description of rich politicians and businessmen who drove about in Mercedes-Benz cars. Successful politicians were also able to dispense patronage on a large scale, providing their followers and friends with jobs, contracts and other favours, thus improving their standing in the community. In parliament and at public meetings, leading politicians still issued promises about social equality and referred sympathetically to the needs of the common man, but with less and less conviction. For the vast majority of the population, independence brought few of the changes they had been led to expect. 'A peasant's life,' noted Abel Goumba, a prominent critic of the government in the Central African Republic, 'is worth a month and a half of that of a member of parliament.'

Whatever difficulties and disappointments the new states of Africa encountered in the early years of independence, on an international level they still excited the attentions of the world's rival power blocs. The position that each newly independent country adopted in its relations with the West or the East was viewed as a matter of crucial importance. Africa in the early sixties was considered to be too important a prize to lose. While the old colonial powers sought to strengthen the special relationships they had mostly formed with their former colonies, the Eastern blocs embarked on major campaigns to gain influence in the new states. The competition between the two sides, at a time when the Cold War in other parts of the world was at one of its peaks, was often intense. The West tended to regard with suspicion and distrust any links between Africa and the socialist world. But an even fiercer contest for influence was waged between the Russians and the Chinese. So frantic did their feud become that Nyerere, addressing a conference of the Afro-Asian People's Solidarity Organisation in Moshi, northern Tanganyika, in February 1963, felt obliged to warn of the dangers of a 'second scramble for Africa', more insidious than the first. 'I wish I could honestly say that the second scramble for Africa is going to be a scramble only between the capitalist powers,' he said. The battles fought between the Russians and the Chinese in Africa were but one aspect of the wider Sino-Soviet dispute, but in part they also occurred because the Russians were worried that China's emphasis on revolutionary activity would lead to greater Western intervention, as had happened in the Congo, and would also alarm moderate governments which the Russians valued as trading partners. Trade and aid were important elements in Soviet foreign policy towards Africa, whereas the Chinese, lacking the economic resources to compete on the same level, hoped to gain more by spreading revolutionary ideology. Their presence in Africa was small, insignificant when placed alongside the West's many contingents. Their activities were also largely unsuccessful. They sought out dissident groups, like the Sawaba movement in Niger, Tutsi exiles in Burundi, Mulelist rebels in the Congo, and the Odinga faction in the Kenya government, usually moving on the fringes of African politics and never achieving any lasting result. Yet the reputation they gained throughout much of Africa at the time, in African eyes as much as in the Western view, was of a dangerous breed of men, capable of any feat of subversion. When premier Chou En-lai made a tour of African states between December 1963 and February 1964, his very presence was taken as an ominous sign. The Lagos *Daily Times* described him as 'one of the world's most dangerous men'. His parting speech in Mogadishu, the capital of Somalia, in February 1964, seemed to confirm the worst fears about China's intentions. Speaking of the 'earth-shaking changes' that had already occurred in Africa, Chou En-lai went on to assert that 'revolutionary prospects are excellent throughout the African continent'. In the version more commonly used, his words were translated as 'Africa is ripe for revolution'. Yet whatever plans China had for aiding revolution in Africa, or for simply establishing an influential role there, little came of them. Only in Tanganyika did the Chinese prosper and there they succeeded by confining themselves to aid and training projects. The West nevertheless remained suspicious, as Nyerere wryly noted: 'I gather that even the suits I wear have been adduced as evidence of pernicious Chinese influence,' he remarked in 1965.

The first upheavals, when they did occur, sprang not from revolutionary agitation, but from circumstances altogether more bizarre. President Sylvanus Olympio of Togo, a small, impoverished West African state which had gained independence from France in 1960, had established a reputation abroad as a politician of liberal views and democratic attitudes. At home, however, he ran a repressive regime, packing the jails with political prisoners and tolerating no opposition. One year after independence, he set up a one-party system. What caused Olympio's downfall was his intemperate handling of a group of Togolese soldiers demobilised from the French army at the end of the Algerian war. Returning to Togo in 1962, they applied to join the Togolese army, which then consisted of 250 men. Olympio, who was in the middle of an austerity programme, saw no reason to employ even the extra sixty men requested by the soldiers' leaders. On 13 January 1963 he was shot dead at the gates of the American embassy in Lomé by a group of ex-servicemen led by a 25-year-old sergeant, Etienne Eyadema, who had seen service in Indo-China and Algeria. Olympio's assassination, marking as it did black Africa's first *coup d'état*, was denounced vociferously throughout Africa, though in Togo itself there was little mourning. In order to lend respectability to the coup and to reassure the Togolese population that the country was in responsible hands, the Military Insurrection Committee, as the coup leaders called themselves, installed as president a prominent politician, Nicolas Grunitsky, Olympio's brother-in-law and political rival. Grunitsky's first priority, naturally enough, was the expansion of the army to 1,200 men.

Later that year, Congo-Brazzaville, another former French colony, ran into trouble. Since its independence in 1960, Congo-Brazzaville had been governed by Abbé Fulbert Youlou, a flamboyant and ambitious figure who had served as a priest for ten years before taking to politics. His regime was notoriously corrupt. Most ministers were heavily involved in their own business affairs, setting up ventures like bars and nightclubs in Brazzaville and diamond smuggling rackets. A television station was established for less than three hundred sets. Towards critics of his regime, Youlou reacted vigorously. Once when the opposition tabled a motion of censure on his government in the National Assembly, he pulled out a revolver from under his soutane and pointed it at the deputies responsible. In 1963 he announced plans to introduce a one-party state. Unions and youth groups took to the streets in anti-government demonstrations which lasted for three days. In desperation, Youlou telephoned de Gaulle asking for French troops stationed in Congo-Brazzaville to crush the demonstrations, but de Gaulle refused. French officers in command of the Congolese army were ordered to remain neutral and Congolese officers decided to withhold the army's support. On August 15, two senior African officers met Youlou to demand his resignation. Youlou signed, fell into a faint and, upon recovering, telephoned de Gaulle. 'J'ai signé, mon général,' he announced tearfully. He later sought exile in France but was turned away, and settled in Madrid, dying there in 1973. In his place, Alphonse Massemba-Debat, a former schoolteacher and president of the national assembly, was appointed.

Former French colonies seemed especially susceptible to disorder and civil strife. French army units stationed in Africa as a result of defence cooperation agreements which France signed with almost all its former colonies, were called upon time and again for help. Sometimes their intervention was needed merely to restore public order. In 1962, for example, French troops were used in Congo-Brazzaville and Gabon to break up fighting between each country's nationals after a disputed football match. At other times, they were brought in to quell tribal warfare and agitation, or to snuff out anti-government plots. In Cameroon, French forces were actively involved in suppressing the Bamileke rebellion which had begun before independence. In Chad, they were used increasingly in an attempt to defeat local insurgency. The disposition of French troops in Africa gave France considerable power in determining the fate of precarious African governments in accordance with French interests. When de Gaulle turned down Youlou's request for French intervention in Congo-Brazzaville in 1963, he effectively terminated his regime. The following year in Gabon, a small West African state rich in mineral resources, French troops were used by de Gaulle to reinstate President Léon M'Ba, who had been briefly deposed by an army *coup d'état*. M'Ba had been in the process of eliminating opposition candidates from a forthcoming election when a section of the 400-man Gabonese army, led by four lieutenants, seized the presidential palace in Libreville, forced M'Ba to resign and installed in his place a popular opposition leader, Jean-Hilaire Aubame. However, the rebel soldiers neglected to secure the airport. French troops were flown in from Chad and Congo-Brazzaville, took control of the airport, the radio station and the presidential palace and routed the rebels in their army camp at Baraka. A French spokesman explained that it was not possible 'for a few men carrying machine guns to be left free to seize a presidential palace at any time'.

It was in East Africa, though, that the most violent eruption occurred. The revolution in Zanzibar, a lush, tropical island lying twenty-two miles off the coast of Tanganyika, had its roots in deep-seated racial antagonism between Arab and African inhabitants, which flared up during the race for power before independence. Zanzibar, together with the neighbouring island of Pemba, twenty-five miles to the north, had become an Arab colony early in the nineteenth century. When the British established a protectorate there in 1890, they continued to treat Zanzibar as an Arab state, under the control of an Arab dynasty. The Arab minority, amounting to about one sixth of the population, owned large clove and coconut plantations, played a dominant role in government affairs and filled the higher ranks of the civil service. Asian immigrants were encouraged by the Sultan to settle in Zanzibar and they soon established a hold over commerce and trade. The African population, consisting mainly of indigenous islanders known as Shirazis but increased by immigrant groups from the African mainland, occupied the lowest rungs in Zanzibar society, working as manual labourers, farmhands, fishermen and craftsmen. In the drive for independence, it was the Arab elite who led the way, establishing the first political party, the Zanzibar Nationalist Party (ZNP). There were many Africans who were prepared to accept Arab leadership and the ZNP gained a large African membership. Most African support for the ZNP came from the northern areas of Zanzibar island and from the island of Pemba. In opposition to the ZNP, African politicians founded the Afro-Shirazi Party (ASP) with the explicit aim of transforming Zanzibar into an African-ruled state. The ASP drew its support mainly from African mainlanders and from central and southern areas of Zanzibar islands where the local population had been more directly affected by Arab settlement. But it was badly organised and prone to factional disputes. Its leader, Abeid Karume, a former merchant seaman, was a man of dour temperament and little education. In the middle there emerged a third group, the Zanzibar and Pemba People's Party (ZPPP), whose followers came mostly from Pemba. Because of the large African majority on the islands, the ASP was convinced that it would triumph at the polls. But in the last election before independence in July 1963, even though the ASP obtained a majority of the total votes cast, taking some fifty-four per cent, it won only a minority of seats. Whereas the support it gained in a few areas was massive—in the African quarter of Zanzibar Town and in the southern half of Zanzibar island—elsewhere it met with little success. On Pemba island it won only two of fourteen seats. To the immense frustration of ASP supporters, the new government was formed by a coalition between the ZNP and ZPPP, which obtained eighteen of the thirty-one seats in the National Assembly. Thus, when independence day arrived on 10 December 1963, it was overshadowed by a mood of intense racial animosity, made worse by the open contempt that Arab politicians, once in power, showed towards the African population. In Ngambo, the crowded African quarter of Zanzibar Town, it was referred to as *Uhuru wa Waarabu*—

independence for Arabs. There, there were no celebrations.

Several plots were soon under way. But the revolution, when it started, came from a totally unexpected quarter. Unknown to either the authorities or to Karume's Afro-Shirazi Party, a hitherto obscure African immigrant, John Okello, had decided to form his own small private army. In the early hours of 12 January 1964, Okello led his men, armed with axes, spears, bows and arrows, in an attack on a police armoury in Zanzibar Town. Having overcome police resistance, they distributed guns to their supporters and went on to seize the unguarded radio station, from where Okello made several broadcasts inciting an uprising against the Arab population. Within a few hours, Okello's coup had succeeded. The Sultan fled on his yacht, government ministers surrendered, the police capitulated and Okello, appointing himself Field Marshal, was left in control. A wave of terror was then unleashed against the Arab population. Probably well over 5,000 Arabs were killed, thousands more were interned, their houses, property and possessions seized at will. At a later stage, many hundreds of Arab families were forcibly deported, packed into requisitioned dhows and sent off to the Arabian Gulf. As a community, the Arabs virtually disappeared. Twelve days after Okello's action, a Revolutionary Council was named. It was led by Karume and included several leading radical figures, notably Abdulrahman Muhammed Babu, a Marxist who had once worked as a correspondent for the New China News Agency, and Kassim Hanga, a teacher who had studied in Moscow and married a Soviet citizen. Okello himself, though appointed a member, was soon eased out and forced to return to his native Uganda. While Britain and other Western countries withheld recognition of the new regime, China, Russia and East Germany, encouraged by Babu and Hanga, were quick to offer aid, assistance and military training. For the Russians who had previously portrayed the Arab-led ZNP as a popular anti-imperialist mass movement, the Revolution required some hasty revision of policy. Hundreds of Communist technicians duly arrived in Zanzibar, promoting Western fears that the islands might become an African 'Cuba'. On mainland Tanganyika, Nyerere too distrusted the growing influence of foreign Communists there and he was further worried that Zanzibar might be drawn directly into the Cold War or engulfed in the Sino-Soviet dispute. Partly to avoid either eventuality, partly wishing to exercise a moderating influence, he proposed a union between Tanganyika and Zanzibar. This union, to which Karume agreed in April, was later named Tanzania.

The revolution in Zanzibar was followed swiftly by a series of army mutinies in Tanganyika, Uganda and Kenya, creating an even wider circle of alarm about the stability of East Africa. Behind each mutiny lay grievances over pay, promotions and the continuing presence of senior British officers, rather than political resentment against the three governments. In each case, British troops were required to intervene to bring the mutinies to an end. The worst example was in Tanganyika. There, on 19 January, soldiers from Colito Barracks, eight miles outside the capital, Dar es Salaam, led by a sergeant, arrested their British and African officers and proceeded to take control of the radio station, the airport, police stations and State House, the residence and office of President Nyerere. Nyerere himself went into hiding for two days, leaving the country leaderless. The mutiny spread to a second barracks at Tabora, 400 miles west of the capital, thus involving virtually the whole army. When negotiations failed, Nyerere was obliged to call for help from British commandos, who landed from a carrier lying off the Tanganyika coast. The Tanganyika mutiny set off a chain reaction a few days later at barracks in Uganda and Kenya, though the mutinies there were on a lesser scale. In the case of Tanganyika, the army was disbanded.

A variety of other troubles afflicted Africa in the early years. A religious uprising broke out in Zambia a few months before independence, leaving more than 700 dead; Tutsi exiles based in Burundi invaded Rwanda in an attempt to overthrow the Hutu-led government and restore Tutsi rule, provoking terrible reprisals against Tutsi communities still living there; in southern Sudan, there was also rebellion. Intermittently the Congo rumbled on like some diseased part of the continent. Yet many of the troubles, like the East African mutinies, once they had passed, seemed not so fearful as they had done at the time and served in some cases as tests of stability. Then, towards the end of 1965 running into the new year, a spate of coups occurred. Once again, former French colonies were involved: Dahomey, the Central African Republic and Upper Volta. None of the coups caused much surprise. Indeed, a country like Dahomey seemed to be encumbered with every imaginable difficulty. Some thought of it as ungovernable. But the sudden sequence of coups was nevertheless unsettling.

A small strip of territory jutting inland from the West Coast, Dahomey was crowded, insolvent, beset by tribal divisions, huge debts, unemployment, frequent strikes and an unending struggle for power between three rival political leaders. The government's budget, permanently in deficit, was dependent on French subsidies. Two thirds of state revenues were spent on maintaining a huge bureaucracy and, despite the country's desperate financial plight, further large sums were lavished on prestige projects such as a glittering palace in Cotonou for the president. Previously, in 1963, in response to trade union demands, the army commander, Colonel Christophe Soglo, who had served in the French army for thirty years, had briefly taken control from the squabbling politicians while a new government was formed. In November 1965, during another round of strikes, demonstrations and political deadlock, Soglo stepped in again, appointing a new interim president. When this failed to restore order, he intervened for a third time on 22 December 1965, deciding to ban politics altogether and set himself up in power.

The coup in the Central African Republic ten days later had similar features. The Central African Republic was an impoverished, landlocked state, burdened with a vast and costly bureaucracy and dependent on French subsidies. Its president, David Dacko, a former schoolteacher, who had set up a one-party system in 1962, though well-intentioned proved to be an inept and ineffectual leader. Ministers and civil servants devoted most of their time to their own business ventures; some were notoriously corrupt, embezzling state funds with impunity and using their official positions to operate diamond-smuggling rackets. The economy, meanwhile, remained stagnant. While Dacko grew increasingly tired and dispirited by the trials of office, two contenders for power made their separate plans to replace him. One was the chief of the *gendarmerie*, Commandant Jean Izamo; the other was the army commander, Colonel Jean-Bedel Bokassa, like Soglo a French army veteran. Ostensibly to celebrate New Year's Eve, Izamo invited Bokassa and other senior officers to a party at his house. Bokassa, suspecting a plot to arrest him, asked Izamo to call first at his office to sign some documents. When Izamo arrived, he was arrested. Bokassa then collected his troops, surrounded the president's palace and persuaded Dacko to resign. In justifying his coup, Bokassa referred to the level of corruption and to the 'bad associates' who surrounded Dacko, adding 'I gave him valuable advice which he did not heed.'

Three days later, on 3 January 1966, President Maurice Yaméogo of Upper Volta was removed, after crowds of demonstrators in Ouagadougou had implored the army to intervene. Yaméogo, like so many other African politicians of that era, had begun his regime popularly elected, determined to maintain an efficient administration and outspoken in his condemnation of corruption. 'Government is not a gang of old pals having it good on nice fat jobs at the expense of the people,' he said. Upper Volta was a landlocked state with scant resources, one of the poorest countries in the world and heavily dependent on French aid and remittances from migrant labour. Though Yaméogo had won the 1959 election with a commanding majority, taking sixty-four of seventy-five seats in the Legislative Assembly, he was intolerant of opposition. Opposition leaders were interned, exiled or sent abroad as ambassadors. From 1960, his *Union Démocratique Voltaique* became the only legally sanctioned party in the country. His regime also became noted for corruption. Yaméogo himself, while issuing ringing calls for public sacrifice and renewed dedication, lived in a luxuriously furnished presidential palace and indulged in other extravagances. In Ouagadougou, a television station was built to serve a mere one hundred private sets. To the outrage of the local Catholic church, he dispensed with his first wife in 1965, ostentatiously married a twenty-two-year-old beauty queen and hastened off to a honeymoon in Brazil. On his return in December, he pushed through the National Assembly an austerity budget cutting back the salaries of government employees, though not in any way reducing his own salary or expenses. On 1 January 1966 civil servants called for a general strike and students and trade unionists took to the streets in protest against the government. Yaméogo, from the comfort of his palace, refused to meet any delegations, declared the strike illegal and blamed the disorder on 'Communist' agitators. The demonstrations persisted. Thousands gathered at army headquarters demanding an army takeover. Reluctantly, the army commander, Colonel Sangoulé Lamizana, another French army veteran, agreed to take control. Yaméogo was later convicted of embezzling more than one million pounds.

The sequence of coups did not stop there, however. Like a contagion, they spread across the continent, striking down regimes debilitated by internal political quarrels, economic difficulties or corrupt leadership. Nor were they confined to inherently weak and unstable countries. For the giants of Africa, too, came crashing down, in some cases with the most terrible consequences.

CHAPTER TWENTY

The Fall of Nkrumah

As prime minister of the newly independent state of Ghana, Kwame Nkrumah chose as his official residence a seventeenth-century castle built by Danish slave traders on a rocky promontory on the outskirts of Accra and named by them Christiansborg. A succession of British Governors had lived there, presiding over the affairs of state with imperial dignity, and by moving there himself, Nkrumah seemed personally to mark the capture of this final citadel of colonial power. He also acquired the remoteness of a ruler. For Christiansborg Castle was a place of solitude, where the most familiar sound was the insistent roar of the surf pounding against its ancient walls.

Finally free to pursue the dreams that he had nurtured since his student days in London, Nkrumah conceived one grand scheme after another. He was impatient for results on a spectacular scale. Having successfully challenged the might of British rule in Africa and opened the way to independence for a score of other African countries, he saw himself as a revolutionary leader destined to play an even greater role. At home he wanted to transform Ghana into an industrial power, a centre of learning, a model socialist society which other states would want to emulate. But his most ambitious ideas concerned the whole of Africa. He dreamed of making Africa a giant in economic, military and political terms, as united and powerful as the United States or the Soviet Union, with himself as leader. For a while his sweeping visions of a brave new world, his restless energy and above all the remarkable charm that he could bring to bear, won him many friends and admirers. On the world stage he became a familiar figure, mixing with the rich and powerful, relishing the fame it brought him. Queen Elizabeth was among those who found him a fascinating character. In 1959 he was invited as her personal guest to the royal residence at Balmoral, a rare favour for a foreign head of state, and there one morning, after a walk on the moors to watch Prince Philip shooting grouse, he was affirmed a member of 'Her Majesty's Most Honourable Privy Council'. The picture taken of him with the Queen at Balmoral became a favourite possession. He ordered thousands of copies to be printed. From the Queen too he acquired the habit of drinking Malvern water, which was imported for him from England at considerable cost to the government.

The dreams soon turned sour. In the process of building his new society in Ghana, Nkrumah resorted increasingly to dictatorial methods. Within a year of independence, new laws were introduced which allowed the government to detain anyone without trial for up to five years. In theory, the detention laws and other similar measures that followed were to be employed only at times of emergency; in practice, they were used arbitrarily to silence the government's critics and its political opponents and even, in some cases, to pay off petty scores. The opposition press, too, was soon muzzled. In defence of such measures, Nkrumah argued that newly independent states needed strong government to unify the country, to mobilise resources, to demonstrate the change of regime. But the result was to concentrate power in Nkrumah's own hands and to his own advantage. Through the activities of his Convention People's Party, his personal control grew until it reached into every aspect of Ghanaian life, into trade unions, farmers' associations, youth movements and the civil service. His presence became inescapable: his profile embellished coins, banknotes, postage stamps; his statue stood outside parliament; his name appeared in neon lights; his birthday became a public holiday; framed photographs adorned offices and shops.

Indeed, the personality cult which surrounded Nkrumah soon reached grotesque proportions. He assumed grand titles—Man of Destiny, Star of Africa, His High Dedication and, most famous of all, Osagyefo, a name which meant 'victor in war', but which was often more loosely translated as 'redeemer'. Every day the press extolled his intellectual brilliance, his foresight, his integrity. His importance was compared to that of Lenin, of Lincoln, of Gandhi. 'When our history is recorded,' said the *Evening News* in a typical example in 1961, 'the man Kwame Nkrumah will be written of as the liberator, the Messiah, the Christ of our day, whose great love for mankind wrought changes in Ghana, in Africa and in the world at large.' Taking the personality cult to further heights, Nkrumah created an official ideology, calling it Nkrumaism, and built an ideological institute in his name costing millions of pounds. There a staff of mostly left-wing expatriates worked diligently, constructing elaborate political theories. But despite their efforts, 'Nkrumaism', though frequently quoted in public, was never clearly defined. When it was launched in 1960, at the same time that Nkrumah became president, 'Nkrumaism' was described by the *Evening News* as 'a complex political and social philosophy', to which Nkrumah would add from time to time. Five years later, it was said to be based on 'scientific socialism'. But nothing more original emerged. Nkrumah himself, since his student days, always borrowed heavily from other ideologies. Indeed, large parts of the books to which he lent his name were written for him by other authors.

The adulation that Nkrumah received was absurd, but not particularly costly. What set Ghana on a far more ruinous course was his grand design for industrialisation and the system of corruption that went with it. With reckless speed, Nkrumah pressed ahead with one project after another—with factories, steelworks, mining ventures, shipyards, highways, almost any idea, in fact, that caught his imagination. Some schemes were started simply for reasons of prestige. Nkrumah wanted, for example, to build the largest drydock in Africa, regardless of its viability; once built, it was rarely used. The state airline, equipped with a fleet of jet aircraft, was required to fly to destinations such as Cairo and Moscow, for which there were few passengers; it ran up heavy losses. A modern motorway was constructed between Accra and the port at Tema, though little traffic used the route.

Other schemes were impractical. An enterprising Rumanian-born businessman who struck up a friendship with Nkrumah convinced him of the need to build a huge set of concrete silos to store cocoa, so that the price of cocoa could be controlled more effectively; once built, the silos were condemned as unusable. After a visit to Soviet bloc countries in 1961 had greatly impressed him, Nkrumah decided that state-owned enterprises should provide the spearhead for Ghana's industrialisation programme. Accordingly, more and more state enterprises were launched—the State Steelworks Corporation, the State Gold Mining Corporation, the State Fibre Bag Corporation, the Ghana Fishing Corporation, the State Farms Corporation. By 1966 more than fifty state enterprises had been set up. Most of them were badly managed, weighed down by inefficient bureaucracies and run at a huge loss. In the rush to modernise, much worthwhile progress was made: the Volta river hydro-electric scheme provided a lasting source of cheap power, though on terms which greatly favoured its American financiers; schools, hospitals and roads were built; locally manufactured goods replaced imports. But the overall effect was to burden Ghana with a vast, unwieldy and unprofitable industrial structure which the country could not hope to sustain.

From 1961, Ghana's economy fell ever deeper into disarray. The steady decline in world cocoa prices from that time seriously reduced the country's foreign earnings just when the government was heavily committed to such ambitious development plans. Ignoring the danger, Nkrumah would not hold back. From his office the ideas, the schemes, the instructions poured forth. When the government's reserves ran down, Nkrumah decided, against the advice of his own officials, to press ahead by using suppliers' credits. In effect, he was mortgaging Ghana's revenues for years ahead. Ghana's foreign debt soared. No-one could ascertain precisely to what extent the government was in debt because complete records of the contracts were not kept in government files. Nkrumah often awarded contracts personally, without reference to the cabinet, the appropriate minister, or the cabinet's contracts committee. In later years, odd items—a £5 million warship for the navy, a 7,500-ton luxury boat built for Nkrumah himself—kept turning up. In some cases the delivery of goods for which Ghana signed was never made. Faced with mounting economic difficulties, the government eventually responded by imposing import controls, but they were administered in such random fashion that further chaos ensued. Steadily, the grand industrial programme, hampered by shortages of raw materials and spare parts, ground to a halt. Agriculture, too, fell into sharp decline. Nkrumah favoured mechanised state farms and diverted government resources—financial support, technical assistance and import allocations—for their benefit, neglecting the needs of traditional peasant farmers. But the state farms made huge losses and their yields were less than one fifth of peasant agriculture. Meanwhile, peasant farmers, disgruntled by low cocoa prices offered by the government and by the state monopoly of cocoa-buying which tended to provide government officials with an unduly good living, grew less and less produce.

What made Ghana's difficulties even worse was the level of corruption which spread throughout the government. At an early stage of Nkrumah's tenure of office, the problem of high level corruption had become noticeable. A commission of inquiry in 1956 had revealed how the CPP had established control of the Cocoa Purchasing Company and used it to ensure that government-funded loans were granted to party sympathisers. After independence, the system of corruption grew, along with the government's development programme. Foreign businessmen seeking lucrative contracts were only too ready to contribute large payments to a special company, the National Development Corporation, set up by Nkrumah as a clearing house for funds for the party. The Israeli shipping line, Zim, for example, paid £300,000 for a contract for eight merchant ships; a West German company gave £200,000 for a locomotive contract. The list, in fact, was endless. But it was not only the party that benefited. Nkrumah's ministers were willing enough to push through contracts for a ten per cent fee. 'It was the order of the day,' one of Nkrumah's officials later admitted, 'for every minister connected with a government contract to take a cut for himself.' Almost any foreign businessman, therefore, with a bright idea and a ready bribe, stood a reasonable chance of obtaining a contract. Soon everyone—the Russians and the East Germans as much as Western businessmen—was lining up signing deals that were often overpriced, with terms of repayment that were exorbitant, for equipment that was sometimes obsolescent.

The rush for private gain among Nkrumah's circle was conspicuous and, in some cases, openly flaunted. Government ministers and high party officials acquired large houses, filling them with expensive, imported furniture and *objets d'art*, and lived in flamboyant styles. One minister, Krobo Edusei, gained particular notoriety when his wife ordered a £3,000 gold-plated bed from a London store. In the ensuing scandal, she was obliged to send it back. Edusei confessed in later years that he owned fourteen houses, a luxurious beach house, a long lease on a London flat, several expensive cars and six different bank accounts. Nkrumah made little effort to deal with corruption. He spoke critically of 'a new ruling class of self-seekers and careerists'. But his toughest stricture about such activities was that no party member should own more than two houses and two cars, conditions to which no-one paid attention. Indeed, Nkrumah himself became a wealthy man, controlling such companies as the National Development Corporation and using, when necessary, government funds for personal as well as business purposes.

All this was achieved while the mass of the population, beset by rising prices, higher taxes and consumer shortages, suffered increasing hardship. An official survey showed that by 1963 the standard of living of unskilled workers in towns had fallen in real terms to the levels of 1939. In rural areas, cocoa farmers, forced to accept successive cuts in crop prices, saw their incomes reduced by half over a ten-year period. Resentment against the government, in particular against the profligate manner in which Nkrumah's ministers lived, inevitably increased. But towards any sign of opposition Nkrumah reacted ruthlessly. In 1961, as a result of the fall in cocoa export prices and the country's diminishing reserves, the government introduced new and severe taxes. Protesting against the sharp rise in the cost of living, dock and railway workers went on strike and the opposition United Party added its own call to the government to adopt a more 'sensible' economic policy. Nkrumah's response was to arrest strike leaders and jail them without trial. In a radio broadcast, one of his ministers denounced the strikers as 'despicable rats'. Through a mixture of force, intimidation and bribery, the strike was eventually broken. Next Nkrumah turned on the hapless United Party and ordered the arrest of leading politicians, including Dr Danquah, the prominent lawyer for whom Nkrumah had worked on his return from London. He then purged his own Cabinet of more conservative ministers who were showing doubts about the direction of government policies. Among them was Komla Gbedemah, an able finance minister who ten years before, while Nkrumah was serving his prison sentence under British rule, had been largely responsible for organising the famous 1951 election; prudently, Gbedemah went into exile. Finally, to control any future disturbance, Nkrumah set up special courts to deal with political offences, with judges appointed by himself, from which there was no right of appeal.

The course on which Nkrumah was now embarked was fraught with peril. As his grip over the government became ever tighter, Ghana was caught in a succession of plots, palace intrigues, reprisals and repression. In August 1962, while Nkrumah was passing through the small village of Kulungugu in northern Ghana, a bomb was thrown at him: four people were killed outright, fifty-six others were injured, but Nkrumah escaped unscathed. Convinced that party radicals had been plotting to overthrow him, he ordered the arrest of Tawia Adamafio, then one of his closest associates, and two other ministers. They were tried on charges of conspiracy before a special court headed by the Chief Justice, Sir Arku Korsah. When the Chief Justice returned a verdict of not guilty and ordered the accused men to be discharged, Nkrumah dismissed him and rushed a new law through parliament enabling him to set aside the verdict of the special court when it was 'in the state's interest'. Another assassination attempt was made in January 1964 by a police constable. Suspecting this time that the police service at large was involved, Nkrumah ordered the police to be disarmed, sacked several officers and detained the Commissioner and his deputy. For protection he now relied increasingly on a personal security service recruited largely from his home district in the southwest corner of Ghana and trained with the help of Soviet advisers.

In his final years Nkrumah became increasingly isolated and remote from the realities of the crisis that Ghana faced. Many of his old friends and colleagues had left him, some like Gbedemah heading for exile, others falling victim to the detention laws for which they had once enthusiastically voted. Opposition politicians, harassed and persecuted, fell silent. Dr Danquah, the doyen of the old guard elite, arrested again in 1964, was fated to spend the last year of his life a sick and disheartened man, in solitary confinement with no adequate medical treatment. He died in prison in February 1965. Among the hundreds of political prisoners, many others suffered ill-health; some remained in detention, forgotten. Except for a rare outburst in parliament, public debate and discussion were stifled. The only voices heard were those in praise of Nkrumah. In everyday life, too, critics of the government were careful of what they said, for fear of the presence of spies and informers. Not even the University of Ghana, with a long tradition of academic freedom, escaped Nkrumah's attentions. To bring the University to heel, expatriate lecturers were deported, other faculty members were arrested, controversial debates were prohibited and party thugs were let loose on the campus. In 1964, a party committee was set up to purge university and school libraries of books deemed to be of a 'capitalist' or 'reactionary' nature. In what was virtually a formality, Nkrumah decided in 1964 officially to make Ghana a one-party state. A referendum on the issue was allowed, but in advance of the vote, the government press threatened reprisals against anyone who did not participate and anyone who did not vote in favour. Even then, the result was blatantly rigged. According to official figures, some 96 per cent of the total registered electorate voted, a far higher proportion than had ever voted during any previous election. Of these, only 0.1 per cent were said to have voted 'No'. In the Ashanti region, previously one of the main centres of opposition, not a single 'No' vote was recorded. The result hardly mattered. For the CPP had long ceased to have any serious function, except as a massive propaganda machine, and all opposition had anyway been silenced. Nor did elections matter any more. In the general election in 1965, all CPP candidates, previously picked by Nkrumah and a small party committee, were returned unopposed, without even the formality of a vote. Nkrumah announced over the radio the names of those he had chosen.

From the pinnacle of power that he had constructed,

Nkrumah presided in lonely seclusion, ruling by edict and surrounded by elaborate security precautions. On his decision and judgement the machinery of government now largely depended. At Flagstaff House, the main presidential compound in the northern suburbs in Accra, Nkrumah concentrated more and more functions of state, establishing there 'secretariats' which bypassed the work of government ministries and gave him direct control over a wide range of government business. Under his personal auspices came such matters as higher education, foreign trade, internal security, African affairs, parliamentary business, the civil service and, finally, defence. At Flagstaff House he also built a private zoo, to which various friends made contributions: Emperor Haile Selassie sent a lion; President Tubman of Liberia, a hippo; and Fidel Castro, a boa constrictor. But in the months after the assassination attempt in 1964, Nkrumah, moody and introspective, withdrew more and more to the solitude of Christiansborg Castle. Friends noted how he cut himself off even from his most intimate associates, doubting their loyalty and preferring to keep the company of those who simply flattered him, or to meditate alone. Foreign advisers, on whom Nkrumah had always relied, gained access to him more readily than his own compatriots. With ministers bearing reports of economic setbacks he was impatient and dismissive, and they found increasing difficulty in arranging a hearing.

His abiding passion remained African affairs. As preoccupied as ever with distant goals, he pressed constantly for complete African union. The idea of a continental government became an obsession. Great expense and effort was involved to ensure that Nkrumah played a leading role in the major African issues of the time—in the Congo, Rhodesia, southern African liberation, in negotiations setting up the Organisation of African Unity and with plans to establish an African High Command. In the wider field of foreign affairs, Nkrumah strove tirelessly to act as a world statesman by offering his services as a mediator in international crises. In support of these ambitions, he built up a vast diplomatic network which included fifty-seven embassies. But, once again, the reality proved to be far different from what Nkrumah had in mind. Other African leaders did not share his absolutist view of African unity. Nor did they take kindly to the vain and arrogant manner which Nkrumah adopted towards those who disagreed with him. He quarrelled sharply with Nyerere of Tanganyika over his plans for an East African federation, since it conflicted with Nkrumah's own concept of African unity. He also took to denouncing the policies of 'African socialism' which other African leaders favoured after he had decided that 'scientific socialism' was the 'correct' road. Even more serious were the disputes that he fell into with his neighbours—Togo, the Ivory Coast, Nigeria, Upper Volta and Niger. As well as setting up guerrilla training camps for African exiles from southern Africa, Nkrumah readily supported the activities of subversive groups from neighbouring countries in the hope of helping them to power. The Niger president, Hamani Diori, accused Ghana of supporting an assassination attempt against him. Nkrumah's foreign policy, in fact, was often erratic. He constantly attacked Western governments or business corporations, but then appealed for their help or finance. He devoted much time to warning of the danger of 'neo-colonialism', but ended by leaving his country in pawn to foreign interests to a greater extent than any other contemporary African ruler.

Still in pursuit of foreign prestige, Nkrumah embarked on a scheme which for later generations stood as a symbol of his fondness for extravagant gestures. Though at the time factories were starved of raw materials, food queues in towns were a common sight, hospitals were short of drugs, state companies were bankrupt and the country's cocoa income had fallen sharply, Nkrumah ordered the construction of an £8 million palace to house a single conference of the heads of state of the Organisation of African Unity in 1965. He himself was captivated by its details and proudly boasted of them to parliament—the sixty self-contained suites that would have satisfied the demands of millionaires, the banqueting hall capable of seating 2,000 guests, the fountains operated by seventy-two jets with a multi-coloured interplay of lights, rising to a height of sixty feet. It was, he told parliament, a magnificent complex of buildings. The conference was only partially successful. Because Nkrumah's foreign policy had upset so many people, many governments were reluctant to attend the conference. Nkrumah was obliged to give an undertaking to refrain from assisting dissident groups from neighbouring countries. In the end, twenty-eight out of thirty-six members of the OAU attended the meeting, but only thirteen were represented by heads of state.

What eventually brought Nkrumah down, however, was not the muddle and mismanagement into which the government had fallen, nor the high level corruption which was so conspicuous, nor even the country's desperate economic plight, but his fatal decision to interfere with the military. Brought up in the Sandhurst tradition, the army command, though concerned about Ghana's mounting difficulties, stood aside until the time when its own interests were threatened. Nkrumah's attempts to bring the army into line with his own purposes, as he had done with every other part of the state, produced within the army command a deep and dangerous resentment which grew at each successive stage. During the leftward turn the government took in 1961, Nkrumah instructed the army to take up a Soviet offer to train 400 recruits. Most officers disliked the idea, fearing that it might lead to the emergence of rival groups within the army. But at Nkrumah's insistence, some recruits were eventually sent to Russia. There was further discontent over moves by the CPP to infiltrate the army and set up party branches and over the presence of party spies in army messrooms. But the most serious cause of resentment was the growing strength of an elite unit, the President's Own Guard Regiment, which Nkrumah detached from the army command and placed under his own control and which was trained separately with the help of Soviet and East European advisers. The President's Own Guard Regiment soon came to be regarded as Nkrumah's private army. Its 1,200 officers and men were equipped with modern weapons, they were paid at special rates and received preferential treatment, while the rest of the army suffered from serious shortages of clothing and equipment and was forced to take cuts in allowances, pay and social amenities. In the police command, too, there was discontent with Nkrumah's regime, particularly over the humiliating way in which Nkrumah dealt with the police after the 1964 assassination attempt. From among the senior ranks of the army and the police, a group of conspirators linked up in 1965 with the aim of overthrowing Nkrumah. Suspecting the existence of an army plot, Nkrumah dismissed two generals in August 1965. But their abrupt departure served only to further antagonise the army command.

To the very end, Nkrumah was preoccupied with his foreign adventures. When Ian Smith declared Rhodesia's UDI in November 1965, Nkrumah rushed through parliament legislation giving him authority to send Ghana's armed forces to 'wherever the peace and security of Africa is threatened'. All military leave was cancelled, and recruitment centres were opened to enrol volunteers for a Rhodesian invasion. When the army finally struck on 24 February 1966, Nkrumah was on his way to Hanoi at the invitation of Ho Chi Minh, carrying new proposals for ending the war in Vietnam.

The coup was accomplished with little resistance. Nkrumah's ministers and his supporters swiftly deserted him. On the streets of Accra and Kumasi, large crowds gathered to welcome the soldiers and celebrated by ripping down the framed photographs which adorned houses, offices and factories. Outside parliament, Nkrumah's statue was battered to the ground. Some ragged, barefoot urchins were allowed to scamper on top of it. Then it was smashed to bits.

CHAPTER TWENTY-ONE

Nigeria's Civil War

The sense of optimism about Nigeria's future, so much in evidence when the country was launched as an independent state in 1960, remained buoyant in the early years of independence. As the most populous nation in Africa, led by politicians widely applauded for their long experience of government, endowed with a strong, diversified economy and possessing an efficient civil service, Nigeria was clearly marked out as one of Africa's emerging powers. Whatever disputes between the country's three regions had occurred during the closing stages of British rule seemed largely resolved with the advent of independence. The federal constitution, over which there had been such fierce argument, in its final form was regarded as a sensible compromise, effectively balancing the country's rival political interests and well able to contain the strains and stresses which the hurly-burly of Nigerian politics invariably produced. At the helm of the Federal government was a coalition of Northern and Eastern politicians from the conservative Northern People's Congress (NPC) and the more radical National Council of Nigerian Citizens (NCNC), providing a broadly-based administration that avoided the danger of either the North or the two regions of the South holding power exclusively. It was led by a moderate Northerner, Sir Abubakar Tafawa Balewa. Western politicians in the Action Group meanwhile settled for the role of parliamentary opposition in the traditional British manner. At a regional level, each of the three major parties remained in control of regional government. By outward appearances, therefore, Nigeria provided a promising example of a carefully balanced and stable parliamentary democracy.

Behind this reassuring façade, however, politicians on all sides were engaged in a scramble for power and profit conducted with such reckless abandon that it led finally to the downfall of civilian rule within six years. The advantages of political office were used at every opportunity by Nigeria's leaders to accumulate empires of wealth and patronage with which to improve both their personal and their party's fortunes. In return for political support, party and government bosses were able to provide their followers and friends with jobs, contracts, loans, scholarships, public amenities; indeed with any favour that came within their purview. Public funds were regularly commandeered for political and sometimes personal gain. At every level, from the Federal government to Regional government down to local districts and towns, the system was worked by politicians in office to ensure that their own areas and members of their own tribe benefited, while opposition areas suffered from neglect. Politics thus degenerated into a corrupt and bitter struggle for the spoils of office. Each region was locked in competition, for a larger share of federal revenue, for the location of industries, for appointments to public office, for political advantage, often in an atmosphere of such cut-throat antagonism that tribal fears and mistrust inevitably became more deeply rooted. By nature, Nigerian politics tended to be mercenary and violent. Political debate was routinely conducted in acrimonious and abusive language; and tribal loyalties were constantly exploited. The tactics employed were often those of the rough-house variety. The eventual consequence of these rash and profligate years, however, was that Nigeria was led into sudden upheaval and, ultimately, towards a tragedy of monumental proportions.

It was the Western Region which became the centre of political turbulence. There, Chief Awolowo's Action Group remained in control of the Regional government, but found itself at considerable disadvantage, in terms of patronage, by standing in opposition to the Federal government. In 1962, the Action Group broke into two factions during a dispute over its future role. One group, led by Chief Akintola, the premier of the Western Region and the party's deputy leader, advocated a change in policy which would enable the Action Group to participate in the Federal coalition—a move which was also favoured by the Federal prime minister, Sir Abubakar Tafawa Balewa. The other group, led by Awolowo, the head of the party and leader of the opposition in the Federal House, argued that there was more to be gained by keeping the Action Group out of the coalition and working to win the next Federal election with the aid of a programme of radical reform. When it came to the vote, Awolowo gained the upper hand. At a meeting of the party's executive, delegates decided unanimously to remove Akintola from the party hierarchy and from his post of premier of the Western Region. Subsequently, a majority of the party's parliamentary group elected as his replacement one of Awolowo's loyal supporters, Dauda Adegbenro. At the end of May, Adegbenro was duly sworn in as premier of the Western Region. But when parliament next assembled to give Adegbenro a formal vote of confidence, Akintola's supporters sought to disrupt the proceedings. One member flung a chair across the floor of the House; another seized the Mace, attempted to club the Speaker, but missed and smashed the Mace on a table; more chairs and tables were thrown; a Minister, hit on the head, was rushed to hospital. Finally, police had to use teargas to clear the House. For several hours the Speaker suspended the sitting, hoping for an orderly resumption, but when members reassembled, similar scenes of uproar occurred and again the police intervened using teargas.

Taking advantage of these disturbances to strike a blow at the opposition, Balewa's Federal government hastily summoned the Federal parliament, imposed a state of emergency in the Western region, suspended the constitution and appointed a sole Administrator to run the Region on behalf of the Federal government until the end of the year. These measures drew widespread criticism and were condemned by Awolowo as 'a gross misuse of power'. But thereafter the Federal government continued to harass and discredit the Action Group at every opportunity. Leading party members were served with restriction orders and the party's business and political empire was put under close official investigation, revealing to the public a vast web of corruption and malpractice. In September, Awolowo and his senior colleagues were put on trial, charged with conspiring to overthrow the government. After a hearing lasting nine months, Awolowo was found guilty and sentenced to ten years' imprisonment, though his own role was left in some doubt. While the trial was still in progress, the state of emergency in the Western Region came to its end and, without the test of an election, Akintola was installed as prime minister of a coalition government, leaving the Action Group in opposition in its former stronghold as well as in the Federal arena, shorn of most of its leaders and cut off from the spoils of power with which to maintain its support. As a final blow to the Action Group's fortunes, the Western Region was carved up into two parts through the creation of a new Mid-West Region.

These manoeuvres placed the ruling Federal establishment and its various allies in a seemingly unassailable position, with control of each of the country's four Regions as well as the Federal government. But the increasingly assertive manner which Balewa and his Northern colleagues used to maintain their hold over Federal affairs soon revived old grievances and rivalries among the coalition's partners. The North's intention from the outset had been to dominate Federal politics. Balewa had shown, by his handling of the Action Group opposition, to what extent he was prepared to go to enforce his control. What lay behind the ruthless tactics he employed was the North's ingrained fear of a strong Southern coalition threatening its identity and independent way of life. The overriding aim of the North's powerful and autocratic prime minister, the Sardauna of Sokoto, Sir Ahmadu Bello, was to prevent the influence of skilled and enterprising Southerners from spreading to the North. But, in turn, the North's grip over Federal affairs was resented in the South, by Easterners as much as by Westerners. As the Eastern Region's main political party, the NCNC had joined Balewa's Federal coalition, anxious to share in Federal spoils, but it became increasingly embittered by its treatment as a mere junior member.

The one hope of Southern politicians, ambitious for a change in the power structure, was that Nigeria's population figures, on which representation in the Federal parliament was based, would alter in the South's favour. The North had been able to dominate Federal politics by virtue of its huge population. But a new national census was due in 1962 which Southerners hoped would prove that the South's combined numbers now outweighed the North's and so bring an end to the North's control of the Federal parliament. When the figures were eventually collected, the unofficial results suggested evidence of inflated returns, especially from some Eastern districts. While the North's population was shown to have risen over a ten-year period from 17.3 million to 22.5 million, an increase amounting to 30 per cent, returns from some Eastern areas claimed increases as high as 200 per cent and rising on average 71 per cent; the Western returns also gave an increase of over 70 per cent. In the ensuing controversy, Balewa ordered a new census. When the figures for the 1963 census were produced, they showed the North's population to have risen to nearly 30 million—seven million more people had been found—while the South's combined population was counted as nearly 26 million. In political terms, the census result was a clear victory for the North.

All the latent antagonism between the North and the South, never far below the surface, now broke out in a wave of bitter wrangling and recrimination that wrecked the government coalition. The Eastern Region government, along with the Mid-West government, both under the control of the NCNC, rejected the results; the Northern government and Akintola's regime in the West accepted them. As the 1964 election approached, new alliances were formed. In a concerted attempt to break the Northern stranglehold, the two established Southern parties, the NCNC and the Action Group, joined to form the United Progressive Grand Alliance (UPGA), confident that they would sweep the Southern constituencies and hoping that, with the help of Northern minority parties, they would gain enough seats in the North to win a majority in the Federal parliament. Against them was ranged the Nigerian National Alliance (NNA), consisting of the Sardauna's NPC, Akintola's Nigerian National Democratic Party (NNDP) and minor Southern parties.

No proper election was held. When nominations closed on 19 December, eleven days before the election, the results showed that in sixty-one constituencies in the North, although UPGA candidates had presented themselves for nomination in each constituency, NPC candidates had been returned unopposed. The UPGA leaders subsequently claimed that widespread electoral malpractices had occurred and produced a collection of affidavits to support their case. One affidavit described how three abortive attempts had been made to nominate a candidate in Prime Minister Balewa's constituency. At the first attempt, the nominators were arrested; the second time they were carried away by thugs; on the third occasion they were kidnapped and held until the lists closed. Fearing that defeat was inevitable, the UPGA incautiously called for an election boycott. This tactic was effective in the East, where no election was held at all. But elsewhere it merely strengthened the NNA victory: the NPC swept the Northern seats; and in the West, Akintola's NNDP gained a dubious majority.

In the constitutional crisis that followed, Nigeria went to the verge of breaking apart. Asserting that he was dissatisfied with the conduct of the election, the President, Nnamdi Azikiwe, a former NCNC leader, refused to call on Balewa to form a new government and for two days, while he held firm, the risks of a deadly confrontation remained high; in the army, officers considered the possibility of a coup, while in the Eastern Region, political leaders secretly discussed the idea of secession. In the end, a compromise was reached under which Balewa agreed to form another coalition government and the NCNC, preferring to remain close to power and patronage rather than join the Action Group in opposition, resumed its role as a junior partner. But once again the South had suffered a severe defeat at the hands of the North, leaving many Southerners in a sullen and frustrated mood.

One last opportunity remained for Southern politicians to challenge the hegemony of the North. In 1965, new elections were scheduled for the Western Region where Akintola's term of office was due to expire. By winning these elections in another joint effort, the two main UPGA partners—the NCNC and the Action Group—stood to gain control of all three Southern Regions as well as Lagos. Though this outcome still would not enable them to circumvent the NPC majority in the Federal House of Representatives, it would give them control of the Senate and thereby a hold over the passage of legislation.

The election, accordingly, was fought by all sides with ruthless and brutal tenacity; bribes, threats, assaults, arson, hired thugs and even murder were commonly used. At every stage of the election, during the nomination of candidates, the polling, the counting of votes and even during the announcement of results, Akintola's NNDP used its position in government to try to rig the result and secure a return to power. Electoral officers disappeared or refused to receive nomination papers of opposition candidates and declared NNDP candidates elected unopposed; other officers had their appointments revoked after they accepted the nomination of opposition candidates. The hapless Federal Election Commission reported that its officers had been kidnapped and threatened with death. When nominations closed, sixteen NNDP candidates were duly declared 'returned unopposed'.

The polling itself was irregular. Large numbers of ballot papers disappeared from police custody; opposition party agents were obstructed; three electoral officers and two party polling agents were shot dead. But the most blatant tactics were used when the counting of votes was finished. Returning officers refused to declare the result of the poll after the count, enabling false results to be broadcast from the regional capital, Ibadan. In several cases, when returning officers did declare opposition candidates elected, the official results broadcast on the radio announced that NNDP candidates had been elected. Both sides claimed victory. But when the UPGA leader, Adegbenro, stated he would form a government, he was arrested and obliged to retract his remarks. The official results gave Akintola's NNDP seventy-one seats; the Action Group, fifteen; and the NCNC, two.

Once Akintola had been reinstated as prime minister, the Western Region descended into lawless turmoil in which hundreds died. Spreading from rural areas to the towns, a wave of riots, arson and political murders gradually engulfed the whole area bringing administration to the verge of collapse; taxes went uncollected, local courts ceased to function, law and order crumbled. But despite these desperate circumstances, the Federal Government stood by impassively. Whereas Balewa had been only too ready to intervene in the Western Region in 1962 after a few unruly incidents had occurred in parliament, in order to crush the Action Group government, when faced with a real emergency, he refused to take any measures that would harm his corrupt ally, Akintola.

The end of civilian rule came with sudden and violent finality. On 15 January 1966, after three months of chaos in the Western Region and mounting disgust with the flagrantly corrupt and avaricious manoeuvres of the country's politicians, a group of young army majors attempted to mount a revolution, overthrowing the entire order. In the early hours of the morning, rebel officers in Lagos seized the Federal prime minister, Sir Abubakar Tafawa Balewa, took him outside the city and executed him by the side of the road, dumping his body in a ditch; in Ibadan, the capital of the Western Region, Akintola was killed by rebel troops after a brief gun-battle; and in Kaduna, the Sardauna of Sokoto, premier of the Northern Region, was shot dead at his residence. Senior army officers, also on the deathlist, were killed.

But the revolution then faltered and finally failed. In Lagos, the army commander, Major-General Aguiyi-Ironsi, alerted by the wife of one of his murdered officers, rallied loyal troops and began to consolidate his control over the army. By noon only one city—Kaduna—was in the hands of the rebel group. In a broadcast from Kaduna, Major Chukwuma Nzeogwu, one of the leading conspirators, declared martial law, announced that the Regional government and assembly had been dissolved and instructed civil servants to run the administration. 'Our enemies,' he said, 'are the political profiteers, swindlers, the men in the high and low places who seek bribes and demand ten per cent, those that seek to keep the country divided permanently so that they can remain in office as ministers and VIPs of waste, the tribalists, the nepotists.' He then listed ten proclamations, one of which decreed the death penalty for such offences as embezzlement, bribery, corruption, rape, homosexuality and 'obstruction of the revolution'. But Nzeogwu's position after the failure of other rebel groups was untenable. Two days later, having obtained from Ironsi guarantees of safe conduct and immunity from prosecution for rebel soldiers, Nzeogwu surrendered. He was then flown to Lagos and imprisoned along with other ringleaders.

The military regime which now assumed power, with General Ironsi at its head, was greeted with popular acclaim in many parts of Nigeria. In the South, as discredited ministers and politicians were swept out of office, there were scenes of wild rejoicing. Within days the spate of violence which had gripped the West for the past three months subsided. In the North, the reaction was more subdued, but radical Northerners and minority groups welcomed the downfall of the Sardauna's autocratic regime, and traditional emirs came forth with pledges of loyalty to the new government. In the aftermath of the majors' coup, however, as Northerners began to weigh up the full impact, their doubts and suspicions about the motives behind it began to take hold. All but one of the seven principal conspirators, it was noted, were from the East's major tribe, the Ibo. In the murders that they had organised, the North had lost its two most important political leaders—Balewa and the Sardauna of Sokoto—and virtually all its senior army officers. Yet no Ibo politician, neither of the two Ibo regional premiers for example, had been killed and only one senior Ibo officer, the quartermaster general, had died and that had only happened, so it was said, because he had refused to hand over the keys of an armoury. Moreover, the result of the coup had been to wrest power away from the North and to install a military government led by an Ibo, General Ironsi. Brooding over their suspicions of these events, Northerners became more and more convinced that the majors' coup in January, far from being an attempt by radicals to rid the country of a corrupt and profligate regime, was in fact part of an Ibo conspiracy to gain control. The evidence which undermined this theory was of no account. As more myths and sinister rumours embellished the notion in the following months, fear and resentment in the North steadily mounted.

Ironsi was ill-prepared to survive such dangerous cross-currents. A bluff, forty-one year old officer who had risen from the ranks of the old colonial army, he had been thrust unexpectedly into a position of power, lacking any kind of political instinct. Once in command, he acted simply by administrative fiat. One decision after another, taken in what he thought were the interests of efficiency or sensible administration, served only to alienate Northerners further. Believing that 'regionalism' was the root cause of Nigeria's problems, Ironsi proclaimed himself in favour of a united Nigeria and appointed a commission to inquire into the 'unification' of the regional civil services. 'In the new order there should be no place for regionalism and tribal consciousness,' he declared in February. Yet for Northerners, control over their own regional civil service was prized as a crucial safeguard against domination by the more experienced Southerners. In a unified Nigeria, they feared, Northerners would fare badly competing against the huge, educated Ibo elite for government jobs, and risk losing administrative power. To make matters worse, Ironsi named an Ibo civil servant to head the commission. Indeed, though Ironsi showed no particular favour to the East—he chose a bodyguard of Northern soldiers—many of the key advisers who surrounded him were Ibo civil servants, creating the impression of an Ibo clique at the centre of power.

Some of the issues facing Ironsi were unavoidably contentious. Army promotions were needed to fill gaps left by the January events and, since the majority of senior officers were Ibos, Ibo officers benefited substantially from the new appointments. Whereas before January Ibos had held five out of twelve operational command posts in infantry battalions, by May they held ten out of thirteen. To the Northern rank and file, already aggrieved by the loss of popular Northern commanders in January, these promotions were taken simply as examples of a growing Ibo takeover. Ironsi was further beset by difficulties over the fate of the January conspirators, still held in detention. In the North, and especially among the Northern rank and file of the army, there were vehement views that they should be brought to trial for murder and mutiny. In the South, where they were seen as heroes, there were persistent demands for their release. Ironsi's answer was to prevaricate. But criticism of his regime, from the South for failing to move decisively enough, from the North for moving too fast, became increasingly vocal.

At the end of May, Ironsi took action precipitately and with disastrous consequences. Without waiting for official reports from his advisory commissions, he suddenly promulgated a new constitution. Nigeria, he declared in a broadcast, had ceased to be a federation, the Regions were abolished, and the Regional civil services were to be unified. In addition, all political and tribal organisations were proscribed and political activity was banned for two years. The reaction to these measures came swiftly. In the North, civil servants and students staged anti-government demonstrations which soon flared into popular riots against Ibos living in the *sabon garis*, the strangers' quarters sited outside the walls of Northern towns. Armed thugs crossing into the *sabon garis* went on the rampage attacking Ibos and destroying their homes and property. Several hundred Ibos were killed. Shaken by the riots, Ironsi gave assurances that there would be no major constitutional changes made without public consultation, but he seemed otherwise unaware of how intense were the pressures building up among Northerners and within the army. The May riots, however, were but a token of the deep hatreds and fear that had taken hold in the North and that were to burst out again and again in far greater waves of vengeance.

The North struck back ferociously at the end of July. In a counter-coup led by junior Northern officers, Ironsi was seized, flogged and executed; scores more Eastern officers and other ranks were rounded up and murdered. For three days, Nigeria was left without a government and without leadership, while a group of senior Northern officers, meeting in an army barracks near Lagos, argued heatedly over the future of the country. The Northern troops who had staged the coup, having taken their revenge, wanted the North to secede. The advice of civil servants brought into the discussions was that secession would lead to social and economic disaster in the North and involve insuperable problems for the army. In the tense disputes that followed, the army chief of staff, Lt-Colonel Yakubu Gowon, gradually gained the upper hand. Gowon, a thirty-one year old Northerner from a minority tribe in the Middle Belt and a devout Christian, was closely aligned with the young modern Nigerian elite which opposed dissolution of the Federation, but he was also acceptable to the Northern secessionists as a new army commander. By a narrow margin, the threat of secession was averted and Gowon was chosen as Supreme Commander. But the fate of the Federation remained far from clear.

The Northerners' coup had succeeded in the North, the West and in Lagos, but not in the Eastern Region where the existing government under the military governor, Lt-Colonel

Emeka Ojukwu, an Ibo officer, retained control. Ojukwu refused to accept Gowon's position as Supreme Commander and made clear his view that the July coup had effectively divided Nigeria into two parts. Because tribal killings inside the army still continued, the commanders on both sides agreed to the repatriation of Northerners from the East and Easterners from the North in what amounted to a formal division of the army. To help decide the political future of the country, Gowon convened a constitutional conference in Lagos in September to which each Region sent civilian representatives. The delegates from the North, the West and the East all brought with them proposals for a loose confederal arrangement that would separate the Regions further; only delegates from the small, multi-tribal, Mid-West wanted to retain a Federation with a strong central government, but one that would be altered by the creation of new states to divide up the three main Regions. During the conference proceedings, however, the Northern delegates produced a new set of proposals dramatically different from their original ones. They now pressed, like the Mid-West representatives, for a strong central government and the creation of more states. This sudden change was brought about partly through the influence of Northern civil servants in Lagos who saw clearly the economic and administrative disadvantages of breaking up the Federation, and partly because of the rising importance of minority tribes, like those of the Middle Belt, with large contingents in the army, which wanted local autonomy for themselves yet a strong central government that could protect them from powerful neighbours. Before the conference could reach any conclusion, however, another violent upheaval engulfed the North.

This time the killing was on a far more terrible scale, and the purpose was not simply to seek vengeance but to drive Easterners out of the North altogether. All the envy, resentment and mistrust that Northerners felt for the minority Eastern communities living in their midst burst out with explosive force into a pogrom that the authorities made no attempt to stop. Disgruntled local politicians, civil servants and students were active in getting the mobs onto the streets and this time Northern troops joined the rampage. In the savage onslaught that followed, thousands of Easterners died or were maimed, and as others sought to escape the violence, a massive exodus to the East began. Abandoning all their possessions, hundreds of thousands of Easterners—traders, artisans, clerks and labourers—fled from their Northern homes. From other parts of Nigeria, too, as the climate of fear spread among Ibos living there, thousands more, including civil servants and academics, joined the exodus. By the end of the year, more than a million refugees, many of them wounded, exhausted or in a state of shock, had sought safety in the East. And amid a sense of outrage and bitterness at the fearful sequence of events that had occurred—the downfall of Ironsi, the return of Northerners to power, the murder of Eastern officers, the months of persecution and the massacres of September and October—Eastern leaders made plans for secession.

The key figure in the East was now Ojukwu. Until the Northerners' coup in July, he had been unpopular as military governor of the Eastern Region, but afterwards he came to be acclaimed as the saviour of the Ibo people. An ambitious and clever man, 34 years old, the son of a wealthy Ibo businessman, with an Oxford degree and training in Britain as an army officer, he relished the exercise of political power and skilfully rallied the Ibos behind him. Spurred on by an inner circle of Ibo advisers, mostly displaced civil servants and academics who had become fervent Ibo nationalists, Ojukwu began to sever the remaining links with the Federation. Though there were still possibilities for concilation that could have given Easterners the security they sought, he made little effort at compromise. In October he ordered the expulsion of all non-Easterners from the Region on the grounds that he could no longer assure their safety. He refused to send back Eastern delegates to the constitutional conference which had resumed in Lagos, or to travel there himself for negotiations, saying that he feared for his life, and he called on Easterners still living in other parts of the Federation to return home. In January 1967, at a conference in Ghana, Ojukwu and Gowon met face to face, but their discussions proved abortive. In April, Ojukwu issued decrees appropriating all Federal revenues collected in the East and giving the East control of

Federal corporations, railways, schools and courts. While this process of gradual withdrawal was underway, the government radio and press kept popular opinion at fever pitch with a constant stream of propaganda, stressing details of the atrocities that had taken place and warning of the threats of genocide. As the stories were told and re-told, the numbers that had died in the North, once reliably estimated at about 7,000, were raised higher and higher, until in later years Ojukwu asserted that 50,000 had perished. The effect of the propaganda, as well as binding Ibos together against the Northern threat, produced a momentum of its own towards secession.

For the East, secession was a far more viable proposition than for the landlocked North. The Eastern Region contained seaports and rich oilfields that were beginning to produce valuable revenues. By April 1967, after six months of preparation, Ojukwu's government had built up a full administration, trained its own armed forces, purchased arms supplies and acquired local sources of revenue, all sufficient to sustain an independent state. Yet the East was far from being a united, homogenous area. Just as in the North the power and the influence of the Hausa-Fulani were resented by minority tribes in the Middle Belt, so in the East the dominant role played by the Ibo was disliked by minorities such as the Ibibio, Ijaw and Efik, which altogether represented more than one third of the East's thirteen million population and which in the past had often campaigned for their own separate states. In the aftermath of the 1966 massacres in the North, when these minorities had been caught up in the waves of vengeance directed mainly at the Ibo, sympathy and support for the Eastern cause was strong, but this sense of solidarity soon dissipated, and among the minorities there was far less enthusiasm for the idea of an Eastern secession that would leave them permanently under Ibo control. Yet without the minority areas, secession was unviable, for it was in the minority areas that the seaports, the rich oilfields and half of the land lay.

As Ojukwu made his final moves before breaking away, Gowon, determined to hold the Federation together, struck decisively at this weakness in the East's position. Having first obtained the agreement of the North and the West, he issued a decree on 27 May abolishing the four Regions and creating in their place twelve new states. The North was divided into six and the East into three separate states. Thus, in one fell swoop, the old power blocs dominated for so long by the Hausa-Fulani, the Yoruba and the Ibo were broken apart, giving minority tribes a voice of their own and placating Southern fears of Northern hegemony. Gowon's measures came too late to affect the launching of Biafra, but by offering the Eastern minorities new states of their own freed from Ibo rule, he gave them new cause to remain loyal to the Federation, thus undermining Ojukwu's strategy for survival. Three days later, on 30 May 1967, a year after the first riots against Ibo in the North, Ojukwu proclaimed amid high jubilation the independence of the new state of Biafra.

The Nigerian civil war began in fits and starts in July 1967, with bizarre and confusing episodes, fought haphazardly by two armies with raw and inexperienced troops. Gowon looked on it at the time merely as a 'police action'; Ojukwu too was confident that the fighting would be resolved in a matter of weeks. But it grew into a terrible war of attrition that lasted two and a half years, arousing passionate argument and controversy around the world, and in the end cost nearly a million lives.

Both sides took the initiative. Attacking from the north and along the southern coastline, Gowon's Federal forces made rapid advances into Biafran territory. But in a surprise counter-attack Ojukwu sent a flying column of a thousand men, riding in an assortment of private cars, 'mammy wagons', cattle trucks and police and army vans, across the Niger river into the Mid-West state, with the hope of reaching Lagos. In the air a single, aged Biafran B26 bomber, one of two Ojukwu had purchased in Europe, circled over Lagos dropping several crude explosives; other towns were bombed in similar fashion. But the Biafran advance towards Lagos was halted and, after occupying the Mid-West for two months, Biafran forces withdrew eastwards across the Niger river, never to threaten the Federal side again.

The Biafrans suffered further setbacks. In October the capital, Enugu, close to the northern border, and the southern port of Calabar fell to Federal forces and, once the eastern border with Cameroon had been sealed off by Federal troops, Biafra became an encircled, embattled enclave, bombed and strafed daily by Gowon's newly acquired air force and surrounded by an army of 100,000 men which grew ever larger. At intervals there were prolonged lulls in the fighting and local stalemates on the ground, but steadily Biafra was forced to concede more ground. By mid-1968, after the fall of Port Harcourt, Biafra had lost half of its territory, all its major towns and airports, its oil refinery and most of its oilfields. Furthermore, the funds which Ojukwu had used to purchase arms supplies abroad were all but exhausted. Only an occasional planeload of arms reached the enclave; in the front line, Biafran troops were rationed to four rounds each. Reduced to a landlocked, impoverished region of only 5,000 square miles, crowded with refugees, short of food, running out of ammunition, Biafra seemed on the point of defeat.

But Ojukwu remained defiant. Though the scale of suffering was reaching appalling heights, he doggedly held fast to the idea of an independent state. Even when international efforts were made to mediate between the two sides, he showed no willingness to compromise. The strategy for survival he chose instead proved to be remarkably effective. Initially, at the beginning of the war when Ojukwu was confident of success, Biafra was portrayed as a strong and resilient nation which deserved support. 'There is no power in this country, or in Black Africa, to subdue us by force,' he declared in May 1967. After the fall of the capital, Enugu, in October, however, as Biafra came under siege, a different ploy was used. With brilliant success, Ojukwu's Directorate of Propaganda set out to convince the Ibos inside the enclave and foreign opinion in the world outside that the Lagos government was bent on a policy of mass slaughter.

This theme of genocide became one of the most potent weapons in the war. For the Ibos, gripped by memories of the Northern pogroms of 1966, the fear of genocide was real enough and provided every reason to fight on, whatever the odds against them appeared to be. In the outer areas of Biafra where minority tribes lived, Federal troops made comparatively rapid progress and in some places their arrival was actually welcomed by local inhabitants; but in the hard core of Biafra—the Ibo heartland, as it was known—the Ibos, often poorly armed and equipped, fought on with extraordinary tenacity and determination, believing that otherwise they would be wiped out. Such courage on its own, however, was not sufficient to keep Biafra alive and what prevented imminent defeat, and therefore prolonged the war, was the growing intervention of foreign sympathisers.

The plight of Biafra during 1968 produced waves of alarm and anxiety in Europe and America. Hitherto Ojukwu's efforts to attract international support or attention had been unsuccessful. But early that year he mounted a publicity campaign, with the help of a Geneva public relations firm, Markpress, and of Biafran envoys who toured the world stressing that Biafra was now fighting against genocide and that without international support the survival of the Ibo people was in jeopardy. Ojukwu believed that provided Biafra could hold out for long enough, international pressure would eventually force the Federal government to accept a ceasefire and a political settlement that would guarantee Biafra's autonomy. From early 1968 foreign support for Biafra steadily mounted. Church organisations, notably the Catholic Church whose missionaries had stayed behind in Biafra, became actively sympathetic; foreign visitors too came away from Biafra impressed by the stature of Ojukwu and the strength of Ibo nationalism. But what finally galvanised Western opinion was the spectre of mass starvation among refugees in Biafra as the Federal noose slowly tightened. Biafra for the West became a symbol of suffering and persecution. Its very determination to fight on under such terrible conditions lent credence to the fear of genocide. In Europe, no other foreign issue at the time aroused such deep emotion. In the United States, Biafra rated as the most important foreign issue after Vietnam. And what followed from the public outcry in the West about the fate of Biafra was the largest privately organised relief operation in history.

Relief missions to Biafra had started in January 1968 with a few church organisations improvising a supply run by buying space on planes carrying military supplies for Ojukwu from Europe. Later the churches and other agencies acquired their own aircraft. But the scale of relief soon needed was enormous. By mid-year, the small remaining pocket of Biafran territory held eight million people—one third of them refugees, many packed into fetid camps, dying in hundreds and later in thousands every day. In response to this catastrophe, the relief agencies organised a major airlift of food and medical supplies, using the same routes as the gun-runners. At its height in mid-1969, more than forty relief flights every night were made into Biafra. In all, they totalled nearly 8,000. The conditions under which the flights were made were hazardous. After the fall of Port Harcourt, the last major airport, in May 1968, the only landing strip available for relief flights was a makeshift runway near Uli. At Ojukwu's insistence, the relief flights heading for Uli were allowed to operate only at night, for then they provided cover for arms flights making the same run into Biafra. Though the Federal side was willing to approve a daylight flight scheme, Ojukwu refused to accept one. Nor would he agree to a supervised land corridor for relief supplies, for this would have rendered unnecessary the heroic airlift which had come to dramatise to the outside world Biafra's plight, as well as depriving the arms flights of their cover. So, until the end of the war, the same risky Biafra run was made.

The relief operation was vital to Biafra not only in providing food and medical supplies for a desperate civilian population, but also as an invaluable source of revenue for Ojukwu. All the expenses that the relief agencies incurred inside Biafra—the purchase of locally grown food, the hire of transport, the cost of building materials for refugee camps—all these were paid for in foreign currency in Europe which Ojukwu then used to buy military supplies and other foreign purchases. Indeed, in mid 1968, when Biafra was on the verge of collapse, the foreign currency which the relief agencies paid over was Ojukwu's only source of income. To this extent, the relief effort was used to finance the war and keep Biafra in the field.

In the critical months of 1968, as the impact of the Biafran war spread around the world, other help was forthcoming. Four African states—the Ivory Coast, Gabon, Tanzania and Zambia—hoping that their actions would improve the chances of a ceasefire, announced diplomatic recognition of Biafra. Though of little practical effort, their support, coming at a time when spirits were low, lifted morale and seemed to constitute a breakthrough in the struggle for survival. Even more significant were signs of encouragement from France. Partly in response to domestic political pressures and public opinion which was running strongly in Biafra's favour, partly because it suited French interests in Africa, de Gaulle at the end of July 1968 expressed his sympathy for the Biafran cause and subsequently authorised the clandestine supply of French arms for Biafra routed indirectly through the Ivory Coast and Gabon. By the end of September, large deliveries of French arms were arriving in Biafra. Despite this show of support, however, de Gaulle's interest in Biafra was no more than marginal, and the arms supplied to Ojukwu, though helping him to fight on, were enough only to help sustain a war of attrition. While de Gaulle was dealing unofficially with the Biafrans, at the same time he maintained diplomatic relations with Nigeria. Indeed, during the Nigerian civil war, France held its place as Nigeria's fourth most important trading partner. One other foreign state, Portugal, the last colonial power in Africa, provided indispensable assistance throughout the war. Portugal allowed air traffic for Biafra to use Portuguese staging posts in Guinea-Bissau and São Tomé, an island 300 miles southeast of the Nigerian coastline. Most of the traffic was controlled from offices in Lisbon. Portugal's purpose was to keep African states in disarray, and its assistance was forthcoming strictly on business terms; but without those vital lifelines, Biafra would have met defeat at the outset. Whatever the motive was, the foreign aid that Biafra received—relief supplies, French arms, diplomatic recognition, staging posts—all helped to sustain the war effort and reinforced Ojukwu's determination to fight on.

Ojukwu's intransigence, however, eventually stirred disagreement inside the Biafran camp. Moderate Biafrans, like Nnamdi Azikiwe, the highly respected nationalist leader and former President of Nigeria, who had done much to win international support for Biafra at the outset, argued that the scale of suffering had reached such heights that a negotiated compromise was preferable to a war which clearly could no longer be won. In 1969, in a major blow to the Biafran cause, Azikiwe switched to the Federal side. Foreign supporters were also dismayed by Ojukwu's unwillingness to seek terms and international sympathy for Biafra began to wane. After a team of foreign military observers had concluded in 1968 that there was no evidence to support Biafran claims about genocide, the propaganda machine that the Biafrans had used so successfully to arouse concern for their plight lost much of its impact. In military terms, Biafra was faced at best with a grinding war of endurance. The Federal government by 1969 possessed an army of 250,000 men, an air force equipped with Russian and Czech planes and a supply system backed up by Britain and Russia. And though at times the Nigerian military was inert, cumbersome and poorly led, it had every advantage on its side. Against such an army, Biafra was fighting with makeshift tactics and means. White mercenaries were hired; a miniature air force of light aircraft was raised with the help of an elderly Swedish aristocrat, Count von Rosen, and used to bomb Federal positions. But such efforts were of little avail.

Biafra collapsed suddenly in January 1970. Weary, demoralised and short of food, its people were desperate for peace. On 10 January, two days before Biafra formally surrendered, Ojukwu fled to exile in the Ivory Coast, still defiant, still warning of the threat of genocide. In a final statement, he explained that he had departed 'knowing that whilst I live, Biafra lives'. The aftermath of the war, however, was remarkable for its compassion and mercy, and the way in which the memories of Biafra soon faded. In Lagos, Gowon vigorously pursued a policy of clemency, pledging a general amnesty for those who had fought against the Federal government and encouraging Ibos in the tasks of reconstruction. No medals for services in the war were awarded; no reparations were demanded. Biafran rebels were reabsorbed in the Federal army; civil servants returned to their posts in the Federal government; and property belonging to Ibos in the north and other Federal areas was restored to them. 'In the history of warfare,' the writer, John de St Jorre, remarked, after observing the transition to peace in Biafra, 'there can rarely have been such a bloodless end and such a merciful aftermath.'

CHAPTER TWENTY-TWO

The Plight of Uganda

Uganda began its independence in 1962 in a climate of goodwill and great promise. Its position as one of the most prosperous and well managed states in East Africa seemed assured. What difficulties had occurred over the status of the kingdom of Buganda before independence had been resolved in a spirit of compromise which augured well for the country's future. Under a carefully constructed federal constitution, Buganda was allowed a measure of internal autonomy, retaining its own parliament, the Lukiiko, and monarchic traditions, while the central government in Kampala remained in effective control nationally. Since none of the three parties contesting the 1962 elections had gained a clear majority, the independence government consisted of a coalition between the largest party, the Uganda People's Congress, headed by Milton Obote, and the Baganda royalist party, the Kabaka Yekka. Though only a marriage of convenience between two ill-assorted partners, one with nationalist aspirations, the other tied firmly to tribal tradition, the coalition provided a government broadly representative of the whole country, which Obote led as prime minister initially with due regard for conservative interests. This spirit of cooperation was endorsed in 1963 when the Kabaka, Sir Edward Mutesa, was chosen with Obote's support as head of state.

As a political leader, Obote was a lacklustre figure with limited popular appeal, but he was ambitious, resourceful and a skilful tactician, and with considerable flair he set out to gain absolute control. Patiently he lured members of parliament away from the Kabaka Yekka and the opposition Democratic Party, persuading them to defect to his UPC, until by 1964 he had gained an outright majority in the National Assembly. With new confidence, he then began to speak out on the virtues of a one-party state. 'Organised opposition against the government is a typical capitalist notion,' he declared in January 1964. His argument, commonly used by politicians advocating a one-party system, was that tribal and factional groupings tended to threaten the stability of the country and that a one-party state was needed to forge a sense of national unity. Obote's tactics proved remarkably successful. By August 1964, after further defections to the UPC, he had acquired a two-thirds majority in the National Assembly, and that month he disbanded his increasingly fractious alliance with the remnant of Kabaka Yekka. By the end of the year, after the Democratic Party leader and other opposition politicians had crossed the floor, Obote's position in parliament was seemingly impregnable.

His achievement, however, was deceptive. As well as alienating the Baganda, Obote's drive for a one-party state and the increasingly autocratic and secretive manner he adopted in government aroused within the UPC a great deal of dissension and intrigue and opened up tribal rifts within the party. Since its formation in 1960, the UPC had represented little more than a coalition of local political groups; it lacked both a strong organisation and a popular mass following. Its role as the country's major political party was complicated by the intricate mosaic of tribal interests on which Uganda was founded. The broad division occurred between the Bantu tribes of the south, such as the Baganda, and the Nilotic and Sudanic tribes of the north, such as the Acholi and the Langi, to which Obote belonged; but as much rivalry was to be found amongst southerners or amongst northerners as between the north and the south. In the crisis that developed over Obote's leadership, the main split was between northerners who supported Obote and favoured radical policies and a group of southerners, led by Grace Ibingira, a government minister and high party official, who preferred a more moderate course, especially in dealings with Uganda's hereditary rulers like the Kabaka. For Obote, the crisis nearly proved fatal. What saved him from defeat was the close relationship he had prudently developed since independence with the police and the army and in particular with a senior army officer named Idi Amin.

Amin, who was destined to become the most notorious African dictator of modern times, had risen with spectacular speed in the hierarchy of the Ugandan army. Recruited during British rule in 1946 to serve in the King's African Rifles, he was virtually illiterate, with only a rudimentary education and limited intelligence, yet he possessed those qualities of loyalty, stamina and leadership ability which marked him out as ideal material for the ranks of the British colonial army. A man of huge physique, he excelled at sport and marksmanship and for nine years he held the national title of heavyweight boxing champion. Serving in the *Mau Mau* campaign, he was promoted to corporal and in the following years he rose steadily until he reached the rank of sergeant-major, the highest position then open to African soldiers. When the search for potential African officers began before independence, Amin was an obvious possibility, yet however outstanding British officers had found him as an NCO, his lack of education was clearly a serious obstacle to further promotion. On special army education courses to which he was sent, he made little headway. In the press of events leading to independence, however, such drawbacks were overlooked. In 1961, at about the age of thirty-five, Amin was given a commission.

Further problems then arose to cloud his career. In 1962, after a military operation in Kenya's Northern Frontier District in which Amin participated, complaints were made to the Kenyan authorities that he had murdered three Turkana tribesmen. British officials in Nairobi dealing with the case wanted criminal charges brought against Lieutenant Amin, but the Governor of Uganda, Sir Walter Coutts, pointed out that to put on trial for murder one of the only two African officers in the Ugandan army some six months before independence would be politically disastrous. He asked instead that Amin should be returned to Uganda to face a court martial or other proceedings. The final decision on Amin's future was left to Obote, then in his first months in office as prime minister. When the matter was put to him, Obote recommended that Amin should merely be reprimanded. Thus reprieved, Amin continued his climb to the top, and even faster than before. Because British officers were withdrawn from the army rapidly after the 1964 soldiers' mutiny, Amin was promoted to the rank of lieutenant-colonel, given command of his own battalion and appointed deputy commander of the army. He soon became a familiar figure in the capital, Kampala, introduced into Obote's inner circle, invited frequently to State House, provided with a Mercedes car and other perquisites and clearly trusted by Obote as a bluff, loyal and simple soldier who would do his bidding without too much scruple.

Amin received his first special assignment from Obote in secret at the end of 1964. His mission was to travel to the Congo to assist the Stanleyville rebels in their campaign against the central government in Léopoldville. Obote had decided on this course of action without the knowledge of his cabinet, consulting only two ministers, one of whom was a cousin. Inside the Congo, Amin achieved some success. Coming himself from a border area of north-west Uganda which had close tribal ties with the Congo and the southern Sudan, he was able to enlist a large number of dissidents. He was also entrusted to smuggle out of the Congo consignments of gold, ivory and coffee to be used to pay for arms and equipment for the rebel cause. But rumours of his activities soon abounded in Kampala and were seized upon by Obote's critics both inside and outside the government.

In March 1965, an opposition MP, Daudi Ocheng, an outspoken northerner who also served as secretary-general of the Kabaka Yekka, claimed in parliament that Amin, Obote and the two ministers privy to the Congo operation had been dealing illicitly in gold and ivory smuggled from the Congo, and as evidence he produced what purported to be a copy of Amin's bank statement showing deposits in a period of less than a month amounting to £17,000. Ocheng was promised a government investigation, but for nearly a year Obote succeeded in obstructing the issue. On 4 February 1966, however, Ocheng, who by then was mortally ill, returned to the attack. Brandishing the same copy of Amin's bank statement before parliament, he presented a motion demanding that Amin should be suspended from duty while his bank account was investigated. He accused Amin of plundering gold, ivory and coffee from the Congo and sharing the proceeds with Obote and his two colleagues. He went further, claiming that Amin was planning to seize power on

Obote's behalf. 'The reason why Colonel Amin has not been subjected to the searching eyes of the law,' he declared, 'is because he is the man through whom a few individuals in the Government are planning a coup to overthrow the Constitution.' To general astonishment, one UPC member after another, including six ministers, rose in support of Ocheng's motion demanding Amin's suspension and an official inquiry. The motion was tantamount to a vote of no confidence in Obote. Only one dissenting vote was cast.

Assured of support from Amin and the police, Obote struck back decisively. On 22 February, while the Cabinet was meeting to consider the terms of reference for a commission of inquiry into Ocheng's allegations, armed police burst into the Cabinet room and surrounded the ministers there. On Obote's signal, five leading ministers, including Grace Ibingira, the UPC secretary-general and Obote's most prominent critic, were seized, handcuffed, dragged out of the Cabinet meeting and thrown into prison. Obote then issued a statement declaring that he was temporarily assuming all powers. Two days later, he abrogated the constitution, suspended the National Assembly and dismissed the Kabaka as president. The army commander, Brigadier Shaban Opolot, who was related by marriage to the Kabaka, was removed from operational control, then later dismissed and arrested. In his place, Amin was appointed as the new army commander. On 15 April, at one day's notice, Obote reconvened the National Assembly and, while truckloads of Amin's troops patrolled the streets outside and air force jets wheeled overhead in formation, he gave parliamentarians the outlines of a new constitution. The main point was that Obote was to become executive president of a unified state endowed with immense powers. When he had finished speaking, the MPs were told that a vote would immediately be taken on the new constitution. None of them was given an opportunity to see the constitution; nor were they allowed to debate the matter. They were merely informed by Obote that copies of the constitution would shortly be placed in their pigeonholes. Members of the opposition walked out, but the remaining MPs, in a duly compliant mood, approved the new constitution by fifty-five votes to four.

The impact of the new constitution was felt most directly in Buganda. Many of the safeguards for which the Baganda had fought so tenaciously before independence—their autonomous powers, their control over local administration, law courts and finance and the right they retained to hold indirect elections to the National Assembly—all these were swept away. The Kabaka and the other three hereditary kings of Uganda were transformed into purely ceremonial figures, barred from holding any other public office. In the misguided belief that Obote could be challenged by legal action, the Baganda parliament, the Lukiiko, passed a resolution asserting that Obote's constitution was illegal and that the Kabaka still remained the country's rightful president. To force the issue further, the Lukiiko passed another resolution on 20 May requiring Obote's central government to leave Baganda territory, and hence Kampala, within ten days. It was a futile and dangerous gesture to make. The Baganda, however resourceful, were a minority tribe, constituting no more than sixteen per cent of the population, whose pre-eminent role in Uganda's affairs had long been resented elsewhere in the country. They had neither allies nor any means with which to defend their actions against a powerful and determined central government. And the Lukiiko's defiant manoeuvre merely gave Obote the opportunity he had long sought to crush the Baganda in the name of national unity.

Obote's immediate response was to order the arrest of three prominent Baganda chiefs, primarily responsible for organising the Lukiiko's motion. As news of their arrest spread, government cars were stoned and the Kabaka's supporters threw up barricades on the roads leading from Kampala to the Kabaka's palace on Mengo Hill, three miles from the capital, and rallied in large numbers to the palace compound. Meeting with his advisers in Kampala, Obote decided on military action and instructed Amin to attack the palace. Early on the morning of 23 May, Amin's troops advanced, but met unexpected resistance from the palace guard. On Amin's orders, the palace was then shelled by artillery and Amin himself led a second and stronger attack. The palace was ransacked and several hundred Baganda died. But during a torrential rainstorm, the Kabaka managed to escape after climbing a high perimeter wall and hailing a passing taxi. Walking westwards, he succeeded four weeks later in reaching the Congo, then travelled on to the kingdom of Burundi, from where he flew to London, arriving destitute and penniless. He spent the rest of his life in exile in London, living in a flat in Bermondsey lent to him by a friend, dependent on the dole and the generosity of friends, and died there of alcoholic poisoning in November 1969, a sad and lonely figure at the age of forty-five.

Whatever further resistance the Baganda attempted, Obote dealt with ruthlessly, determined to show that they were in effect a conquered people. Amin's troops were billeted in the Kabaka's palace; the Lukiiko was turned over to the Defence Ministry for use as offices; martial law was declared in the province; hundreds of Baganda were detained without trial; and Baganda political parties were outlawed. Finally, in a new constitution which Obote produced in 1967, awarding himself still greater powers, the four kingdoms of Uganda were abolished and Buganda was divided into four districts. When the Kabaka died in exile in 1969, Obote used the army to prevent the Baganda from paying their respects in the traditional manner at the Royal Tombs at Kasubi.

Once again, Obote's position seemed impregnable. His opponents were either in exile, or in detention, or remaining prudently quiet within the UPC. Opposition parties were no longer of any concern. And the powers now at his disposal were formidable. Having dispensed with the need to conciliate conservative factions, Obote declared a sharp move to the left, proposing a wide degree of state participation in industry, commerce and agriculture, and lauding the cause of the common man. Yet his regime depended largely on coercion to maintain control and the measures which Obote employed to keep himself in power became increasingly repressive. Through a secret police organisation known as the General Service Department, Obote built up an elaborate informer system which was widely feared and resented. He appointed as its commander a trusted cousin, Akena Adoko. After an assassination attempt by Baganda conspirators in December 1969, Obote imposed a nationwide emergency, banned all opposition parties and gave the General Service Department a free hand to arrest and imprison suspected opponents. In his nine years in office, he allowed neither a general election nor even a single parliamentary by-election for the score of seats that had fallen vacant.

Well aware that his survival in office had come to rest largely on the loyalty of the army, Obote was careful to build up a personal following in the officer corps and to look for support from among the large contingents of Acholi and Langi troops. His manoeuvres were matched by those of Amin, who in matters of his own safety was invariably shrewd and cunning. From his home district in the far northwestern corner of Uganda, Amin enlisted loyal groups of Kakwa, Madi and Lugbara tribesmen and he also recruited heavily from Nubian communities scattered in towns around Uganda. Descendants of southern Sudanese mercenaries used by the British authorites to pacify areas of Uganda, the Nubians were related directly to Amin's own tribal group from the West Nile region.

From a relatively small, cohesive force of about 1,000 men at the time of independence, the Ugandan army within ten years expanded to nearly 9,000 men. Its discipline was often poor and the rival attentions of Amin and Obote split it dangerously into factions. Both men became suspicious of each other's intentions. Amin resented the activities of the paramilitary General Service Department, recruited largely from Obote's Langi tribesmen, and he also disliked the manner in which Obote cultivated links with several senior Langi officers. Obote, in turn, began to look on Amin as a potential threat. Their differences were brought out into the open as a result of the assassination attempt made on Obote's life in December 1969. When soldiers arrived at Amin's house to tell him what had happened, Amin, mistaking their intentions, fled through the back of the house, scrambled over a fence and made his way to a secure barracks twenty miles away. His abrupt disappearance for several hours at the moment of crisis aroused doubts about Amin's loyalty and led to suspicions that he might have been involved. At a meeting of senior officers some weeks later, the army's deputy commander, Brigadier Pierino Okoya, an Acholi officer who supported Obote, quarrelled violently with Amin, accusing him of desertion and cowardice. A few days later, Okoya and his wife were found murdered.

Again Amin was suspected, but the evidence implicating him which came to light several months later was too flimsy to warrant action against him. Obote, however, cautiously began moves to dispense with Amin. In September 1970, while Amin was on an official mission to Cairo, Obote reorganised the military hierarchy. Amin was promoted and, in effect, deprived of direct operational control of army units. In his place, a brigadier loyal to Obote was given operational command. Confident that the army was secure, Obote left Uganda for Singapore on 11 January 1971 to attend a Commonwealth conference. Soon after he arrived there, he received reports from his officials in Kampala warning that Amin was involved in a plot to assassinate him on his return to Uganda. Obote's response was to order Amin's arrest. Learning of the order, Amin alerted his own network of loyal officers and troops. On the night of 24 January they seized control of Kampala.

Amin's coup was carried out with remarkably little resistance from within the army and greeted in many parts of Uganda with relief and enthusiasm. Throughout Buganda, the news of Obote's downfall brought rejoicing and popular demonstrations. Enjoying the role of a national hero, Amin began by adopting conciliatory measures that won him yet further applause. He released political prisoners, lifted the state of emergency and made arrangements for the body of the Kabaka to be brought back from England for a traditional burial. The Cabinet that he appointed consisted mainly of highly qualified civilians drawn from the ranks of the civil service, the legal profession and Makerere University. After the first Cabinet meeting, Amin's new ministers came away impressed, so they remarked, by his good nature and common sense. 'He was a model of decorum and generosity,' wrote Henry Kyemba, then secretary to the Cabinet and previously Obote's private secretary, whom Amin had allowed to return from Singapore to take up several key posts in the new government. Indeed, many of Amin's ministers and officials, even after they had fled from Uganda in fear for their lives, like Kyemba, recalled how affable and courteous at times he appeared. 'Face to face, he is relaxed, simple and charming,' wrote Godfrey Lule, a former Minister of Justice, in exile. 'He seems incapable of wrongdoing or of sanctioning any crime.' Amin's early pronouncements encouraged a sense of optimism. He stressed the temporary nature of military rule, disbanded the secret police, the General Service Department, promised free elections and lower taxes. In the first week of his regime, he spent much time travelling by helicopter and by car from one district to another, listening to elders, addressing meetings, covering more ground than Obote had done in nine years in office.

Yet Amin never felt secure. His coup had been carried out by only a small section of the army, principally with the support of an armoured battalion based in Kampala, and though the rest of the army offered little resistance, Amin lived in constant fear of a counter-attack by troops supporting Obote. Amin knew when he struck that most of the officer corps would remain loyal to Obote. Scores of officers were thus hunted down, captured, killed or imprisoned; others fled into exile in neighbouring Tanzania. In their place, Amin promoted men from his own West Nile district and Nubians, some of them from the ranks of the army, some who were not even professional soldiers but raw civilians recruited merely to serve as Amin's henchmen. To bolster his control among the rank and file, he arranged for the enlistment of thousands more men from his own tribal area and slowly edged out the large contingents of Acholi and Langi troops which he suspected were still loyal to Obote. Several hundred Langi and Acholi officers in the police, the General Service Department and the army were murdered in the first months of his regime. Then in mid-1971, the mass killing of Langi and Acholi troops in the army began. Between May and July, several thousand died in army barracks. The last survivors—more than five hundred held in a prison in southern Uganda—were murdered in groups in January 1972.

Throughout the eight years that he remained as President, Amin was preoccupied with brutally consolidating his power, always quick to perceive any threat and ruthless in eliminating it. The army he built rapidly into a force of 20,000 men, giving it powers of arrest and immunity from the law. Vast sums were spent on military equipment, airfields, barracks and armour, regardless of cost. The possibility of an attack by Obote's supporters from bases in Tanzania, which President Nyerere had authorised soon after the coup, constantly nagged him. On visits to Britain and Israel in 1971, he asked without success for military aircraft with which to attack Tanzania. But the main apparatus that Amin came to rely on to watch for any sign of dissent or opposition and to deal with it, consisted of three special units—the Military Police, a police group known as the Public Safety Unit, and an intelligence organisation called the State Research Bureau. These three units were staffed mainly with Amin's own Kakwa tribesmen, with Nubians and with southern Sudanese. They owed no loyalty other than to Amin; they were given unlimited powers; and they came to be regarded with utter dread.

What hope there had been that Amin's coup might mark a change for the better soon dwindled. Amin had no interest in the business of government, nor indeed any understanding of it. He ruled by whim, broadcasting his orders over the radio and plundering at will what he needed from the treasury. In cabinet meetings, ministers quickly learnt that to argue against him was both unprofitable and dangerous. The profligate manner in which he diverted funds for military use exacerbated the economic difficulties that the government had inherited from Obote. Foreign exchange reserves ran short; prices soared; consumer goods became unobtainable; and disillusionment with Amin's regime steadily spread.

To improve his popularity, Amin turned vindictively on Uganda's Asian community. As a wealthy, aloof, immigrant minority, controlling much of the country's trade and industry, the Asians were profoundly disliked. Some 30,000 Asians, though mostly born and brought up in Uganda, had chosen to retain British nationality. In August 1972, Amin ordered them to leave the country within three months. Their expulsion was acclaimed by much of the African population in Uganda and indeed in other African countries with unpopular Asian communities. But the real benefit was derived not by the expectant African populace but by Amin's army. The shops, the businesses, the property which the Asians were forced to leave behind, even their personal possessions, were taken as spoils by Amin's cronies. Many Asians, as they departed, were harassed, humiliated and robbed by soldiers. Within a few months, the huge amounts of Asian wealth had vanished. Shops were stripped then left bare; factories broke down; trade was severely disrupted. The decline in government services was equally sharp. For in the general exodus of the Asian community that occurred—some 50,000 left in all—a large proportion of the country's doctors, engineers and professional staff was lost.

In the middle of the Asian upheaval, in September 1972, Obote's supporters in exile invaded from Tanzania, hoping to provoke a general uprising against Amin. Poorly trained and ineptly led, their force of a thousand men was quickly routed. The revenge that Amin took for this escapade was horrific. In the first wave of reprisals that followed his coup in 1971, the killing had been confined largely to the army. Now Amin sought to eliminate civilians who were suspected of opposing him. Thousands died at the hands of his special squads. Again Langi and Acholi were among the prominent victims. But no-one was immune. The Chief Justice was dragged away from the High Court, never to be seen again. The University's Vice-Chancellor disappeared. Scores of prominent Ugandans were murdered. Others fled in hundreds into exile. Periodically, whenever a new threat emerged, more purges were carried out. In 1977 the Anglican Archbishop, Janan Luwuum, and eighteen other bishops signed a memorandum courageously speaking out about the 'suspicion, fear and hidden hatred' which the civilian population felt towards Amin's forces. They referred to 'a war against the educated' and accused the State Research Bureau of killing at will innocent citizens. A few days later, shortly after Amin had publicly denounced him, the Archbishop was murdered, his bullet-riddled body still in ecclesiastical robes dumped at the mortuary of a Kampala hospital. Amin claimed he had died in a car accident.

Uganda became a country where the rule of law and all notion of orderly government ceased to exist. Amin used the state and its resources simply to keep himself in power and his army satisfied. As one by one his civilian ministers were dismissed or fled into exile, bearing tales of atrocity and torture, Amin replaced them with military colleagues, mostly untrained and in some cases barely literate. The civil service, once the most advanced in East Africa, was reduced to a mere shell, its senior members either purged or escaping to safety abroad. As industry and commerce steadily deteriorated, Uganda reverted more and more to a subsistence society. What foreign exchange was earned from the country's declining agricultural exports like coffee was used mainly to buy military equipment and consumer goods for the army.

Ruling by fear, Amin constantly felt the need to demonstrate how powerful and important his position was. He promoted himself to the rank of field marshal, made himself president for life, and awarded himself military medals and titles like the Conqueror of the British Empire. He took sadistic pleasure in exploiting advantage over others, particularly ministers or civil servants, men with wide education and experience, for whom he held an instinctive distrust. To make sure that his first group of highly respected ministers recognised their proper place, he ordered them to enrol as cadets in the armed forces and to submit to military discipline, and he then proceeded to undermine their authority by telling privates in the army that they were entitled to arrest ministers on suspicion of subversive activities.

His treatment of expatriates living in Uganda, especially the British, was sometimes similar. A group of British residents, inducted as army reservists, were required to kneel in Amin's presence when they took the oath of loyalty, as a sign of his power over his former colonial masters. To impress African diplomats at a grand Kampala reception, Amin staged his entrance on a wooden litter borne by British carriers. When a British lecturer, Denis Hills, was arrested in 1975 for possessing a manuscript in which he described Amin as 'a village tyrant', Amin extracted as much advantage as possible. Hills was tried by a military tribunal, found guilty of treason and sentenced to death by firing squad. Using him as a pawn, Amin became the centre of world attention. Pleas for clemency arrived from the British prime minister, the Archbishop of Canterbury, the Pope and some fifty heads of state. Queen Elizabeth wrote him a personal letter which was conveyed to Uganda by a British general. When Hills was finally reprieved the British Foreign Secretary, James Callaghan, flew out to Kampala to collect him. All such events were duly recorded by photographers and cameramen for Amin's benefit.

However cruel, brutal and capricious many of Amin's actions may have seemed in some parts of the world, in much of Africa he was regarded as something of a hero. By expelling the Asian community, by nationalising foreign companies, by forthright attacks on Western imperialism, he was seen to be valiantly asserting African interests. The bizarre cables he sent to foreign leaders—wishing President Nixon 'a speedy recovery from Watergate', offering Edward Heath a post as bandmaster after his election defeat in Britain, advising Israel's Golda Meir 'to tuck up her knickers' and run to Washington—all these were taken as examples of Amin's fearless nature. At meetings of the Organisation of African Unity, of which he was chairman for one year in 1975, Amin's appearances inspired enthusiastic applause. Weighed down with his own medals and gold braid, a figure towering over other presidents, he was undoubtedly a star attraction. Only two African leaders—Nyerere of Tanzania and Kaunda of Zambia—saw fit to denounce him as a crude and vicious dictator.

Nor did Amin lack foreign backers. In 1972, one year after gaining power, he formed a profitable relationship with Libya's Colonel Gaddafi which endured until the last days of his regime. In return for funds from Libya, Amin, a Muslim, undertook to promote the Islamic cause in Uganda and to align his government firmly behind the Arab campaign against Israel. Though Uganda was a predominantly Christian country, with no more than six per cent of the population classed as Muslims, Amin's efforts earned him considerable support from the Arab world. Saudi Arabia as well as Libya was generous with loans. To replace an Israeli military misson, Amin turned to the Soviet Union for help with training and the supply of equipment. Amin's subsequent attacks on Israel were notoriously crude. At a Soviet embassy reception at which he was the guest of honour, he announced his intention to erect a monument in Uganda in commemoration of Hitler. In a telegram to the United Nations Secretary General, with a copy dropped to the Palestinian leader, Yasir Arafat, he praised the action of Palestinian guerrillas who had murdered Israeli participants at the Olympic Games, and he went on to extol Hitler's extermination of the Jews. The Palestinians were allowed to set up training facilities in Uganda and accorded official recognition. They were also recruited to help with Amin's dreaded State Research Bureau.

It was Amin's involvement with the Palestinians that led to his greatest humiliation. In June 1976, a group of pro-Palestinian terrorists hijacked an Air France airliner on a flight originating from Tel Aviv, flew to Entebbe and, with Amin's cooperation, holding hostage a hundred passengers, they demanded the release of Palestinian prisoners in Israel. In a dramatic and daring raid on 4 July, Israeli commandos routed a force of Ugandan soldiers guarding the airfield and rescued the hostages. The only revenge that Amin could take was against a lone elderly passenger, Dora Bloch, who had been taken to hospital in Kampala after choking on a piece of meat that was lodged in her throat. After the Israelis had left, two men from Amin's State Research Bureau hauled her out of bed and, in full view of hospital staff, dragged her screaming to a waiting car. Her body was dumped twenty miles from Kampala. In the following months Amin, still smarting from his humiliation, turned vindictively on the Christian churches in Uganda, ordering the expulsion of missionaries and arranging for a hostile radio broadcast to be made on Christmas Day. The climax of his campaign came with the murder of Archbishop Luwuum in February 1977.

At least a dozen assassination attempts were made on Amin, but with uncanny luck he survived them all. Guerrilla activity was also ineffective. The result in both cases was invariably to bring terrible reprisal. For Uganda's population, cowed and demoralised, there seemed no future other than to endure Amin's macabre tyranny. When he finally did run into trouble, it came not from Obote's guerrillas, or popular revolt, but from within the ranks of the army.

Amin had overcome several challenges from army factions in the past. In 1972 a group of Lugbara officers from northwestern Uganda, plotting to seize power, were killed. Two years later an uprising led by officers from Amin's own Kakwa tribe was bloodily suppressed. In 1978, rivalry and squabbling within the military hierarchy broke out anew, but this time the consequences were more serious. Amin fell out with his closest collaborators, removing some from office and arresting others. In August, an army battalion sought to overthrow him. Hoping to distract the army from growing disorder, Amin embarked on a desperate diversion which proved to be his undoing. In October, he ordered the invasion of the Kagera Salient in northern Tanzania, allowing his troops to loot and plunder at will. Hundreds of Tanzanian civilians were killed; others were captured and taken back to Uganda. After an orgy of destruction, Amin's troops withdrew.

In retaliation, Nyerere assembled a force of 45,000 troops and in January 1979 sent them across the Ugandan border with orders to attack and destroy two towns in southern Uganda, Masaka and Mbarara. Having accomplished that aim, Nyerere then decided to oust Amin altogether. As Tanzanian troops advanced towards Kampala, Amin in desperation appealed to Gaddafi for help. Gaddafi dispatched a thousand men, many of whom were thrown straight into battle, but to no avail. Amin's army, after initial resistance, broke and ran. Amin himself abandoned the capital, Kampala, without a fight, fleeing northwards to his home in the West Nile district, then seeking refuge in Libya and finally Saudi Arabia. On 10 April, Tanzanian troops entered Kampala, greeted by cheering, ecstatic crowds. Days and nights of looting followed. To complete their conquest, Tanzanian units moved northwards from Kampala in pursuit of the remnants of Amin's army. They arrived at the northern border at the beginning of June, after encountering little opposition. Most of Amin's soldiers simply retreated into the southern Sudan and Zaire, carrying with them what loot they had taken on the way.

Amin's rule had left Uganda ravaged, lawless and bankrupt. But there was to be no respite. No sooner had exiled politicians returned to Kampala to set up a new government than squabbling and intrigue began once more.

CHAPTER TWENTY-THREE

Coups and Dictators

The succession of coups in Africa swept on so rapidly that many episodes passed by in little more than a blur. In the first two decades of African independence, there were some forty successful coups and countless attempted coups. Dahomey, over a period of ten years, went through six coups, five different constitutions and ten heads of state. Not once was there an occasion when an African government was peacefully voted out of office. In justifying their actions, coup leaders invariably referred to the morass of corruption, mismanagement, tribalism, and other malpractices into which previous regimes had sunk. Only the military, it was said, with their background of discipline and dedication, were in a position to restore national integrity and bring about a return to honest and efficient government.

Many of the early coup leaders in francophone Africa, men like Soglo in Dahomey and Lamizana in Upper Volta, both of whom were former French army officers, saw themselves in the tradition of de Gaulle and the Fifth French Republic, replacing ailing regimes with a salutary spell of military rule. After taking power in 1966, Lamizana remarked: 'We had been taught two things by the French army: discipline and how to save the state's finances. This lesson we have not forgotten.' For African officers brought up in the Sandhurst tradition which disapproved of the idea of military intervention, there were sometimes greater qualms. 'I have always felt it painful to associate myself with a coup to overthrow a constitutional government, however perverted that constitution may be,' wrote Colonel Afrifa, one of the coup leaders who ousted Nkrumah. '(It was) . . . painful, therefore to come to the conclusion that the coup was necessary to save our country and our people.'

Coup leaders invariably emphasised as well the strictly

ry nature of military rule. All they required, they said, icient time to clear up the mess which had prompted intervene. Even Amin, for a few days at any rate, saw ve that assurance. Yet the military often turned out to nore competent, no more immune to the temptations of ption, and no more willing to give up power than the es they had overthrown. And the initial relief which times greeted their arrival in power quickly turned sour.

few military regimes were noted for ruling effectively. e example was provided by General Eyadema, the former ench army sergeant who had taken part in the assassination President Olympio of Togo in 1963. Four years later, yadema seized power from the civilian government of resident Grunitsky, which he had previously helped to nstall. Eyadema's regime was rigid and authoritarian. He deliberately encouraged a personality cult: giant portraits of him appeared on billboards, and officials took to wearing Eyadema lapel badges. No public criticism was tolerated. Yet Eyadema was effective in overcoming tribal divisions between north and south, his economic policies were generally beneficial, he kept Togo notably free of corruption and in the long run he gave the country a degree of stability rarely achieved elsewhere in West Africa. He also allowed in due course a measure of political participation. In 1979, elections for a National Assembly were held under a one-party system. Eyadema, standing as the sole candidate, was elected president. His grip over Togo remained tight, yet he still managed to achieve some popular support.

Niger provided another example. Though one of the poorest countries in the world, surviving precariously on the southern fringes of the Sahara desert, Niger gained a reputation after independence for being relatively stable, and its president, Hamani Diori, was highly regarded in international circles. At home, however, the government was controlled by a small, tribally-based elite which tolerated no opposition, held no proper elections and spent considerable time accumulating personal fortunes. One of the most successful entrepreneurs was the president's wife, Madame Diori, sometimes known to local students as 'L'Autrichienne' after Marie Antoinette. She owned numerous properties in the capital, Niamey. Like other countries in the Sahel region, Niger was devastated by drought in the early 1970s. In 1973, when the drought was in its third year, nearly half a million starving refugees swept over the border from Mali into Niger; a similar number fled from Niger into Nigeria; Tuareg tribesmen in the north lost almost all their cattle herds; and hundreds of thousands of people were left without shelter or means of support. The Niger government was ill equipped to handle such a disaster, but made matters worse through its own incompetence and inertia and by the blatantly corrupt way in which relief aid was handled. Vehicles supplied by international relief agencies were used as taxis on the streets of Niamey; stores of grain were hoarded by profiteers waiting for prices to rise. As public agitation over the country's plight mounted, the government retaliated harshly, calling out the army to deal with demonstrators and handing down severe jail sentences to its opponents. When the army moved to take control in 1974, the only serious resistance they encountered was from Madame Diori who urged the president's personal bodyguard, a force of Tuareg warriors, to fight to the last. Thus they perished, along with Madame Diori.

In contrast to Diori's regime, the military government that followed was austere and puritanical. Its leader, Colonel Seyni Kountché, demanded efficiency and discipline and dealt swiftly with anyone who did not comply. He was renowned for paying sudden early morning visits to government offices and private factories to make personal checks on staff there. He also made determined efforts to root out corruption, ordering vigorous audits of government departments. Government spending was kept on a tight rein. Within five years of the great drought, Niger was self-sufficient in food, the only one of eight Sahelian countries that no longer required emergency food donations. A boom in the uranium mining industry in the mid-1970s helped balance the government's finances after years of chronic budgetary deficits. In trying to create a new society for Niger, Kountché cared little whether his regime was popular or not; nor did he show any interest in reviving political activity.

What attempts were made by the military to hand back control to civilian governments rarely prospered. In Ghana, the officers who overthrew Nkrumah stayed in power for nearly three years. They took no serious initiatives other than to increase the pay of soldiers and to prepare for a return to civilian rule. A new government, under Kofi Busia, one of Nkrumah's former opponents, was elected in 1969, but ran headlong into economic difficulties. Ghana was already struggling under the burden of debts incurred during the Nkrumah era; merely to service the debts cost one third of the country's foreign earnings. To make matters worse, during Busia's regime, cocoa prices on the world market fell to their lowest level in ten years. The country's economic plight was further compounded by Busia's erratic policies. First he attempted to liberalise trade, thus accumulating even greater debts. Then he reacted with austerity measures which aggravated unemployment, drove up the cost of living and precipitated strikes. By the end of 1971 economic conditions were worse than they had been at the time of Nkrumah's downfall. In January 1972 the military threw him out.

The next military regime, under General Acheampong, began with good intentions and it was helped fortuitously by record prices for cocoa. But Acheampong's regime soon degenerated into a brazen scramble for the spoils of power. Senior army officers were heavily involved in smuggling operations and the black market and in setting up profitable deals for themselves with local and foreign entrepreneurs. The economy, meanwhile, ran out of control, inflation soared, food shortages were common and, despite the record cocoa prices, foreign exchange difficulties prevailed. So reckless did Acheampong's regime become that in 1978 his fellow officers, worried about the army's reputation, removed him. Officially he was accused of being corrupt and despotic, of giving building contracts and import licences to his girlfriends and of dabbling in juju. More accurately, he could be said to have plundered the country.

The next military regime, under General Akuffo, set about more seriously the business of returning Ghana to civilian rule. But two weeks before elections were due to be held, a new phenomenon arose. On 4 June 1979, a group of junior officers and other ranks led by a thirty-two year old air force pilot, Flight-Lieutenant Jerry Rawlings, seized power and embarked on what was described as a 'house-cleaning exercise'. Eight senior army officers, including three former heads of state, Generals Afrifa, Acheampong and Akuffo, were executed by firing squad; traders accused of profiteering were publicly flogged; the main market in Accra was razed to the ground; and impromptu People's Courts were set up to deal with scores of army officers and businessmen. As a champion of the poor, Rawlings gained huge popularity. He was trusted, more so perhaps than any previous Ghanaian leader, as an honest and well-intentioned man. Yet he had little understanding of how deeply rooted the decay in Ghana was, after so many years of graft, incompetence and mismanagement. With idealistic fervour, Rawlings believed that a dose of sharp corrective punishment, whether for corrupt army leaders or market mammies, would lead to a return to an orderly system of government. What Ghana had become, though, was a wasteland, a society that was crumbling in ruins at every level.

The elections proceeded on schedule and, after four months in office, Rawlings handed over in September 1979 to a civilian government led by Hilla Limann, a former diplomat. On the evening of his inauguration, while reviewing with colleagues Ghana's economic difficulties, Limann paused at one point, wearily rubbed his brow and remarked: 'The enormity of it all.' He survived for little more than two years, an amiable but ineffective politician, plagued by political squabbles and beset by a further slide in the economy. Cocoa exports sank to their lowest level since independence, twenty-two years before; factories short of raw materials operated at ten per cent of capacity; schools lacked textbooks; hospitals ran out of drugs; supermarket shelves were bare; roads, railways and ports were in need of serious repair. To the sound of a few shots on 1 January 1982, the entire government collapsed and Rawlings, in a muddled and haphazard coup, returned to power. 'I ask for nothing less than a revolution,' he declared in a radio broadcast. Yet still he had little idea of how the 'revolution' should proceed. Nor was his second coming greeted with the same popular fervour as before.

The road back to civilian rule in neighbouring Upper Volta proved equally difficult. Initially General Lamizana had been reluctant to take power at all, even when crowds in

Ouagadougou were beseeching him to do so; then he declared that it would be for only three months. Four years later, when he announced that the army intended to stay in power, he precipitated a general strike. Under pressure from the powerful union movement, he agreed to hold elections for a new parliament. A mainly civilian government took office in 1970, but was soon caught up in protracted political feuds. In 1974 Lamizana intervened again, dissolved the National Assembly and reimposed military rule. Once more, union strikes forced him to agree to new elections. In 1978 Lamizana himself stood as a presidential candidate against two other candidates and narrowly won. Upper Volta's multi-party democracy—a rare feature in West Africa at the time—lasted for only three years. In 1980, after a wave of strikes had paralysed his government, Lamizana was overthrown in a bloodless military coup.

Sierra Leone's experience of military rule was altogether more bizarre. It began when the prime minister, Sir Albert Margai, discovered to his consternaton that even after a rigged election he had still failed to gain a majority in parliament. Sir Albert had become prime minister in 1964 on the death of his brother, Sir Milton Margai, whose Sierra Leone People's Party had won the previous general election in 1962. During his tenure of office, Sir Albert Margai gained a reputation for avarice and corruption and the SLPP lost much of its former influence and popularity. To strengthen his position, he resorted to a variety of stratagems: he packed the higher ranks of the civil service and the army command with members of his own Mende tribe, introduced proposals for a one-party system and harassed the opposition All Peoples' Congress at every opportunity. Despite these tactics, Sierra Leone remained a relatively open society, with a free press and an opposition party which continued to thrive. When the 1967 elections were due, Margai tried every kind of manipulation to stay in power. Opposition and independent candidates were disqualified by returning officers on the most flimsy pretext. One was rejected for committing a mild misspelling of the name of his constituency; two others for signing nomination papers with their middle names, when these were not in the register. During polling day on 17 March, there were numerous incidents of intimidation and election fraud. Yet still the APC, with strong support from the northern Temne tribe, managed to gain a majority of seats.

The Governor-General, Sir Henry Lightfoot-Boston, at first tried to arrange a coalition between the two parties. But when this failed, he invited the opposition leader, Siaka Stevens, to form a government. For the first time in black Africa, so it seemed, a government had been changed through the ballot box. But half an hour after Stevens was sworn in as prime minister by the Governor-General at State House, the army commander, Brigadier David Lansana, one of Margai's closest associates, stepped in with a small detachment of troops, arrested them both, and declared martial law. Demonstrators protesting against his action on the streets of Freetown, the capital, were brutally suppressed. Lansana held power for only forty-eight hours, when he in turn was arrested by a group of army officers. These officers set up a government known as the National Reformation Council, banned all political activity, introduced austerity measures and imposed control over the press. A commission of inquiry established to inquire into the affairs of Sir Albert Margai found that in his three years as prime minister he had received at least £200,000 beyond his lawful income.

The National Reformation Council was soon faced with mounting opposition and widespread demands for a return to civilian rule, but it sought to delay the process. Then on 17 April 1968, after little more than a year in power, the National Reformation Council was overthrown by a group of mutinous soldiers and warrant officers, disgruntled over pay and conditions of service. They arrested virtually the entire officer corps, set up an Anti-Corruption Revolutionary Movement for a few days and then handed over power to Siaka Stevens. Stevens' regime, starting in 1968, saw four states of emergency, two more coup attempts and two assassination attempts. In an ironic twist, in 1978 he pushed through a referendum that outlawed the opposition SLPP and created a one-party state.

The one outstanding example of a country successful in returning to civilian rule appeared to be Nigeria. But the transition there was accomplished only with considerable difficulty and much scepticism; and in the end civilian rule survived for little more than four years. General Gowon, who achieved so high a reputation for promoting reconciliation at the end of the Biafra war in 1970, ended his career in ignominy, presiding over a military administration that was renowned for its lethargy, incompetence and corruption. He initially insisted that the military would require six years in office, a period which seemed inordinately long to ambitious politicians waiting restlessly in the wings. When he announced in 1974 that an even longer period of military rule was necessary, his popularity plummeted. The following year, while he was representing Nigeria at an OAU conference abroad, Gowon was removed from power by fellow officers. (He went off to study politics at a university in England.) His place was taken by General Murtala Mohammed, an energetic and forceful officer, who started by sacking all state governors, notorious for their lavish lifestyles, and by purging the government's overweight bureaucracy of thousands of employees in an efficiency drive. He also gave a firm commitment to hand back power to the politicians by October 1979.

Though Mohammed was assassinated in 1976 by a dissident army faction during an abortive coup, his successor, General Obasanjo, carried out the promise. The first elections for fourteen years took place on schedule in 1979 in an orderly fashion, free from the previous thuggery and bitterness. As the results showed, tribal loyalties were still a powerful force. Each of the three major parties did best in its own tribal stronghold. Yet under the new constitution they were also compelled to seek votes in all nineteen states into which Nigeria had been divided. The winning party, the National Party of Nigeria, led by Shehu Shagari, gained eighty per cent of the vote in the north, but also collected a large proportion of votes outside northern states. In the presidential election, Shagari succeeded again by attracting support from 'minority' tribes. He was an unusual figure to lead a nation renowned for rough-house politics. A mild-mannered, unassuming and rather ascetic character who came from a northern Fulani family, his ambitions in the past had been limited to worthy posts rather than powerful ones. Indeed, he showed little interest in either the power or the profit which so attracted most Nigerian politicians in their race for office. When the National Assembly proposed that his salary as president should be raised by a modest amount, he opposed the move. Failing to get his way, he gave the extra sum to charity. In 1983, Shagari was re-elected president for a second four-year term. But after only a further four months in office, he was overthrown by the army, his government accused of corruption and mismanagement.

For Uganda, there was no deliverance. The downfall of Amin in 1979 brought neither an end to violence nor a return to orderly politics. Even with the economy in ruins, with drought and famine afflicting the northeast of the country, with banditry and lawlessness rife in the capital and in every province, the struggle for power between rival political factions continued unabated. No less than twenty-two groups were involved in forming a National Consultative Council to act as an interim parliament, but they soon fell out in bitter disagreement. The first president they chose, Yusufu Lule, an elderly, conservative academic, who wanted sweeping executive powers, lasted for no more than sixty-eight days before he was deposed. His successor, Godfrey Binaisa, a British-trained lawyer, was overthrown within a year.

Much of the manoeuvring centred around the ambitions of Milton Obote, the former president living voluntarily in exile in Dar es Salaam, who was determined to regain power. Though he was vehemently opposed by the Baganda and by other political groups in Uganda, Obote started out with several decisive factors in his favour. In the first place, he had the crucial support of President Nyerere, whose troops stationed in Uganda after the defeat of Amin represented the only real centre of authority that the country had at the time. Nyerere played a direct role in the removal of Lule as president in June 1979. He also sanctioned the coup which ousted Binaisa in May 1980. Once Binaisa had been deposed, the way was open for Obote's return. The Ugandan military commission that took power was led by Paulo Muwanga, an ardent Obote supporter. It also included the army chief of staff, Brigadier David Oyite Ojok, a loyal Obote officer largely responsible for raising the new Ugandan army. Most of the government ministers appointed by the military commission were Obote associates. Thus, when Obote flew back from exile in May 1980 to contest new elections, the first since 1962, he was already in a highly advantageous position. At every stage of his election campaign he received unstinting help from the authorities. The radio service gave his Uganda People's Congress full publicity while ignoring opposing candidates. Government vehicles were put at the party's disposal. Ministers campaigned on his behalf. In due course, Obote's UPC was pronounced the winner of the December elections. But the elections were so riddled with malpractice that they left Uganda even more divided than before. Opposition parties provided evidence of intimidation, fraud and obstruction at every level, but they were unable to challenge the results. Obote's victory was resented especially in Buganda and other areas of southern Uganda which had voted overwhelmingly against him. In Kampala a sullen and mutinous mood prevailed. Within a few weeks Obote faced guerrilla attacks and sabotage in and around the capital. The reprisals that his unruly army took were as terrifying as anything that had happened during Amin's rule. Murder, brutality, detention without trial and the torture of prisoners were commonly recorded by human rights organisatons. For Uganda, it seemed almost that killing had become a way of life.

Among the multitude of coups in Africa, there were many that were accomplished without violence. Indeed, some countries established a tradition of peaceful coups. In Dahomey—later renamed Benin—all six coups after independence were bloodless. In Upper Volta, where political activity was confined to such a small circle that incoming ministers tended to be related to those who had just been thrown out, politicians took pride in the fact that no-one there had ever been killed for political reasons. There was considerable disquiet, therefore, when during the country's fourth coup in 1982, rival army factions clashed; shooting had never occurred before. In other cases, however, as with the majors in Nigeria in 1966 and with the Rawlings' group in Ghana in 1979, the purpose behind coups was not just to seize power but to deal vengefully with previous governments.

The Liberian coup in 1980 provided a particularly ruthless

example. Liberia, founded under United States' sponsorship in 1847 for freed American slaves, had been ruled ever since by a small black settler elite, the Americo-Liberians, who controlled politics and business, amassed most of the country's wealth and kept doggedly to a nineteenth century version of political life. One political party, the True Whig Party, had run the country unchallenged for more than a century, dispensing patronage and deciding on public appointments. Since Liberian law stipulated that only property owners were entitled to a vote, the majority of indigenous Africans were effectively left without one. No political opposition was tolerated. President William Tolbert, a wealthy, deeply religious Baptist minister, who had taken office in 1971, attempted hesitantly to introduce some reforms. He abandoned the top hat and tail coat traditions favoured by his predecessor, William Tubman, and lately he had permitted the registration of an opposition political party. But the disparity between the ostentatious lifestyle of the rich elite and the overwhelming majority of impoverished tribal Africans grew ever more noticeable. In 1979—the same year that Tolbert spent an amount equivalent to half the national budget while acting as host to an OAU heads of state conference—demonstrators took to the streets in protest against food price increases. On Tolbert's orders, armed police and troops opened fire killing dozens of demonstrators. A year later, in April 1980, a small group of soldiers led by a twenty-eight year old master-sergeant, Samuel Doe, broke into the presidential palace and killed Tolbert in his bedroom. Tolbert's body was dumped in a mass grave along with twenty-seven others who died defending the palace. Sergeant Doe then ordered the execution of thirteen more ministers and officials. These revenge killings produced an outburst of criticism from other African states and, for a while, Doe was treated as a pariah. He proclaimed he was leading a revolution but made few changes other than to award soldiers a pay increase, and he soon settled comfortably in power. Two years later he was respectable enough to be received by President Reagan at the White House in Washington.

There were, too, regimes which became notorious, like Amin's, for their sheer brutality. In Zanzibar, Abeid Karume, the former seaman thrust into power by the 1964 revolution, ruled the islands as a cruel and irascible despot. Members of his Revolutionary Council ordered arrests, imprisonment without trial, torture and execution as they saw fit and seized at will property and estates. The once prosperous Asian community, which survived the revolution largely intact, was picked on for victimisation. Asians accused of minor offences were publicly flogged; a number of Asian girls were forced into marriage. Karume's style of government grew increasingly erratic. A man of little education, he was given to making rambling speeches and issuing personal decrees. He banned contraceptives and authorised forced labour. His end came in April 1972, when a Zanzibar army officer bearing a personal grudge against him shot him as he was relaxing in his favourite club.

The tiny central African state of Burundi, during Colonel Michel Micombero's regime, witnessed one of the most organised tribal massacres of modern times. Burundi had been ruled traditionally, like the neighbouring state of Rwanda, by the minority Tutsi tribe, which acted as feudal overlords to the majority Hutu. But whereas in Rwanda the Hutu had succeeded by 1961 in gaining power, in Burundi the minority Tutsi, no more than fifteen per cent of the population, managed to retain control, though only with considerable difficulty. Two of the first three prime ministers were assassinated. Seven governments came and fell in quick succession. In 1965 a mutiny by Hutu army and *gendarmerie* officers led to terrible reprisals against Hutu leaders. When Micombero came to power in a coup in 1966, he and his Tutsi associates set out to remove the 'Hutu threat' once and for all. The army and government were purged of Hutu members. Leading Hutu politicians and scores of soldiers were executed. In 1972 Micombero was threatened by a Hutu uprising in which hundreds of Tutsi died. What followed was not so much repression as slaughter. Hutu tribesmen with any kind of education—teachers, church leaders, bank clerks, nurses, traders, civil servants—were rounded up by Micombero's army and killed. In a campaign which was described as selective genocide, the Hutu elite was virtually eliminated. Possibly as many as 200,000 died. Thus the Tutsi continued in power. Micombero himself was overthrown in a palace coup in 1976.

The tyranny of President Macías Nguema in Equatorial Guinea, a former Spanish colony in West Africa, reached such grotesque proportions that one of the few outside investigators who penetrated the country in later years described it as no better than a 'concentration camp'. In the eleven years that he survived as dictator, Macías turned Equatorial Guinea into a land of fear and devastation. Thousands were tortured and executed or perished in overcrowded jails. As much as one third of the population fled the country in terror as refugees, mainly to neighbouring Cameroon and Gabon. No normal system of government existed; there was no education, no medical services; towards the end not even a currency. In the words of one international agency report, Equatorial Guinea 'slowly dropped out of the world'. What had once been a relatively prosperous colony with thriving cocoa and coffee plantations and a tourist trade, descended into a state of primitive brutality. Though popularly elected as president at the time of independence in 1968, Macías quickly established himself as a dictator, eliminating political opponents and relying heavily on the army and police to enforce his control. A man of limited education, bearing a pathological hatred of 'intellectuals', he ruthlessly suppressed all forms of opposition and wreaked vengeance on the pre-independence intelligentsia. Within a few years, all senior civil servants and two thirds of the national assembly had been murdered, imprisoned or driven into exile. Ten of the twelve ministers in the first government were killed.

Macías also turned against the influential local Catholic Church. In 1974 all mission schools were closed, effectively ending all formal education. Children from then on were taught only political slogans. Later churches were shut by presidential order and Catholic services were banned. The population was told to change Christian names to African names.

For a wide range of offences the penalty was death. Guineans could also be punished for such crimes as giving aid to missionaries, failing to attend manifestations of praise and joy, or merely for being '*discontento*'. The judicial process broke down completely. The Spanish community fled soon after independence, abandoning their plantations and businesses. In the capital, Malabo, on the island of Fernando Po, rows of shops stood shuttered; consumer goods were unobtainable; electricity supplies were erratic; and the population there rapidly dwindled. Cocoa and coffee production dropped dramatically. As the market economy collapsed, Equatorial Guinea reverted to a level of rural subsistence.

The government meanwhile was left in the grip of a man who was clearly paranoid and a few of his relatives whom he made ministers. Macías honoured himself with grand titles such as 'Great Maestro of Popular Education, Science and Traditional Culture' and 'the only miracle of Equatorial Guinea'. Many Guineans thought he was endowed with supernatural powers. No proper administration survived. The only people to be paid regularly were the president, the army, the police and the militia. Most ministries—including those dealing with education, agriculture, construction and natural resources—had no budgets at all and their offices in Malabo were shut. The national bank too was closed after the director was publicly executed in 1976. All foreign exchange was delivered instead to Macías, who hoarded it along with large amounts of local currency in his various palaces on the island of Fernando Po and in the mainland province of Rio Muni. Eventually no money at all was left in general circulation in Fernando Po. Macías himself retreated from the island to live in his remote native village on the mainland, Nsangayong, among his fellow Fang tribesmen. He took with him most of the national treasury, storing huge wads of bills in bags and suitcases in a bamboo hut next to his house. Some of the money rotted in the ground. Towards the end of his regime, even his close associates thought he was mad. In August 1979, Macías was overthrown in an army coup, put on trial and executed.

In the Central African Republic, Bokassa's regime became renowned not so much for its brutality, though this was to be the cause of his downfall, but for extravagance and folly on a scale unsurpassed in modern Africa. Soon after seizing power in 1966, Bokassa began to think in grandiose terms. He liked to describe himself as an 'absolute monarch' and forbade mention of the words democracy and elections. He promoted himself to the rank of general and then, like his friend and ally Amin in Uganda, took the title of Field Marshal. For public appearances he insisted on wearing so many medals and awards that special uniforms for him had to be designed to accommodate them. Among the display were a few genuine decorations, for in his twenty-three years of service in the French army, as he rose from the rank of private to captain, he had performed with distinction. The greatest moment of his life had been when he was decorated by General de Gaulle in person. Bokassa worshipped de Gaulle, addressing him as 'Papa' even after he had become president of the Central African Republic. At de Gaulle's funeral, he was inconsolable.

Bokassa's other hero was Napoleon, a man whom he described as his 'guide and inspiration', and it was in an attempt to emulate Napoleon that Bokassa conceived his most ludicrous venture. In December 1976 he declared the Central African Republic an empire and himself Emperor of its two million subjects. The following year, using as a model the ceremony in which Napoleon had crowned himself Emperor of France in 1804, he arranged for his own coronation. No expense was spared. From France Bokassa ordered all the trappings of a monarchy: a crown of diamonds, rubies and emeralds; an imperial throne, fifteen feet high, shaped like a golden eagle; thoroughbred horses; carriages; coronation robes; brass helmets and breastplates for the Imperial Guard; and tons of food, wine, fireworks and flowers for the festivities. To the strains of Mozart and Beethoven, mixed with the throb of tribal drums, Bokassa duly crowned himself Emperor in Bangui's sports stadium on the mosquito-infested banks of the Oubangui river. The cost, amounting to $22 million (£12 million) was nearly equivalent to one quarter of the entire national revenue for the previous year. Most of the bill in the end was paid by France, which regularly provided subsidies to cover half of the government's normal budget.

The spectacle of Bokassa's lavish coronation in a country with few government services, a high infant mortality rate, widespread illiteracy, only 260 miles of paved road and in serious economic difficulty, aroused universal criticism. None of the invited foreign heads of state deigned to attend. However, Robert Galley, the French Cooperation Minister who represented President Giscard d'Estaing, attacked critics of the coronation. 'Personally,' he said, 'I find it quite extraordinary to criticize what is to take place in Bangui while finding the Queen of England's Jubilee ceremony all right. It smacks of racism.'

Bokassa's excursions into violence and brutality, however, were another matter. Though his reputation as a cruel and capricious tyrant was based on relatively few incidents, they were memorable enough for him to be mentioned in the same category as Amin. In 1972, in a campaign against theft, Bokassa published a decree prescribing mutilation for thieves. Dissatisfied with the results of these measures, he then ordered 'merciless punishment' and personally led a detachment of soldiers to the local jail where they beat convicted thieves with wooden staves for ten minutes. As the convicts screamed in agony, Bokassa turned to a foreign newspaper reporter to observe: 'It's tough, but that's life.' Three men died and several others seemed barely alive. The next day the forty-two thieves who had survived the beating, together with the corpses of the three others, were put on display under a blazing sun on a stand in Bangui's main square. When the United Nations Secretary General, Kurt Waldheim, protested at the atrocity, Bokassa called him 'a pimp' and 'a colonialist'.

The events which led to Bokassa's downfall started little more than a year after his coronation. In January 1979, student riots broke out in Bangui. Ostensibly the students were protesting against an imperial order instructing them to buy and wear uniforms bearing Bokassa's name and portrait which were manufactured by a textile firm owned by the Bokassa family. But the deeper causes of the riots lay in widespread discontent over inflation, bureaucratic inefficiency and Bokassa's imperial pretensions. The riots were brutally suppressed by troops, but strikes by teachers, students and civil servants continued. When Bokassa's own car was stoned in April, he ordered the Imperial Guard to round up school children. At Ngaragba prison near Bangui, about one hundred children were killed in a massacre in which Bokassa himself took part, as an independent judicial inquiry subsequently confirmed. When the results of the inquiry were known to the French government, an envoy was sent to Bokassa advising him to abdicate, since France would no longer support him. Bokassa struck out at the envoy with his stick. The French government at first suspended financial aid, but then resolved that Bokassa should be removed altogether. On 29 September, while Bokassa was on a visit to Libya requesting aid from Colonel Gaddafi, French troops stationed in Gabon and Chad as part of a special strike force, flew into Bangui to support a bloodless coup. The man they installed as the new president was David Dacko, whom Bokassa had overthrown thirteen years before. Bokassa himself sought exile in France, but was turned away. He found refuge instead in the Ivory Coast. At a trial which later took place in Bangui in his absence, he was accused of murder, embezzlement and cannibalism, and sentenced to death.

CHAPTER TWENTY-FOUR

Areas of Conflict

No other area of Africa endured such profound upheaval and such prolonged conflict as the Horn of Africa. It was an area accustomed by its history to great episodes of conquest, revolt and religious strife. But the struggles which erupted along the mountain ranges and deserts of the Horn in the 1970s were made all the more dangerous and complex by the involvement of foreign powers, which valued the Horn for its strategic location alongside the Red Sea and the Indian Ocean, and by the nearby cauldron of Middle Eastern politics. The centre of gravity in the Horn lay, as it had done for centuries, in the Ethiopian Empire, an ancient Christian kingdom whose origins could be traced back to the first century but whose modern boundaries were shaped only after a period of imperial expansion in the late nineteenth century, at the same time that European powers were involved in the scramble for Africa. What precipitated the modern upheavals in the Horn was the declining authority of Ethiopia's ageing Emperor, Haile-Selassie. After a lifetime's rule, he was no longer adept at the business of government; nor had he managed, even by the age of eighty, to arrange for an orderly succession to the throne.

Haile-Selassie had ruled Ethiopia for more than fifty years, first as Regent from 1916, then as Emperor from 1930. For a period of five years his reign had been rudely interrupted by Mussolini's grand design to enlarge Italy's African empire at his expense: in 1935, Italian forces invaded Ethiopia from Eritrea, an adjoining Italian colony on the Red Sea coast, and after a seven month long campaign captured the capital, Addis Ababa. Haile-Selassie fled into exile and remained abroad until 1941, when the British army defeated the Italians and reinstated him. Once back on the throne, he set out to strengthen his personal control over the further reaches of his feudal empire, laying the foundations of a civilian administration and building up a modern army. Some reforms were introduced. A parliament was elected in 1957, filled mostly by provincial nobles. But the basic character of the Empire remained unchanged. Haile-Selassie continued to govern as an autocratic monarch, dispensing titles, appointments and land in return for loyal service, and holding together the Empire and its twenty-seven million subjects through a vast network of personal ties. His royal palaces in Addis Ababa still constituted the centre of power from where all government affairs were directed. His divine right to rule was devoutly upheld by the Orthodox Christian Church through its multitude of monasteries, churches and priests. And his authority was further enhanced by the mystique which surrounded a monarchy whose origins were said to be rooted in biblical times. According to the Ethiopian constitution, the Emperor was descended directly from the marriage of Solomon and Sheba, and among the titles with which he was graced was that of 'Elect of God'. Thus the ancient heritage of his kingdom, the elaborate traditions of the royal court, the religious ceremonies performed by patriarchs and priests, all served to endow Haile-Selassie with an aura of high esteem. What was equally important, though, in sustaining the power of the monarchy was the considerable extent to which the Emperor, together with the Coptic Church and influential aristocratic families in the provinces, owned and controlled land and thereby the livelihood of millions of peasants who worked it.

The Empire remained a difficult place to govern. Despite Haile-Selassie's attempts to strengthen the bonds of his control from Addis Ababa and to establish a modern bureaucracy, his power in the provinces was often weak, dependent on the cooperation of local potentates or on the disposition of his army. The inner core of the Empire, bound together by ancient ties of history and religion, was formed around the mountains and plateaus of central Ethiopia where two dominant peoples—the Amharas and the Tigreans—had traditionally vied for ascendancy. Since the late nineteenth century, Ethiopia had been ruled by an Amhara dynasty from Shoa, the southernmost Amhara province, and it had been part of Haile-Selassie's strategy for enforcing his control on other areas of the Empire to impose the Amharic language and culture there. The outer regions of the Empire, however, were added mostly as a result of military conquest in the late nineteenth century, when the size of Ethiopia doubled, and in these areas local revolts and rebellions against the authorities in Addis Ababa frequently broke out. Parts of southern Ethiopia, where Oromo tribesmen had lost much of their land to armed Amhara settlers and absentee landlords, proved particularly troublesome. In the 1960s Haile-Selassie was obliged to send an expeditionary force to Bale province in the south to quell an Oromo uprising there which lasted for seven years. But the greatest threats to his Empire came from other areas on its periphery, from Eritrea in the north and from the Somali border region.

Eritrea had been incorporated into the Ethiopian Empire only after protracted controversy and a good deal of devious manoeuvring on the part of Haile-Selassie. As an Italian colony for fifty years, called Eritrea after the Latin name for the Red Sea, Mare Erythraeum, it had gained a distinct identity of its own. When the Italians were defeated in 1941, the British military administration which provisionally took control of the territory further stimulated a sense of Eritrean identity by encouraging the creation of political parties, labour unions and a free press, none of which was to be found in Ethiopia. Its future after the war, given to the United Nations to decide, proved difficult to resolve. Ethiopia laid claim to Eritrea on the grounds that historically the territory, or parts of it, had previously belonged to the Empire. For strategic reasons, too, the Emperor was anxious to gain control over the Eritrean ports of Assab and Massawa to give Ethiopia direct access to the outside world.

The Eritreans themselves, numbering about three million, were divided over the issue. The Christian half of the population, mostly Tigreans who inhabited the Eritrean highlands surrounding the capital, Asmara, tended to support unification with Ethiopia, with which they already had religious and ethnic ties. The Muslim half of the population, also found in the highlands but mainly occupying the harsh desert region along the Red Sea coast and the western lowlands, tended to favour independence. As a compromise, the United Nations devised a form of federation linking Ethiopia and Eritrea under which the Ethiopian government was given control of foreign affairs, defence, finance, commerce and ports, while Eritrea was allowed its own elected government and assembly to deal with local affairs. Eritrea was also permitted to have its own flag and official languages, Tigrinya and Arabic. An election held under British auspices in 1952, shortly before the British departed, resulted in a roughly equal division of votes between Christian and Muslim, but left a unionist party with a majority. From the outset, Haile-Selassie looked on the federation as nothing more than a step towards unification. Through a mixture of patronage, pressure and intimidation, Ethiopian officials steadily consolidated their control over the territory, relying for support for their manoeuvres on amenable Christian Tigrean politicians. The various freedoms which Eritreans had briefly enjoyed—political rights, unions, an independent press—all were consistently undermined. In 1958, the Eritrean flag was discarded; in 1959, the Ethiopian law code was extended to Eritrea; political parties were banned; the labour movement was destroyed; censorship was introduced; and Amharic replaced Tigrinya and Arabic as the official language. Finally, in 1962, the Eritrean assembly was persuaded to vote for the dissolution of federation and its own existence in favour of annexation to Ethiopia. From then on, Eritrea was treated no differently than any of the other thirteen provinces of Ethiopia. Amhara officials were awarded senior posts in the administration. The principle of parity between Christian and Muslim officials, once carefully observed, was abandoned. In effect, Eritrea became simply another acquisition of the Empire. The result was the longest running African war in modern times.

Starting in 1961 with small-scale raids carried out by Muslim guerrillas seeking independence from Ethiopia, the war in Eritrea slowly gathered momentum, attracting support from Christians as well as the Muslim population, until a whole division of Haile-Selassie's troops was involved in containing it. The guerrillas received training, funds and equipment from Arab sources which looked on the Eritrean war as an Arab cause and saw a strategic advantage in establishing a new independent state on the Red Seas which would give the Arabs total control of the coastline. Syria and Iraq were prominent supporters at an early stage and neighbouring Sudan allowed its territory to be used as a base and a refuge; in later years a variety of other willing helpers came forward, ranging from Libya and the Palestinians to Cuba. As the Eritrean movement expanded, however, it was beset by a series of tribal, religious and ideological feuds. A major split occurred in 1970, dividing the Eritreans into two factions, the Eritrean Liberation Front (ELF), which had first launched the guerrilla war with Muslim support, and the new Eritrean Popular Liberation Front (EPLF), in which young Christian radicals played a leading role. By 1972, these two rival groups were engaged in internecine warfare in which hundreds died. The Eritrean movement was further weakened in 1972 as the result of an agreement between Ethiopia and Sudan under which Sudan undertook to withdraw its assistance from Eritrean guerrillas, while Ethiopia agreed to stop supporting Anya Nya rebels in southern Sudan. In the early 1970s, therefore, Ethiopian forces were able to make major advances in the Eritrean campaign. But the brutal methods of repression they employed in Eritrea, burning and bombing villages and inflicting reprisals against the civilian population, served only to alienate ever increasing numbers of Eritreans and fan the flames of Eritrean nationalism.

The Somali dispute proved equally intractable. By one of those cruel twists of fate that occurred so often during the scramble for Africa in the nineteenth century, the Somalis, a people sharing a common language, culture and religion, were divided up by the boundaries of new territories decided on by imperial powers. The French settled for French Somaliland, a bleak enclave of lava-strewn desert surrounding the port of Djibouti at the southern entrance to the Red Sea; the British acquired northern Somaliland, initially to ensure that the British garrison at Aden was kept regularly supplied with meat; the Italians established themselves in the Italian colony of Somalia, with a capital in Mogadishu; further south, Somali communities were incorporated within the boundaries of the British colony of Kenya; and to the west, on the Ogaden plateau, they came under Ethiopian jurisdiction. Ethiopia's claims to the Ogaden, an area used by Somali nomads as pastures for their herds of cattle, dated from the conquests made during the reign of Emperor Menelik in the late nineteenth century by one of his most able generals, Ras Makonnen. After occupying the ancient Muslim city of Harar in 1887, Ras Makonnen set out to extend the frontiers of the Empire across the Ogaden and southwards into Oromo territory. Makonnen's son, Ras Tafari, destined to become Emperor in 1930 as Haile-Selassie, was born in Harar in 1892. For many years, Ethiopia's authority in the Ogaden did not extend much beyond the scattered military outposts that the army established there. But its claims to the Ogaden were nevertheless recognised in treaties with Britain and Italy.

The overriding ambition of Somali nationalists in the postwar era, when the future of Italian Somalia and British Somaliland was under discussion, was to recover their 'lost lands' and to establish a 'Greater Somalia'. In 1960, when the two former colonies were joined together to form an independent Somalia, the new Somali government persisted with irridentist claims to the Ogaden, to Kenya's Northern Frontier District and to French Somaliland, where about one third of the four million Somalis lived, and refused to accept the validity of any of the existing borders. In the case of Ethiopia, the Somali claim amounted to about one third of Ethiopia's territory. This desire for Somali unification was enshrined in the Somali constitution and emblazoned on the Somali flag, which bore as its emblem a five point star representing the five segments of the Somali people. Despite the extreme poverty of Somalia, its lack of resources and its dependence on foreign aid, the main energies of the Somali government from independence onwards were directed towards the goal of unification. Both Kenya's Northern Frontier District and the Ogaden became Somali targets.

The Northern Frontier District, an arid, sparsely populated region extending across one third of Kenya's territory, included a large Somali community which actively favoured joining Somalia. A British commission sent out to Kenya in 1962, shortly before Kenya's independence, to ascertain the strength of public opinion in the Northern Frontier District, reported that Somali tribesmen there, more than half of the population of about 400,000, 'almost unanimously' preferred secession from Kenya; in five of six districts there were large majorities supporting secession. The British authorities, however, were obliged to take into account the adamant views of Kenya's nationalists, including Kenyatta, who insisted that the Northern Frontier District was an inalienable part of Kenya, and they finally announced in March 1963 that the area would be incorporated into Kenya. In retaliation, the Somali government in Mogadishu severed diplomatic relations with Britain and encouraged Somali nationalists in the Northern Frontier District to embark on a guerrilla campaign against the Kenya government. Thus a *shifta* or bandit war, as it was known in Nairobi, broke out in northern Kenya, continuing for four years.

Simultaneously, the Somali government was involved in supporting insurgents in the Ogaden. Shortly after Somalia's independence in 1960, a Western Somali Liberation Front (WSLF) was established in Mogadishu, claiming to represent the Somali population and other tribes in eastern Ethiopia. The WSLF, as well as aiding Somali secessionists, supplied arms to Oromo dissidents in Bale province in their campaign against the Ethiopian government. Periodic clashes erupted along the border between Ethiopian and Somali forces, culminating in a brief full-scale war in 1964 which the Ethiopian army won in a matter of days.

Lacking an effective army with which to advance its plans for a Greater Somalia, the Somali government sought assistance from foreign powers. For three years after independence, negotiations on arms were conducted with the United States, West Germany and Italy, but the most they were willing to provide was equipment and training for an army of 5,000 men intended to deal with nothing more serious than internal security and civic action. So when the Soviet Union came forward in 1963 with an offer to establish an army of some 10,000 men, together with a small air force, the Somalis swiftly accepted it. At the time, the Soviet Union looked for no particular advantage in Somalia; nor did it support the government's plans for a Greater Somalia. But after a military coup in Mogadishu in 1969, the Russian involvement in Somalia increased dramatically. The new

Somali leader, General Mohammed Siad Barre, proclaimed Somalia as a Marxist state, embarked on a nationalisation campaign, and accepted a large number of Soviet advisers in government ministries and agencies as well as in the military. The Russians in turn began to look at Somalia with greater interest for strategic reasons, as part of their reassessment of the importance of the Indian Ocean and the Red Sea and their search for military facilities in the area. In exchange for the use of the northern Somali port of Berbera as a military base, the Russians agreed in 1972 to provide Somalia with increased military aid. By 1974, Somalia had acquired an army of 22,000 men, armoured personnel carriers, and a modern air force with jet fighters. Its army, in the view of military observers at the time, was better equipped than the Ethiopian army.

Ethiopia's armed forces had traditionally been supplied and supported by the United States. Under an agreement signed in 1953, the United States had obtained a twenty-five year lease for a communications and intelligence gathering base near Asmara, named Kagnew, and in return it had agreed to train and equip three Ethiopian military divisions. A second agreement, made in 1960, provided for the training and equipment of a fourth division and brought the size of the army to 40,000 men. American officials regarded the cost of their military assistance programme to Ethiopia essentially as rent for the Kagnew station, which formed a vital link in a chain of communications and defence bases that the United States maintained around the world. In 1970, Kagnew was a major installation employing some 3,000 military and civilian employees, but from 1973 its importance to the Americans declined and its size was drastically reduced. The American commitment to Ethiopia, however, continued. By 1974, more than 2,000 Ethiopian officers had received training in the United States, and the army, air force and navy were totally dependent on American support. The effectiveness of the military became all the more crucial when the Ethiopian government found itself dealing with both the insurgency campaign in Eritrea and the threat posed by a powerfully-equipped Somali army across the eastern border. Yet within the ranks of Ethiopia's armed forces, as elsewhere in the country, a mood of restlessness and discontent was spreading.

Haile-Selassie reached the age of eighty in July 1972, having held absolute power for longer than any other figure in contemporary history, but without making known any plans for his succession. His son, the Crown Prince, Asfa Wossen, suffered a stroke the following year and repaired to Switzerland to recuperate, leaving the succession in even greater doubt. Meanwhile the Emperor's ministers allowed the government to drift on indeterminately, taking no initiative to deal with agrarian or political reform and responding with indifference to the pressing problems that Ethiopia faced. When drought and famine overtook the province of Wollo in 1973, claiming the lives of tens of thousands of peasants, the government, though aware of the disaster, made no attempt to alleviate it by using its own resources, nor did it seek help from international agencies for fear of damaging the country's reputation. The diplomatic community based in Addis Ababa knew well enough of the scale of suffering but refrained from interfering for reasons of protocol. When Haile-Selassie belatedly paid a visit to the area, after an international outcry broke out, he merely referred to the 'natural disasters beyond human control' which had often afflicted Ethiopia and implied that little could be done to prevent them. Among the educated Ethiopian elite, already dissatisfied with an archaic system of government and their own lack of influence over it, the government's inertia over the Wollo famine caused a wave of exasperation. Yet there were no signs of overt opposition to the Emperor's rule except among students in Addis Ababa, who represented no threat to the government. On the surface, as 1974 began, Ethiopia remained comparatively tranquil.

The Ethiopian revolution in 1974 grew from a few small and random incidents. On 12 January, enlisted men at an army outpost at Neghelle in southern Ethiopia mutinied against their officers. The soldiers' water pump was out of order, but the officers refused to allow them the use of their own well. The officers were arrested. When an army general was sent there as the Emperor's personal envoy to investigate the matter, he too was detained and forced to share the soldiers' crude rations. The news of the Neghelle mutiny spread through the army's radio network to every unit in the country. On 10 February, airmen at an air force base near Addis Ababa staged a similar revolt, holding officers hostage, in protest against pay and conditions. In mid-February, a series of spontaneous civilian protests erupted on the streets of Addis Ababa: students demonstrated over plans for educational reform; teachers went on strike demanding higher pay; taxi drivers struck in protest against fuel price increases; labour unions took to the streets to voice grievances over pay, food price rises and union rights. On 23 February Haile-Selassie offered concessions, postponing changes in the educational system, reducing fuel price increases and implementing price controls to check inflation. He also announced pay rises for the armed forces and the police. But dissidents in the army were not satisfied. On 25 February, noncommissioned officers and enlisted men in the Second Division based in the Eritrean capital of Asmara mutinied, took control of the radio station and broadcast demands for more pay and improved conditions of service. Haile-Selassie responded with more concessions. On 27 February he dismissed the prime minister, Aklilu Habte-Wold, who had served him for fifteen years, and appointed in his place another Cabinet Minister, Endelkachew Makonnen, an Oxford-educated aristocrat with a more liberal reputation. Haile-Selassie also agreed to revise the constitution to make the prime minister responsible to parliament, a change which in Ethiopian terms amounted to major reform. For the armed forces, he offered still further increases in pay and allowances and sacked a bevy of senior officers. The army appeared satisfied.

In the towns and cities of Ethiopia, however, a chaotic profusion of strikes and demonstrations broke out. One group after another raised its demands amid the general clamour: civil servants, teachers, students, journalists, even priests and prostitutes. A massive Muslim demonstration was held in protest at official discrimination against Islam and calling for the separation of Church and state. Parliamentarians, once renowned for their docility, spoke out now for press freedom. The most persistent demand was for the arrest and trial of former ministers and palace officials on charges of negligence and corruption. The outbursts were unplanned and uncoordinated, but insistent on the need for widespread reform. The new prime minister, however, paid scant heed to the demands, other than to permit finally the arrest of some of his former colleagues and palace officials as a token gesture. He attempted no serious reform and instead turned to loyal units of the army for help in curbing strikes and demonstrations. For a brief while the old aristocratic establishment held control, fully expecting that Ethiopia, under their command, would evolve gradually towards a parliamentary democracy.

Within the armed forces, though, a more radical movement was emerging. In an arcane manoeuvre at the end of June, an armed forces 'committee', known by its Amharic name, the 'Derg', took control of the government. For many months, the 'Derg' remained a shadowy organisation: none of the names of its members was announced and its activities were kept hidden from the public. Initially it consisted of representatives chosen by units of the armed forces, numbering in all 126, mostly junior officers and noncommissioned officers. It offered no clear programme of action, but its first pronouncements were notably moderate and included pledges of loyalty to the Emperor. Then, stage by stage, growing in confidence the Derg began to dismantle the whole imperial structure. The new prime minister, Endelkachew Makonnen, was forced out and replaced by a more radical figure, Mikael Imru. Palace functionaries, high government officials and prominent aristocrats, including Haile-Selassie's closest advisers and confidants, were arrested in one wave after another, until all leading members of the *ancien régime* had been removed. One by one, old imperial institutions such as the Emperor's private exchequer were abolished. The Emperor's residence, the Jubilee Palace, where he was being held a virtual prisoner, was nationalised and renamed the National Palace. Finally, the Emperor himself, as well as his entourage, was subjected to a barrage of attacks through newspapers, on radio and television, accused of corruption and negligence and, above all, of responsibility for the disaster of Wollo province the previous year. On 12 September, Haile-Selassie was deposed without a sign of public dissent and without a shot being fired. A group of officers from the Derg went to the National Palace and summoned the eighty-two year old Emperor to the library where the proclamation deposing him was read out. Then he was put in the back of a small, blue Volkswagen and driven away to army barracks in Addis Ababa. He died in captivity a year later.

Ethiopia thus formally came under the control of a committee of soldiers, none of whom was known to the public. The Derg set up a government which it named the Provisional Military Administrative Council (PMAC) and appointed as its chairman General Aman Andom, a popular former army commander, remembered for his victory over the Somali army in the brief border war in 1964. But still no clearly defined policies emerged. The Derg, though stripping the monarchy of its power and titles such as 'Elect of God', hesitated to abolish it outright and invited the Crown Prince Asfa Wossen, who was still convalescing in Switzerland, to return to Ethiopia and to replace his father as constitutional head of state. The Crown Prince declined the offer. The PMAC outlawed strikes and demonstrations and firmly rebuffed demands by students and unions for a 'people's government'. For two months, factions within the Derg argued over the direction of government policy and over the issues of civilian rule, the fate of royal prisoners and the war in Eritrea. The arguments culminated in a violent struggle for power between radical members of the Derg and Aman Andom, an independent-minded officer with ambitions of his own. As an Eritrean himself, Aman Andom favoured a negotiated settlement in Eritrea; he was also opposed to the execution of prisoners. The outcome was that on 23 November Aman Andom was killed in a gun battle at his house in Addis Ababa by troops who had been sent there by the Derg to arrest him. The same night, the Derg ordered the execution of fifty-seven prominent prisoners, mostly officials and army officers associated with Haile-Selassie's regime, including two former prime ministers, Aklilu Habte-Wold and Endelkachew Makonnen. The Derg also agreed to send troop reinforcements to Eritrea with orders to launch a new onslaught in the guerrilla war. The Ethiopian revolution had entered a more violent and more radical phase that was to bring the country to the verge of disintegration.

The bloody events of November 1974 also marked the point at which a young ordnance officer from the Third Division in Harar, Major Mengistu Haile Mariam, emerged as one of the most powerful figures in the country. Mengistu came from a poor background, he had received little formal education, but he was intelligent, ambitious and quite ruthless. Since the Derg's formation, he had played a prominent role in its affairs as an advocate of radical policies and he had also acquired the post of vice-chairman of the PMAC. Mengistu's radical group, now in the ascendant, soon made its mark with a programme of revolutionary reform. In December the Derg proclaimed the advent of Ethiopian socialism; in January 1975, banks and insurance companies were nationalised; in February, large industries were taken over. Then in March, in the most sweeping measure of all, the Derg abolished by proclamation all private ownership of rural land and the whole system of land tenancy, thus destroying at a stroke the economic power of the old regime. The monarchy, too, was formally abolished. Urban land and rented property in towns were expropriated by decree in August. At a later stage, the Derg proclaimed Marxism-Leninism as Ethiopia's official ideology.

As rival groups across the country sought to sustain the revolution or destroy it, Ethiopia was engulfed in strife and turmoil. Landlords organised armed resistance to the reforms; royalists and the nobility raised the banner of revolt; peasants and farmworkers fought for their rights to land; in one province after another, rebellions against the central government over long-held grievances flared up. The most intense struggle was waged in Addis Ababa between the Derg and left-wing civilian groups demanding civilian control of the revolution. The Derg had no intention of giving way. On May Day in 1975, demonstrators agitating for an immediate return to civilian rule were shot down by soldiers.

Opposition to the military steadily intensified. A clandestine group, the Ethiopian People's Revolutionary Party (EPRP), emerged in August with demands for a mass movement, democratic rights and a Marxist ideology, and rapidly established cells in other towns and cities. Its demands were supported by unions which in September organised a general strike. In an attempt to solve the differences between the military and radical civilian factions, Mengistu, as vice-chairman of the PMAC, appealed to them in April 1976 to join the Derg in carrying out a 'national democratic revolution'. His proposal was accepted by one faction, the All-Ethiopian Socialist Movement, usually known by its Amharic acronym, *Meison*, but it was rejected outright by the EPRP, which embarked on a campaign of urban terror to try to wrest control from the military. Scores of officials and supporters of the Derg were murdered. The Derg sent out its own murder squads. Rival factions then developed within the ranks of the Derg, Mengistu favouring uncompromising action against the Derg's opponents, other officers preferring a more conciliatory approach.

In February 1977, in an hour-long gun battle at the old palace of Emperor Menelik, which the Derg used for its headquarters, eight senior officers, including the PMAC chairman General Teferi Bante, were killed, leaving Mengistu in undisputed control. Having dispensed with his rivals on the Derg, Mengistu turned ruthlessly against his civilian opponents, embarking on what he referred to as a campaign of 'red terror'. 'It is an historical obligation to clean up vigilantly using the revolutionary sword,' he told his supporters in 1977. 'Your struggle should be demonstrated by spreading red terror in the camp of the reactionaries. Turn the white terror of reactionaries into red terror.' Thousands died in the red terror, thousands more were imprisoned, many of them tortured and beaten. Determined to root out EPRP cells from every neighbourhood, Mengistu organised urban militia squads and workers' units in factories and government offices, instructing them to set up road blocks, search houses and hunt down the Derg's opponents. Months of urban warfare, assassination and indiscriminate killing followed as supporters of the EPRP, Meison and the Derg struggled for control. On the streets of Addis Ababa, printed posters were put up carrying the message: 'Intensify Red Terror'. Bodies of murdered victims were left lying where they fell with signs attached to their clothing marking them as 'counter-revolutionaries'. The peak of terror was reached in December 1977 and the following January. By mid-1978, the EPRP was virtually destroyed.

While these violent struggles for power were taking place in Addis Ababa, in other parts of the country the government was steadily losing control. In the northwestern province of Begemdir, a conservative opposition party, the Ethiopian

Democratic Union, led by former aristocrats, raised an army, succeeded in capturing towns close to the Sudan border and advanced towards the provincial capital of Gondar. In the northeast, Afar tribesmen formed the Afar Liberation Front and mounted guerrilla attacks on traffic using the main road to the port of Assab on the Red Sea coast, where the country's only oil refinery was located. In Tigre province, a large guerrilla force was established by the Tigre People's Liberation Front with the help of the Eritreans. In the south, the Oromo Liberation Front was launched with support from Somalia. The Somalis also revived the Western Somali Liberation Front, which had lain dormant for five years, and began to infiltrate arms and equipment into the Ogaden, preparing for a new initiative to recapture their 'lost lands'. But the most immediate crisis facing the Derg was in Eritrea.

The Derg's decision in November 1974 to prosecute the war in Eritrea, instead of seeking a negotiated settlement as General Aman Andom had wanted, provoked a savage outbreak of fighting. Hundreds of guerrillas infiltrated the provincial capital, Asmara, at the end of January 1975 and for three weeks fought ferociously to capture the town. Their attempt failed, but it marked the beginning of a guerrilla initiative that was nearly to succeed in driving the Ethiopian army out of Eritrea altogether. As Ethiopian troops retaliated with a campaign of brutal repression, the Eritrean guerrilla movement gained massive support from the local population, from Christians in the highlands as well as from Muslim communities. The ranks of the guerrillas, filled with young Christian recruits, rose from 6,000 in early 1975 to nearly 40,000 within two years, greatly outnumbering Ethiopian troops in the province. By mid-1976, the guerrillas controlled most of the countryside and were laying siege to small garrisons. In a desperate attempt to reverse the tide of the war, the Derg recruited a huge peasant army from other provinces, hoping that sheer numbers would overwhelm the guerrillas, but, poorly trained and armed only with ancient rifles, it was routed on the Eritrean border even before it had been deployed. The Eritreans also received vital help from foreign sources. Saudi Arabia, worried about the impact of a revolutionary Marxist regime in Ethiopia so close to its own

Red Sea borders, supplied the guerrillas with funds and the Sudanese leader, General Nimeiri, announced his open support for the Eritrean movement and for the conservative Ethiopian Democratic Union in Begemdir province, after discovering that the Derg had been involved, with Libya, in assisting Sudanese rebels in an attempt to overthrow his government in July 1976. The Derg had agreed to support the Libyan scheme in return for Colonel Gadaffi's agreement to withdraw his support for the Eritrean movement. From early 1977, the Ethiopian army in Eritrea, weary, demoralised and outnumbered, receiving no reinforcements for its depleted contingent of 25,000 men, began losing major towns and garrisons to the guerrilla forces. By mid-1977, Ethiopian troops controlled little more than Asmara and the ports of Massawa and Assab.

At this critical juncture, Mengistu turned to the Soviet Union for help. The Russians had followed the course of the revolution with avid interest, but they only became directly involved in Ethiopia as a result of Mengistu's desperate need for arms. A secret arms deal was negotiated in Moscow in December 1976. In February 1977, when Mengistu emerged triumphant from the gun battle at Menelik's palace in Addis Ababa, the Russians acted swiftly with messages of support. They were averse, however, to playing a major role as Ethiopia's military sponsor while Ethiopia retained military links with the United States. The Americans too had responded to the Derg's difficulties in Eritrea by providing emergency deliveries of arms in 1976. But under the new Carter administration, the United States took a more critical view of the Derg's policies. In February 1977, the United States government condemned human rights violations in Ethiopia and cut its military aid grants. In April the US announced it would reduce its military assistance team in Ethiopia and close its communications base at Kagnew near Asmara by September. Mengistu responded by ordering the expulsion of the American military assistance team and the immediate closure of the Kagnew facility. The Americans then suspended all military supplies to Ethiopia. Thus Mengistu was left heavily dependent on the Russians.

The gamble that the Russians took in Ethiopia was a

considerable one. Mengistu's regime was facing the possibility of military defeat in Eritrea. It was beset by revolts in several other provinces and by internecine warfare on the streets of Addis Ababa. Only with massive amounts of military aid was it likely to survive. Yet by arming Ethiopia, the Russians risked alienating the Somali government, its main ally in Africa, which provided bases and airfields highly valued by the Russian navy and air force. The Russians endeavoured at first to juggle with both sides. While providing Mengistu with the arms he so badly needed, they also tried to mediate between Ethiopia and Somalia, proposing a federation of all Marxist-Leninist countries on the Red Sea: Somalia, Ethiopia and the People's Democratic Republic of Yemen on the other side of the Straits of Bab el Mandeb. The Cuban leader, Fidel Castro, was also active as an intermediary. But the idea proved abortive. Mengistu and Siad failed to come to terms. The Russians thus found themselves in the awkward position of arming both Somalia and Ethiopia as the two sides drew close once more to war over the Ogaden.

Taking advantage of the Derg's preoccupation with Eritrea, where half of the Ethiopian army was under siege, Somali guerrillas renewed their attacks on the Ogaden early in 1977, probing Ethiopian defences and capturing government outposts. In July 1977, Siad, judging that the time was right for a full-scale invasion, committed Somali regular forces to the Ogaden. Their advance was swift and effective. By August, the Somalis controlled most the Ogaden. In September they captured Jijiga, an Ethiopian tank base, and pressed on towards the town of Harar and the rail and industrial centre of Dire Dawa, the third largest city in Ethiopia. Outside Harar, the Somali forces were checked. When Siad requested more Soviet arms, he was turned down. In November, Somalia abrogated its Treaty of Friendship and Cooperation with the Soviet Union and expelled all Russian personnel. The Somalis were left in possession of all of Ogaden except for two strategic towns, but without the support of any major arms supplier.

Shortly after Somalia broke with the Soviet Union, the Russians committed themselves to Ethiopia on such a massive scale that the course of the wars in the Ogaden and in Eritrea was changed. Starting from the end of November, a huge airlift and sealift was mounted by the Russians, ferrying tanks, fighter aircraft, artillery, armoured personnel carriers and hundreds of military advisers to Ethiopia. In December, Cuban combat troops were sent there. Armed with Soviet weapons and trained by Cuban instructors, new regular forces and militia units were added to the Ethiopian army. By the end of the year, Mengistu had at his disposal some 250,000 men. But the Ethiopians' main striking force consisted of Cuban troops, which at their peak numbered 17,000. In February 1978, the Ethiopian counter-offensive in the Ogaden was launched, led by Cuban armour. After falling back towards the town of Jijiga, the Somalis suffered a crushing defeat there early in March, and four days later they announced their withdrawal from the Ogaden.

The full force of the Ethiopian army, supported once more by Russian and Cuban logistics, was now turned on Eritrea. While the Ethiopians had been fighting to block Somali advances in the Ogaden, they had come close to a major defeat in Eritrea. In December 1977, Eritrean guerrillas had nearly succeeded in capturing the port of Massawa, gaining possession of most of the town and leaving the Ethiopians holding only the port itself. Outside Asmara, guerrilla forces controlled the road network and sporadically shelled the capital's airport. But as more and more reinforcements were dispatched to Eritrea, Ethiopian forces steadily regained control of the towns and much of the countryside.

Mengistu thus succeeded in holding the old Empire together. His regime, brutal but effective, was deliberately portrayed as following a tradition of strong Ethiopian rulers. Indeed, Mengistu came to be compared with the Emperor Tewodros, a nineteenth century ruler who started his career as a minor local chieftain, fought his way up to take the Crown and then strove to reunite the Empire after a period of disintegration. Mengistu chose as his headquarters Menelik's palace and he took to presiding over official functions from an ornate velvet chair favoured by Haile-Selassie, while members of the Derg stood respectfully to one side. Many of the reforms he implemented, on land redistribution, on medical care, on literacy campaigns, were successful. But neither in Eritrea nor in the Ogaden were the rebellions suppressed. Guerrilla warfare continued and remained as troublesome to Mengistu as it had been to his predecessor.

*

At about the twelfth parallel, there is a broad belt running across Africa which marks a generic change in the nature of the terrain and the peoples living thereabout. To the north lie the great desert regions of Africa, the domain of Muslim, often nomadic people, influenced by Arabic culture and traditions. To the south lies tropical Africa, populated by black negroid tribes with multifarious languages and religions. This fault line, as it is sometimes called, provides a constant source of friction. In the case of two countries which straddle it—Sudan and Chad—the enmity aroused between the north and south has led to prolonged conflict.

The Sudan was often thought of as a country of two halves. For most of the colonial era, it was governed, on behalf of an Anglo-Egyptian condominium, by two separate British administrations, one which dealt with the relatively advanced North, the other with the remote and backward provinces of the South. The two halves were different in every way: the North was hot, dry, partly desert, inhabited by Arabic-speaking Muslims who accounted for three quarters of the country's population; the South was green, fertile, with a high rainfall, populated by diverse African tribes, mostly animist in belief but including a small Christian minority which had graduated from mission schools. There was even a physical barrier between the two regions, a vast swamp known as the *sudd* stretching across thousands of square miles, where the channels of the Nile were lost in a mass of floating papyrus, almost as impenetrable in modern times as it was during the nineteenth century. What links of history there were between the North and South provided a source of grievance. In the nineteenth century, Northern traders had plundered the South in search of slaves and ivory. Tales of the slave trade were passed from one generation to the next in the South, sustaining a legacy of bitterness and hatred towards Northerners which endured beyond independence. The Northerners, meanwhile, tended to treat Southerners as contemptuously as they had done in the past, referring to them as *abid*—slaves—even until modern times.

When the British authorities set the Sudan on the road to self-government, they endeavoured to link together the North and the South in what was hoped would eventually become an equal partnership. The change of policy was announced in 1946, when ample time still seemed available. In 1948, Southern members were appointed to the Sudan's legislative assembly. From the outset, though, Southern politicians expressed fears that Northerners, because of their greater experience and sophistication, would soon dominate and exploit the South. The South was ill prepared for self-government. There were no organised political parties there, nor any sense of national consciousness uniting its disparate tribes. When negotiations over self-government for the Sudan were conducted in 1953, Southerners were neither consulted nor represented. The first Southern political party was launched only in 1953, the same year that self-government was granted. Southern politicians immediately began to campaign for federal status for the South. Their worst fears about Northern domination were realised when new civil service appointments, replacing British officials with Sudanese, were made in 1954. Out of a total of some 800 senior posts, only six were awarded to Southerners. The presence of Northern administrators and traders in the South, often abusive in their dealings with the local populace, soon rekindled old resentments. In July 1955, demonstrations over a labour dispute at Nzara erupted into violence; at least twenty people died when security forces opened fire, an event which some Southerners marked as the outbreak of conflict between the North and the South. In August, the Southern Corps of the army, commanded by Northern officers but consisting almost entirely of Southern troops, mutinied. The mutineers, led by Southern junior officers and NCOs in league with disgruntled Southern politicians, succeeded in gaining control of the whole of Equatoria province except for the capital, Juba, and received widespread local support. Northern officials and traders were hunted down and several hundred were killed. The Khartoum authorities reestablished their control by dispatching some 8,000 troops from the North. Some mutineers surrendered, others fled into the bush with their arms. In December, the Sudanese parliament adopted a resolution agreeing to give full consideration to Southern demands for federal status after independence, due in January 1956. But the prospects for an amicable solution to the dispute, as the British departed, seemed slim.

The Southern campaign for federal status continued after independence, but to no avail. In 1958, an army coup brought to power General Abboud, who set out to suppress opposition in the South, as in the North, believing that the Southern problem could be overcome by introducing firm measures. Military governors and administrators in the South spent much energy on efforts to promote Islam and the use of Arabic, on the grounds that this would encourage national unity. Several Islamic Institutes were opened and the day of rest, previously observed on Sunday in the South, was changed to Friday to concur with the Muslim practice in the North. Christian missionaries, who became critical of the government's policies, were expelled *en masse* from the South in 1962, accused of interfering in political affairs. Meanwhile leading Southern politicians, fearful of arrest, escaped abroad, set up exile organisations and, with help from Christian churches, began to canvass for international support. Intermittently, bands of dissidents, mostly former soldiers from the Southern Corps, carried out raids on army and police posts, but their efforts initially had little effect. In 1963, however, they joined together, taking the name of Anya Nya, derived from words meaning 'snake venom', and launched a sustained guerrilla campaign.

The secessionist war in the southern Sudan continued for ten years, claiming hundreds of thousands of lives. Like most civil wars, it was fought with particular ruthlessness. Neither side took prisoners. 'We do not want mercy and we are not prepared to give it,' said the Anya Nya when outlining their objectives. The guerrillas obtained arms from Congolese rebels and also received support at a later stage from Ethiopia and Israel. An attempt to solve the South's grievances was made at a conference in Khartoum in 1965, after Abboud's regime had fallen; it ended in failure but exposed to many Northerners for the first time the depth of mistrust and bitterness that educated Southerners felt towards them. When General Nimeiri, an officer who had seen service in the South, seized power in 1969, he continued to prosecute the war vigorously but, recognising the need for a political solution, he offered Southerners more favourable terms. In peace negotiations between the Khartoum government and the Southern Sudan Liberation Front, conducted under Haile-Selassie's auspices in Addis Ababa in February 1972, Nimeiri agreed to make major concessions allowing the South a wide measure of local autonomy. The three Southern provinces were linked together as a separate region endowed with its own elected assembly and executive authority, while Anya Nya guerrillas were accepted into the ranks of the Sudanese army. The peace agreement was successfully implemented due largely to the immense popularity and prestige that Nimeiri gained in the South by making it possible. In 1983, however, anti-government activities broke out anew.

*

The conflict in Chad too sprang from ancient hostility between Northerners and Southerners, dating from the days when Muslim chieftains raided the South for slaves. But it was made infinitely more complex by the way in which the North itself became divided between rival warlords and by the extent to which foreign governments sought to meddle in the warfare for their own advantage. Indeed, Chad came to resemble a jigsaw of so many ethnic, religious and regional antagonisms that at times it seemed inherently ungovernable. The French had succeeded in maintaining control effectively for forty years, relying on an army of no more than 2,000 men. But once they had departed, old rivalries and hatreds rose to the surface, eventually tearing the country apart into warring fiefdoms.

In Chad, it was Southerners rather than Northerners who emerged in control of the government at independence in 1960. They had welcomed the advent of French rule as a protection against slave raids from the North, accepted French education and worked their way up through the lower ranks of the administration into political life, and finally into national government. As peasant farmers, they had also built up a thriving cotton trade. About half of Chad's population of three million lived in the southernmost prefectures, mostly members of the Sara tribe, some of whom were Christian, others animist. The Northerners, meanwhile, preferred their nomadic existence, resisting French endeavours to draw them into the modern world. In the far north lived the fiercely independent Toubou, black Muslims of the Sahara, who had fought on against the imposition of French rule until 1930. Their Saharan zone—the provinces of Borkou, Ennedi and Tibesti, usually referred to as the BET—remained under the control of French military officers until 1965, five years after independence.

Chad's first President, François Tombalbaye, a former teacher from the southern Sara tribe, began his regime with a high reputation, but became increasingly autocratic and ended up running one of the more notorious tyrannies in Africa. He was intolerant of opposition, banned political parties and arbitrarily arrested opponents. Chad became a one-party state in 1962. The Muslim population, whom he disliked and distrusted, was dealt with particularly harshly. Muslims were gradually edged out of public life. The authority of their sultans and chiefs was reduced to its lowest level. As French officials in Muslim areas were withdrawn, their place was taken by Sara administrators, often poorly qualified, who enforced government measures with a heavy hand, regardless of Muslim traditions. Tax collectors gained particular notoriety for their harassment of the local population. The army, too, recruited mainly from Southern tribesmen, was known for its brutality and indiscipline. Overall, Tombalbaye's regime was marked by corruption and incompetence, but its impact was felt most forcefully on the sultanates of central Chad.

The first revolt against the government broke out in Malgalmé, an isolated region in central Chad, in 1965. Muslim peasants rioting against tax collectors were fired on by government troops and many subsequently fled to take up arms. The rebellion spread eastwards, gathering momentum. Bands of Muslim dissidents roamed about the countryside, attacking administrative and military posts, murdering government officials and local collaborators, stealing cattle and burning crops. The government in Fort Lamy, the capital, referred only to acts of banditry, but in reality local administrators had been forced by 1967 to retreat to the safety of the towns. Further trouble erupted in the far north soon after French military officers were withdrawn in 1965, handing control over to Tombalbaye's army. Sara troops stationed in the BET provinces acted as an occupying force. New restrictions were imposed to control the unruly Toubou. These included a ban on the wearing of turbans and on meetings of more than three persons. The movement of livestock was regulated. Attempts were made to force nomads into fixed settlements. Both men and women offenders were given humiliating punishments. In 1965, the entire population of the settlement of Bardai was arrested after a soldier had been killed during an affray between Toubou and the army. The following year, a prominent Muslim leader, the Derde of Tibesti, fled to Libya with a thousand followers when government troops were sent to arrest him for protesting against the diminution of his office. In 1968, Toubou Nomad Guards in Aazou mutinied and attacked the small local garrison manned by Southern troops.

The rebellions in the east and in the north had reached such a scale by 1968 that Tombalbaye was compelled to appeal for help from the French army, under the terms of a defence treaty between France and Chad signed in 1960. Accordingly, French paratroops, followed by the Foreign Legion and marines, were dispatched to Chad, but only on the condition that Tombalbaye also accepted a French civilian mission to investigate what reforms needed to be made. The mission produced a report that was highly critical of Tombalbaye's regime. Among the reforms he was required to introduce were measures restoring to Muslim chieftains many of their original powers. Under French pressure, Tombalbaye also agreed to release political prisoners and to broaden his administration by appointing Muslim ministers excluded from office since 1963. French troops, meanwhile, succeeded in driving back rebel groups in the east and in the north, although they were never entirely defeated. In 1971, French forces began to pull out.

The calm in Chad did not survive for long. No sooner had French troops restored control than Tombalbaye was beset by political plots and intrigues, amongst the Sara now as well as his Northern opponents. Once more he reacted by ordering arbitrary arrests. He also tried to exert control over the Sara by embarking on a cultural revolution, replacing French customs with a revival of the cult of Yondo, the traditional Sara initiation rites. Yondo ceremonies, involving gruesome ordeals in the bush for weeks on end, were made compulsory for Sara youths and for candidates seeking admission to the civil service or appointment to high public office. Tombalbaye later tried to extend the Yondo campaign by inducting senior civil servants, politicians and high-ranking military officers. In southern Chad, Yondo acquired the status of a semi-official religion. All individuals were obliged to assume authentic indigenous names and register them. Tombalbaye changed his first name from François to Ngarta, and the name of the capital from Fort Lamy to Ndjamena. Christians who refused to submit to the Yondo campaign were persecuted. The eventual result of Tombalbaye's cultural revolution was that he provoked opposition at every level, from urban officials, university students, army officers and Christian missionaries. When he then attempted to purge the army officer corps of suspected opponents, the army struck back In 1975, Tomalbaye was killed during an army *coup d'etat*.

Chad's new military leader, General Félix Malloum, a Southern officer whom Tombalbaye had imprisoned two years previously, pursued a more conciliatory course, but found his administration increasingly harassed by rebel Muslim groups which showed no interest in negotiating a settlement. The fortunes of the rebels, since they had been subdued by the French army, had fluctuated. Their common aim was to overthrow the central government in Ndjamena, dominated as much by Southerners under Malloum as under Tombalbaye, and to seize power for themselves. But they were riven by implacable jealousies and rivalries. Attempts to form a united front had met with little success. Initially in 1966, dissident Muslim politicians living in exile had established Frolinat, the *Front pour la Libération du Tchad*, with the aim of uniting active opposition to Tombalbaye. Rebel groups fighting Tombalbaye adopted the name of Frolinat, but in practice they were only loosely connected with it. In the east, the insurgents came to be known as the First Liberation Army; in the far north, they assumed the title of the Second Liberation

Army, or, alternatively, the *Forces Armées du Nord* (FAN). Periods of internecine warfare were common. In 1976, a fatal rift developed within the leadership of FAN between two men whose struggle for supremacy was to engulf Chad in endless strife: Hissène Habré and Goukouni Oueddei. Both men came from the northern Toubou tribe; though from separate clans. Their backgrounds, however, were completely different. Habré, born in 1942, had gained a degree in social science from a French university and had briefly served as an administrator during Tombalbaye's regime, before joining the rebels. Goukouni, a son of the Derde of Tibesti, was a skilful and tenacious guerrilla commander, but illiterate. In their dispute, Goukouni gained the upper hand. Habré was expelled from FAN's war council and, taking about three hundred followers with him, he moved out of the far north—the BET provinces—into eastern Chad. Despite this rift in the insurgents' ranks, General Malloum's forces were faced with an increase in guerrilla attacks. What accounted for the upsurge in rebel activities was the growing interest that Colonel Gaddafi in neighbouring Libya was taking in Chad's affairs.

Gaddafi's policy towards Chad in the past had varied from open support for the rebels to moves for a rapprochement with Tombalbaye. But he soon demonstrated that he had territorial ambitions there. In 1973, Libyan troops clandestinely took control of the Aazou Strip, a narrow wedge of land on the northernmost edge of the BET, adjacent to the Libyan border. Gaddafi's deployment into the Aazou Strip was the main cause of the rift between Habré and Goukouni: Habré insisted on reclaiming the area from Libya; Goukouni preferred to accept the aid that Gaddafi was willing to offer the rebels. Having won the contest, Goukouni benefited from substantially increased supplies of weapons from Libya. His forces, as a result, made steady advances in 1977 across the BET provinces in the far north. At the same time, Gaddafi supported an insurgent group in eastern Chad known as the Volcan army, which had taken over from the First Liberation Army. In a joint offensive launched in 1978, Goukouni's forces and the Volcan army, supported by Libyan troops, made a rapid thrust southwards towards the capital, Ndjamena. To stave off defeat, General Malloum called for help from France. A thousand French troops and combat aircraft were thrown into battle and routed the rebel forces on the road to Ndjamena.

In the aftermath of the 1978 clashes, a new alliance was formed between General Malloum and Habré, giving Northerners a major role in the government for the first time. Habré's fortunes had changed dramatically since he had left the far north. From his new base in eastern Chad, he had raised a tough, well disciplined force, gained support from Sudan and established a strong enough position in negotiations with Malloum to obtain the post of prime minister in a new 'government of national union'. The alliance did not last long. In February 1979, in what became known as the first battle of Ndjamena, Habré's forces and Malloum's national army fought for supremacy. French troops stationed in the capital made no attempt to intervene. The national army, weak and demoralised, was driven out and headed southwards, but before retreating, Southern troops massacred thousands of Muslim civilians. When Northern soldiers took possession of the city, they retaliated with equal ferocity against Southerners. Thousands of Sara residents fled southwards, leaving the administration to collapse. As the cycle of revenge continued, thousands of Muslim traders in the south were killed. In the following months, Chad had no government at all.

A host of international mediation attempts—by France, Nigeria, Sudan and Libya—was launched to try to devise a solution. Eventually, in November 1979, a shaky coalition government comprising no less than ten Muslim factions together with Southern representatives, was formed; Goukouni was chosen as president, Habré as minister of defence and the Southern leader, Colonel Kamougue, a French-trained officer, as vice-president. In Ndjamena, troops from five different armies patrolled the streets. Within a matter of weeks, the bloody struggle for power was resumed. Habré's forces clashed with pro-Libyan factions. In April 1980, Habré was ousted from the coalition government. Sporadic fighting continued for months longer. Finally, in December 1980, Libyan troops, backed by tanks and combat aircraft, combined with Goukouni's forces to drive Habré's army out of the capital. Habré fled to Cameroon; Goukouni was installed as president. Libya's intervention provoked an outcry among African states which feared Gaddafi's expansionist schemes and, after remaining in Chad for nearly a year, Libyan troops were withdrawn and replaced by an OAU peace-keeping force. As the Libyans withdrew, Habré's forces, which had regrouped in Sudan, crossed the eastern frontier and occupied eastern Chad. In June 1982, supplied with funds from the United States, they advanced on Ndjamena. Goukouni fled to Cameroon; Habré was installed as president. In 1983, Goukouni's forces, supported by the Libyans, occupied northern Chad and then advanced on Ndjamena. In response to Habré's appeals for help, French troops and aircraft were sent to Chad to act as a buffer between the rival armies. France thus resumed responsibility for deciding Chad's fate.

CHAPTER TWENTY-FIVE

The Collapse of the Portuguese Empire

The prospects for Portugal's African empire as it entered the 1960s seemed auspicious. After years of economic neglect, the two main Portuguese territories, Angola and Mozambique, were proving to be valuable assets to the metropolitan power. Angola, in particular, with the discovery of oilfields, the expansion of mining and the buoyant revenues from its coffee industry, was enjoying boom conditions. Both territories were attracting new foreign investment. The cities of Portuguese Africa—Luanda, Lourenço Marques, Beira, Lobito, Benguela—were among the most modern on the continent, well served by their own newspapers, broadcasting stations, sports clubs and museums. By 1960 Luanda, the capital of Angola, had become the third largest city in the Portuguese domain after Lisbon and Oporto; and the white population of Angola had risen to 200,000, the largest white community in tropical Africa. While other colonial powers were beset by the ferment of African nationalism, the tranquillity of Portuguese Africa seemed convincing proof to the authorities in Lisbon that Portugal alone possessed a particular talent for creating multi-racial communities which obviated the dangers of such unrest. What signs of political opposition there were to Salazar's dictatorship, among whites as well as blacks, were dealt with effectively enough by the secret police, the *Polícia Internacional de Defesa do Estado* (Pide), which had established branches in Portugal's African territories in 1957. By 1960, most clandestine nationalist groups formed in the 1950s had been forced underground or driven into exile.

Thus the explosion of violence which struck Angola in 1961 caught the Portuguese administration unprepared. In mid-March, roving bands of Africans armed with machetes, homemade muskets and other crude weapons attacked isolated European settlements and plantations, killing several hundred whites, including women and children, and massacring African migrant workers. The attacks erupted in two areas, one along the frontier with the Congo, the other about one hundred miles south in the Dembos Hills. From these two areas the uprising spread until, by June, it affected most of northwestern Angola. Some fifty administrative posts and settlements were overrun. When the violence started, there were no troops stationed in northern Angola, nor did the Portuguese administration have large enough forces elsewhere in the country to deal with such a widespread rebellion. Reinforcements were despatched from Lisbon. By August, with 17,000 men in the field, the Portuguese military succeeded in driving back the rebels into the two pockets of territory in which the first attacks had been made. By October they had reoccupied all the lost settlements and administrative posts. The wave of repression that was unleashed against the local population was brutal and often indiscriminate. Even areas not involved in the violence met with reprisals. White militia groups roamed the countryside killing at will. Tens of thousands of refugees fled to the Congo. In the six months that the uprising lasted, probably some twenty thousand Africans and about seven hundred whites died.

The magnitude of the 1961 uprising in Angola shook the very foundations of the Portuguese empire. It had been organised in part by an Angolan exile group based in the Congo, the *União das Populaçõs de Angola* (UPA), with the aim of driving the Portuguese out of Angola. The UPA had built up strong support among the Bakongo of northern Angola. Party agents had been sent across the border into Angola with instructions to foment an uprising. But the extent to which the rebellion spread, flaring up in areas beyond Bakongo territory, and the sudden and spontaneous character of much of the violence indicated massive discontent with Portuguese rule. There were many causes lying behind the 1961 uprising. In northern Angola, strong local grievances had arisen over the loss of African land acquired by Portuguese farmers for their coffee and palm plantations, and over the harsh treatment often meted out by Portuguese settlers and traders. It was an area, too, directly affected by the independence of the Belgian Congo some nine months before, which had aroused excitement among the Bakongo living on both sides of the border. Angolan exiles living in the Congo clearly expected that the Portuguese in Angola, like the Belgians in the Congo, would leave rather than fight to stay. Whatever its origins, the impact of the uprising led the Portuguese to make the first major reforms in their colonial policies for more than sixty years. Decrees were announced abolishing all forms of compulsory labour and prohibiting illegal land expropriation. Equal rights were accorded to 'civilised' and 'non-civilised' citizens of the Empire. In an attempt to win the support of the African population in northern Angola, the Portuguese authorities launched an ambitious programme of social rehabilitation, education and economic development.

But Salazar refused to contemplate any political reforms or to relax his grip over political activity. With the same rigid determination that he had shown in the 1930s, he held that Africa remained an inalienable part of the Portuguese nation. In one territory after another, therefore, nationalist groups turned to guerrilla warfare. Guerrilla activity in Angola continued after the 1961 uprising had been suppressed; it broke out in Guinea-Bissau in 1963 and in Mozambique in 1964. In each case the wars were started by exile groups using neighbouring African territories as their bases from which to recruit and train supporters and to gather arms. Initially, guerrilla attacks were confined to border areas, then they slowly spread deeper into the interior. In Angola and Mozambique, however, the guerrilla campaigns had little overall effect. For many years, the Portuguese army was successful in containing the guerrillas in remote areas, far from the main towns and economically productive regions. And the guerrilla movements themselves were frequently wracked by bouts of internal dissension, personal feuds and tribal antagonisms.

The Angolan nationalists were divided almost from the outset. At first two principal movements competed for ascendancy, then three. The result was to undermine much of the effectiveness of the guerrilla campaign against the Portuguese, and eventually to lead to civil war. The UPA had started its existence as a Bakongo tribal organisation, launched in 1957 in Léopoldville by Angolan Bakongo with the idea of resurrecting the old Kongo kingdom, and though it subsequently proclaimed nationalist objectives, it remained predominantly a Bakongo party, attracting little support from other areas of Angola. Its leader, Holden Roberto, named after a British Baptist missionary, had spent most of his life in exile in the Congo. For eight years he had worked as an accountant in the Belgian administration. Roberto had been converted to the nationalist cause while attending the All-African People's Conference in Accra in 1958, where he met Nkrumah and George Padmore. The following year he travelled to New York, where he established contact with American organisations. After the Congo's independence in 1960, Lumumba allowed him to establish a base in Léopoldville and to use Radio Léopoldville for propaganda broadcasts to Angola, urging revolt against Portuguese rule. The 1961 uprising in northwestern Angola then propelled the UPA to prominence. Help was forthcoming from Tunisia and the Algerians, and recognition from the Organisation of African Unity. The Americans, too, showed an interest in the movement. Under the Kennedy administration, government officials took a sympathetic view of African nationalism and sought out nationalist leaders free from Communist association. The UPA was cleared by the Central Intelligence Agency as being a suitable venture for American support. From 1962, Roberto received covert American assistance in the form of money and arms, and even when this aid was cut off in 1969, Roberto himself continued to receive from the CIA an annual retainer of $10,000. Above all, the UPA depended on the assistance of the Congolese government, which allowed it to establish headquarters in Léopoldville and training camps and refugee centres in the lower Congo close to the border with Angola. But the initial impetus achieved by the UPA, or the *Frente Nacional de Libertação de Angola* (FNLA) as it was called from 1962, was soon lost through spasms of internal dissension. Roberto ran the UPA as his personal fiefdom, controlling all finance and administration and tolerating no rivals. He rarely ventured into Angola, preferring a comfortable *émigré* lifestyle in Léopoldville where he had extensive business interests. Weakened by splits and desertions, the FNLA's guerrilla campaign had virtually come to a halt by 1965.

The other main nationalist organisation, the *Movimento Popular de Libertação de Angola* (MPLA), had quite different origins. It was founded at a secret meeting in Luanda in 1956 by a group of radical Angolan intellectuals, with the aim of overthrowing Portuguese rule. Its leaders were mostly *mesticos* (mixed race) but included a number of white Angolans. Some had links with the underground Angolan Communist Party. The MPLA attracted a following among dissident civil servants and students in Luanda and other towns in the Kimbundu hinterland. For several years it managed to operate clandestinely but most of its leading members were caught in a wave of arrests carried out by the Pide in 1959 and again in 1960. The MPLA thus became an exile organisation, establishing offices first in Paris, then moving in 1959 to Conakry, the capital of Guinea, where Sékou Touré provided it with a headquarters, then in 1961 transferring to Léopoldville. The MPLA's leader, Agostinho Neto, was a physician and an accomplished poet, widely admired for his opposition to Portuguese rule. While studying medicine in Portugal he had been arrested on several occasions for his involvement in opposition politics. After graduating as a doctor of medicine, he had returned to Angola in 1959, but he was arrested in the Pide sweep in 1960, deported to the Cape Verde islands, then transferred to Lisbon, where he lived under restriction. In 1962 he escaped from Portugal and resurfaced in Léopoldville, and it was there in 1962 that he was elected as the MPLA's president.

The MPLA was regarded at the time as a largely ineffective organisation lacking an adequate military wing and debilitated by internal power struggles and dissension. Its attempts to infiltrate men into Angola from the Congo were persistently blocked by the FNLA. Roberto also rejected the MPLA's proposals for an alliance. Expelled from Léopoldville in 1963, the MPLA set up offices on the other side of the Congo river in Brazzaville. It was largely kept alive by support from Soviet bloc states. Help was also forthcoming from Cuba. The Cuban revolutionary Ché Guevara met Neto in Brazzaville in 1965 and was sufficiently impressed to provide the MPLA with

Cuban instructors. Guerrilla recruits were sent to Cuban and Soviet bloc states for training. Unable to break through northern Angola and reach Kimbundu areas where its main support lay, the MPLA opened a new front in eastern Angola in 1966, using Lusaka, the capital of Zambia, as headquarters. Initially, the eastern campaign made some headway, though the area was thinly populated and of little strategic significance. But a series of Portuguese counter-offensives between 1968 and 1973 resulted in major defeats for the MPLA there. And once again the party was brought to the verge of collapse by internal wrangling.

A third nationalist group, formed in 1966, also chose to launch a guerrilla campaign in eastern Angola, using Zambia as a rear base. The *União Nacional para a Independência Total de Angola* (Unita) was founded by Jonas Savimbi, one of Holden Roberto's former associates who had broken with the FNLA in 1964. Unita attracted support from the Ovimbundu, Angola's largest tribe, concentrated in the central highland districts of Huambo and Bié. Savimbi was unable to secure much foreign assistance, his guerrilla bands were poorly equipped and they were further harassed by attacks from the MPLA, which claimed eastern Angola as its own preserve. Unita was eventually driven out of the east and retreated to a small base area in central Angola.

In Mozambique, the progress made by nationalist guerrillas, after a decisive start in 1964, was equally limited. In the initial stages of its campaign, the *Frente Libertação de Moçambique* (Frelimo) made major advances in the two northernmost provinces, gaining widespread support among the Makonde. But Frelimo then failed to penetrate further south, mainly because of opposition from the Makua, Mozambique's largest tribe, which regarded Frelimo as a party of the Makonde, their traditional foes. Frelimo had been formed in 1962 in Dar es Salaam, the capital of Tanganyika (later Tanzania), as a coalition between three small nationalist groups. Its leader, Eduardo Mondlane, born in the southern Gaza district, had been the first African from Mozambique to enter the University of Lisbon. He had later studied at American universities and worked as a United Nations research officer. At the time of Frelimo's formation, he was a professor of anthropology at Syracuse University in New York State. Frelimo attracted support from the Soviet bloc, which supplied arms, and from China, which provided military instructors. The Americans, too, showed an interest, as they had done in Angola. In 1963, Mondlane received a payment of $10,000 from the CIA. Frelimo's main training bases were in Tanzania, but it became sufficiently well established in the two northern provinces of Cabo Delgado and Niassa to set up a rudimentary administration there. Like the nationalist organisations in Angola, Frelimo was constantly afflicted by splits, personal rivalries and defections to the Portuguese. Mondlane was killed in Dar es Salaam in 1969 by a parcel bomb, probably a Portuguese device planted by his opponents within the party. But Frelimo's greatest failure in the early years of the war was its inability to break out of its home base in the far north. The two northern provinces were sparsely settled, remote areas, nearly a thousand miles from the capital, Lourenço Marques. Guerrilla activity there had little effect elsewhere in the country, and never interfered with daily life in the south where most of the white population lived. And though the armed forces found it difficult to dislodge Frelimo from the north, the guerrillas there represented no serious threat to the Portuguese administration.

Only in Guinea-Bissau, a small enclave in West Africa, did the nationalists succeed in gaining control over large areas of the country, driving Portuguese forces back to a string of fortified camps and surrounding the major towns. Guinea-Bissau was the least valuable of the Portuguese colonies; it had little economic or strategic importance and it attracted only a few thousand white settlers. Yet for reasons of prestige and for fear of setting a precedent, the Portuguese were obliged to commit huge forces to stave off collapse there. The war had been started in 1963 by the *Partido da Independência da Guiné e Cabo Verde* (PAIGC), which became one of the most effective nationalist movements ever founded in black Africa. Infiltrating across the border from Guinea-Conakry, PAIGC guerrillas rapidly established bases in southern areas of the colony. A Portuguese counter-offensive in 1964 failed and from then on PAIGC forces in the south were never again seriously threatened. By 1965 the guerrillas had control of as much as one third of Guinea-Bissau and the areas under their occupation steadily expanded. The architect of the PAIGC campaign was Amilcar Cabral, a Portuguese-trained agronomist who had helped form the PAIGC as a clandestine nationalist group in 1956. In 1960, Cabral established a base in Conakry and it was from there that he directed the PAIGC campaign, laying strong emphasis on political mobilisation. Once the guerrillas had consolidated their hold, he organised schools, hospitals, a judicial system and even elections. In a counter-move designed to win over the support of the local population, a new Portuguese commander, General Spinola, posted to Guinea-Bissau in 1968, embarked on a massive programme of social and economic development. But overall Spinola's efforts made little difference to the Portuguese position. More than half of the country remained under PAIGC control.

At the beginning of the 1970s, Portugal was engaged in nationalist wars in each of its African territories, adamantly refusing to consider any form of political compromise. Salazar's successor, Marcello Caetano, who took office in 1968, continued the same colonial strategy as before, holding fast to the notion of an indivisible Portuguese nation. He informed General Spinola that he would prefer defeat in Guinea to any negotiation that might provide a precedent for Mozambique and Angola. In terms of manpower, the wars involved a heavy burden. Portugal deployed in all some 140,000 men in Africa: 50,000 in Angola, 50,000 in Mozambique, and 40,000 in Guinea. Yet, apart from the case of Guinea, the wars did not constitute a serious threat. Casualties were relatively low. And the counter-insurgency tactics employed by the army in Mozambique and Angola were largely effective. At intervals, large-scale sweeps would be mounted against the guerrillas. In an operation in northern Mozambique in 1970 named 'Gordian Knot', which involved the use of 35,000 troops, Frelimo forces were driven back towards the Tanzanian border. The army's strategy of constructing fortified villages, known as *aldeamentos*, was also useful in depriving guerrillas of contact with the local population. The Portuguese were successful, moreover, in recruiting large numbers of Africans into the ranks of the army and local militias. In Guinea, African commando units set up by Spinola gained a fearsome reputation. In Mozambique, African recruits formed a high proportion of paratroop and commando units and specialist counter-insurgency groups. In the 1970s, Africans formed up to sixty per cent of the colonial armies. The possibility of military defeat or withdrawal was considered to be remote. Even in Guinea, the PAIGC was unable to force a resolution of the conflict. A secret American appraisal of the Portuguese wars, made for the National Security Council in 1969, forecast a period of continued stalemate. 'The rebels cannot oust the Portuguese and the Portuguese can contain but not eliminate the rebels,' it concluded.

From 1972, however, the Portuguese suffered serious setbacks. In Mozambique, Frelimo guerrillas, using Zambia as a rear base, infiltrated into the central Tete province, endangering the construction of the giant Cabora Bassa hydro-electric scheme on the Zambezi river and spreading their attacks slowly southwards towards the Beira region. Reinforcements had to be sent to Mozambique from Angola. In early 1974 a sudden increase in attacks on whites in rural areas in central Mozambique, in which five civilians were killed, sent a shock wave through the white community. No longer was the war in Mozambique a remote affair for the whites, and in fear and anger they turned against the army for failing to guarantee their protection. White demonstrators took to the streets in the towns of Vila de Manica and Vila Pery; and in Beira, whites hurled stones at military installations and demanded the closure of a luxury military hotel. In central Mozambique, the army still maintained local superiority, and the southern half of the country was unaffected by guerrilla activity. But its confidence was shaken and its morale rapidly declined.

In Guinea, too, the army was forced to give further ground. By 1973, the PAIGC controlled about three quarters of the country. Many army forts could only be maintained through air supply. Though Amilcar Cabral was assassinated in Conakry in January 1973 by PAIGC dissidents working with the Portuguese, the guerrilla campaign continued as forcefully as before. In September 1973, the PAIGC declared the independence of Guinea and within a few weeks it had been recognised as the legitimate authority in the country by more than sixty governments.

Weighed down by the burden of colonial wars which had lasted for thirteen years and about which there was an increasing sense of futility, the Portuguese officer corps grew resentful of Caetano's dictatorship. Initially, the opposition movement that developed within the armed forces was started by officers who were concerned only about their own professional grievances. The government's attempt in July 1973 to increase the number of army officers by offering non-career officers the same conditions and privileges as those of professional officers with combat experience in Africa produced an immediate outcry among career officers. In November, however, the Armed Forces Movement, influenced by a group of left-wing officers, plunged into radical criticism of the whole Portuguese regime. Among junior officers, there was profound disillusionment with Portugal's authoritarian government, its economic backwardness and especially with its debilitating colonial wars. A new generation within the army was inspired less by the grandiose ideas of Portuguese nationalism that Salazar and Caetano tried to inculcate than by policies of economic progress that other European states pursued. Africa, even in terms of trade, was of declining importance to Portugal. And the wars there were seen as unwanted legacies from the past. The military hierarchy, too, no longer believed that the wars could be won. In February 1975, General Spinola, regarded by the public as a national hero because of his war record, published a book entitled *Portugal and the Future* in which he stated that military victory was not possible. His book reflected the views of most of the officer corps. Caetano dismissed him as the army's deputy chief of staff.

On 25 April 1974, the Armed Forces Movement overthrew Caetano's regime and chose Spinola to head the new military junta. The coup in Lisbon was eventually to change the face of southern Africa, but for several months its effect on the fate of the Portuguese empire was far from clear. Spinola had no intention of abandoning the colonies. He was committed only to finding a political solution to the wars. Indeed he believed that the retention of Angola and Mozambique was vital to Portugal's own interests. What he hoped to achieve was a form of home rule for the colonies within a federal framework. He spoke privately of a timetable for self-government extending over 'a generation or so', during which time the process of democracy could be gradually introduced to Africa. The junior officers who had carried out the coup, however, soon made their own views felt. They saw no further advantage in clinging to the Empire and they established amicable contacts with African nationalist organisations. In the struggle for power between Spinola and the radical wing of the Armed Forces Movement that followed the coup, Spinola eventually lost. In July he publicly agreed to negotiations over the transfer of power in the Portuguese colonies, and a few weeks later he resigned.

In the colonies, the immediate impact of the Lisbon coup was to cause confusion and disorder. With the collapse of Caetano's regime, the entire colonial administration fell into disarray. Portuguese army units in the field mostly retreated to barracks, ignoring official orders from Lisbon to continue the wars. In Guinea, the transfer of power was negotiated relatively swiftly. Portuguese troops in the field quickly established their own ceasefire and began to withdraw. By September, Guinea was recognised as an independent republic. In Mozambique, parts of the country were thrown into chaos. Hundreds of white settlers in rural areas, fearing revenge by the guerrillas and frightened by Frelimo's revolutionary Marxist image, abandoned their homes and fled to the coast. From early May, a mass white exodus from Mozambique began. The Portuguese army, weary and dispirited, withdrew from the field, allowing Frelimo to pour guerrillas into central Mozambique unhindered. Since most Portuguese troops refused to fight, an undeclared ceasefire prevailed. Negotiations between Portugal and Frelimo were protracted. Some whites, meanwhile, hoped to keep Mozambique as Portuguese territory; some wanted an autonomous white-ruled state and talked of staging a coup; others simply fled. Black groups opposed to Frelimo were launched belatedly, but made little headway. On 7 September, the Portuguese government signed an accord with the Frelimo leader, Samora Machel, paving the way for the establishment of a transitional government in which Frelimo was to play a predominant role. The following day, right-wing whites launched an abortive revolt. The white exodus gathered pace. By the time that Mozambique gained its independence in June 1975, the country had lost not only most of its administrators and officials, but also managers, technicians, artisans and shopkeepers. No links with Portugal remained.

The transition from Portuguese rule in Angola turned into disaster on a far greater scale. It originated from the contest for power between Angola's three rival nationalist factions which then grew into a massive civil war, causing the flight of almost the entire white population, and drawing the world's major powers and a host of other countries into perilous confrontation. The Portuguese abandoned all attempt to control the transition. On the eve of independence in November 1975, with much of the country engulfed in violence, the Portuguese high commissioner, Admiral Leonel Cardoso, held a brief ceremony in Luanda at which he announced he was transferring power to the 'Angolan people'. Not a single Angolan was present to witness the proceedings.

No serious effort was ever made by the nationalists to reconcile their differences. The race for power in Angola from the outset was conducted more in terms of an armed struggle than through political bargaining. At every stage of the conflict, each faction tried to gain advantage by appealing for support from foreign interests. The two principal foreign powers involved in the conflict, the United States and the Soviet Union, had no direct strategic interest in Angola. But both were determined, for reasons of their own prestige and because of their preoccupation with the global balance of power, to ensure that the Angolan factions they supported were triumphant. It was because the nationalist parties were so weak and disorganised in the first place, however, that foreign involvement in Angola acquired such crucial importance.

At the time of the Lisbon coup in April 1974, the faction that was strongest in military terms was Roberto's FNLA. His guerrilla army, after passing through a period of internal dissension and mutiny at its bases in Zaire (as the Congo was now called), had been reorganised and retrained with the help of President Mobutu's army. Mobutu had ambitions to play a pan-African role and he had taken advantage of the upheavals within the FNLA to bring it more directly under his own supervision. His personal relationship with Roberto had also grown closer as the result of Roberto's marriage to a kinswoman of his wife. In December 1973, Roberto had flown to Peking and persuaded the Chinese government to support the FNLA with military instructors and arms. In June 1974, an advance party of a team of 120 instructors arrived at Kinkuzu, the FNLA's main military base in Zaire, and a consignment of Chinese arms followed shortly afterwards. Roberto also retained his links with the American CIA. The difficulty facing the FNLA was that politically it was weak. Its support was confined to the Bakongo of northern Angola numbering about 700,000, and no effort had been made to win a following in other areas of the country. Roberto, from the comfort of his exile in Zaire, had been content to run little more than a border war against the Portuguese. His leadership in the past had been the cause of much of the infighting within the FNLA. Indeed, during a mutiny at Kinkuzu in 1972, it was only through the intervention of Mobutu's troops that he had managed to remain in control. Nevertheless, by comparison to the other factions, the FNLA was favourably placed. In September 1974, as Portuguese forces disengaged, newly trained and equipped FNLA troops were able to establish an occupied zone in northwestern Angola.

The MPLA, at this crucial juncture, was on the verge of collapse. The party had fragmented into three rival groups; guerrilla activity was at a standstill; and Soviet military supplies had been suspended for fear that they would be used for internal fighting. One of the MPLA's most ardent supporters, President Nyerere of Tanzania, had become so disillusioned with the party that he had used his influence with the Chinese to persuade them to support Roberto and the FNLA instead. It was largely through Nyerere's offices that Roberto had obtained Chinese assistance. At an acrimonious party conference in Lusaka, the capital of Zambia, in August 1947, Neto's leadership was openly assailed. The most serious challenge he faced came from one of the MPLA's most successful field commanders, Daniel Chipenda, a former professional soccer star who had organised the eastern campaign and who could count on larger guerrilla forces in his support than could Neto. Chipenda and his men subsequently broke with the MPLA and linked up with Roberto's FNLA, using southern Angola as a base. But Neto's fortunes then began to improve. In October, the Russians, fearing that China's success with the FNLA in Zaire and the subsequent deployment of FNLA troops in northern Angola would eclipse their own efforts in Angola, resumed their military supplies to the MPLA, hoping to rebuild it as a credible armed force. They were already concerned about the progress that China was making elsewhere in the southern African arena, particularly with liberation movements. The MPLA also began to make headway, mobilising its popular support in Angola. Its leaders, coming mostly from an urban, left-wing background, attracted African support in many towns. Luanda, the capital and the key to any bid for power, was regarded from the outset as an MPLA stronghold. The party was firmly rooted, too, in Kimbundu areas lying east of Luanda. Moreover, it gained vital help both from the Portuguese Communist Party and socialist groups then influential in Lisbon and from sympathetic Portuguese officials in Luanda. The head of the Portuguese military council in Angola, Admiral Rosa Coutinho, posted to Luanda after the Lisbon coup, was an active supporter of the MPLA. Despite these advantages, the MPLA remained essentially a regional party. Neither in the north among the Bakongo, nor in the south among the Ovimbundu, did it acquire much of a following.

Savimbi's Unita, at the time of the Lisbon coup, consisted of a force of no more than about one thousand poorly armed men operating in a small base area in the central highlands. The only significant foreign support it had received was from China, which had supplied small quantities of arms. Its potential, however, was considerable. The Ovimbundu, from whom Unita drew support, were the largest tribal group in the country, numbering about two million, and Savimbi, a charismatic figure who, alone among the nationalist leaders, had remained with his guerrilla forces in the field during the war, was regarded as a local hero. Unita was the first nationalist group to obtain a formal ceasefire with the Portuguese and Savimbi rapidly made overtures to Angola's whites, seeking their support. An OAU assessment of the strengths of the three movements early in 1975 estimated that Unita enjoyed the most support, followed by the FNLA, and then by the MPLA.

Under pressure from the OAU, the three nationalist leaders, Roberto, Neto and Savimbi, were brought together in January 1975 in Kenya, where they agreed to mutual recognition and to open negotiations on the transition from Portuguese rule to independence. On 10 January the negotiations moved to the Algarve in Portugal and they were concluded there on 15 January with a settlement known as the Alvor agreement. According to the Alvor agreement, Angola was to be administered by a coalition government composed of the three nationalist groups and the Portuguese until independence day set for 11 November 1975. Elections for a constituent assembly were to be held in October. During the transitional period, Portugal would retain a 24,000-man army in Angola. The three nationalist movements, meanwhile, would contribute 8,000 men each towards establishing a national army. The nationalists also agreed to place a freeze on their military positions as at January 1975. At the time of the Alvor agreement, the FNLA had a distinct military advantage. It possessed an armed force, estimated at 15,000 troops, which was relatively well equipped, and it was further supported by Daniel Chipenda's guerrilla army, several thousand strong, which had defected from the MPLA. The MPLA, by comparison, had about 3,000 trained guerrillas under its command, although it was rapidly expanding its forces through recruitment mainly in the Luanda area. Unita was also heavily recruiting among the Ovimbundu.

On 31 January, the new transitional government took office in a climate rife with suspicion and mistrust. On the following day, the first clash occurred in Luanda between the FNLA and MPLA troops. Seven people, including two officers in a Portuguese patrol who had tried to restore order, were killed. Further minor clashes broke out during February. In March, the Russians delivered substantial military supplies to the MPLA, intending to bolster it against the superior forces of the FNLA. An outbreak of heavy fighting between the two factions occurred in March after FNLA troops had attacked MPLA positions and massacred a group of MPLA supporters at Caxito, a town north of Luanda. Portuguese civilians, fearing that civil war was imminent, started to flee in thousands to Portugal, causing the collapse of government services and the economy; in the following six months, some 300,000 whites left Angola, the largest exodus of whites from Africa since Algerian days. The battle for the control of the capital continued for several months. The MPLA recruited to its side a force of about 4,000 armed Katangese, former Tshombe supporters based in exile in Angola, with an abiding hatred of Mobutu, whom the Portuguese had used in their war against the FNLA. The MPLA also turned to Cuba for help with training. The Cubans had provided instructors for the MPLA since 1965. In response to Neto's request for assistance made in May, a group of 230 Cuban instructors arrived in Angola in June to set up four military training centres. The centres were operational by August. Strengthened by the influx of Russian weapons and supported by the Katangese, the MPLA drove the FNLA and Unita out of Luanda in July and gained tentative control over other major towns, including the ports of Lobito, Benguela and Moçâmedes. It also held the Cabindan exclave, where the oilfields lay. The transitional government duly collapsed. From then on, the government in Luanda, with Portuguese consent, remained effectively in the hands of the MPLA.

At that stage, the Angolan civil war developed into a major international conflict. Much of what actually happened was obscured from view at the time and also deliberately distorted by propaganda campaigns which were waged simultaneously with the fighting. For many years after the violence had subsided, Angola was held up by some as an example of Russian and Cuban aggression in Africa, with sinister implications for the rest of the continent; President Kaunda of Zambia, who played a side role in the conflict, referred at the time to 'a plundering tiger and its deadly cubs'. Others later pointed to Angola as an example of the reckless adventures into which the American CIA was prepared to plunge; among such critics was the CIA's Angolan task force director, John

Stockwell, repenting of his own involvement in the affair. Yet others used Angola as an early illustration of South Africa's willingness to destabilise its African neighbours. The Angolan conflict had many facets. It was unquestionably a tragedy of great magnitude. And it was made ultimately worse by the way in which the ground was laid for a prolonged struggle between rival factions which continued well into the 1980s.

The Americans at first took only a passing interest in events in Angola. In July 1974 the CIA resumed some covert funding for the FNLA, but requests for arms from both the FNLA and Unita were turned down. When Russian assistance to the MPLA was resumed, the CIA lobbied in Washington for greater American support for the FNLA. In January 1975, after the Alvor agreement had been signed, the CIA was authorised to make a covert grant of US$300,000 to the FNLA, mainly to help Roberto make his mark in the transitional government. The money, made available in March, was used by the FNLA partly to acquire a television station and a daily newspaper in Luanda. These conspicuous deals immediately drew attention to the possibility that the CIA was seriously entering the fray. But still no military supplies were authorised.

By mid-July, however, not only had the balance on the battlefield in Angola shifted decisively in the MPLA's favour, but America's perspective of the Angolan conflict had radically altered. The American defeat in Vietnam in April 1975 had severely damaged its prestige in the world, and it had left the United States Secretary of State, Henry Kissinger, anxious to find ways of reasserting American power. Kissinger had never before taken any interest in African issues. Indeed he had always considered Africa, compared to the great theatres of Vietnam and the Middle East, to be a bore. But the rise of Soviet influence in Angola caught his attention. Kissinger argued that unless America countered Soviet activities in cases like Angola, then the larger global balance of power between the two superpowers would be impaired. He was convinced that Soviet objectives in Angola were to impose a government of its own choice on the country and to carve out a new sphere of influence. He maintained that if the West allowed that to happen unopposed, then the confidence of neighbouring pro-

Western states such as Zaire and Zambia would be severely shaken and US prestige around the world would again be adversely affected.

The influence of Zaire was a strong factor in American thinking. Zaire at the time was regarded as the key to US policy in black Africa and the Americans were as keen in the 1970s to keep Mobutu in power as they had been in the 1960s. Mobutu aspired to play a leading role in the Angolan drama and he therefore used what influence he had in Washington to persuade the Americans to support the FNLA. Zaire itself was already involved directly in Angola, not only through its own links with the FNLA, over which it exercised considerable control, but also because of Mobutu's decision to use his own troops in the conflict. Zairian officers had supported FNLA actions in Angola since February 1975; they had participated in the March round of fighting; and Mobutu was willing to commit further forces.

In deciding what action to take, Kissinger's options were limited. In the wake of the Vietnam defeat, neither Congress nor American public opinion was ready to tolerate another foreign adventure, particularly in a part of the world in which the United States had no apparent interest. Kissinger's own African experts in the State Department warned him to steer clear of Angola. Ignoring their advice, Kissinger and the CIA set up a major covert operation in Angola, while denying to Congress the extent of their involvement. The advantage of such a covert operation was that as well as avoiding any embarrassment with Congress, it reduced the possibility of a clash between the two superpowers. As Kissinger later put it, it kept American 'visibility' to a minimum. On 17 July, the National Security Council's 40 Committee approved a programme for Angola, in cash and arms worth $30 million, to be used in support of the FNLA and Unita. More funds were committed later. During August and September, a vast flow of American arms was secretly despatched to Angola through Zaire. Indirect aid for the Angolan movements was also channelled through Zaire. In July, Mobutu committed armoured car units to Angola. They were followed by Zairian paratroop companies in August, by two Zairian battalions in September, and another battalion in late October.

Meanwhile, a second scheme to defeat the MPLA, involving South African support for the FNLA and Unita, was taking shape. For the South Africans, the end of Portuguese rule in Africa carried major implications. Angola and Mozambique had long provided buffer zones shielding South Africa from direct contact with black-ruled states to the north and their transfer into the hands of black governments altered South Africa's entire defence strategy. In the case of Mozambique, even though Frelimo came to power as a revolutionary party proclaiming Marxist policies, the South Africans had quickly established an amicable working relationship with the authorities there. Much of Mozambique's foreign earnings depended on South Africa's use of its port and rail facilities and on the earnings of Mozambiquan workers in the South African mines. South Africa in turn relied on Mozambique for providing a large part of its labour force and for power from the Cabora Bassa hydro-electric scheme on the Zambezi river.

In the case of Angola, the South African attitude was quite different. The South Africans saw Russian involvement in Angola as part of a communist plan to dominate southern Africa. They also had a direct interest in Angola to the extent that nationalist guerrillas from the South West Africa People's Organisation (Swapo) used Angolan territory from which to launch attacks into South West Africa (Namibia), which South Africa controlled. The South Africans thus responded readily to approaches from the FNLA and Unita for help, in the hope that it might lead to the emergence of a moderate, pro-Western government in Luanda, amenable to South African interests. In May, Daniel Chipenda, whose headquarters were sited at Menongue in southern Angola, met South African intelligence officials in Windhoek, the capital of South West Africa; in July, Holden Roberto met South African officials in Zaire; and in August, Savimbi travelled to South Africa. The outcome was that in August South Africa in secret began to establish training facilities in southern Angola for the FNLA and Unita and to supply arms to the FNLA. South African troops were also moved north of the South West African border to occupy the site of the Cunene river hydro-electric project which they were financing.

By August, therefore, the Angolan conflict had become

decidedly complex. On one side, the MPLA retained control of the capital, Luanda, it had a tenuous hold over most of the towns of central and southern Angola, and it possessed the Cabindan exclave. It was supported by Russian arms, Cuban instructors and former Katangese *gendarmes*. On the other side, in opposition to the MPLA, an array of forces was involved. The FNLA held northwestern Angola and areas of southern Angola where Chipenda's wing was active. It was supported from its Zaire base by Chinese arms and instructors, by a covert CIA operation, and by units of the Zairian army; in the south, it was assisted by South African arms and instructors. It was allied to Unita which was strongly rooted in areas of southern and central Angola. Unita was supported by Zambia, by the CIA and by South African arms and instructors. Scattered about the country were demoralised units of the Portuguese army mostly anxious to avoid any active role.

As independence day drew near, the contest for power in Angola began in earnest. In coordinated actions, columns of FNLA and Unita troops, backed by forces from South Africa and Zaire, together with an assortment of white mercenaries and foreign advisors, advanced from the north and from the south on the capital, Luanda, and other towns held by the MPLA. The southern operation made spectacular progress. Starting from the South West African border area on 14 October, the main southern column moved rapidly up the coast, supplied *en route* by air and accompanied by South African helicopters. The South Africans on the way also attached an armoured car squadron and mortar units. They planned to disguise their involvement by representing it as a mercenary venture. The column advanced for 500 miles, capturing the port of Benguela, before it was checked by the Queve river, north of Novo Redondo, about 120 miles short of Luanda. Meanwhile, regular South African army units had crossed into Angola and joined other columns of FNLA and Unita troops and Portuguese mercenaries advancing northwards. At the peak of the campaign, the South Africans committed more than 5,000 troops to Angola. In the north, FNLA forces, assisted by Mobutu's troops and supplied by an airlift of American arms to airfields in northwestern Angola, penetrated to the outskirts of Luanda. By the time that independence day had arrived, the MPLA controlled little more than the capital and a narrow stretch of territory running eastwards.

What turned the tide was massive intervention from Cuba and Russia. In late August, partly in response to the deployment of Zairian forces in northwestern Angola, the Cubans had decided to send combat troops to Angola to strengthen the MPLA. The first Cuban troops arrived on 27 September and they were engaged in action in early October. By the beginning of November they numbered about 2,000. The supply of Russian arms greatly increased. When the battle for Benguela was lost, the Cubans decided that only reinforcements on a large scale would prevent the collapse of the MPLA. On 8 November, the first Cuban reinforcements were flown into Luanda and thrown immediately into action. On 11 November, Angola's independence day, a FNLA force, supported by two Zairian battalions and a South African artillery unit, launched an assault on Luanda. Under a barrage of rocket and artillery fire from Cuban troops, the FNLA force broke and ran, retreating northwards. Thousands more Cuban troops arrived, flown in in a Russian airlift, along with Russian tanks and huge quantities of equipment. In a desperate attempt to shore up the FNLA campaign, the CIA organised contingents of French and Portuguese mercenaries for Angola and supplied Roberto with funds to recruit British and American mercenaries. The CIA was thwarted from taking further action when the funds it had available for covert operations ran out. Kissinger was thus obliged to ask Congress for more funds, but Congress proved uncooperative. On 19 December the Senate voted to block all additional covert funds, forcing the CIA to abandon Angola and its allies there.

The war was soon over. By January the MPLA had the support of a striking force of some 15,000 Cubans and a vast arsenal of Russian weapons. In the north, the FNLA retreated in disarray, while Zairian troops straggled towards the border, looting and raping on the way. On 11 February the last FNLA stronghold, São Salvador, was captured. In the south, the South Africans fell back and eventually withdrew into South West Africa. The Unita capital, Huambo, was captured on 11

February. The FNLA-Unita campaign had long since lost all credibility. Once the extent of South Africa's involvement in the war was realised, African opinion turned swiftly against them. African leaders, who had previously been critical of Soviet and Cuban intervention, without knowing at the time of either South Africa's involvement or the CIA's role, now saw the Soviet action in a different, more acceptable light. Whereas Nigeria, for example, had readily denounced Soviet intervention in November, by February the Nigerian leader, General Murtala Mohammed, was angrily warning of what he said was a far greater danger of other outside powers acting there in collusion with 'the obnoxious apartheid regime in Pretoria'. Far from winning friends in Africa, therefore, Kissinger's excursion into African politics resulted in a humiliating setback for American policies. Meanwhile for Angola, years of internal strife and violence lay ahead.

CHAPTER TWENTY-SIX

Rhodesia's War

Rhodesia's rebellion against Britain in 1965, though it was eventually to have fateful consequences, was accomplished at the time with little difficulty. The Rhodesian establishment—the civil service, the police and the armed forces—stood firmly behind Ian Smith's government. Apart from a few minor disturbances, the African population remained passive or indifferent. As a gesture towards those whites who still wanted to retain links with the Crown, Smith announced that Rhodesians would continue to fly the Union Jack and sing the British national anthem. He was careful to portray his unilateral declaration of independence as an act of defiance not against the British monarch but against the British government.

Britain's reponse to UDI was muddled and ineffective. Expecting that white resistance would quickly crumble, Prime Minister Harold Wilson applied economic sanctions on a piecemeal basis; when one set of sanctions failed to make the right impact, he resorted to more extensive measures. But far from weakening the resolve of white Rhodesians, sanctions helped to close their ranks. Businessmen opposed to UDI found themselves engaged in elaborate schemes to evade them and become proud of their ingenuity in outmanoeuvring Wilson as he sought to block one loophole after another. Each success that the Rhodesians had bolstered their confidence and their determination to win. In December 1965, Wilson delivered what was expected to be the *coup de grâce* by banning oil imports into Rhodesia. But with tacit help from South Africa and from the Portuguese authorities in Mozambique, and by resorting to petrol rationing, Rhodesians overcame this hurdle. By 1971, oil supplies through South Africa and Mozambique were flowing so freely that Rhodesia was able to end petrol rationing altogether. The effect of sanctions on ordinary life was otherwise barely discernible. Favourite brands disappeared from the shops; there was a chronic shortage of Scotch whisky and good brandy; luxury goods became scarce; but there was little unemployment or reduction in earnings, and if the white standard of living did suffer mildly, it was so high as to make the difference bearable. Sanctions, in time, became no longer a threat but a routine. By 1972, the level of total exports had climbed higher than in 1965. Foreign tourists arrived in ever increasing numbers and so, to the delight of Smith, did thousands of new white immigrants. By 1973, the white population of Rhodesia had reached 273,000.

The early years of UDI were punctuated by a series of negotiations between Britain and Rhodesia which reflected Smith's growing confidence. At every stage of the negotiations, he managed to extract more concessions from the British government until, finally, he reached an agreement that gave him almost everything that he wanted. In December 1966, Smith and Wilson met on board the British cruiser, HMS *Tiger*, and debated the future of Rhodesia while sailing in circles in the Mediterranean off Gibraltar. Wilson was ready to offer Smith a settlement which would have postponed majority rule beyond the end of the century, but the two men differed over the issue of how Rhodesia would return to legality and the talks foundered. In October 1968, they met again in Gibraltar, this time on board the assault ship, HMS *Fearless*. The British terms were similar to those presented in HMS *Tiger*, except that Wilson by then had abandoned all preconditions for the return to legality. The *Tiger* negotiations failed when Wilson insisted that as a guarantee against any retrogressive amendment of the constitution Rhodesians should have the right to appeal to Britain's Privy Council, an issue that Smith was unwilling to concede.

In the interval before the next round of negotiations, Smith introduced a new constitution for Rhodesia, designed to entrench political power permanently in the hands of the whites. The 1969 constitution, in Smith's own words, 'sounded the death knell of the notion of majority rule'. Although Africans were allocated sixteen seats and whites fifty seats in the new parliament, a ratio almost identical to that of the 1961 constitution, the rate of increase allowed for African representation was so slow that it would probably have led to no change in representation for the rest of the century. Ultimately, a limit was fixed on African representation so that it could only equal but never exceed white representation. The 1969 constitution also eliminated several previous clauses safeguarding African interests. Simultaneously, a new Land Tenure Act was introduced, imposing new restrictions on the African population and permanently dividing land on a racial basis: white and black areas in future consisted equally of 45 million acres. In a referendum in June 1969, the electorate voted overwhelmingly in favour of the new constitution and, at the same time, gave their approval for Rhodesia to become a republic.

It was an example of Smith's remarkable tenacity and of Britain's desperate willingness to be rid of the Rhodesian issue that during the next round of negotiations, he obtained a settlement with the British government that was based on the 1969 constitution. The Anglo-Rhodesian agreement of 1971, negotiated in Salisbury between Smith and the British Foreign Secretary, Sir Alec Douglas-Home, represented a clear victory for Smith. Although the new constitutional proposals were complex and ambiguous, they certainly meant a continuation of white rule until at least the end of the century. Sanctions were to be lifted and Smith's 1969 constitution was to remain in force with few amendments. There were no external safeguards to prevent Smith from altering the agreement at a later stage; no provision for the repeal of the government's sweeping security laws; no guarantee that racial discriminatory measures would be abandoned; and no assurance that political detainees would be released. Smith's main concession was to give up the idea of parity, enshrined in the 1969 constitution, and accept the principle of majority rule. But the rate of African political progress envisaged was still so slow and the possibility of African rule so remote, that he felt the price was worth paying. Smith left his final meeting with Home, as he said, 'a very happy man'. And when he later appeared with Home on the verandah of the Prime Minister's office in Salisbury on 24 November to announce their agreement, the awaiting crowd clapped and cheered. Throughout Rhodesia the white population was jubilant at news of the agreement, and also relieved that six years of isolation had finally ended. In London, shares with Rhodesian interest had millions of pounds added to their market value within minutes.

There remained one further hurdle: the test of the settlement's acceptability to the people of Rhodesia as a whole, a condition to which Smith had agreed in negotiations with the British government in 1964. At the time that the agreement was signed, the test of acceptabiltiy was thought to be no more than a formality. Smith was confident enough to boast that Rhodesia had 'the happiest Africans in the world'. African political activity had been notably subdued since the nationalist parties had been banned seven years before. When nationalist guerrilla groups based in neighbouring Zambia had infiltrated across the Zambezi river into Rhodesia, they had found little local support; indeed, their presence was often reported to the authorities. No nationalist organisation existed within the country which could be used to stir up African opposition to the settlement and nationalist leaders like Nkomo and Sithole remained safely locked away. Moreover, both the British and Rhodesian governments expected that the African population would be favourably impressed by the offer of a programme to increase African education and employment that was included as part of the settlement terms. It was an opportunity for advancement that they believed could not sensibly be refused.

The nationalists themselves held out little hope that in the few weeks available before the test of acceptability was carried out, they would be able to mobilise enough African support to defeat the settlement. Only a small group of hardcore nationalists were at liberty in Rhodesia; many of them were former detainees still restricted to an area within a few miles of their homes. Yet they threw themselves back into the nationalist fray with a determination that took government officials by surprise. In December 1971, less than four weeks before the test of acceptability was due to start, they launched a new nationalist organisation, the African National Council (ANC) and persuaded a little-known bishop, Abel Muzorewa, to step in as leader. Muzorewa was a mild-mannered, bespectacled cleric, with a reputation for speaking out against racial injustice from the pulpit, but with no past political association; he was therefore acceptable as a figurehead to both rival nationalist factions and also as someone whose church credentials would lend the ANC a mantle of respectability. The task facing the ANC was daunting. The new party had no proper headquarters, few funds and only a rudimentary organisation. And it confronted a government that was able to use its vast apparatus to promote the settlement, through radio broadcasts, in leaflets, and at meetings with chiefs, headmen and councillors, constantly stressing the advantages of more schools, jobs and land development that would accrue to the whole African population.

The ANC's campaign against the settlement spread across the country with a speed that not even the nationalists had expected. For the first time in history, the African population was being consulted about its future, and the event generated an intense momentum. There was deep resentment that African political leaders had been excluded from the negotiations and a growing wariness about the government's promotion of the proposals. By the time that the team of British commissioners led by Lord Pearce arrived in Rhodesia in January 1972 to carry out the test of opinion, a strong groundswell of frustration and discontent had built up. Riots broke out in Gwelo, Salisbury and Umtali, and elsewhere there were at times rowdy crowds to greet the commissioners. The barrage of grievances they heard reflected not just a simple rejection of the settlement but monumental distrust of the government. At one meeting after another, many of them quiet and orderly occasions, persistent doubts and fears about the settlement were raised. Smith tried to counter the nationalist campaign by claiming in dossiers presented to Lord Pearce that, but for intimidation by the ANC, the African people would overwhelmingly approve of the proposals. A counter-offensive was also launched by the white network of business and professional assocations, commerce, industry and the civil service, which bombarded the Pearce Commission with petitions advocating acceptance of the proposals and expressing concern for the welfare of their African employees if the settlement should fail. After collecting evidence for two months, Pearce retired to consider his verdict and in May 1972 he handed his report to Home. It concluded that, although the great majority of whites accepted the proposals, the majority of Africans rejected them. 'In our opinion,' he wrote, 'the people of Rhodesia as a whole do not regard the proposals as acceptable as a basis for independence.'

The Pearce Commission marked a decisive turning point in the history of Rhodesia, for it provided a catalyst for the resurgence of African nationalism. Smith was never again to suppress black political activity as successfully as he had done for seven years. Yet the lessons of the Pearce Commission, and what the unexpected show of African strength might mean for the future, were entirely lost on Smith and most of the white population. Few whites acknowledged the deep undercurrents of discontent rising among the African population—the 'repressed fear, restless silence, forced tolerance and hidden hatred' to which Bishop Muzorewa referred at the time. Smith was convinced that the Pearce Commission had simply blundered by paying too much attention to the loud and violent activities of a handful of agitators, a view that he hoped the British government, too, would eventually come to accept and thus honour the agreement that he had made with Home. In the meantime, the whites, in a vindictive mood over the loss of their prized settlement, were determined to make the Africans pay for their defiance. By the end of the year, a deluge of discriminatory legislation had been presented to parliament. There were tougher pass laws; new powers for the authorities to control entry into urban areas; provision for separate facilities at post offices and for the segregation of public swimming pools and recreational areas; measures which threatened the continuation of multi-racial education in church and private schools and barred Africans from drinking in white areas after dark. The legislation in fact amounted to a concerted move in the direction of South Africa's apartheid policies, which many leading members of the Rhodesian Front favoured.

If the lessons of the Pearce Commission made little impact on white Rhodesia, for the exiled guerrilla organisations beyond Rhodesia's borders they provided a new source of encouragement. The early guerrilla incursions launched in the 1960s by both nationalist factions, Zapu and Zanu, from their bases in Zambia had all ended in failure. The guerrillas lacked any overall political or military objective; they received little local support; and they were quickly routed by Rhodesian security forces. The ineffectiveness of the nationalist strategy caused severe dissension among the guerrillas in exile and brought guerrilla activity in Rhodesia to a halt. But the African response during the Pearce Commission's visit indicated that the time was ripe for another attempt at insurgency. During 1972, Zanu guerrillas began to lay the groundwork for a new offensive in areas of northeastern Rhodesia. Instead of having to cross the Zambezi river from Zambia, as earlier insurgent groups had done, the guerrillas were able to infiltrate across the border through Mozambique's Tete province, using bases and supply routes that Frelimo had established in their war against the Portuguese. The region beyond was sparsely inhabited and largely neglected by the Rhodesian authorities, and the mountainous terrain gave ideal cover for guerrilla activity; in some parts of the border region, Rhodesian army patrols took seven days to cover a distance of thirty-five miles. Over a period of six months, Zanu guerrillas worked carefully to establish support among the local population, recruiting hundreds of tribesmen for training and as porters and building up a network of arms caches. During that time, no word of their activities reached the Rhodesian authorities. The local population was won over to an extent which later astonished Rhodesian officials.

The guerrilla campaign began in December 1972, with sporadic attacks on isolated white farmsteads and road ambushes in northeastern Rhodesia. The white farming community there was shaken by the attacks, but rapidly adjusted to the dangers of living amid a guerrilla war. Their determination to remain on the land held firm. Once the extent of guerrilla penetration was realised, the government concentrated its counter-insurgency campaign on efforts to stamp out local support for the guerrillas. Smith was convinced that the guerrillas had managed to establish themselves only by using intimidation against the local population, which the government could best counteract by replying with forceful action. Accordingly, government officers were given wide powers to impose collective fines on

African villagers if any of them were suspected of assisting guerrillas. Cattle were frequently seized to pay for the fines imposed. In some cases, villagers were evicted from their homes in the northeast and deported to other districts. In the border area alongside Tete province, thousands of tribesmen were removed from their villages so that the army could create a *cordon sanitaire*. At a later stage in the war, hundreds of thousands of Africans were placed in protected villages to deprive the guerrillas of local support. The government's policies achieved considerable success. As the counter-insurgency measures took effect, intelligence from the local population about guerrilla activities flowed more readily. By calling up white reservists and recruiting more African troops and police, and by strengthening local administration, the government was able to provide the northeast with far more effective cover. In the field, the military introduced highly mobile tactics, rushing helicopter-borne commandos and paratroopers to any area where a guerrilla presence was detected. Yet the guerrilla threat was never entirely rooted out. And though most of Rhodesia remained unaffected by the war, the disruption it caused was widespread. Commerce and industry suffered serious setbacks from the increasingly prolonged periods that white employees were required to serve in the security forces. Defence expenditure soared. White immigration figures showed a marked fall and the rate of white emigration increased.

Because of pressure from the white community, especially from business and industry which constantly harped on the need for a settlement with Britain, Smith was eventually persuaded to open negotiations with Bishop Muzorewa, the leader of the ANC. Smith's purpose was to obtain African sanction for his 1971 agreement with Britain by adding whatever extra benefits were needed as an inducement. His talks with Muzorewa began in July 1973, continued at a leisurely pace and ended abortively ten months later. The most that Smith was willing to concede was an additional six seats for Africans in parliament, an offer which the ANC executive dismissed in June 1974 with derision. Smith was not unduly dismayed. He himself saw no particular urgency for a settlement. Nor did he believe that the government had lost the support of the African population. 'There are a few who are politically motivated, yes, the agitators, who are political leaders,' he remarked in 1974, 'but the vast majority of them openly say: "We've always lived under a system where you have governed the country and we're satisfied with what you've done. We are happy under our tribal system. Why don't you leave us alone?"'

The fortunes of Rhodesia, however, were to be irrevocably changed as a result of the *coup d'état* in Lisbon in April 1974. The end of Portuguese rule in Mozambique, depriving Rhodesia of a long-standing ally and bringing to power there a left-wing nationalist movement, meant that Rhodesia's entire eastern border, some 760 miles long, was potentially vulnerable to infiltration by Rhodesian guerrillas. Instead of using just Zambia as their main rear base, the guerrillas would now be able, with Frelimo's approval, to establish bases in Mozambique as well. Frelimo's accession to power in Mozambique also emboldened Rhodesian nationalists to believe that in Rhodesia too guerrilla warfare would succeed in overthrowing white rule.

Indeed, the Lisbon coup and its consequences in Africa changed the whole structure of white power in southern Africa. And though Smith was unwilling to alter course, the South Africans saw every reason to revise their strategy. Hitherto, the South Africans had looked on Angola, Mozambique and Rhodesia as a valuable buffer separating them from contact with black Africa, a *cordon sanitaire* which it was in their own interests to strengthen. The withdrawal of the Portuguese from Angola and Mozambique, however, not only destroyed this premise but also endangered the survival of white Rhodesia. In the South African view, Rhodesia was no longer important as a frontline defence, for the winds of change had finally reached South Africa's own frontier. The South African prime minister, John Vorster, calculated that in the long run Smith's position, without an open-ended South African military and economic commitment, was untenable. In his long range assessment, white rule in Rhodesia was ultimately doomed and Smith's stubborn resistance to any change in policy only added an unwelcome note of uncertainty, likely to attract communist attention. An unstable white government in Rhodesia was therefore less preferable than a stable black government, heavily dependent on South African goodwill. With this objective in mind, Vorster now began to apply pressure on Smith.

South Africa had played a crucial role in enabling Smith's UDI to succeed. Though the South African government had deep misgivings at the time, popular enthusiasm for UDI among South Africa's white community was strong. South Africa subsequently supported Rhodesia's trade, its finances and sanctions-busting operations, including the supply of oil, and when guerrilla activity started, it despatched contingents of paramilitary police to help in the counter-insurgency campaign. Indeed, without South Africa's support, Smith would have been unable to survive. But in attempting to force Smith to come to terms with the Rhodesian nationalists, Vorster was obliged to act circumspectly, for fear of antagonising his own electorate and provoking an outcry in Rhodesia. Fortuitously, he found an ally in Zambia's President Kenneth Kaunda, who had become increasingly concerned about the disruption caused in Zambia by the Rhodesian imbroglio and about the dangers of a widening guerrilla war there. Through a series of secret contacts carried out in 1974, Vorster and Kaunda devised a scheme that would draw Smith and the nationalists into negotiation, bring an 'honourable' end to the war, and install, over an acceptable period of about five years, a moderate black government. Vorster's role was to apply sufficient pressure on Smith to force him to the negotiating table; Kaunda's task was to produce a united front among the nationalists.

As a preliminary part of the scheme, Vorster told Smith to allow the detained nationalist leaders, Joshua Nkomo and Ndabaningi Sithole, to fly to the Zambian capital, Lusaka, in conditions of strict secrecy, so that Kaunda could instruct them, along with Muzorewa, on their part of the deal. Accordingly, in November 1974, Nkomo and Sithole were taken to Lusaka, told of the plan, and then returned to detention in Rhodesia. At the beginning of December, they were flown back to Lusaka to join a second, final meeting of all the nationalist factions. Under strong pressure from Kaunda and President Nyerere of Tanzania, the rival nationalist leaders—Nkomo, Sithole and Muzorewa—together with a fourth splinter group, Frolizi, agreed to form a united front to conduct negotiations with Smith. Once their agreement was signed, Smith, much against his better judgement, was obliged to release the nationalist detainees, many of whom had served ten years' imprisonment.

Eight months of wrangling, intrigue and manoeuvre followed before Smith and the nationalists finally sat down to negotiate. Neither Smith nor the nationalists believed that negotiations would serve much purpose. Only pressure from Vorster and Kaunda had induced them to hold a conference. The nationalists, despite their agreement in Lusaka, remained chronically divided. Within the Zanu guerrilla movement, a fierce outbreak of internal dissension culminated in the murder of the guerrilla leader, Herbert Chitepo, causing Kaunda and Nyerere to detain hundreds of Zanu guerrillas. By the time a conference was arranged, Smith was even less inclined than before to give any ground. The conference opened in August 1975 imaginatively enough in a line of railway carriages parked on the Victoria Falls bridge, which spans the border between Rhodesia and Zambia. Despite the presence of Kaunda and Vorster, who threatened and cajoled both sides, the conference made no headway and broke up after the first day in disarray.

Though the detente exercise initiated by Vorster and Kaunda ended in failure, it had a marked effect on the course of the Rhodesian conflict. The release of nationalist leaders like Nkomo, Sithole and Mugabe, from ten years' detention, effectively broke the logjam of nationalist politics, even though they remained permanently at odds with each other. Once freed, the more militant nationalists, like Mugabe, who believed that only war would bring down the white regime, lost no time in surreptitiously organising a recruitment campaign for Zanu's guerrilla army. Thousands of recruits were sent across the border into Mozambique. In April 1975, Mugabe joined them there. In the months following the abortive Victoria Falls conference, Zanu's guerrilla army was reorganised and re-equipped; it moved its main rear base from Zambia to Mozambique and from there it prepared for a major offensive across the eastern border.

In the meantime, a new round of negotiations had begun between Smith and Nkomo. Smith looked on Nkomo as the most skilful of the nationalist leaders, a moderate politician, agreeable to change which would safeguard white interests and influence. Nkomo's Zapu guerrilla forces, based in Zambia, were largely ineffective and had played no part in the guerrilla war, and he was amenable therefore to the idea of negotiating a separate settlement with Smith which would leave him well placed to gain power. Their talks started in December 1975 and continued until the following March. The end result was the same. Nkomo wanted a firm commitment from Smith that would lead to majority rule. Smith, though prepared to make some concessions involving a power-sharing arrangement, was still unwilling to go that far. 'I have said we are prepared to bring black people into our Government to work with them,' he said after the talks had failed, 'and we have to accept that, in future, Rhodesia is a country of blacks and whites, and that it will be governed by blacks and whites. But I don't believe in majority rule, black majority rule, ever in Rhodesia, not in a thousand years.'

While Smith and Nkomo were holding their talks in Salisbury, the guerrilla war entered a new and more perilous phase. From bases in Mozambique, hundreds of Zanu guerrillas infiltrated into eastern Rhodesia in early 1976, attacking white homesteads, robbing stores, planting landmines and subverting the local population. At first only border areas were affected. But by mid-1976 the guerrillas were aiming at targets deeper inside Rhodesia. When Nkomo's talks with Smith broke down, Zapu guerrillas joined the war, opening a new front in western Rhodesia, along the borders with Zambia and Botswana, and recruiting heavily among the Ndebele and Kalanga people for training in exile. Nkomo too went into exile. The government shored up its defences by calling up more white reservists, extending their periods of military service, enrolling more Africans in the security forces and encouraging foreign volunteers to enlist. Retaliatory raids were launched against Zanu camps in Mozambique. But the strain of the increased war effort on white Rhodeisa was immediately apparent. With every able-bodied man under the age of thirty-eight liable for military service, commerce and industry were seriously disrupted. Higher taxes had to be levied for defence purposes. To Smith's dismay, the outflow of white emigrants rose significantly.

Though Rhodesia's army commanders still expressed confidence in their ability to defeat the guerrilla menace, in many parts of the world it seemed that Smith was embarked on an increasingly risky venture to sustain white rule, which endangered the stability of the whole region. Among those whose attention was drawn to the Rhodesian war was Henry Kissinger, the United States Secretary of State. In the wake of the Angolan débâcle, Kissinger was particularly alert to the dangers of how nationalist guerrilla wars could widen the circle of conflict, drawing in neighbouring countries and providing the Soviet bloc with opportunities for intervention. Already the Rhodesian war affected Mozambique and Zambia, and to a minor extent Botswana. The Soviet bloc and China were involved, supplying arms to Zapu and Zanu and training their guerrillas. The longer the war went on, the more the guerrilla organisations would come to rely on Communist help, and the more likely they were to adopt a radical or revolutionary ideology. This process of radicalisation, Kissinger believed, could eventually spread throughout Africa. He was anxious, therefore, to use American influence to secure an orderly transition to majority rule in Rhodesia and to encourage the emergence of a black moderate government there. He found the South African prime minister, John Vorster, in a similar frame of mind, increasingly worried about the possibility of Soviet and Cuban intervention in the Rhodesian conflict, and impatient with Smith's intransigence. At meetings in Europe, the two men agreed on a plan to force Smith to accept majority rule.

Kissinger's strategy was twofold. He relied on Vorster to apply the necessary pressures on Smith, and he looked to the African 'frontline' states, Zambia, Mozambique, Botswana and Tanzania, to sort out the rival claims for leadership among the nationalists and to provide a united front capable of playing a constructive role in the transition to majority rule. The pressures that Vorster exerted on Rhodesia were rapidly felt. In August 1976, after Smith authorised a major raid against a Zanu base in Mozambique, contrary to South African advice,

Vorster made clear his displeasure by withdrawing all South African helicopter pilots and technicians who had been secretly lent to Rhodesia to assist in counter-insurgency operations, a sanction which effectively cut the air force strike capability by half. Other South African measures were taken to delay Rhodesia's import and export traffic and to cut back on oil shipments and supplies of arms and ammunition. Unable to ignore the designs of the joint South African and American strategy, Smith hoped to be able to convince the Americans that Rhodesia was engaged in a struggle against communist forces aiming to take over the whole of southern Africa; he felt sure that in a personal meeting with Kissinger he could persuade him of the merits of the case.

In September, Kissinger flew to Pretoria in South Africa for a meeting with Smith, determined to break his resistance. Smith forcefully defended the need for a white-led Rhodesia to fight against communist encroachment; he pleaded for American aid, not pressure. Kissinger was not prepared to listen. He coldly analysed the severe economic and military difficulties that Rhodesia faced. Rhodesia, he said, could not resist the growing military thrusts from Mozambique and Zambia, while the guerrillas could rely on increased Soviet and Chinese aid. Certainly, neither South Africa nor the United States were willing to intervene on his behalf. He had brought with him, he said, a package deal. It had been devised by British and American officials, with the approval of Kaunda and Nyerere acting on behalf of the nationalists, and it would be given the full legal authority of the British government. Smith's choice was simply to accept it or reject it. If he decided to reject the deal, it was Kissinger's estimate that he could survive for no more than three months. South Africa, he said, would no longer provide logistical support for the war, nor guarantee the smooth running of Rhodesia's sanctions-busting operations, in particular the supply of fuel. Kissinger handed Smith a typed list of five points that he said must be used as the basis for a Rhodesian settlement. The first point covered Smith's acceptance of majority rule within two years; other points related to the way in which an interim government would be set up, consisting of an equal number of representatives nominated by Smith and the nationalists.

Smith took the document away to give it some thought, initially dismayed at the terms of surrender.

On consideration, Smith and his advisers found that Kissinger's terms were not so entirely bleak. They would allow the whites a two-year period to preserve white influence and give ample time for black rivalry to take root. The whites would play a major role in drafting a new constitution and could ensure that their interests were entrenched. Moreover, sanctions would be lifted and the war would end. In further discussions with Kissinger, Smith asked that certain functions in the interim government, such as the portfolios of defence, internal security and finance, should be allocated specially to whites, citing the danger that rival nationalist factions might use government powers against their opponents, as they had done during the transition in Angola. Kissinger thought that Smith's requests were reasonable and gave them his temporary assent, but cautioned that final approval would only be forthcoming after he had consulted Presidents Kaunda and Nyerere. After seven hours of talks, Smith finally gave way. He was ready, he said, to recommend the package to his government. Kissinger wanted him to announce his acceptance publicly then and there in Pretoria, but Smith said he would have to wait until the terms had been approved by his colleagues in Salisbury.

Smith returned to Salisbury on 19 September. By prior arrangement with Kissinger, he planned first to consult his cabinet and then the parliamentary caucus before announcing his acceptance of the Kissinger deal in a nationwide broadcast on 24 September. Kissinger meanwhile travelled to Lusaka and Dar es Salaam to obtain approval from Kaunda and Nyerere for inserting the additional clauses that Smith wanted. On 22 September, Smith received a message from Kissinger confirming that Nyerere, as chairman of the frontline states, found the five-point plan 'an acceptable basis for settlement' and permitting Smith to add to his speech the extra clauses. Kissinger did not say specifically that the Presidents had approved of these insertions but that was the impression he gave. On the basis of that message, Smith convinced his cabinet and his parliamentary caucus that Kissinger's deal should be accepted, pointing to the more favourable aspects of its terms. On radio and television on 24 September, to the stunned disbelief of most of the white electorate, Smith duly announced that the days of white rule in Rhodesia were over.

The Kissinger deal immediately ran into trouble. For Kissinger, in order to get Smith to publicly accept the principle of majority rule, had deceived him in several vital respects. In Pretoria, Kissinger had led Smith to believe that the proposals he put forward had already been accepted by the African presidents on behalf of the nationalists. Indeed, Smith had agreed to the deal only on the understanding that the proposals made to him, once accepted, were strictly observed. But in fact Nyerere and Kaunda had been given no more than an outline of the terms by Kissinger, when he was on his way to Pretoria. While approving of Kissinger's mission, they maintained that his task should be confined to obtaining Smith's commitment to majority rule. They did not consider that Kissinger was authorised to make offers about the composition of an interim government. Neither the African presidents nor the nationalists were willing to accept a political framework drawn up by British and American officials without their consultation. Such matters, they argued, could only be decided upon at a constitutional conference. Kissinger therefore had not informed them of what his exact intentions were, for fear that their objections then would wreck the whole exercise. On leaving Pretoria, Kissinger was obliged to compound the deception. Though the African presidents strongly objected to Smith's demands for specific portfolios in the interim government, Kissinger indicated in his message that in fact they approved of them. His central purpose was to get Smith to consent publicly to majority rule. Once that had been achieved, he believed that the Rhodesian crisis would be transformed. It would be impossible for Smith to revive white morale and confidence in the indestructability of white rule. Smith's announcement, he felt sure, would produce a momentum of its own, which would make the chances of a settlement more favourable.

No sooner had Smith announced the terms of the Kissinger deal than the nationalist leaders and their African sponsors disputed them, and demanded that Britain, as the responsible colonial authority, should convene a constitutional conference at which the structure and functions of an interim government could be decided upon. With some reluctance, Britain agreed to convene a conference in October, choosing Geneva as a suitably neutral location. From the outset, its chances of success were remote. Smith insisted that there could be no deviation from the Kissinger plan and his position was supported by the South Africans, who considered that he had done everything required of him. The nationalists, however, wanted a completely new start to negotiations; the purpose of the conference, in their view, was to arrange the transfer of power to a black government on their own terms. The more militant nationalists within Zanu saw little point in negotiating at all, and preferred that the outcome should be determined by guerrilla warfare. Four nationalist factions were invited to Geneva: one was led by Muzorewa, as leader of the ANC; another by Nkomo, as leader of Zapu; a third by Mugabe, who had become the acknowledged leader of the Zanu guerrilla army; and a fourth by Sithole, who still claimed the leadership of Zanu. It was the uncompromising stand taken by Mugabe's group which largely influenced the course of the conference. After seven weeks of desultory negotiations, the conference broke up without any progress made.

In the aftermath of the Geneva conference, the prospects of Rhodesia looked increasingly bleak. By mid-1977, the war had spread like a cancer across the entire country. Sporadic guerrilla raids were made around the central towns of Que Que, Gwelo and Shangani. In Bulawayo, Rhodesia's second largest city, the security forces had difficulty in tracking down small Zapu groups which periodically raided the black suburbs. In the rural areas, civil administration began to break down. Schools, hospitals, clinics and African councils were frequent targets in the guerrilla campaign. By July, three hundred schools, most of them in eastern Rhodesia, had been forced to close. The network of mission hospitals and clinics, which provided the backbone of rural health services, also suffered. Missionaries were harassed by both sides and many started to leave the country. Local African councils faced similar disruption. Council buildings and equipment were wrecked and safes robbed. Officials in some rural areas found it impossible to collect dues from tribesmen and dozens of councils verged on bankruptcy. African councillors, worried about the possibility of guerrilla reprisals, refused to participate in the administration of their districts. Attacks on isolated white farmhouses were commonplace. Farmers also had to contend with large-scale cattle rustling and attempts by guerrillas, often successful, to force African labour off their farms. Many white farms were consquently abandoned.

The government responded by tapping the last reservoir of white manpower. All reasonably fit men between the ages of thirty-eight and fifty were required to enlist for periods of military service; above the age of fifty, whites were urged to volunteer for special police duty. Other whites had their length of service extended to as much as six months of the year. More black troops were recruited. The disruption to business was severe. Many firms found that at one time half of their skilled staff might be called up. Small businesses frequently went bankrupt. Entire shopping complexes in the suburbs of Salisbury and Bulawayo became vacant. The burdens of war, of sanctions, higher taxes, a faltering economy and the uncertain future produced a mood of despair and demoralisation among the white community that was unprecedented. Each month the white exodus from Rhodesia gathered momentum.

For several months, British and American officials toured African capitals in a joint endeavour to find a solution that would end the war acceptable to both Smith and the guerrilla organisations, Zapu and Zanu, now linked together in a loose alliance known as the Patriotic Front. The stumbling block was no longer the issue of majority rule, for Smith acknowledged that, if there was to be a political settlement, the demand for one-man one-vote had to be conceded. What divided them now was the question of how the transition was to be achieved and the future of the Rhodesian security forces. The Patriotic Front (PF) regarded the security forces as the fighting arm of the Rhodesian Front, distrusted their intention of staying neutral after any settlement, and demanded that the guerrilla forces should take control of internal security. Smith was adamant that the security forces would have to be retained. Without them, he warned, the whites would abandon the country; it was a matter that was simply not negotiable. Between these two stands the British and Americans could find no satisfactory compromise and their initiative failed.

Yet the pressures on Smith to find a political settlement had become intense. South Africa regarded a transfer of power as imperative. The white community, weary of war, was anxious above all for a return to normal life. No longer did the hazards of black rule seem so fearful when set against present dangers. What most concerned the whites now was whether the transition from white to black rule could be accomplished in an orderly fashion. Smith therefore embarked on the search for what was called an internal settlement, an agreement with moderate black leaders willing to concede, in exchange for majority rule, a powerful role for the white community. The two principal candidates whom he had in mind were Muzorewa and Sithole. Muzorewa at the time was regarded as the most popular African leader in the country; he could draw large crowds; his ANC was relatively well organised; and he was known to be a well-meaning though inept politician who favoured white participation. Sithole's support inside Rhodesia, as well as within the Zanu guerrilla movement, had withered away, but Smith believed that his intense personal ambition and intellectual vigour would lend a certain credibility to an internal settlement. Neither Muzorewa nor Sithole possessed guerrilla forces and both were consequently amenable to inheriting the government's security forces. To these two Smith added a compliant tribal chief, Jeremiah Chirau, who, at the government's behest, had set up a conservative black political party and who could be relied upon to nod approval of the government's demands. In November 1977, Smith announced that negotiations on an internal settlement would begin with these three leaders. He calculated that a constitutional agreement based on one-man one-vote would effectively undercut the guerrilla campaign and gain international recognition.

The negotiations were protracted. Smith was determined to gain the most advantageous terms possible for the whites, ignoring the dangers that in the process he might undermine the standing and popularity of the African politicians with whom he was dealing. Indeed, the welfare of the whites was

Smith's overriding concern. The African negotiators, for their part, proved to be maladroit. They made no attempt to form a common front and the rivalry between Muzorewa and Sithole allowed Smith to play off one against the other. In March 1978, Smith emerged with an agreement which gave the whites twenty-eight out of one hundred seats in parliament and left them in control of the administration, the security forces and the economy. The whites were also given the power in parliament to veto changes to entrenched clauses in the new constitution. Smith declared the outcome a 'victory for moderation', and Muzorewa proclaimed himself to be happy with the result. But in the black suburbs of Salisbury, where his support was strong, Muzorewa's performance caused deep disappointment.

Under the terms of the agreement, a coalition government consisting of all four delegations was set up to administer Rhodesia for an interim period. Its main tasks were to arrange a ceasefire, remove racial discrimination, draft a new constitution and conduct an election, before handing over to a black government. But the coalition government made little headway in persuading guerrillas to accept an amnesty and it was soon beset by internal dissension. Smith's main concern was to minimise the impact of any reforms in order to sustain white confidence and to make clear that the whites were really still in control. When one of Muzorewa's ministers spoke out on the need for positive discrimination in favour of Africans to rectify decades of injustice, Smith forced him out of the government, humiliating Muzorewa in the process. Despite African demands for the swift removal of race laws, only slow progress was made. When it became apparent that ceasefire efforts had failed, black and white members of the government sought to blame each other for what had gone wrong.

The war, in fact, far from diminishing, took an ever increasing toll. The plight of many isolated farming communities became desperate. Every day farmers faced the risk of ambush, abduction or landmines. In the more vulnerable areas, scores of farmers decided to leave, making the survival of those who wanted to stay that much more precarious. Sporadic raids on the outskirts of Salisbury and a spate of guerrilla attacks in the black townships aggravated the sense of insecurity that many whites living there began to feel. Ambushes on road traffic were so prevalent that every main road in the country was considered unsafe after dark. Rail traffic, too, was a frequent target. By mid-1978, nearly one quarter of all black primary schools in the country had closed. Health and veterinary services in some areas collapsed. Several hundred thousand head of cattle died as animal diseases spread unchecked. Doctors reported that malnutrition in African adults and children was extensive in areas where stores had been closed and travel was dangerous. In an attempt to curb guerrilla activity inside Rhodesia, the security forces struck repeatedly at guerrilla targets in Mozambique and Zambia, but never to any lasting effect. The government allowed Muzorewa and Sithole to recruit supporters into what amounted to private armies, in the hope that they would stem the guerrilla advance in rural areas, but they made little impact. South Africa secretly provided troops for operations in southern areas of the country, but still guerrilla attacks there spread. Smith also tried to lure Nkomo into joining the internal settlement, but a secret meeting between the two men in Lusaka in August ended abortively.

The main hope of saving the internal settlement, in the government's estimation, therefore depended heavily on the success of the election. A reasonably high poll would be taken by the outside world as evidence of the popularity of the new government, thus boosting the campaign for international recognition and dealing the guerrilla organisations a damaging blow; a low poll would obviously have the reverse effects. The election, scheduled for April 1979, therefore became a trial of strength between the government, which needed to get Africans to vote, and the guerrilla organisations whose objective was to stop them. The government launched a massive publicity campaign, bombarding the public with slogans urging a high turnout. The message insistently put across was that by voting in strength the blacks would bring peace and prosperity to the country; a majority rule government would gain international recognition, sanctions would be lifted, and there would be more jobs, schools and clinics. Both Muzorewa and Sithole claimed that fighting would stop a few months after the election when the guerrillas were satisfied that a black government was firmly in power. For the election period, the government also mobilised as many men as it could spare to provide maximum protection for polling stations, so that the black population would be encouraged to turn out and vote. Commerce, industry and the civil service were stripped of all available whites. In all, nearly one hundred thousand men were placed at the government's disposal. The effect was immediately apparent: rather than risk confrontation, most guerrilla units decided simply to lie low.

The voting performance was mixed: in some areas, there were enthusiastic queues; in other areas, the response was subdued, with a low poll. But on a national basis the turnout far exceeded the government's expectations. According to the government's figures, some sixty-four per cent of the estimated black electorate voted. Muzorewa emerged with a commanding lead, gaining nearly seventy per cent of the votes cast; Sithole trailed behind; Chirau was eliminated. Undoubtedly a degree of coercion was used by all sides in the election. The fact that Zapu and Zanu were banned also affected the outcome. But the view of most independent observers was that overall the result represented as accurate a reflection of African opinion as could be obtained in the circumstances. However much disappointment there was with a new constitution that entrenched white privilege, the opportunity to vote for a black leader who promised peace was considered worth having.

Thus, on 31 May 1979, amid a civil war in which some twenty thousand lives had been lost and which showed no signs of abating, white rule came to an end after eighty-eight years. It was an occasion marked as much as foreboding as by hope. Even the name chosen for the new state—Zimbabwe Rhodesia—signified the conflicting aspirations of its peoples: the whites treasured the name of Rhodesia; the blacks wanted Zimbabwe, the site of stone ruins in the centre of the country, formerly the capital of an ancient African monarchy. There were no public celebrations, no new flag or national anthem, no grand speeches, no public holiday, no foreign dignitaries to offer their congratulations.

The tasks facing Muzorewa's government were daunting. A

'campaign for peace' that he launched soon after taking office proved a dismal failure. The presence of Smith as a minister in his government—an appointment upon which Smith had insisted during their negotiations—only made it more difficult for him to demonstrate to the African population that a genuine transfer of power had taken place. Muzorewa's attempts to get sanctions lifted and his search for international recognition were no more successful. In the United States, the Carter administration insisted that any political settlement which excluded the Patriotic Front was unviable. In Britain, the new Conservative prime minister, Margaret Thatcher, was more sympathetic to his appeals, but she was eventually persuaded by her Foreign Secretary, Lord Carrington, that recognition of Muzorewa's government would only alienate African and Commonwealth states, as well as the Americans, while failing to stop the war.

Carrington instead launched a new initiative in one last endeavour to find a negotiated settlement. At the time, no-one—least of all Carrington—believed that it could succeed. Neither side in the war was yet in desperate enough straits to make the kind of compromise which seemed necessary for an agreement to be reached. Nor did Carrington have any clear idea of how to proceed. What happened to alter that deadlock was largely fortuitous. But the one factor that made a crucial difference to the outcome was Carrington's decision to reassert Britain's responsibility for devising a Rhodesian solution and to bear whatever risks for Britain that course entailed. Ever since Smith's UDI in 1965, the British government had been wary of the dangers of being caught up in Rhodesian affairs without either the political or economic power to enforce its decisions. On its own Britain had no effective means of ensuring the collaboration of the administration or the security forces or the African nationalist factions vying for power. Carrington's plan, however, was based on the premise that, if necessary, Britain should take direct control of Rhodesia for a limited period to manage the transition to independence, regardless of those risks.

The British strategy evolved in stages. Carrington's idea was that Britain should first draw up a new constitution and present it at a constitutional conference to which the

Muzorewa government and the Patriotic Front would be invited. He believed that many of the objections to the Muzorewa regime could be attributed to the way in which the constitution Muzorewa had negotiated with Smith allowed the white minority such a powerful role; and that a new constitution which scrapped the white veto in parliament and reduced white control over the civil service, the judiciary and the security forces would be more acceptable to British and international opinion and, possibly, to the Patriotic Front. If the two sides agreed on the constitution, a ceasefire would be negotiated and Britain would then supervise new elections, monitored by Commonwealth observers to ensure impartiality, before granting independence. If, however, the Patriotic Front did not accept the terms of a new constitution of which Britain approved, while Muzorewa did, then Carrington was prepared to come to a separate agreement with Muzorewa and risk a collision with African and Commonwealth states which supported the Patriotic Front.

The conference opened at Lancaster House in London in September 1979. Among Muzorewa's delegation was Smith, as obdurate as ever and unwilling to make any further concessions. But Muzorewa himself, anxious above all to secure an early release from sanctions and to obtain international recognition, was ready to fall in line with Carrington's suggestions. His main hope was that the Patriotic Front, in pursuing extreme demands, would break away from the conference, leaving him to come to a separate deal with Carrington. Before the conference opened, however, both Nkomo and Mugabe had been given some sharp lessons by the frontline presidents in the diplomacy that would be required of them at Lancaster House. Neither Zambia nor Mozambique could afford to sustain their side of the war for much longer. Each month that passed brought greater dislocation to their economies. The pressure they continued to exert during the conference had a marked effect on the Patriotic Front's strategy. None of the presidents saw grounds for the conference to break down over arguments about the constitution if it was in line with other independence constitutions that Britain had devised for colonies with white minorities, nor about arrangements for the transition to independence. Nkomo, for his part, preferred that negotiations should succeed. But for Mugabe, Rhodesia was an unfinished revolution. Alone among the nationalist leaders, he saw the war as a opportunity not just to defeat white rule but to bring down the capitalist structure that the whites represented and to replace it with an egalitarian people's state. Mugabe made no secret of his admiration for the principles of Marxism-Leninism; nor of his hopes to establish in Zimbabwe a one-party Marxist system. Throughout the conference the demands he pursued were the most uncompromising. And his final stand against the Rhodesian settlement was broken only when Mozambique privately threatened to withdraw its support for his guerrilla army.

Thus, to Carrington's surprise, and the consternation of Muzorewa's officials, the negotiations stumbled through to success. After fourteen weeks of arduous manoeuvre, the Lancaster House conference ended on 21 December in a short ceremony at which Muzorewa, Nkomo, Mugabe and Carrington signed their agreement in the genteel atmosphere of the Grand Gallery. The Lancaster House agreement, however, had been won mainly through skilful diplomacy employed by Carrington and his officials in London. Its actual implementation was to be carried out in circumstances fraught with peril, amid a scramble for power that was bound to be conducted on all sides by ruthless means. Under the terms of the Lancaster House agreement, a British governor, Lord Soames, was sent to Salisbury, armed in theory with full executive and legislative powers and assisted by a team of British civilian and military advisers, to manage the transition to independence and to ensure that elections were held in conditions as fair and as orderly as possible. But in practice Soames was heavily dependent on help for running the country on the Rhodesian administration and police, which had every interest in making sure that a few months of British rule did not lead to an election victory by the Patriotic Front. Similarly the guerrilla organisations were determined to see that their military gains in seven years of war were not wiped out.

The arrangements made at Lancaster House for a ceasefire were inevitably precarious. In theory the security forces and the guerrillas were to disengage from the rural areas and to be confined to separate locations: the security forces to their existing bases; the guerrillas to special assembly points set up in rural areas by a ceasefire monitoring group composed mainly of British troops but also of small military units from other Commonwealth states. The ceasefire monitoring teams would be only lightly armed and would face considerable risks. If the ceasefire broke down, as almost everyone expected it would, the only resort available to Soames in practice was to call for assistance from the Rhodesian security forces. He was given no independent force to which he could turn.

The ceasefire exercise was soon enmeshed in controversy. Some 22,000 guerrillas responded to the ceasefire call, moving into heavily defended camps at assembly points, but Mugabe held back more than one third of his forces, dispersing them in villages, so as to influence the election campaign and to resume the war if the result was not to his liking. Thousands of Zanu guerrillas also crossed the border from Mozambique in contravention of the ceasefire agreement. As a result, Rhodesian army commanders insisted that their own forces should be redeployed. Reluctantly, Soames agreed. As well as the regular forces that returned to the bush, auxiliaries loyal to Muzorewa were deployed. Their harassment of the local population became so notorious that draconian methods were used to restore discipline. The greatest measure of intimidation, however, was attributed to Mugabe's Zanu supporters and to his guerrillas. Soames's election supervisors reported that in five of Rhodesia's eight electoral provinces conditions for a free election no longer existed, mainly because of Zanu's activities. Soames called Mugabe to Government House and threatened to impose sanctions on Zanu unless intimidation was curbed. The result was that by the time the election was due to start—on 27 February—the level of intimidation had fallen considerably. Moreover, against all predictions, the ceasefire had held up well enough to allow voting to take place in an orderly manner.

The Rhodesian election of 1980 was essentially a contest between two men: Muzorewa and Mugabe. Both were competing for the Shona vote which represented three quarters of the electorate. Neither expected to win many votes among the minority Ndebele and Kalanga tribes of western

Rhodesia, which was Nkomo's stronghold. In view of Muzorewa's showing in the 1979 election, Rhodesian officials were confident that either Muzorewa would win, or at least that he would gain enough seats to lead a moderate alliance which included the whites, with the twenty seats in parliament they had been allocated under the Lancaster House agreement, and possibly Nkomo. The result, however, was an overwhelming victory for Mugabe. With sixty-three per cent of the national vote, he took fifty-seven of the eighty black seats in parliament. Nkomo's showing—twenty-four per cent of the vote and twenty seats—was confined almost entirely to the Ndebele and Kalanga areas of the country. The Muzorewa vote—eight per cent and three seats—simply collapsed.

More than anything else, it was a vote for peace. Muzorewa's failure to bring an end to the war, as he had promised in 1979, destroyed whatever chance he had of being re-elected. The war-weariness that gripped the black population had been as much the cause of his own victory in 1979 as it was of Mugabe's ten months later. Any other result, as most blacks well knew, would have led almost certainly to a resumption of fighting. Indeed, the most potent feature of the election compaign was Zanu's warning that unless the blacks voted for Mugabe the war would continue. But an equally clear motive in the vote for Mugabe was the belief that he would take possession of the country in a way which Muzorewa, locked in his fateful alliance with Smith, seemed incapable of achieving.

The shock for the whites when the results were announced on 4 March was all the more profound because they had been convinced, until the last minute, that Muzorewa would win. A black Marxist government had been their greatest dread all along; yet suddenly, so it seemed, one was upon them. In despair and despondency, many whites prepared to leave. But when Mugabe appeared on television that evening, far from being the Marxist ogre that the whites feared, he impressed them as a model of moderation. To most whites he appeared as thoughtful and conciliatory, anxious that white representatives should be included in his government. Even Ian Smith who, a few weeks before, had denounced Mugabe as 'the apostle of Satan', now found him 'sober and responsible'. So calmly did the transfer of power take place in fact, to a man who had hitherto been renowned as a Marxist revolutionary, that some whites, though their fears about the future remained, wondered at the time why the war had been fought, what the cause was for which there had been so much suffering and grief.

The honeymoon period, however, did not last long.

CHAPTER TWENTY-SEVEN

The Long Distance Men

The generation of African leaders that took power at independence produced many notable survivors. There were some leaders who succeeded in establishing stable and orderly regimes, with programmes of economic and social development that fulfilled many of the promises they had made at independence. The esteem in which men like Jomo Kenyatta and Félix Houphouët-Boigny were held remained high throughout their long tenures of office. Indeed, the death of Kenyatta in 1978 was an occasion for genuine national mourning. Botswana, under Seretse Khama's leadership, provided a rare example of a multi-party democracy, where elections were regularly contested and political life was free from corruption; his death too, in 1980, was mourned by his countrymen. Julius Nyerere of Tanzania was regarded for many years as a politician of international stature, whose socialist strategy attracted widespread interest. There were other leaders, like Sékou Touré of Guinea, whose regimes were frequently under threat and who survived mainly through the use of coercion and violence. The common feature of almost all African leaders was that, for however long they had held power, they remained reluctant to step down. In a quarter of a century of independence, only two African presidents—Léopold Senghor of Senegal and Ahmadu Ahidjo of Cameroon—took the decision, after long periods in office, to retire gracefully, Africa thus witnessed a small and diminishing band of old stalwarts of the independence generation, clinging determinedly to power and often shaping the destiny of their countries with a degree of personal control that was rarely seen outside Africa. The results were varied.

*

Sékou Touré was undoubtedly the most persistent survivor of all. His regime was born amid chaos and confusion, cast adrift by the French government in reprisal for defying de Gaulle's plans in 1958 to establish a Franco-African Community, in the hope that, without French aid and without French personnel to run the country, the new state of Guinea would quickly founder. Touré overcame that hurdle by turning to the Soviet bloc for help and he emerged from his contest with de Gaulle with massive popular support in Guinea and with a reputation in much of Africa as a fearless champion of the anti-colonial cause. Yet Guinea was condemned to live in an atmosphere of plots and purges. Touré himself spoke frequently of what he called a 'permanent plot' to overthrow his regime, a vast conspiracy, so he claimed, organised by Western powers and other enemies of the 'Guinean revolution'. Some plots were undoubtedly real; some were contrived; others were simply fictitious. Touré used plots as a pretext for liquidating his opponents, whether there was evidence against them or not. Few of Touré's close associates escaped unscathed. His regime became notorious for show trials, for public executions, for arbitrary imprisonment and the use of torture. More than fifty ministers were shot or hanged, or died in detention, or served prison sentences. About one fifth of Guinea's population emigrated to neighbouring African countries, mostly to avoid Touré's harsh domestic policies. Through it all Touré battled on, as one historian noted, rather like 'an eighteenth century prizefighter blinded by his own blood'.

The plots started in 1960. Touré announced that he had discovered a conspiracy by French nationals and Guinean dissidents to assassinate him, and arrested scores of people; some died under torture. In 1961, a 'teachers' plot' was unfurled after teachers had demanded equal pay for equal work and criticised government policies; union leaders and prominent intellectuals were detained and the Soviet ambassador was summarily expelled. When a group of traders attempted to form an opposition party in 1965, Touré discovered a plot involving the traders and arrested those involved. Other plots in the 1960s led to the imprisonment of ministers and senior army officers. In 1970, an invasion force of Portuguese troops from neighbouring Portuguese Guinea, together with Guinean exiles, landed in Conakry with the aim of destroying the headquarters of Amilcar Cabral's PAIGC and overthrowing Touré. The invaders were driven back from the presidential palace where Touré was staying. Touré used the occasion to carry out a massive purge. On the pretext that a 'fifth column of internal enemies, stooges of imperialism and neo-colonialism' was at work, hundreds of people, including ministers, ambassadors and party leaders were arrested and put on trial before a 'supreme revolutionary court'. They were given no opportunity to defend themselves nor to retain lawyers nor even to see or talk to their judges. Some fifty-eight accused men were later hanged in public in what the government called a 'carnival atmosphere'. In 1972, a medicine shortage was described by Touré as a 'plot by the physicians to discredit the Revolution'. He also interpreted news of a cholera epidemic in Guinea in 1973 as a counter-revolutionary plot. Even Guinea's defeat in the finals of the African soccer championship in 1976 was viewed as a plot. Another major purge, carried out in 1976, included Touré's distinguished Justice Minister, Diallo Telli, a Guinean diplomat who had served as the first secretary-general of the Organisation of African Unity. Telli was jailed, tortured and then subjected to '*la diète noire*', a drawn-out form of execution commonly used in Guinea which consisted of depriving a prisoner of food and water until he died.

The economic strategy that Touré pursued proved a disaster. He was attracted from the start by the idea of extending state control over every sector of the economy so as to free Guinea from its subordination to France and to prevent the rise of an elite entrepreneurial class in the country. Accordingly, a huge state trading monopoly was set up to replace the activities of thousands of independent traders; new state industries were launched as part of an ambitious industrialisation programme; agricultural cooperatives were established; and public works were expanded. Yet there was no coherent planning behind the schemes and few trained Guineans to manage them effectively. At independence Guinea possessed no more than a dozen university-level graduates. The result was a string of state corporations that were badly managed, heavily in debt, rife with corruption and inefficiency and crippled by low production. A sympathetic critic of Guinea, Claude Rivière, wrote in exasperation: 'To set up a cannery without products to can, a textile factory that lacked cotton supplies, a cigarette factory without sufficient locally grown tobacco, and to develop . . . a forest region that had no roads and trucks to carry its output—all these were gambles taken by utopian idealists and ignoramuses.' The agricultural cooperatives also failed and, as a result of low crop prices set by the government, food production declined. Thousands of farmers and their families preferred to emigrate to Senegal and the Ivory Coast in search of work. Whereas at independence Guinea was almost self-sufficient in food, with huge agricultural potential, within a few years it became heavily dependent on food imports. Many essential commodities were constantly in short supply and could only be obtained through the black market. Hospitals often lacked even the most basic medicines.

Touré's campaign against small African traders and transporters continued unabated. They were frequently portrayed as bourgeois traitors to the Revolution. In 1977 a government decree closed all village markets—a major feature of life in Guinea—and accorded state stores, run by local party and government officials, a total monopoly of local trade. All farmers were required to deliver their crops to these stores. This decree and other grievances over the shortage of goods and the rough treatment dealt out by Touré's 'economic police' led to protest demonstrations by market women, which began in rural centres, then spread to provincial towns and finally erupted in the capital. When market women in Conakry marched on the presidential palace, government troops were instructed to fire on them. The party newspaper, *Horoya*, described the incident as part of the 'historical struggle between revolution and counter-revolution'. Touré himself resorted to blaming 'the fifth column.'

Amid all the muddle, incompetence and corruption, what saved Guinea, and Sékou Touré, from ruin were the revenues derived from the country's giant bauxite mines. Guinea possessed one third of the world's reserves of bauxite and Touré was careful to leave mining operations in the hands of foreign companies. The bauxite industry accounted for ninety-five per cent of export revenues and a third of the gross domestic product. One Western mining consortium alone provided Guinea with seventy per cent of all its foreign currency. It was an ironic comment on a man who chose for one of his many titles 'The Terror of International Imperialism, Colonialism and Neo-Colonialism'.

Like most African dictators, Touré built up a personality cult and retained tight personal control over every aspect of his regime. He was referred to as the *Guide Suprême de la Révolution.* In every field, from agriculture to philosophy to soccer, he was portrayed as an expert. More than twenty volumes of his speeches and reflections upon Guinean and African development were published and made compulsory reading. Students were required to memorise his long didactic poems to ensure success in their examinations. No major decision could be taken without his approval. Though a National Assembly existed, it met briefly twice a year formally to sanction legislation and approve the budget. Touré himself was the source of all authority, ruling by decree, intervening at his own discretion in legal cases and deciding the verdict when necessary in the name of the people. Yet despite the unbridled personal power he possessed, despite the repression and economic chaos that marked his regime, Touré stood out from the run of more brutal dictators through his efforts to mobilise the Guinean population towards socialist goals. In the early years of his rule, he was seen as a dynamic, popular figure, supported by a well organised mass political party, the *Parti Démocratique de Guinée*, engaged in defending a beleaguered socialist outpost. And though the vision soon disintegrated, the PDG remained an active organisation and Touré himself was always able to draw huge and enthusiastic crowds throughout the country.

After twenty years of fierce socialist rhetoric, Touré changed course. In 1978 he permitted some private business and trading firms to operate, disbanded the 'economic police' and allowed contraband goods to appear freely in the markets. He also began to make overtures to western investors. 'For the first twenty years, we have concentrated on developing the mentality of our people,' he explained in 1979. 'Now we are ready to do business with others.' The atmosphere of fear and tension in Guinea eased. Hundreds of prisoners were released from jail. In 1982 Touré travelled to New York to appeal to Wall Street financiers for increased private investment in Guinea; and later that year he visited Paris for the first time in twenty-four years. In old age, the *enfant terrible* of West Africa, as he was once known, wanted to adopt a more mellow image. Sékou Touré died in 1984, not at the hands of an assassin, as many had expected, but undergoing a heart operation in an American hospital.

*

Even by African standards, Hastings Banda's regime was remarkable for the extent of personal control that he exercised in Malawi. His grip extended not just over the government and the economy of the country but even over the moral standards under which the population was required to live. No other African leader imposed his personality with such vigour and force on to the country he ruled. Banda ran Malawi as his personal fiefdom and insisted on directing even the smallest details of its affairs. 'Everything is my business. Everything,' he once said. 'The state of education, the state of our economy, the state of our agriculture, the state of our transport, everything is my business.' He was equally blunt about what power lay at his disposal. 'Anything I say is law. Literally law. It is a fact in this country.' No-one was permitted to question his authority or his decisions. Any politician who attempted to assert himself or who gained too influential a role incurred his displeasure and was swiftly undercut. Banda wanted no understudies, even when old age and infirmity began to take their toll. As his official title made clear, he was president for life, both of the nation and the Malawi Congress Party, the only political organisation permitted in the country. He personally controlled portfolios of foreign affairs, defence and justice and other departments as the need arose. He appointed or dismissed at will members of parliament, party officials, ministers and civil servants. His quest for absolute control extended to the courts. Banda gave himself the discretion to interfere with legal proceedings and frequently used it. His instructions were expected to be fulfilled without question, whatever their nature. The strict puritan code which he so admired became the nation's way of life. Men were forbidden to wear long hair; women were forbidden to wear short skirts or trousers. Films, foreign newspapers, magazines and books were strictly censored to prevent 'decadent' Western influences from harming the population. Drinking was strongly discouraged. At an elite secondary school that Banda established in 1981 for carefully selected students, Latin was made a compulsory subject. Victorian values of hard work, thrift, obedience and discipline were what Banda required in Malawi.

Banda's autocratic nature was evident from the start of his regime. He acquired the habit early on of referring condescendingly to ministers as his 'boys' and of lecturing them during cabinet meetings. Within a few months in 1964 he faced a cabinet revolt. A group of young ministers accused him, as he later put it, of 'running the government as if it were my personal estate'. The ministers were also critical of the slow pace at which Banda wanted to replace British expatriates with Malawians in the civil service. There were further disagreements over the direction of foreign policy. Infuriated by the challenge, Banda dismissed three of his eight cabinet ministers. Three others resigned in sympathy. All six eventually fled the country. From then on, Banda never tolerated any sign of dissent, either within the government or in the country at large. He encouraged youth activists—members of the Young Pioneers—to hunt down dissidents, giving them licence to act virtually as they saw fit. Loose talk became dangerous. Scores of people were detained. Banda was characteristically forthright about his objective. 'If, to maintain the political stability and efficient administration, I have to detain ten thousand or one hundred thousand, I will do it,' he remarked in 1965. One group singled out for reprisal was the Watchtower movement, a religious sect whose members refused to salute the national flag or to buy party cards. Thousands were persecuted and driven into exile. The small Asian community also suffered. In 1976 a large group of Asians was expelled from Malawi after a radio broadcasting a speech by the president was switched off during an Asian wedding reception.

Banda's foreign policy was equally forthright. He was

openly contemptuous of the Organisation of African Unity and of African liberation movements. Alone among black African leaders, he established diplomatic relations with South Africa and paid an official visit there in 1971. The racial problems of southern Africa, he argued, were best tackled through dialogue rather than by violence and boycotts. He relished his reputation for being, as he said, 'the most unpopular person in the continent of Africa', and declared that he was willing to make an 'alliance with the Devil' if it was in Malawi's interest. The South Africans were duly grateful, providing him with finance for the construction of a new capital city at Lilongwe and an additional rail link to the coast in Mozambique.

The personality cult which surrounded Banda gave him a god-like status. Newspapers and the radio continuously lavished praise on his accomplishments. Parliamentary sessions were often devoted to the same purpose. At public appearances he was surrounded by ululating women, wearing dresses displaying his portrait and loudly proclaiming his virtues. The name by which he was popularly known was 'Ngwazi' meaning conqueror. Yet, as well as being a vain and arrogant man, Banda was shrewd in his use of political control. The Malawi Congress Party was kept alive in every village and district. Banda himself made frequent tours of rural areas, a familiar figure invariably dressed in a dark three-piece suit and a homburg hat, even under the hottest sun, exhorting crowds to make greater efforts, and keeping track of every development. His whole life was devoted to the business of government. He never married, he had no close family ties, no social life, no known recreations. Banda personified his country to an extent that no other African leader achieved. The society he produced was tightly controlled, but it was also ordered and disciplined and largely successful in improving the living standards of many Malawians. His programme of rural development was often cited abroad as an exemplary model. His strategy of providing strong support for peasant smallholders while encouraging large-scale farming activities by foreign companies made Malawi self-sufficient in food supplies and an exporter of agricultural crops. The country's overall record of economic growth in the 1960s and the 1970s was impressive.

In the latter years of his regime, Banda relaxed his grip. In 1977, about one thousand political prisoners were released. In 1978, parliamentary elections were held, the first for seventeen years. Another round of elections occurred in 1983. Banda, of course, picked the candidates entitled to stand.

*

Kenya, during the fifteen years of Jomo Kenyatta's rule, stood out as one of the most stable, tolerant and prosperous countries in tropical Africa. Its record in agricultural development, economic growth and the provision of government services like education was widely admired. The capital, Nairobi, flourished as an international business and conference centre, its skyline constantly changing with the construction of new hotels and office blocks. Foreign tourists flocked to the country's spectacular wildlife parks and coastal resorts, providing a major source of revenue. Though Kenya became a one-party state, lively debates still continued in parliament. The local press, too, was allowed a wide measure of freedom. Political detainees were few. The judiciary remained firmly independent. The civil service was competently run. And the army was small, well trained and loyal to civilian control. By most African standards, therefore, Kenya was a paragon of orderly government.

The stability that Kenya enjoyed was largely attributable to Kenyatta's massive authority. Even critics of the government accorded him due respect. His stature alone was sufficient to command the allegiance of the population in most parts of the country. He ruled not so much by exercising direct control over the government as by holding court with an inner circle of loyal ministers and officials who themselves were entrusted with the administration of the country. Kenyatta's court moved with him wherever he chose to stay. His favourite residence was his country home at Gatundu, in the hills above Nairobi, where he was born; but he was also to be found at State House in Nairobi or at lodges in Mombasa on the coast and at Nakuru in the Rift Valley. Wherever he was resident, he held regular audiences. His court was open to delegations, petitioners and visitors of all kinds. Sometimes they arrived in huge numbers, accompanied by teams of dancers. For Kenyatta delighted in displays of dancing, and many evenings were spent watching them. He himself performed expertly as a dancer until he suffered from a heart attack in 1972, six years before his death.

Despite the tranquillity of Kenya during Kenyatta's lifetime, there always flowed beneath the surface strong undercurrents of tension that were never resolved. The issue of land hunger, which had given rise to the *Mau Mau* rebellion, constituted as potent a grievance during Kenyatta's regime as during the colonial era. In the last years of British rule, while the transfer of power was made to an African government, colonial officials had been greatly alarmed by the possibility of renewed rebellion over the land issue. A plan to seize land at independence was made by former *Mau Mau* supporters who regrouped together as a Land Freedom Army. Their influence over the Kikuyu was considerable. In some Kikuyu areas, government officials reported, the atmosphere was approaching 'boiling point'. The government's response was to devise settlement schemes for Africans on land purchased from European farmers with finance provided by Britain. The first schemes were launched in 1962. By 1971, a total of 1.5 million acres, about one fifth of the former White Highlands, had been acquired for settlement schemes involving some 500,000 people. A further area of 1.6 million acres was sold privately into African hands. The land came mostly from mixed farming areas. Many of the large coffee, tea and sisal plantations and cattle ranches remained under European control. Despite the land transfer programme, the problem of land hunger continued. Less than twenty per cent of Kenya's land was arable, and the large proportion of the population packed into that area grew at one of the fastest rates in the world. In 1960, the population stood at six million. By 1980, it had reached sixteen million.

While the land transfer programme was largely successful in defusing demands for a takeover of white-owned land, it soon gave rise to bitter controversy. Several prominent politicians were critical of Kenyatta's government for allowing large areas of the land made available to pass into the hands of individual Africans, some of whom were able to amass considerable landholdings. The principal beneficiaries were an elite group of politicians, civil servants and businessmen, who constituted the new Kenyan establishment. One leading critic of the government was Bildad Kaggia, once a key figure in the organisation of the *Mau Mau* rebellion. Kaggia warned of the dangers of letting a new class of African landholders replace European settlers, while landless Africans were struggling to survive. He argued that the land transfer programme benefited departing European farmers by providing them with full compensation, yet burdened new African farmers with the high cost of land purchase. He wanted instead land to be made available without compensation. A more general attack on the direction of government policies was made by a prominent Luo politician, Oginga Odinga, whom Kenyatta had appointed vice-president after independence. As well as a more radical approach on the land issue. Odinga proposed a moderate socialist programme which would reduce the extent of foreign control of the economy and provide for a more equitable distribution of wealth. Odinga's faction met with little success. A parliamentary motion introduced in 1965 urging that a limit should be placed on individual land purchases was rejected. In 1966, Odinga resigned from the government and the ruling Kenya African National Union, taking with him a small core of supporters including Kaggia, and set up an opposition party, the Kenya People's Union. The KPU started out with hopes of providing a broad-based alternative to the government, but it soon dwindled to little more than a Luo faction. Kaggia and other Kikuyu supporters left in 1969. That same year, the party was banned.

In the 1970s, the government was faced with a more formidable critic. A young and ambitious Kikuyu politician, J. M. Kariuki, who had once been detained by the British authorities during the *Mau Mau* era, emerged as a champion of the poor and the landless, with a popular following that came close to rivalling Kenyatta's own. Kariuki's goal, quite openly, was to inherit the presidency after Kenyatta's death. He built his popularity with a sustained attack on the scramble for land and wealth that so occupied the Kenyan elite. 'A stable social order,' he said, 'cannot be built on the poverty of millions. Frustrations born of poverty breed turmoil and violence.' In truth, Kariuki was not a particularly admirable figure. He was a playboy, an inveterate gambler; he himself owned two farms, a racehorse, a light aircraft and several cars, and he also had a reputation for sharp business practices. But he possessed an unerring popular touch and he skilfully exploited the groundswell of discontent that was building up over the greed and corruption clearly evident at the top of Kenyan society. Kenyatta himself was never a target for such criticism, but members of his own family—the 'royal family', as they were known—aroused strong resentment. The focus of attention rested mainly on the activities of two particular members, his young wife, Ngina, and his daughter, Margaret, the Mayor of Nairobi. Both operated business empires and ruthlessly used their link with Kenyatta for personal gain. Ngina Kenyatta became one of the richest individuals in the country, with business interests that extended to plantations, ranches, property, hotels and the ivory trade. In his role as champion of the poor, Kariuki persistently attacked the role of Kenya's rich elite. He never mentioned names, but no-one was left in any doubt to whom he was referring when he said 'We do not want a Kenya of ten millionaires and ten million beggars.' Kariuki also dwelt provocatively on the issues over which the *Mau Mau* rebellion had been fought, a topic which in public was virtually forbidden. 'Our people who died in the forests died with a handful of soil in their right hands, believing that they had fallen in a noble struggle to regain our land . . . (but) . . . we are being carried away by selfishness and greed.' The end result, he warned, would be violence. 'Unless something is done the land question will be answered by bloodshed.' To many people in the government, Kariuki was clearly considered to be a threat. In March 1975 he was murdered, his body dumped at the foot of the Ngong Hills outside Nairobi. In outrage at his death, parliament insisted on setting up its own inquiry. The evidence that a parliamentary committee obtained implicated men in the highest ranks of the government.

In the last years of his remarkable life, Kenyatta showed less and less interest in the business of government, leaving it to his trusted lieutenants to conduct. Much of his time he spent pottering about his two farms, either at Gatundu or at Rongai in the Rift Valley. In private, his thoughts turned to religion; he was given to lecturing visitors on the finer points of theology. And he liked to recall the past—the dour Scottish missionaries who so influenced his childhood. His favourite relaxation, though, was to construct complex riddles—the peculiar delight of the Kikuyu people—with his brother-in-law, Mbiyu Koinange. Then at times he would feel lonely and complain with emotion of his old friends deserting him. The morning was his best time. He would rise at dawn and occasionally place an early telephone call to his ministers. In the evening, he still enjoyed watching tribal dancers. He would retire to bed early, sometimes even dropping asleep in front of the television news. His aides would creep in to switch off the set. He died on 23 August 1978.

*

When Joseph-Desiré Mobutu was first propelled to prominence in the Congo in September 1960 as the army chief of staff who stepped forward to separate the squabbling politicians, he appeared as a nervous and hesitant figure clearly daunted by the confusion and chaos into which the Congo had sunk. He had held the post of army chief of staff for only two months, during which time the Congolese army had disintegrated into a rabble. His only previous military experience had been in the early 1950s, when he had served as a clerk in the *Force Publique* during the days of Belgian rule. And he had dared to take control and dismiss the prime minister, Patrice Lumumba, only because of the active encouragement of the American Central Intelligence Agency and the connivance of United Nations officials in Léopoldville. Worried about his safety, he often sought the company of United Nations officials, paying nocturnal visits to 'Le Royal', the UN headquarters in Léopoldville, arriving there exhausted and sometimes in despair, and staying late into the night, drinking heavily. The UN representative in the Congo, Rajeshwar Dayal, saw him at the time as a 'young man who was so troubled by his unfamiliar and onerous responsibilities and overwhelmed by the problems of his country.' In his memoirs, Dayal wrote: 'Mobutu gave the impression of Hamlet torn between opposing loyalties, unsure of himself and full of doubts and fears. His mobile face was gloomy and preoccupied, his dark glasses adding to his mournful appearance.'

By the time that Mobutu came to stage his second coup in 1965, he had gained considerably in confidence. The early years of his regime were marked by largely successful attempts to restore the power and control of the central government in Léopoldville and to revive the economy. In suppressing disorder and dissent, Mobutu acted ruthlessly but effectively. Four prominent politicians who were accused of plotting to overthrow his government were hanged in public. The leader of a rebellion in Kwilu province in 1964, Pierre Mulele, who returned to the Congo under the impression that he had been granted an amnesty, was executed. When units of the former Katangese *gendarmerie* serving with the national army in the eastern Congo turned against Mobutu, they were brutally crushed. A white mercenary revolt also failed. Regional opposition was suppressed. Within five years, Mobutu managed to impose law and order of some kind on most parts of the country. His economic strategy was equally effective. Inflation was halted, the currency was stabilised, output increased and the government's debts were kept low. The giant copper mining industry was nationalised successfully. By 1970, the Congo under Mobutu was no longer regarded as an object of ridicule and despair but as a viable state which seemed about to realise its vast potential.

The Congo's riches excited the imagination of an increasing number of foreign investors. Its resources of copper, cobalt, industrial diamonds and other minerals provided a glittering basis for economic expansion. For foreign investors there was the added attraction of a generous investment code laid down by the government in 1969. Encouraged by the United States government, American banks led the way in offering finance for new projects. When Mobutu visited Washington in 1970, President Nixon received him warmly and made much of the Congo's political and economic importance. In the early 1970s, the Congo's prospects seemed ever brighter. The price of copper soared, providing the government with huge revenues. By 1974, American and European financiers were involved in a headlong rush to invest in the Congo. Some $2 billion was committed, mainly for mining and industrial enterprises.

Mobutu's political ambitions grew at the same time. He created a single national political party, the *Mouvement Populaire de la Révolution*, set himself up as its sole guide and mentor, and laid down an ideology to which everyone was instructed to adhere. The ideology was known at first as *authenticité*, but its official name was later changed simply to 'Mobutuism'. Though never clearly defined, Mobutuism had the full force of law. Any 'deviationism' was treated as a constitutional offence. In an endeavour to create an 'authentic' national spirit, Mobutu ordered a wide variety of names to be changed. The Congo was renamed Zaire. Towns with European names were given local ones: Léopoldville was changed to Kinshasa; Elisabethville to Lubumbashi; Stanleyville to Kisangani; the province of Katanga to Shaba. Zairians with Christian names were ordered to drop them for African ones. Mobutu himself took the name of Mobutu Sese Seko Kuru Ngebendu Wa Za Banga, and warned that any priest who was caught baptising a Zairian child with a European name would face a five-year jail sentence. A new flag and national anthem were introduced. In time, Mobutu accumulated vast personal power, appropriating at will government revenues, deciding on all appointments and promotions and ruling by decree. The personality cult which surrounded him became all-pervasive. He assumed grand titles like 'Guide' and 'Messiah'. His deeds were endlessly praised in songs and dances; officials took to wearing lapel badges with his miniature portrait. The television news was preceded by the image of the president descending, as it were, through the clouds from heaven.

In 1973, Mobutu embarked on a campaign designed, so he said, to give Zaire greater economic independence. He confiscated a whole range of businesses, factories, farms and plantations from their European owners, handing them to Zairians. No provision was made for compensation. The main beneficiaries were members of Mobutu's entourage, including the president himself, and politicians and officials whose support he needed. Some became millionaires overnight. In

1974, Mobutu decreed further 'radicalisation' measures and announced: 'I have declared war on the bourgeoisie of our country.' More foreign businesses were expropriated. The results were disastrous. Many businesses went bankrupt. Some were simply stripped of their assets and abandoned; others were ruined by incompetent managers. The disruption caused to commerce, agriculture and trade in rural areas was severe. In 1976 Mobutu was obliged to reverse his 'revolution' and invite back foreign owners, but few returned.

The great bonanza in Zaire soon turned sour. In 1974, the copper price on which the government's finances largely depended began to slide, plunging within a year to one third of its peak level. The cost of oil and imported grain soared at the same time. Zaire was beset by an onrush of massive inflation, fuel shortages, falling revenues, huge debts and severe disruption to commerce and agriculture caused by Mobutu's nationalisation measures. In 1975, the government fell into arrears on repayments of its foreign debts, which by then amounted to nearly $3 billion. Alarmed by the possibility of financial collapse in Zaire, Western bankers came to the rescue by agreeing to stretch out their loans so as to reduce the immediate burden. Even then, Zaire failed to keep to the revised repayment schedule. Its debt service liabilities amounted to nearly half the government's total revenue in 1977. More money was lent to Zaire in the hope that the government would eventually bring its finances under control. The banks had reached the point where they could not afford to let Zaire founder.

Mobutu's entire regime, in fact, soon proved to be precarious. In March 1977, a force of about 1,500 Katangese exiles based in Angola crossed the border into Shaba (Katanga) province and advanced rapidly towards the major copper mining centre of Kolwezi, meeting virtually no resistance on the way. The exiles belonged to the *Front National pour la Libération du Congo* (FNLC), set up in 1968 by former members of Tshombe's Katangese *gendarmerie* and dissidents from the Lunda tribe. Some had taken part in mutinies against Mobutu in 1966 and 1967, when serving in the Congolese army. Based in Angola, they had joined first the Portuguese army as a counter-insurgency unit, then Angola's

MPLA forces during the 1975–76 civil war. Their objective in Zaire was to bring down Mobutu's regime by capturing Shaba province. Despite greatly superior numbers, the Congolese army was incapable of containing the invasion and Mobutu was forced to ask for help from his foreign allies. The Americans provided equipment, the French supplied transport aircraft and teams of military instructors, and Morocco sent 1,500 combat troops. The arrival of French and Moroccan troops in Shaba turned the tide. No major clashes took place, for the rebels vanished as quietly as they had arrived. The following year, though, the FNLC returned in greater strength. In May 1978, in a well executed plan, several thousand rebels attacked Kolwezi and within a few hours captured the town. An elite Zairian unit stationed in Kolwezi collapsed almost at once. The arrival of the rebels was followed by a wave of lawlessness, looting and violence. Europeans were seized as hostages. Nearly one hundred were killed. Once more Mobutu appealed for foreign help, and French and Belgian troops were sent to Kolwezi to evacuate the European population. The rebels retreated across the border. To provide security in Shaba, units from several African armies were posted there. Belgium and France sent teams of military instructors to retrain the Zairian army.

The plight of Zaire by 1978 was once more pitiable. Mobutu's regime had become so weak and decrepit that it survived only as a result of the protection of foreign troops and handouts from foreign bankers. Daily life for most of the population had been reduced to a level of deprivation and misery. Because of inflation, the wages of those who could find employment were worth little more than ten per cent of their value in 1960. Disease and hunger were rife. Relief agencies estimated that forty per cent of Kinshasa's population was suffering from severe malnutrition. In the rural areas, agricultural production had slumped and large imports of food were required to feed the population. Only one per cent of the land was cultivated. A fraction of the rural road network remained usable for motor traffic. Hospitals closed for lack of medicines. Although the population had doubled, employment was lower than in 1960. What made Zaire's degeneracy infinitely worse was the extent of corruption that permeated every level of society. Nothing could be accomplished without a bribe. Mobutu himself frequently referred to this Zairian sickness—*le mal Zairois*—and attacked the manner in which top government officials were obsessed by the drive for personal enrichment. 'To sum it up,' he said in 1977, 'everything is for sale, everything is bought in our country. And in this traffic, holding any slice of public power constitutes a veritable exchange instrument, convertible into illicit acquisition of money or other goods, or the evasion of all sorts of obligation. Worse, even the use, by an individual, of his most legitimate right is subjected to an invisible tax, openly pocketed by individuals. Thus, an audience with an official, enrolling children in school, obtaining school certificates, access to medical care, a seat on the plane, an import licence, a diploma, among other things, are all subject to this tax. . . .'

Yet it was Mobutu himself and his inner circle of friends and associates who were the principal beneficiaries, freely using government funds for private purposes or to dispense patronage and pay off supporters and potential troublemakers; it was from them that the whole system of corruption extended. Many government services allocated a budget were never provided. Civil servants and army officers routinely siphoned off state revenues. One informed estimate by foreign bankers suggested that as much as forty per cent of the government's operating budget was either lost, or diverted to purposes other than those intended. A report in 1979 estimated that two thirds of the country's 400,000 civil servants who were paid regularly every month were in fact 'fictitious'; their wages were merely pocketed by senior officials. Army officers regularly kept for themselves their soldiers' pay and sold food supplies on the black market. The soldiers in turn, extorted money from civilians and set up rural roadblocks to confiscate farmers' produce being taken to market. Teachers went unpaid for months. Hospital medicines and equipment were sold by staff for their own profit.

In despair at the chaotic state of Zaire's finances, the country's foreign creditors in 1978 forced Mobutu to agree to a series of corrective measures. Foreign officials were placed in key institutions such as the central bank, the customs department and the finance ministry; and the government's financial policies were subjected to the strict control of the International Monetary Fund. For all practical purposes, Zaire surrendered sovereignty over its finances. One principal aim of the expatriate teams was to prevent Zairian companies, with links in high places, from evading taxes, import duties and foreign exchange regulations, as they had been doing at great cost to the exchequer for many years. In November 1978, a retired West German banker, Erwin Blumenthal, who had been given effective control of the central bank, issued a list of fifty individual businessmen and corporations whom he prohibited from engaging in all import and export transactions until all their debts had been repaid and all foreign exchange earned from their past operations, amounting to hundreds of millions of dollars, had been repatriated. Another group of fifty individuals and companies were placed under investigation. Virtually all the names appearing on both lists belonged to Mobutu's inner circle. Blumenthal singled out as the worst offenders two corporations owned by Mobutu's uncle, Litho Moboti, who, along with Mobutu, was known to be one of the richest men in the country. The effect of Blumenthal's orders was outwardly encouraging. Several companies complied with his requirements; and Mobutu himself announced that 1979 would be a 'year of moralisation'. But ways and means were soon found to circumvent his instructions. When Blumenthal had completed his year's assignment in Zaire, he compiled a confidential report which gave scant hope to the queue of Zaire's foreign creditors. He catalogued the lavish spending by members of Mobutu's family, illustrating the way in which Mobutu used the central bank as a private account for himself and his family and associates, listing details of his properties in Belgium, France, Switzerland, Italy and in other African states, and explaining how Mobutu personally profited from the sale of Zaire's mineral riches. And he warned: 'There is no, I repeat, no chance on the horizon for Zaire's numerous creditors to get their money back. . . . Mobutu and his government show no concern about the question of paying off loans and the public debt. They are counting on the generosity of their creditors and the indefinite renewal of the loans and their repayment.' He concluded: 'There was, and there still is, one sole obstacle that negates all prospect: the corruption of the team in power.'

Mobutu's use of the presidency had made him one of the richest men in the world. Some estimates of his fortune went as high as $3 billion. He enjoyed flaunting his wealth, building himself lavish palaces and paying frequent shopping visits to Europe. On one memorable occasion in 1982, he arrived in the United States for a vacation in the company of nearly one hundred Zairians and in the space of two weeks, during visits to hotels, stores, a dude ranch and Disney World, spent an estimated $2 million. His people, meanwhile, remained tied to a life of poverty and increasing degradation. Nowhere else in Africa was there such a vivid contrast between the opulence of the ruling elite and the drudgery that the mass of the population faced.

CHAPTER TWENTY-EIGHT

Africa's Economic Spiral

The difficulties and dangers that African states faced as they embarked on independence were daunting. Africa was the poorest, least developed region on earth. Its climate was often harsh and variable. Disease and drought were constant hazards. Most of its population was engaged in primitive subsistence agriculture, without access either to basic education or health services. Death rates for children were the highest in the world; life expectancy, at thirty-nine years on average, was the lowest in the world. Only about one third of the student-age population at primary level went to school; no more than three per cent obtained an education at secondary level. In the late 1950s, just as the independence era was beginning, the entire region, containing a population of about two hundred million people, produced only 8,000 secondary school graduates a year, and nearly half of those came from two countries, Ghana and Nigeria. Few new states had more than two hundred students in university training. Economic resources were equally limited. Only a few islands of modern economic development existed, most of them confined to coastal areas or to mining enterprises in areas like Katanga or the Zambian Copperbelt. Much of the interior remained undeveloped, remote, cut off from contact with the modern world, lacking even a basic infrastructure. Fourteen African states were landlocked, relying on long and tenuous links to the sea hundreds, sometimes a thousand, miles away. Most countries depended for their income on primary products such as cocoa and coffee or on minerals such as copper, iron ore and diamonds, all of them vulnerable to world price fluctuations, over which they had no control. Trade and industry too were largely under the control of foreign companies and businessmen. On average, less than ten per cent of the African population earned a wage; most others subsisted on farming.

In some West African countries, notably Ghana, Nigeria, Senegal and the Ivory Coast, prosperous peasant communities flourished. But for the vast majority of the African population life was a constant struggle for survival in conditions of hardship, destitution and disease. However determined African governments were to develop new societies, they themselves possessed neither the financial resources nor the trained manpower to do so.

The advances that Africa made in those circumstances were remarkable. In the two decades between 1960 and 1980, school enrolment grew faster in Africa than in any other developing region. At primary level, enrolment increased from thirty-six per cent to sixty-three per cent of the age group; at secondary level, it increased from three to thirteen per cent; universities produced thousands of graduates each year. A World Bank study published in 1981 observed: 'The African record is unique: nowhere else has a formal education system been created on so broad a scale in so short a time.' In the field of medical care, similar improvements were recorded. Child death rates fell from thirty-eight to twenty-five per thousand; life expectancy increased from thirty-nine to forty-seven years; the numbers of medical and nursing personnel per capita doubled, despite a large increase in the population. New infrastructures were built at record-breaking pace: ports, railways, roads and buildings. The number of miles covered by all-weather roads tripled, opening up vast areas of the interior for the first time.

Despite these achievements, the magnitude of the problems facing Africa proved overwhelming. Economic growth in much of the continent was slow. In the first two decades, per capita income in nineteen countries increased by less than one per cent a year; in the 1970s it actually fell in fifteen countries. Output per person rose more slowly than in any other part of the world. In many countries agricultural production declined sharply, making them dependent on foreign food supplies. The population meanwhile expanded at one of the fastest rates in the world. As African governments embarked on one development project after another, they accumulated huge and unmanageable debts. During the 1970s many were beset by severe economic crises, threatening to undermine what progress had been made. Hospitals and clinics ran short of medicines; schools lacked textbooks; factories closed through lack of raw materials or spare parts for machinery. Even when the accomplishments were taken into account, Africa remained perilously far behind other areas of the world. Life expectancy was by far the lowest of any region in the world, still twenty-seven years shorter than in industrialised countries and less than in any other developing region. The African child death rate in 1980 was sixty-seven per cent greater than in South Asia, three times higher than in Latin America, and twenty-five times higher than in the developed world. The African population was more exposed to endemic diseases like malaria and to other diseases stemming from poor sanitation, malnutrition and poverty. In the field of education, the advances made were still limited: in about one third of African countries, less than half of the child population received primary education; in only six countries were more than twenty per cent of the age group in secondary school.

The record was not uniformly bleak. A number of countries, either because of effective management or through good fortune, succeeded in establishing more prosperous societies. Malawi, Kenya, Swaziland, the Ivory Coast and Cameroon all provided examples of agricultural development that earned widespread applause. Malawi, in particular, was cited as an example of how a country that was listed as one of the poorest in the world, that was small, landlocked, heavily populated and lacking in mineral resources, could still achieve steady growth not only in agriculture but in industrial development. Kenya, once the domain of wealthy white farmers, was highly successful in promoting smallholder agriculture and diversifying smallholder production into tea, coffee, pyrethrum and other crops. In the Ivory Coast, the pace of agricultural development was so remarkable that it was sometimes termed a 'miracle'. A handful of countries—Nigeria, Gabon, Angola, Congo (Brazzaville) and Cameroon—benefited substantially as oil exporters. Nigeria, by the end of the 1970s, ranked among the ten largest oil producers in the world, with oil revenues reaching higher than $20 billion. Gabon, because of its oil revenues and small population—only 500,000—achieved the highest per capita income in black

Africa. In the case of Botswana, a country consisting mostly of desert, the discovery of large mineral deposits transformed its existence; in the 1970s, copper, diamond and coal mines were developed, giving it the highest growth rate of the decade. Out of the thirty-nine countries in black Africa, ten posted annual growth rates of 2.5 per cent or higher between 1960 and 1979. For the rest, the results were mainly decline and decay.

There were many causes lying behind Africa's plight. Some factors—like drought—were beyond anyone's control. The Sahel zone, bordering the Sahara desert, which included parts of Niger, Mali, Chad, Mauritania, Senegal, Upper Volta and Gambia, experienced a series of droughts between 1968 and 1974 that had a devastating impact. Areas of eastern and southern Africa too suffered periodically from drought. The steep fluctuations that occurred in world commodity prices affected almost every African country, so dependent were they on primary products as a source of income. The effects of large oil price rises in the 1970s were particularly severe on oil-importing African states. Then there was the toll taken by wars, civil strife and disorder, military spending and corruption.

All these factors were disruptive enough in themselves. But what proved to be equally damaging was the widespread failure of government policies. In their eagerness to accelerate economic growth, many African governments, following Nkrumah's example in Ghana, were attracted by plans for rapid industrial development, for large-scale projects and nationalisation of major enterprises that were under foreign control. A substantial proportion of government resources was directed towards establishing new parastatal enterprises in public utilities, manufacturing, trade and transport. The hope was that state-owned corporations would be self-financing institutions that would expand swiftly, generate further funds for investment and stimulate modernisation. But rarely did this strategy succeed. Most parastatal organisations were badly planned, inefficiently managed and overmanned. Huge bureaucracies developed. Heavy debts were incurred. Few countries had enough skilled managers to run them effectively. Mali, a poor country even by African standards, set up twenty-three state enterprises after independence, all of which fell into muddle and chaos, accumulating huge deficits. Senegal's parastatal organisations, numbering in all more than one hundred, were estimated to employ four times the manpower they needed. In Zambia, a new elite emerged in control of the state's industrial sector, demanding houses, cars, expense accounts and foreign travel, burdening their companies with heavy overheads.

Most African governments also spent profligately on prestige projects such as presidential palaces, conference halls, airports, airlines, hotels, grand highways and embassies abroad, providing a further drain on what resources were available. The most glaring examples of lavish spending occurred when governments competed for the privilege of holding the annual conference of the Organisation of African Unity, an event renowned for producing little else than rhetoric. Nkrumah set the precedent in 1965 by building a palace containing sixty luxury suites and a banqueting hall capable of seating 2,000 guests. Others followed suit. In 1977, for example, President Omar Bongo of Gabon, a man much given to gestures of personal grandeur, ordered the construction of several seafront hotels in Libreville especially for the OAU summit and a new palace for himself costing well over $200 million. In 1979, President Tolbert spent half of Liberia's budget to host the OAU summit, which was held shortly after riots broke out over government proposals to increase the price of rice; the following year Tolbert became the first chairman of the OAU, elected annually, to be killed in a coup while in office. In 1980, President Siaka Stevens spent two-thirds of Sierra Leone's budget on holding the OAU summit; he survived. President Eyadema of Togo spent $120 million (half of the 1980 budget) on building a thirty-story hotel and conference centre in Lomé, which included fifty-two presidential suites, an equal number of ministerial apartments, several restaurants and a two-hundred-seat theatre, in the hope of persuading the OAU to transfer its permanent headquarters from Addis Ababa, the capital of Ethiopia, to Lomé. But the OAU did not agree to the move. Togo was thus left with what was called a hotel occupancy problem.

The area where African governments failed most critically, though, was in agriculture. In most of Africa, four out of every five people were engaged in agriculture. It was the principal economic sector. Yet governments, with their attention fixed on industrial and manufacturing programmes and other enterprises, tended to neglect it. Official prices paid to farmers for food crops were kept low in order to provide urban consumers with cheap food. When fixing prices for export crops, governments also set low rates for farmers, so as to profit themselves from their sale on world markets and gain extra revenues. In numerous cases farmers received less than half of the real value of their crops. In some cases, farmers were not paid enough even to cover their costs of production; cocoa producers in Ghana and sisal growers in Tanzania were two examples. A study completed in 1981 showed that rice growers in Mali were paid by the government sixty-three francs for a kilo of rice which cost them eighty-three francs to produce. The agricultural sector was further burdened with inefficient state-run marketing and distribution agencies, which operated at a huge cost but provided a poor service. Farmers were frequently paid months in arrears; crops were not collected in time; fertilisers and seeds were delivered late. Agricultural extension services, though overmanned, were often inadequate. In the case of Congo (Brazzaville), the salaries of the government's agricultural staff by 1971 exceeded the incomes of 600,000 peasants. Some governments encouraged large, capital-intensive farming schemes, but these too suffered from technical and management problems and accumulated heavy losses. State-run cooperatives were usually no more successful. African governments also tended to maintain over-valued exchange rates, which had the effect of making food imports for urban consumers relatively cheap but which limited the price paid to farmers.

When the overall figures for Africa's agricultural sector were compiled, they portrayed a steadily deteriorating position. Africa was the only region in the world where food production per capita over the past two decades declined. The record of the 1970s was considerably worse than that of the 1960s. In the 1960s, the volume of agricultural production increased by 2.3 per cent a year, a level which nearly kept pace with the increase in population. Food production in that period grew by 2.0 per cent a year, at considerably less than the rate of population increase. Agricultural exports, the major source of foreign exchange earnings, grew on average by 1.9 per cent a year, or 20 per cent over the decade. In the 1970s, agricultural production fell from a 2.3 per cent increase to 1.3 per cent; food production fell from a 2.0 per cent increase to 1.5 per cent a year; agricultural exports slumped from a 1.9 per cent increase to a 1.9 per cent decrease, an overall fall of 20 per cent over the decade. During that time the population growth rose from 2.5 per cent a year in the 1960s to 2.7 per cent a year in the 1970s. While food production in Asia and Latin America in the 1970s kept pace with population growth, in Africa food production per head drastically declined. In statistical terms, according to the World Food Council, the fall amounted to 7 per cent in the 1960s and 15 per cent in the 1970s. Of the thirty-nine countries in black Africa, only eight reported an increase in agricultural output per capita during the 1970s; twenty-five countries registered a decline in food production per capita. This decline occurred despite greater attention that governments and international agencies paid to the needs of the agricultural sector. Between 1973 and 1980, about $5 billion in aid flowed into agriculture, half of it from the World Bank. To cover food production deficits, countries once self-sufficient in food came to depend on costly food imports or, when they could not afford them, on food aid. Imports of food grains grew by nearly ten per cent every year from the early 1960s. Food imports in 1979 amounted to 12 million tons. The need to purchase food imports, coupled with the fall in agricultural exports, depleted foreign exchange reserves, contributed to balance of payments crises and put African governments deeper into debt.

In some individual cases, the decline of agriculture was precipitous. In Ghana, cocoa production, which had once formed the basis of the country's prosperity, fell from 566,000 tons in 1965 to 249,000 tons in 1979 as peasant farmers found less and less incentive to grow cocoa. Producer prices lagged far behind other costs. Between 1963 and 1979, the price index of all consumer goods in Ghana rose twenty-two times; food prices rose at about the same rate. In neighbouring countries the price of cocoa rose thirty-six times. But Ghana's farmers received only six times more for their cocoa. Nigeria at independence in 1960 was the world's largest exporter of groundnuts and palm produce. Agriculture formed the backbone of its economy. By the 1970s exports of groundnuts, palm oil, cotton and rubber had all but stopped and the country was dependent on food imports costing $2 billion. While the government concentrated on plans to develop manufacturing and transport industries, agriculture had become a neglected backwater. Low producer prices, inadequate marketing systems, lack of credit, poor extension services and meagre investment, all served to hasten the decline. Farming became a progressively unattractive occupation. Nigeria was saved only by its vast oil revenues. Zambia at independence in 1964 was not only blessed with considerable agricultural potential—fertile land and reliable rainfall—but derived a huge income from its copper mining industry, one of the largest in the world. But instead of concentrating on agricultural development, the government spent heavily on promoting manufacturing production—textiles, chemicals and rubber, all of which were dependent upon imported supplies—and on urban development. What efforts were made with agriculture—with peasant cooperatives and large state farms—were mostly failures. Producer prices were kept low. When the world price of copper began a long-term slide in the mid-1970s, Zambia was overwhelmed by economic crisis. Foreign exchange reserves ran out, imports were cut back, manufacturing output fell and heavy debts were incurred. Zambia, once self-sufficient in food supplies, required food imports.

The difficulties that Africa faced in the 1970s were compounded by a steep rise in oil prices. The real price of oil increased fivefold. World Bank estimates in a study published in 1981 showed that for eight of the region's typical oil importers—Ethiopia, Ghana, Kenya, Madagascar, Senegal, Sudan, Tanzania and Zambia—oil imports as a percentage of export earnings rose from 4.4 per cent in 1970 to 23.2 per cent in 1980. Tanzania, for example, imported 800,000 tons of oil in 1972, using up 10 per cent of the total value of its exports; in 1980, it imported 750,000 tons, using up 60 per cent of the total value of its exports. Part of the increased percentages was explained by declining export volumes. Mineral producers like

Zambia and Zaire also suffered from low commodity prices; both produced copper at a loss. But the terms of trade did not deteriorate for everyone. The World Bank noted that, apart from mineral producers, most African countries experienced either favourable or neutral terms of trade in the 1970s. Oil exporters made spectacular gains and other primary exporters showed a strong upward trend, mainly as the result of a boom in prices for coffee, cocoa and tea between 1976 and 1978. On average, said the World Bank, African oil importers experienced less deterioration in their terms of trade than did most other oil-importing groups in the world. The main causes of Africa's growing financial crisis, it maintained, were not external factors, like the increase in oil prices, but stagnant or negative rates of export growth.

Year by year, Africa's debts mounted. In some cases there was no longer any serious prospect that they could ever be repaid. During the 1970s oil-importing countries ran up current account deficits which by 1980 reached an average of 9 per cent of their Gross Domestic Product—twice the figure for oil-importing developing countries and conspicuously higher than any other region of the developing world. Current account deficits rose from a modest $1.5 billion in 1970 to $8 billion in 1980. The deficits were covered to some extent by loans and grants from foreign governments and international agencies which tripled between 1970 and 1980, but otherwise African governments were forced to borrow heavily at commercial rates or deplete their foreign exchange reserves. Between 1970 and 1980 Africa's external debts rose from $6 billion to $38 billion. By 1982 they had reached $66 billion. At the same time, foreign exchange reserves fell sharply. Several governments were left with almost no reserves of foreign exchange. Some countries ran up debts amounting to 40 per cent or higher of their annual national income. An increasing number were obliged to postpone foreign debt repayments.

What chances there were of economic recovery were constantly undermined by a rapid increase in Africa's population. During the 1970s, while population growth rates in Asia and Latin America slowed down, in Africa they rose on average to 2.7 per cent a year, and in some countries—Kenya, the Ivory Coast and Tanzania—to more than 3 per cent a year, the highest growth rates in the world. On average African women each bore six children. Even with high mortality rates, this meant that Africa's population by the early 1980s was growing by more than one million a month. Between 1960 and 1979, the population rose by 63 per cent to a total of 344 million. At that same rate of growth, Africa's population within thirty years would reach almost 1,000 million. Even if the rate of increase declined to one half of the existing level, the population would still be more than 800 million in the year 2010. The rate of population increase in the 1960s and 1970s had a major impact on agricultural production, on urban growth and on government spending. Governments were simply unable to cope with the demand for more schools, more clinics, more housing and even for basic services. Indeed, some were not even able to maintain existing infrastructures.

As populations grew, the pressures on land intensified. By the 1980s, arable land was no longer in plentiful supply in much of the continent. Peasants thus turned to cultivating more and more marginal land, either in areas of unreliable rainfall or on slopes, increasing the problems of soil erosion and degradation, overgrazing and deforestation. Fallow periods were shortened, weakening the land's productive use. Forests and woodlands were stripped for fuelwood, on which Africans largely depended for cooking and heating. The French agronomist, René Dumont, estimated that nearly 30,000 hectares (74,000 acres) of rain forest disappeared every day. Countries already affected by population pressures—like Kenya, Rwanda and Burundi—faced insuperable difficulties. Kenya's population, growing at the rate of 4 per cent a year, had reached 16 million by 1980. By the year 2000 it was expected to increase to 37 million. Yet the area of land suitable for arable agriculture was no more than 17 per cent of the total. Each year Kenyans burned 27 million tons of wood and 25 million gallons of imported kerosine for heating and cooking. At that level of consumption, no wood would be left by the year 2000 and the country's petroleum needs would be astronomical. In the Ivory Coast in 1956, there were 12 million hectares (29 million acres) of forest; in 1980 only 1.4 million hectares (3.4 million acres) were left. Because of more intensive cultivation and grazing, the long term potential of agriculture was steadily declining.

The Sahel zone provided an example of Africa's crisis in its starkest form. A thin strip of semi-arid land stretching across much of Africa south of the Sahara Desert, the Sahel was listed as one of the poorest regions in the world. Periods of drought or low rainfall were not unusual. Until the mid-1960s, the region was largely self-sufficient in food and produced some agricultural exports. Then, between 1968 and 1973, the Sahel was struck by a succession of devastating droughts causing widespread starvation and death. As many as 250,000 people may have died. Cattle herds were decimated. Vast areas of land deteriorated into desert. In 1973 an international rescue operation was mounted. At first the Sahel disaster was attributed mainly to the effects of the drought. But subsequent studies suggested that drought was only one aspect of the problem. In statistical terms, the Sahel's population was increasing at the rate of 2.5 per cent a year, while food production was growing, at best, by 1.0 per cent. Because of population pressures, peasants pushed northwards into pastoral areas, tilling soil that was too arid for permanent cultivation. As more land was taken over for farming, pastoralists and their herds of livestock were forced into even more arid areas. The overall result was overgrazing, overcultivation and deforestation on a catastrophic scale. Every year some 80,000 square miles of land deteriorated. Massive international aid projects were launched in an endeavour to reverse the crisis. In the ten years after the end of the great 1968-73 drought, some $7.5 billion of aid was poured into the Sahel region. International aid by the late 1970s reached the level of $40 per person, compared with $19 per person for Africa as a whole, and only $6 per person for Asia. But though some projects proved of lasting value, the impact of foreign aid was limited. Much of the aid was directed towards towns and cities, often in the form of food aid to keep civil servants, soldiers and the police content. Some aid was squandered by local elites in conspicuous consumption or passed on to foreign companies for the purchase of goods and services. The region swarmed with experts, commissions and international agencies. In 1981, for example, Upper Volta received no less than 340 aid missions. But it was all to little avail. The process of 'disertification' continued unabated. By 1980 the population reached 30 million. By the end of the century it was expected to rise to 55 million.

Africa's urban areas were similarly affected. Huge migrations from the rural areas to the cities occurred. The urban population of Africa expanded faster than on any other continent. In 1960 there were only three African cities with populations of 500,000; by 1980 there were twenty-eight. In thirty-five African capitals, the population increased annually at 8.5 per cent—a rate which meant that they doubled in size every ten years. In 1960, one African in ten lived in a town; by 1980, the proportion was one in five. If that trend continued, then half of the population was expected to live in towns by the end of the century. African governments, fearful of the consequences of urban unrest, spent heavily on urban development and on food subsidies. But what efforts were made led to little overall improvement. Most urban inhabitants lacked basic amenities like running water, sanitation, paved streets and electricity. Millions lived in slums and squatter settlements, in shacks made from sheets of plastic, packing crates, cardboard boxes and pieces of tin. With no hope of employment, the only means for survival for many of them was crime and prostitution.

What was so striking about Africa's plight was its universality. Whatever economic and political system was devised, whatever ideology was chosen, the same pattern of economic crisis developed. A few states managed to escape by virtue of their oil revenues or through effective management. The rest were chained to dismal prospects. When they embarked on independence, African leaders placed inordinate faith in the power of ideology to provide them with the key to development. In the early 1960s, African Socialism became fashionable. It was thought to offer a third way between Western capitalism and Eastern socialism, catering especially for Africa's needs and giving Africa a special identity. What it meant in practice differed widely. Some states, like Kenya, paid the idea official homage, while continuing to promote a market economy and aggressive free enterprise. Ambitious politicians like Nkrumah tried their own personal versions, hence 'Nkrumaism'. In Zambia, Kenneth Kaunda expounded endlessly on the virtues of 'Humanism', though his government was more noted for being inefficient and corrupt. Nyerere in Tanzania, in launching his 'Ujamaa' programme in 1967, came closest to a serious attempt to implement socialist values. In the 1970s, a number of African governments put their faith in Marxism-Leninism. In the case of Congo (Brazzaville), Benin, Ethiopia and Somalia, 'Marxist-Leninist' states were established simply by proclamation of a military regime. No political movements or popular parties were involved, and the changes that occurred were often no more than cosmetic. In Brazzaville, portraits of Marx, Lenin and Engels adorned public places, and Marxist slogans urging revolutionary struggle and vigilance against Western imperialism proliferated on the streets. But few other countries offered such a profitable environment for foreign companies as Congo. Benin, though adopting a Marxist-Leninist ideology, remained as dependent as before on French assistance and continued its membership of the franc zone.

By the 1980s such ideological distinctions had anyway assumed less and less importance. For as one country after another succumbed to economic crisis, they sought to stave off disaster by courting foreign assistance and investment, principally from the West, adopting whatever measures were necessary to secure it. The priority for many African states had become, quite simply, survival. And the stark reality they faced was that their survival had come to depend more and more on the outside world.

CHAPTER TWENTY-NINE

Tanzania's 'Ujamaa'

Tanzania held the attention of the outside world for longer than any other African country. Its programme of economic and social development, devised by Julius Nyerere in the 1960s, stood out as a beacon of hope in a continent where so many dreams and expectations were faltering. Nyerere himself was regarded as a leader of outstanding ability whose personal integrity and modest lifestyle set an edifying standard for the rest of Africa. His vision of a socialist society, which gave priority to the development of the rural areas and the welfare of the peasant population, won him a huge following at home. Throughout Tanzania, he was known affectionately as *Mwalimu*, a Swahili word meaning teacher. At an international level, he came to be respected as a spokesman not just for Tanzania but for the whole of Africa. His socialist ideals generated as much approval abroad as at home. Tanzania under his leadership was acknowledged to be one of the few African states seriously endeavouring to alleviate the poverty of its rural population. By the 1970s Tanzania benefited from more foreign aid than any other African country. Indeed, in some foreign quarters, Tanzania's socialist experiment was soon surrounded by a cult of uncritical adulation. The political scientist, Ali Mazrui, described it as 'Tanzaphilia'.

Much of the reputation that Tanzania gained was due to Nyerere's skill in articulating African aspirations. He was an ardent exponent of the virtues of traditional African life, depicting pre-colonial Africa as an idyllic society that had been destroyed by colonial rule and urging his countrymen to return to the old values that had once guided them. An essay on African Socialism that he wrote in 1962 gave a glowing account of traditional African society: 'Everybody was a worker. . . . Not only was the capitalist, or the landed exploiter, unknown

... capitalist exploitation was impossible. Loitering was an unthinkable disgrace.' The advent of colonialism had then changed all this: 'In the old days the African had never aspired to the possession of personal wealth for the purpose of dominating any of his fellows. He had never had labourers or "factory hands" to do his work for him. But then came the foreign capitalists. They were wealthy. They were powerful. And the African naturally started wanting to be wealthy.'

The kind of society that Nyerere wanted to establish in Tanzania was one based on African socialism and self-reliance, which would avoid both the evils of capitalism and the pitfalls of doctrinaire socialism. African socialism, he declared, had to be founded upon principles of mutual respect, shared property and the willingness of all members to work for the common good, principles with which he claimed Tanzanians were already familiar. Nyerere termed this indigenous form of socialism as *Ujamaa*, and defined it in English as 'familyhood'. He believed that in time the idea of 'familyhood' and the values it encompassed could be extended beyond the tribe and the community to include the nation and eventually the whole of Africa. It was an idealistic vision of African society, of its past as much as of the future.

Nyerere set Tanzania firmly on a socialist course in 1967, five years after independence. At a conference of the ruling Tanganyika African National Union party he issued a statement of party principles which became known as the Arusha Declaration. The Arusha Declaration called for national self-reliance, emphasised the need for development to begin at the lowest rural level and asserted the state's right to control all major means of production and exchange. It was accompanied by a leadership code designed to prevent the growth of a privileged elite. Senior government and party officials were prohibited from owning company shares, from holding private directorships, from receiving more than one salary and from owning houses for rent. Their fringe benefits were cut and restrictions were imposed on the importation of luxury goods. In pursuance of this new strategy, the government proceeded by stages to take control of virtually every sector of the economy—banking, trade, industry, transport, housing, agriculture, distribution and marketing.

New parastatal corporations were set up to administer the government's holdings and to promote the creation of new industries.

The main thrust of Nyerere's strategy, though, was devoted to rural development. He devised a programme for regrouping the scattered rural population into self-sufficient villages where land was to be owned and tilled on a communal basis. The villagers were to share basic necessities and the cost of social services. These *ujamaa* villages, as they were called, were intended to be voluntary associations. Nyerere was adamant that neither compulsion nor coercion was to be used to establish them. 'An *ujamaa* village,' he wrote in 1968, 'is a voluntary association of people who decide of their own free will to live together and work together for their common good.' Through such cooperative ventures, peasants would be able to increase their total output. They would also make it easier for the government to provide the rural population with basic services such as roads, schools, clinics and water supplies. The *ujamaa* programme steadily grew. At the end of 1968, 350 villages had been registered. By mid-1973, the number had increased to 5,000 villages involving some two million people, or about fifteen per cent of the population. But they were not a success in the way that Nyerere had envisaged. Few were run on cooperative lines. Most peasants preferred to keep to individual farming. Some villages were set up merely to secure government offers of assistance. And far from being self-reliant, *ujamaa* villages attracted a bureaucracy of well-paid party officials, agricultural officers and community development personnel, all determined to assert their own authority and control.

Impatient with the results of the *ujamaa* programme, Nyerere abandoned the idea of establishing voluntary cooperatives and in 1973 announced a massive 'villagization' plan involving the compulsory resettlement of virtually the entire remaining rural population within three years. Between 1973 and 1977 some eleven million people were placed in new villages, in what amounted to the largest mass movement in Africa's history. Nyerere asserted that the movement of villagers was overwhelmingly voluntary. 'Eleven million people could not have been moved by force in Tanzania; we do not have the physical capacity for such forced movement, any more than we have the desire for it.' In some cases, however, peasants reluctant to move were illtreated and punished; houses and food stores were burned down. A French writer, Sylvain Urfer, sympathetic towards the Tanzanian experiment, gave this description in his book, *Une Afrique socialiste: la Tanzanie:*

> 'Between August and November 1974, it was as if a tidal wave had washed over the country, with millions of people being moved in a dictatorial manner, sometimes overnight, on to waste land that they were expected to turn into villages and fields. In many places the army was called in to bring anyone who was reluctant to heel and move them *manu militari*. During the month of October the country seemed to be emerging from some national disaster, with mean huts made from branches and foliage stretching in untidy rows beside the roads.'

The Tanzanian press published similar accounts, depicting scenes of people uprooted from their villages and abandoned in the bush, where they were supposed to find planned villages. 'It would be fair to say,' wrote the French agronomist, René Dumont, 'that the operation took place without any planning at all . . . with the bureaucrats giving orders and "villagizing" on paper with no knowledge whatsoever of the regions affected. . . .'

The disruption caused by the 'villagization' programme nearly led to catastrophe. Food production fell drastically, raising the spectre of widespread famine. Between 1974 and 1977 the deficit recorded was more than one million tons. Drought compounded the problem. The shortfall had to be made up with expensive imports of food which exhausted the government's foreign exchange reserves, and by relying on foreign food donations. A liberal academic, Michael Lofchie, observed in 1978: 'The ujamaa program has placed the Tanzanian government in virtual receivership to its foreign donors. . . . The great historical irony of agrarian socialism in Tanzania is that a program motivated by the principle of national self-reliance and intended to help the country sever its ties of dependence with the international market economy has ended by producing greater dependence than ever before.'

Other aspects of Nyerere's socialist strategy were no more successful. His programme of state control spawned a multitude of state corporations that were inefficient, incompetently managed and mired in debt. By 1979, some three hundred parastatal organisations had been set up—state industries, state banks, state farms, state cooperatives, state marketing boards. Most of them, according to René Dumont in a scathing report he made in 1979, were 'overstaffed, underequipped, poorly run and heavily spendthrift'. Each was burdened with a huge bureaucracy. Among the most notorious were ten state-owned crop authorities. The pyrethrum board, for example, which controlled the production and marketing of pyrethrum, an ingredient used in insecticide, spent more on its administrative costs in 1980 than the total value of the crop it purchased; the sisal's board's overheads in 1980 were higher than the amount Tanzania earned from exporting sisal. Farmers meanwhile were offered inadequate prices and faced long delays in payment, sometimes lasting for up to one year, and eventually they resorted to using the black market or growing subsistence food. The production of export crops like sisal, cashew nuts and pyrethrum fell drastically in the 1970s.

By the end of the 1970s, Tanzania faced a familiar litany of woes. Agricultural and industrial production were in decline. The country's trade deficit was widening all the time; its foreign debt had soared. Oil imports, which had used only ten per cent of the value of exports in 1972, took sixty per cent in 1980. The terms of trade were constantly deteriorating. A ton of exported tea in 1970 bought 60 barrels of oil, but in 1980 only 4.5 barrels. The shortage of foreign currency hampered the running of factories and farms. For want of spare parts and materials, machinery and trucks were idle. Industry operated at only one third of its capacity. A shortage of basic commodities like soap, sugar and cooking oil and other consumer goods produced black markets, petty corruption and smuggling—*magendo*, as it was called. Inflation and drought added to the toll. A further burden came as a result of the war against General Amin in Uganda in 1979, which cost the government $500 million, at least half of it in foreign exchange. In a broadcast in December 1981 to mark the twentieth anniversary of Tanzania's independence, Nyerere admitted: 'We are poorer now than we were in 1972.'

Yet whatever difficulties Nyerere encountered, he was determined to adhere to his socialist strategy. 'People who think Tanzania will change her cherished policies of Socialism and self-reliance because of the current difficulties are wasting their time,' he said in 1979. The possibility that the strategy itself might be flawed was never raised. Indeed, in Tanzania no serious political discussion occurred. No-one questioned the course on which Tanzania was bound. It was held to be a matter of ideological faith. Though parliamentary elections under a one-party system were regularly held, parliament itself remained impotent. Real power lay in State House in Dar es Salaam, in party committees and with a ruling class of bureaucrats, all of which frowned upon opposition. Nyerere was by no means averse to using Tanzania's Preventive Detention Act to silence political critics, and Tanzania for many years remained high on the list of African countries with political prisoners. When Nyerere came to examine Tanzania's economic record on the tenth anniversary of the Arusha Declaration, he was characteristically candid about faults that had occurred. He criticised officials for corruption, workers for slackness and indiscipline, and government departments for overspending. But the overall conception of the government's strategy he held to be valid. He acknowledged that the country was neither socialist nor self-reliant, but he argued that government policy had at least prevented the worst excesses of capitalism, in particular the emergence of a rich and privileged elite. And he compared socialism to a vaccination: 'We are like a man who does *not* get smallpox because he has got himself vaccinated. His arm is sore and he feels sick for a while; if he has never seen what smallpox does to people he may feel very unhappy during that period, and wish that he had never agreed to the vaccination.'

Much was achieved during Tanzania's independence, notably in the field of education, health and social services. Between 1960 and 1980, primary school enrolment increased from one quarter of the school-age population to ninety-five per cent; adult literacy grew from ten per cent to seventy-five per cent; four in ten villages were provided with clean tap water, three in ten had clinics; life expectancy increased from 41 years to 51 years; only half as many children—18 in 100—died before the age of four. Yet what progress was made was financed largely by foreign aid. During the 1970s, Tanzania received no less than $3 billion, mostly from the West. The level of aid increased from $10 million in 1967 to $600 million in 1982, when as much as two thirds of the development budget was derived from foreign funds and grants. Nyerere's achievement, therefore, was related not to the success of his strategy for improving the economic and social welfare of his countrymen, but to his ability to persuade foreign sponsors that his objectives were sincere.

CHAPTER THIRTY

The Ivory Coast's 'Miracle'

In terms of economic progress, the Ivory Coast surpassed every other country in black Africa. A World Bank survey published in 1978 reported: 'Few countries, developed or developing, can match the economic growth record of the Ivory Coast. Its annual growth in real terms of over seven per cent during the past twenty-five years is unique on the African continent.' The results of this economic 'miracle', as it was sometimes called, were to be seen in the towering office blocks which dominated the skyline of Abidjan, the Ivory Coast's capital, in the neat plantations stretching for miles over the countryside, and in the thriving market towns inland.

When compared to the plight of its ill-fated neighbour, Ghana, the prosperity that the Ivory Coast enjoyed was even more striking. In the 1950s both countries were similarly placed, in size and in potential; both depended on agriculture as the mainstay of their economies, but they had taken different paths. While Nkrumah was fired by ambitions to turn Ghana into a major industrial and political power and to lead the rest of Africa in campaigning against colonialism and neo-colonialism, Houphouët-Boigny preferred to retain links with France and to adopt a more cautious approach towards economic development. In 1957, when the two men met in Abidjan and made a wager to compare their fortunes ten years hence, Nkrumah was the triumphant leader of a newly independent state acclaimed throughout the world, while Houphouët was content to serve as a cabinet minister in the French government, wedded to the idea of 'partnership' with France. In all Houphouët served in six successive French governments, insisting at the time that independence from France would bring no real benefits. And though he was eventually carried along by the growing momentum elsewhere in Africa towards independence, when the Ivory Coast did become an independent state in 1960, Houphouët still saw no need for any marked change in its relationship with France. Only through close collaboration with France and with the help of French investors, he maintained, would the Ivory Coast prosper. To men like Nkrumah, Houphouët's continuing links with France amounted to a neo-colonial relationship of the kind that he vociferously denounced. Yet Nkrumah himself ended by leaving his country in pawn to foreign investors to a greater extent than any other contemporary African ruler. And when he was overthrown by the army in 1966, Ghana was already sinking into a decline from which it never recovered.

Houphouët's partnership with France formed the basis of his economic strategy. He relied heavily on French investment, French aid and French personnel. Indeed the French presence in the Ivory Coast became even more noticeable than it was during the colonial era. The number of French residents rose from 10,000 at independence to 50,000. French advisers and *coopérants* were to be found at every level of government, in the presidency, the security services, the military command, government ministries and parastatal organisations. In the 1980s, some 12,000 Frenchmen were still in government service. They also held a wide range of managerial posts in the private sector. Commerce was retained largely in the hands of French and Lebanese businessmen, and about half of the manufacturing sector was French-owned. By offering favourable terms to foreign investors, Houphouët attracted substantial foreign capital and loans. A major advantage for foreign businessmen was the Ivory Coast's continued membership of the French franc zone, under which France guaranteed the convertibility of local currency. In the field of defence, too, the Ivory Coast relied on French assistance. French troops were stationed permanently at a base outside Abidjan, as part of the military network that France maintained in Africa by agreement with its former colonies. Houphouët was unapologetic about the French military presence: 'We have no complexes about this,' he said. 'NATO countries accept American military protection, and eastern European countries rely on the Soviet Union. There is, therefore, no reason why France cannot fulfil its traditional commitment.'

The priority on which Houphouët insisted was economic growth. He wasted little time on politics. Public debate and political criticism he viewed as an impediment to the business of economic development. Not for twenty years were any contested elections held. Hitherto, Houphouët merely arranged for his *Parti Démocratique de la Côte d'Ivoire*, the country's only political party, to present a single list of preselected candidates for each constituency. In 1980, he permitted contested elections under a one-party system, but even then Houphouët's autocratic style hardly changed. Political power was held by a small elite surrounding the president. The party survived mainly as a means of distributing patronage. Houphouët believed above all in the need for management and organisation, rather than political participation, and it was the French to whom he turned to provide it if qualified Ivorians were not available. Yet he was astute in his use of political power, preferring to draw his critics and opponents into the government system rather than to suppress them, while remaining ever watchful. 'I am like the crocodile,' he once remarked, 'I sleep with one eye open.'

Houphouët was one of the few African leaders ever to champion openly the virtues of capitalism. But as well as encouraging foreign and local private initiatives, the government became increasingly involved in sponsoring major development projects. By the 1970s, nearly two thirds of investment came from the public sector. The result was a capitalist economy in which government planning and finance played a prominent role. Houphouët once explained: 'We are not socialists, in that we do not believe in giving priority to the distribution of wealth but wish to encourage the creation and multiplication of wealth first of all. Our major concern is with the human aspect of growth. Our system cannot be described as liberalism either, but it can be likened to a planned economy. We are following a policy of State capitalism.'

The government's drive for economic growth centred on agriculture. Other than good soil, abundant rains and an industrious peasant community, the Ivory Coast had few resources. Not until the 1980s did oil production begin. By any standards, the expansion of the agricultural sector was phenomenonal. In the 1950s, the Ivory Coast produced a single crop, coffee. The government encouraged diversification, guaranteed profitable prices for major cash crops, provided extension services and a marketing organisation. Private enterprise was given free rein. New crops were developed under the direction of parastatal companies. Between 1960 and 1980 agricultural production tripled. The Ivory Coast overtook Ghana as the world's largest producer of cocoa; it became Africa's largest exporter of coffee and a major exporter of pineapples, bananas, palm oil and hardwood; and at the same time it managed to increase food production at a higher rate than population growth. Crops were produced both on large plantations and by smallholders. By the mid-1970s, the number of coffee and cocoa planters reached nearly half a million. The prosperity of the agricultural sector was helped considerably by the flow of cheap immigrant labour attracted to the Ivory Coast from neighbouring territories: by the 1970s, one million foreign African labourers were working in the Ivory Coast, two thirds of them in agriculture; most were poorly paid. Much of the expansion was achieved, too, simply by increasing the area under cultivation rather than by employing more productive farming techniques. Timber resources, in particular, were ruthlessly exploited. The industrial sector, centred mainly on agro-industries and import substitution, also expanded rapidly. Industrial growth as high as fifteen per cent a year was recorded. Overall, in the course of two decades, national output expanded twelvefold. Real incomes in that period doubled at the same time that the population doubled. Per capita income at $1,200 by 1980 was one of the highest in Africa.

Not everything went according to plan. In the late 1970s, when a commodity boom sent state revenues soaring, the government embarked on an ambitious expansion programme which included major projects such as roads, ports and hydroelectric dams. A range of state enterprises was set up to promote further agricultural and industrial diversification. Substantial funds were raised abroad to help finance the programme. Then in 1978 the world price for cocoa and coffee began a precipitous decline. In 1979–80 revenues fell by more than one billion dollars. The government was thus left with a huge foreign debt—nearly six billion dollars—and declining income. For the first time since independence, the balance of payments swung into deficit. To make matters worse, most of the new state enterprises accumulated large losses. In 1980 Houphouët ordered most of them to close, admitting that a fundamental error had been made. 'The almost universally bad management of these state companies has led almost every one of them to make a loss,' he reported. At the same time he curbed public spending and introduced austerity measures. Unemployment and inflation increased. The period of 'miracle' growth was over.

Throughout his long lifetime, whether in times of prosperity or economic restraint, Houphouët's regime was often the target of criticism among young Ivorians. His critics contended that the Ivory Coast, dependent as it was on foreign investment, foreign personnel and foreign markets, had remained virtually in a state of tutelage, as binding as that of colonial rule. They resented the manner in which a small political and business elite had been allowed to accumulate wealth and power and distance itself from the bulk of the population. And they claimed that the conditions of economic growth that the government had created were of benefit mainly to foreign business interests and a privileged minority of Ivorians. Houphouët's own wealth and the extent of his family's business interests also aroused adverse public comment. But Houphouët himself remained indifferent to the criticism and went so far as to boast about his personal holdings. In a remarkably frank speech to the PDCI's political bureau in 1983, he said he had made 'billions' from business in the Ivory Coast, listing among his achievements that he was the country's largest producer of pineapples and avocados. He also admitted that he had 'billions' invested in Switzerland. 'What sensible man wouldn't?'

For all his reputation as an astute and prudent leader, Houphouët embarked on one scheme that was as grandiose as any other showpiece conceived in Africa. As a monument to his career, he planned to transform his birthplace at Yamoussoukro, a small inland village no different from hundreds of others in the Ivory Coast, into a glittering metropolis of grand and luxurious buildings. Other African presidents had pursued similar ideas: Mobutu had built a sumptuous retreat for himself at his home in Gbadolite in northern Zaire; in Cameroon, Ahidjo spent lavishly in his home town, Garoua; Jean-Bedel Bokassa, the 'Emperor' of the Central African Republic, turned his home village of Berengo into a virtual seat of government. But the scale on which Houphouët planned to build the new Yamoussoukro surpassed them all. It was sometimes referred to as an African version of Versailles. The most imposing buildings were the presidential palace and its guest palace. At the entrance stood two huge, gold-painted rams, Houphouët's personal symbol. Sacred crocodiles were kept in the palace pond, fed daily on live chickens, and a sacred elephant was allowed to wander within the walls. At Yamoussoukro, Houphouët also built for himself a mausoleum. It was modelled on the tomb of St Denis, near Paris, where French royalty were laid to rest.

CHAPTER THIRTY-ONE

Epilogue

Shortly after Kwame Nkrumah was overthrown by an army *coup d'etat* in 1966, youth group members who had been trained on such slogans as 'Nkrumah never dies' and 'Nkrumah is the new Messiah' marched through the streets of Accra carrying placards proclaiming 'Nkrumah is NOT our Messiah'. There were many African leaders who, like Nkrumah, aspired to great roles, who saw themselves as possessing unique ability, and whose demise was equally abrupt and ignominious. Whatever their achievements may have been, they were remembered, like Nkrumah, more for the legacy of disorder, confusion and decay that was left behind. Though some African leaders survived for remarkably long periods in office, their legacies were often little different. Only a few were noted for wise, prudent and tolerant leadership. Indeed, Africa was generally ill-served by its political leaders. Once in power, their principal preoccupation became to stay in power, employing whatever means were necessary. Constitutions and laws were cast aside if they stood in the way. Opponents were often imprisoned or murdered. Basic rights were ignored. The most common system of government was a form of personal rule exercised in an arbitrary and authoritarian manner. Because of the internal tensions and rivalries afflicting most African states, it was often said that only strong government could provide the stability they needed to develop and prosper. Yet, in practice, strong governments of the kind employed in Africa—whether personal dictatorships or one-party systems—ensured neither political stability nor effective administration. Where no political outlets existed, the most frequent means used to challenge such governments was their attempted overthrow. A few examples of multi-party democracies survived in the early 1980s—such as Senegal and Botswana—enough to prove that the idea could work. Some one-party states offered relatively tolerant government and occasionally held restricted forms of election. But the vast majority of Africans could expect neither political rights nor freedoms. What was even more crucial was the failure of most African governments to carry through effective economic programmes alleviating the plight of their populations. The rewards of independence all too evidently were reaped for the most part by small, privileged groups at the pinnacle of power. Some individuals, like Mobutu of Zaire, became grotesquely rich. Huge sums were squandered for reasons of pomp and prestige. Meanwhile the gap between the rich and poor grew conspicuously wider. Peasant farmers and urban poor alike suffered from neglect. More than two thirds of the people of Africa were estimated to live in conditions of extreme poverty; and their ranks increased all the time. Added to such misery was the toll taken by natural disasters like drought and famine and by the spasms of violence which persistently wracked Africa. Indeed, by the late 1970s, a mood of despair about the fate of Africa had begun to take hold. The OAU's secretary general, Edem Kodjo, told a group of African leaders: 'Our ancient continent . . . is on the brink of disaster, hurtling towards the abyss of confrontation, caught in the grip of violence, sinking into the dark night of bloodshed and death. . . . Gone are the smiles, the joys of life.'

The predictions made in the 1980s about Africa's future were increasingly gloomy. No solution to its myriad problems seemed available. Experts like the French agronomist René Dumont spoke only in pessimistic terms: 'Most of the countries of tropical Africa, with one or two exceptions, are up to their ears in debt, without any hope of ever being able to repay what they owe,' he said. 'Twenty years after independence these countries are in reality bankrupt, reduced to a state of permanent beggary.' The World Bank noted in a 1983 report that despite billions of dollars of international aid poured into Africa, the region faced 'a deepening crisis'. A study published by the Economic Commission for Africa in 1983, attempting to look twenty-five years ahead, made particularly chilling reading. It predicted that on existing trends poverty in rural areas would reach 'unimaginable dimensions', while the towns would suffer increasingly from crime and destitution. 'The picture that emerges,' it said, 'is almost a nightmare.'

Chapter Notes

The broad nature of this book has meant that, as well as drawing on my own experiences and research in Africa over the course of fifteen years, I have relied on the work of many other authors. Included in these chapter notes are references to some of the books which I found to be of particular interest and value. A more complete list can be found in the select bibliography.

M. M.

Chapter One: The activities of the nationalists in London are chronicled in a variety of biographies, memoirs and histories. Padmore is covered most fully by Hooker; Kenyatta by Murray-Brown; Banda by Short; Nkrumah by his autobiography. Peter Abrahams, in his novel, *A Wreath for Udomo*, portrays Padmore and Kenyatta. Abrahams' remarks on Nkrumah are taken from his essay, *The Blacks*; he also writes memorably there of an encounter with Kenyatta in Kenya in 1952. Ras Makonnen, in conversation with Kenneth King, gives a detailed description of African nationalists in exile. The black American journalist who met Padmore after the war was Roi Ottley. Other writers dealing with this period include Geiss; Langley; Edward Wilson; and Padmore. Three main accounts illustrate British policy at the time: Goldsworthy; Lee; and Pearce. Creech Jones's own writings provide a valuable guide.

Chapter Two: Morgenthau and Mortimer cover French policy during this period. Crowder's essays are particularly helpful; also, Deschamps and Delavignette. Houphouët, explaining his choice of linking up with the Communists, once remarked: 'I thought it advantageous to be able to count on 180 Communist votes every time we had a demand to make.'

Chapter Three: Belgian policy in the postwar era is covered by Anstey; Brausch; Lemarchand; Merriam; Slade; and Young. Lumumba wrote *Le Congo, terre d'avenir—est-il menacé?* during 1956–7, but it was not published until after his death.

Chapter Four: Duffy provides the main accounts; Newitt, a concise overall history of the Portuguese territories; and Abshire and Samuels, much useful information. Henrique Galvâo, the official who reported on forced labour conditions in Angola, in later years was charged with plotting to overthrow the government.

Chapter Five: The most valuable study of Anglo-American relations concerning colonial policy is Wm. Roger Louis's *Imperialism at Bay*. Pearce deals at length with Cohen's endeavours.

Chapter Six: The outstanding work on this period is Austin's *Politics in Ghana*. Also useful are Apter; Bourret; Nkrumah; Pearce and the (Watson) Report on the Commission of Enquiry into Disturbances in the Gold Coast (Col. no. 231, 1948). Arden-Clarke's description of his meeting with Nkrumah is taken from *African Affairs*, January, 1958.

Chapter Seven: A diverse literature covers the 'Mau Mau' rebellion. Murray-Brown follows Kenyatta's part in it. Slater gives an account of Kenyatta's trial. Rosberg and Nottingham provide the most balanced perspective. Of the personal accounts, Kaggia, Itote and Kariuki provide valuable insights from the Kikuyu side: Henderson and Kitson give vivid narrative accounts from the British. The official British government report (Corfield), published in 1960, is still of interest mainly because it illustrates, seven years after the outbreak of the rebellion, how little the colonial authorities understood of what had happened.

Chapter Eight: The early years of the Federation are touched on by several writers, but no comprehensive account of the Federal years yet exists. Of interest are Blake, Bowman, Clements.

Chapter Nine: Coleman provides one of the first political analyses of modern Nigeria. Other references to Nigeria are listed under Chapter Twenty-one; and, to Uganda, under Chapter Twenty-two.

Chapter Ten: Among other guests at the Ghana independence celebrations were Martin Luther King, who suggested to Nixon he should try to pay a visit to the American South to study race discrimination problems there; François Mitterrand, representing France; Garfield Todd, representing Rhodesia; and the Rev. Michael Scott, an anti-colonial campaigner. Todd and Scott were deliberately placed at the same banqueting table, though Todd had signed an order prohibiting Scott from entering Rhodesia. Nixon's entourage included 22 journalists and aides. The Russians complained about the presence of so many Americans and claimed the British were worried about them. The South African envoy broadcast on Ghana radio saying that Ghana could count on the ready cooperation of South Africa.

Chapter Eleven: Woronoff writes about Houphouët's wager with Nkrumah, and follows through with an account of who won. Also, Lacouture, Mortimer, White. Senghor, expressing his gratitude to de Gaulle, remarked: 'He was not only the great Decolonizer of the History of France. Under his firm, lucid direction, France was the nation that brought the most efficacious aid to our young independence.' Houphouët, in a speech at a luncheon for six African presidents given by de Gaulle in July 1965, said: 'If we have been able to achieve some successful results, it is largely thanks to you, thanks to the living example which you represent in this hard and difficult world. It is thanks to you that we have been able to set our people on the path of liberty and happiness. You have been a sort of light-house for us... We who are assembled here and all the others—francophone and anglophone—who turn their eyes towards Paris know as we do that you are our guarantee of peace and security.'

Chapter Twelve: Welensky, in his robust defence of the Federation, blamed Nkrumah for its troubles. Also, Short, Rotberg and the Report of the Nyasaland Commission of Inquiry (*The Devlin Report*) Cmd 814,1958.

Chapter Thirteen: Macmillan's memoirs and Macleod's writings in the *Spectator* and the *Weekend Telegraph* (1964 and 1965) are useful guides. The fear of communist influence was a particularly strong theme at the time. Macmillan: 'As I see it, the great issue in this second half of the Twentieth Century is whether the uncommitted peoples of Asia and Africa will swing to the East or to the West...' To drive nationalism back, he maintained, would be to drive it to communism. Cohen, in his book, *British Policy in Changing Africa*, published in 1959, asserted that 'successful cooperation with nationalism is our greatest bulwark against communism.'

Chapter Fourteen: Blundell provides a vivid personal account. Also, MacDonald and Murray-Brown. MacDonald notes about Kenyatta's government: 'One of Kenyatta's most serious errors is his tacit assent to the acquisitiveness of some of his Ministers and civil servants. Soon after attaining power they began to buy (with money gained by dubious means) large houses, farms, cars and other possessions. This development not only tainted his administration with a reputation for corruption, but also produced a wide division between rich and poor—the governors were a conspicuous privileged class.'

Chapter Fifteen: For the demise of the Federation, Blake, Macmillan, Rotberg, Short and Welensky. Welensky wrote of Macleod: 'From our first meeting on the tarmac at the airport (in Salisbury in March, 1960) until the moment he left the Colonial Office eighteen months later, I found Iain Macleod a very difficult man to get on terms with and to understand. I doubt if we ever talked the same language. He seemed to believe that he had a great and challenging mission, which he was ruthless in carrying out... To me his mixture of cold calculation, sudden gushes of undisciplined emotion and ignorance of Africa was perplexing and discouraging.' Also, the Report of the Advisory Commission on the Review of the Constitution of Rhodesia and Nyasaland (*The Monckton Report*) Cmd 1148, 1960.

Chapter Sixteen: Hall relates the tea-tent incident in Lusaka. Also, Alport, Fisher, Macmillan and Welensky.

Chapter Seventeen: Hoskyns provides a detailed account of the Congo during 1960 and 1961. Kalb uncovers the American role. Also useful is the Report of the Senate committee investigating the CIA: Alleged Assassination Plots Involving Foreign Leaders, an Interim Report on Intelligence Activities, United State Senate, Washington, U.S. Government Printing Office, 1975. Gérard-Libois deals with Katanga's secession; O'Brien writes vividly about his role there. There are at least fifteen different accounts of Lumumba's murder. Heinz and Donnay have made a summary of them. Dayal's personal account is useful; it includes a striking portrait of Mobutu in Léopoldville in 1960.

Chapter Eighteen: Blake provides an erudite history of Rhodesia up to UDI. Also useful are Barber, Bowman and Clements.

Chapter Nineteen: Several writers, as well as Dumont, depict the scramble for power and wealth that followed independence, among them, the distinguished West Indian economist, W. Arthur Lewis: 'What is going on in some of these countries is fully explained in terms of the normal lust of human beings for power and wealth. The stakes are high. Office carries power, prestige and money. The power is incredible. Men who claim to be democrats in fact behave like emperors. Personifying the state, they dress themselves up in uniforms, build themselves palaces, bring all other traffic to a standstill when they drive, hold fancy parades. The money is incredible. Salaries, allowances, travelling expenses, fringe benefits, vast opportunities for pickings in bribes, state contracts, commissions. To be a Minister is to have a lifetime's chance to make a fortune.' The Zanzibar revolution is covered by Clayton and Lofchie. Soglo, Bokassa and Lamizana had known each other since they served in Indochina.

Chapter Twenty: Opinions about Nkrumah remain as sharply divided years after his death as they were during his lifetime. Several people to whom the author spoke remembered him warmly. Michael Shea, a former British Foreign Office official: 'He was very charming. The feeling when he walked into a room was electric. He was enlightened; he was intelligent; he was a most charismatic figure; he had great style.' A sympathetic account is given by Davidson. Genoveva Marais, in her memoir, *Kwame Nkrumah as I knew him* (Janay, Chichester, 1972) recalled: 'The more successful he was politically, the less he seemed capable of trusting his most intimate friends, no matter how loyal they had proved themselves to be. He became so immersed in his own isolation that he withdrew from most people. Instead, he gained the support of party activists who only told him what they thought he wanted to know, to enhance his feelings of superiority.' Jones gives a detached account of Nkrumah's last years. Afrifa and Ocran deal with the army's seizure of power.

Chapter Twenty-one: The prelude to civil war is covered by Luckham, Mackintosh, Miners, Schwarz. St. Jorre gives the best overall account. Stremlau examines international involvement. Crowder provides a standard history of Nigeria.

Chapter Twenty-two: Personal accounts are of most interest: Grahame, a former British army officer who knew Amin well; Kyemba, a former minister in Amin's government; Mutesa and Ibingira. Avirgan and Honey give an eyewitness account of the Tanzanian invasion.

Chapter Twenty-three: In Ghana in 1967, a 27-year-old army lieutenant, Sam Arthur, finding himself in temporary command of an armoured car unit, decided on an attempt to seize power because, he later confessed, he wanted to 'make history' by being the first lieutenant successfully to organize a coup. The coup attempt was given the name 'Operation Guitar Boy'. The armoured car unit drove into Accra but failed to gain control.

Chapter Twenty-four: On the Ethiopian revolution: Gilkes; Halliday and Molyneux; Markakis and Ayele; Ottoway. On Eritrea: Erlich provides a concise, historical account. On Somalia: Drysdale; Lewis. On the Horn: Farer; Marina Ottoway; Selassie.

Chapter Twenty-five: Newitt provides an overall account of the Portuguese territories. On Guinea-Bissau: Chabal; Davidson. On Mozambique: Henrikson; Munslow. On Angola, Marcum's two volumes provide an exhaustive study; Stockwell, the head of the CIA Angola Task Force, discloses American manoeuvres; Klinghoffer examines foreign involvement.

Chapter Twenty-six: The UDI years are based mainly on Meredith; Martin gives Zanu's perspective on the war; Caute looks caustically at the whites in the last years of Rhodesia.

Chapter Twenty-eight: The World Bank's 1981 report provides a valuable summary. A progress report was issued in 1983.

Select Bibliography

Abrahams, Peter, *A Wreath for Udomo*, Faber, London, 1956.
—*The Blacks*, in *An African Treasury*, ed. Langston Hughes, Gollancz, London, 1961.
Abshire, David, and Samuels, Michael, (eds.), *Portuguese Africa: A Handbook*, Pall Mall Press, London, 1969.
Adamolekun, 'Ladipo, *Sékou Touré's Guinea*, Methuen, London, 1976.
Afrifa, Col. A. A., *The Ghana Coup*, Cass, London, 1966.
Ajayi, J. F. A., and Crowder, Michael, (eds.), *History of West Africa*, Volume 2, Longman, London, 1974.
Albright, David E., (ed.), *Africa and International Communism*, Macmillan, London, 1980.
Alexander, H. T., *African Tightrope*, Pall Mall Press, London, 1965.
Allen, Charles, *Tales from the Dark Continent*, Deutsch, London, 1979.
Alport, Lord, *The Sudden Assignment*, Hodder and Stoughton, London, 1965.
Amin, Samir, *Neo-Colonialism in West Africa*, Penguin, London, 1973.
Anstey, Roger, *King Leopold's Legacy: The Congo under Belgian Rule, 1908–1960*, Oxford University Press, 1966.
Apter, David E., *Ghana in Transition;* Second Revised Edition, Princeton University Press, 1972.
Attwood, William, *The Reds and the Blacks, A Personal Adventure*, Hutchinson, London, 1967.
Austin, Dennis, *Politics in Ghana, 1946–1960*, Oxford University Press, 1964.
—*Politics in Africa*, Manchester University Press, 1977.
Avirgan, Tony, and Honey, Martha, *War in Uganda: The Legacy of Idi Amin*, Lawrence Hill, Westport, 1982.
Awolowo, Obafemi, *Path to Nigerian Freedom*, Faber, London, 1947.
—*Awo: The Autobiography of Chief Obafemi Awolowo*, Cambridge University Press, 1960.
Azikiwe, Nnamdi, *My Odyssey, An Autobiography*, Hurst, London, 1970.
Barber, James. *Rhodesia: The Road to Rebellion*, Oxford University Press, 1967.
Barnett, D. L., and Karari, Njama, *Mau Mau from Within*, Macgibbon and Kee, London, 1966.
Bello, Sir Ahmadu, the Sardauna of Sokoto, *My Life*, Cambridge University Press, 1962.
Bender, Gerald, J., *Angola under the Portuguese: The Myth and the Reality*, Heinemann, London, 1978.

Bennett, George, *Kenya: A Political History*, Oxford University Press, 1963.
Beshir, Nohamed Omer, *The Southern Sudan: Background to Conflict*, Hurst, London, 1968.
—*The Southern Sudan: From Conflict to Peace*, Hurst, London, 1975.
Blake, Robert, *A History of Rhodesia*, Eyre Methuen, London, 1977.
Blundell, Sir Michael, *So rough a wind*, Weidenfeld and Nicolson, London, 1964.
Bourret, F. M., *Ghana: The Road to Independence, 1919–1957*, Oxford University Press, 1960.
Bowman, Larry, *Politics in Rhodesia; White Power in an African State*, Harvard University Press, 1973.
Brausch, Georges, *Belgian Administration in the Congo*, Oxford University Press, 1960.
Bretton, Henry L., *The Rise and Fall of Kwame Nkrumah*, Pall Mall Press, London, 1966.
—*Power and Politics in Africa*, Longman, London, 1973.
Brockway, Fenner, *African Journeys*, Gollancz, London, 1955.
Butler, Lord, *The Art of the Possible*, Hamish Hamilton, London, 1971.
Cabral, Amilcar, *Revolution in Guiné*, Stage One, London, 1969.
Carrington, C. E., *The Liquidation of the British Empire*, Harrap, London, 1961.
Cartwright, John, *Political Leadership in Sierra Leone*, Croom Helm, London, 1978.
—*Political Leadership in Africa*, St. Martin's Press, New York, 1983.
Caute, David, *Under the Skin; The Death of White Rhodesia*, Allen Lane, London, 1983.
Centre d'Etude d'Afrique Noire, Institut d'Etude Politique de Bordeaux (ed.), *La Politique Africaines du General de Gaulle*, Pedone, 1980.
Chabal, Patrick, *Amilcar Cabral: Revolutionary leadership and people's war*, Cambridge University Press, 1983.
Clapham, Christopher, *Haile-Selassie's Government*, Longman, London, 1969.
Clayton, Anthony, *The Zanzibar Revolution and its Aftermath*, Hurst, London, 1981.
Clements, Frank, *Rhodesia: The Course to Collision*, Pall Mall Press, London, 1969.
Cohen, Sir Andrew, *British Policy in Changing Africa*, Routledge & Kegan Paul, London, 1959.
Coleman, James, *Nigeria, Background to Nationalism*, University of California Press, 1958.
Coleman, James, and Rosberg, Carl G., (eds.), *Political Parties and National Integration in Tropical Africa*, University of California Press, 1966.
Colvin, Ian, *The Rise and Fall of Moise Tshombe*, Frewin, London, 1968.
Corfield, F. D., *Historical Survey of the Origins and Growth of Mau Mau*, HMSO, London, 1960.
Coulson, Andrew, *Tanzania: A Political Economy*, Clarendon Press, Oxford, 1982.

Cox, Richard, *Kenyatta's Country*, Hutchinson, London, 1965.
Cox, Thomas S., *Civil-Military Relations in Sierra Leone*, Harvard University Press, 1976.
Creech Jones, Arthur, 'The Labour Party and Colonial Policy, 1945–51', in *New Fabian Colonial Essays*, The Hogarth Press, London, 1959.
Cross, Colin, *The Fall of the British Empire, 1918–1968*, Hodder and Stoughton, London, 1968.
Crowder, Michael, *West Africa Under Colonial Rule*, Hutchinson, London, 1968.
—'Independence as a Goal in French West African Politics', in William H. Lewis (ed.), *French-speaking Africa: The Search for Identity*, Walker, New York, 1965.
—*The Story of Nigeria*, Fourth Edition, Faber, London, 1978.
Davidson, Basil, *The African Awakening*, Cape, London, 1955.
—*In the Eye of the Storm: Angola's People*, Longman, London, 1972.
—*Black Star: A View of the Life and Times of Kwame Nkrumah*, Allen Lane, London, 1973.
—*Africa in Modern History*, Allen Lane, London, 1978.
—*No Fist is big enough to hide the sky*. Zed Press, London, 1981.
Davister, Pierre, *Katanga: enjeu du monde*, Editions Europe-Afrique, 1960.
Dayal, Rajeshwar, *Mission for Hammarskjold: The Congo Crisis*, Oxford University Press, 1976.
Decalo, Samuel, *Coups and Army Rule in Africa: Studies in Military Style*, Yale University Press, 1976.
Delavignette, Robert, *French Colonial Policy in Black Africa*, in *Colonialism in Africa*, Volume 2, ed. Gann and Duignan, Cambridge University Press, 1970.
Delf, George, *Jomo Kenyatta*, Gollancz, London, 1949.
Deschamps, Hubert, 'France in Black Africa and Madagascar between 1920 and 1945', in *Colonialism in Africa*, Volume 2, ed. Gann and Duignan, Cambridge University Press, 1970.
Douglas-Home, Charles, *Evelyn Baring: The Last Proconsul*, Collins, London, 1978.
Drysdale, John, *The Somali Dispute*, Pall Mall Press, London, 1964.
Duffy. James, *Portuguese Africa*, Harvard University Press, 1959.
—*Portugual in Africa*, Penguin, London, 1962.
Dumont, René, *L'Afrique Noire Est Mal Partie*, Le Seuil, Paris, 1962.
—(*False Start in Africa*, Deutsch, London, 1966).
Dumont, René, and Mottin, Marie-France, *L'Afrique Étranglée*, Editions du Seuil, Paris, 1980.
—(*Stranglehold on Africa*, Deutsch, London, 1983).
Dunn, John, (ed.), *West African States: Failure and Promise*, Cambridge University Press, 1978.
Erlich, Haggai, *The Struggle over Eritrea, 1962–1978; War and Revolution in the Horn of Africa*, Hoover Institution Press, Stanford, California, 1983.
Eprile, Cecil, *War and Peace in the Sudan, 1955–1972*, David and Charles,

Newton Abbot, Devon, 1974.

Farer, Tom J., *War Clouds on the Horn of Africa: The Widening Storm*, Second Revised Edition, Carnegie Endowment for International Peace, Washington, 1979.

Farson, Negley, *Last Chance in Africa*, Gollancz, London, 1949.

First, Ruth, *The Barrel of a Gun: Political Power in Africa and the Coup d'Etat*, Allen Lane, London, 1970.

Fisher, Nigel, *Iain Macleod*, Deutsch, London, 1973.

Franklin, Harry, *Unholy Wedlock: The Failure of the Central African Federation*, Allen and Unwin, London, 1963.

Galvão, Henrique, *Santa Maria: My Crusade for Portugal*, Weidenfeld and Nicolson, London, 1961.

Gann, L. H., and Duignan, Peter, (eds.), *Colonialism in Africa, 1870–1960; Volume 2:* The History and Politics of Colonialism, 1914–1960, Cambridge University Press, 1970.

—*Burden of Empire: An Appraisal of Western Colonialism South of the Sahara*, Hoover Institution Press, Stanford, California, 1977.

—(eds.) *African Proconsuls: European Governors in Africa*, The Free Press, New York, 1978.

—*Africa South of the Sahara: The Challenge to Western Security*, Hoover Institution Press, Stanford, California, 1981.

Gavshon, Arthur, *Crisis in Africa: Battleground of East and West*, Penguin, London, 1981.

Geiss, Emanuel, *The Pan-African Movement*, Methuen, London, 1974.

Gérad-Libois, Jules, *Sécession au Katanga*, CRISP, Brussels, 1963. (*Katanga Secession*, University of Wisconsin Press, 1966):

Gertzel, Cherry, *The Politics of Independent Kenya 1963–8*, Heinemann, London, 1970.

Gifford, Prosser, and Louis, Wm. Roger, (eds.), *The Transfer of Power in Africa: Decolonization, 1940–1960*, Yale University Press, 1982.

Gilkes, Patrick, *The Dying Lion: Feudalism and Modernization in Ethiopia*, Friedmann, London, 1975.

Goldsworthy, David, *Colonial Issues in British Politics, 1945–1961*, Clarendon Press, Oxford, 1971.

—*Tom Mboya: The Man Kenya wanted to forget*, Heinemann, London, 1982.

Gould, David, *Bureaucratic Corruption and Underdevelopment in the Third World: The Case of Zaire*, Pergamon, New York, 1980.

Grahame, Iain, *Amin and Uganda*; A Personal Memoir, Granada, London, 1980.

Gran, Guy, (ed.), *Zaire: The Political Economy Of Underdevelopment*, Praeger, New York, 1979.

Greenfield, Richard, *Ethiopia: A new Political History*, Pall Mall Press, London, 1965.

Grundy, Kenneth, W., *Conflicting Images of the Military in Africa*, East African Publishing House, Nairobi, 1968.

Gunther, John, *Inside Africa*, Hamish Hamilton, London, 1955.

Gutteridge, W. F., *The Military In African Politics*, Methuen, London,

1969.
—*Military Regimes in Africa*, Methuen, London, 1975.
Hailey, W. M., *An African Survey: A Study of Problems Arising in Africa South of the Sahara*, Oxford University Press, 1938, Revised 1956, London, 1957.
—*Native Administration in the British African Territories*, HMSO, London , 1950–53.
—*Native Administration and Political Development in British Tropical Africa (1940–1942)*, Nendeln, Liechtenstein, 1979.
Hall, Richard, *The High Price of Principles: Kaunda and the White South*, Hodder and Stoughton, London, 1969.
Halliday, Fred, and Molyneux, Maxine, *The Ethiopian Revolution*, Verso, London, 1981.
Hargreaves, John, *The End of Colonial Rule in West Africa*, Macmillan, London, 1979.
Hatch, John, *A History of Postwar Africa*, Deutsch, London, 1965.
—*The History of Britain in Africa*, Deutsch, London, 1969.
—*Africa Emergent*, Secker and Warburg, London, 1974.
Heinz, G., and Donnay, H., *Patrice Lumumba: Les cinquantes derniers jours de sa vie*, CRISP, Brussels, 1966.
Henderson, Ian, and Goodhart Philip, *The Hunt for Kimathi*, Hamish Hamilton, London, 1958.
Henderson, Lawrence W., *Angola: Five Centuries of Conflict*, Cornell University Press, 1979.
Henriksen, Thomas H., *Mozambique: A History*, Collins, London, 1978.
—*Revolution and Counterrevolution; Mozambique's War of Independence, 1964–74*, Greenwood Press, Westport, Connecticut, 1983.
Hoare, Mike, *Congo Mercenary*, Hale, London, 1978.
Hodgkin, Thomas, *Nationalism in Colonial Africa*, Muller, London, 1956.
Hooker, James R., *Black Revolutionary: George Padmore's Path from Communism to Pan-Africanism*, Pall Mall Press, London, 1967.
Hoskyns, Catherine, *The Congo since Independence, January 1960–December 1961*, Oxford University Press, 1965.
Hutchinson, Alan, *China's African Revolution*, Hutchinson, London, 1975.
Ibingira, Grace Stuart, *African Upheavals Since Independence*, Westview Press, Boulder, Colorado, 1980.
Itote, Waruhiu, *'Mau Mau' General*, East African Publishing House, Nairobi, 1967.
Jackson, Robert H., and Rosberg, Carl G., *Personal Rule in Black Africa: Prince, Autocrat, Prophet, Tyrant*, University of California Press, 1982.
Jeffries, Sir Charles, *Transfer of Power*, Pall Mall Press, London, 1960.
Jones, Trevor, *Ghana's First Republic, 1960–1966*, Methuen, London, 1976.
Kaggia, Bildad, *Roots of Freedom*, East African Publishing House, Nairobi, 1968.
Kalb, Madeleine G., *The Congo Cables: The Cold War in Africa—From Eisenhower to Kennedy*, Macmillan, New York, 1982.
Kalck, Pierre, *Central African Republic: A Failure in Decolonisation*, Pall

Mall Press, London, 1971.

Kanza, Thomas, *The Rise and Fall of Patrice Lumumba*, Collins, London, 1978.

Kapuscinski. Ryszard, *The Emperor: Downfall of an Autocrat*, Quartet, London, 1983.

Kariuki, J. M., *'Mau Mau' Detainee*, Oxford University Press, 1963.

Kenyatta, Jomo, *Suffering Without Bitterness*, East African Publishing House, Nairobi, 1968.

Kirk-Greene, A. H. M., (ed.), *The Transfer of Power: The Colonial Administrator in the Age of Decolonisation*, University of Oxford, 1979.

—'Stay by your radios'; *Documentation for a study of military government in Tropical Africa*, African Studies Centre, Cambridge; Afrika–Studiecentrum, Leiden, 1981.

Kirk-Greene, Anthony, and Rimmer, Douglas, *Nigeria since 1970: A political and economic outline*, Hodder and Stoughton, London, 1981.

Kirkman, W. P., *Unscrambling an Empire: A Critique of British Colonial Policy, 1956–1966*, Chatto and Windus, London, 1966.

Kitson, Frank, *Gangs and counter-gangs*, Barrie and Rockliff, London, 1960.

Klinghoffer, Arthur Jay, *The Angolan War: A Study in Soviet Policy in the Third World*, Westview Press, Boulder, Colorado, 1980.

Kyemba, Henry, *State of Blood*, Corgi, London, 1977.

Lacouture, Jean, *Cinq Hommes et la France*, Le Seuil, Paris, 1961.

Lamb, David, *The Africans: Encounters from the Sudan to the Cape*, Bodley Head, London, 1983.

Langley, J. Ayodele, *Pan-Africanism and Nationalism in West Africa, 1900–1945*, Clarendon Press, Oxford, 1973.

Larkin, Bruce D., *China and Africa, 1949–1970*, University of California Press, 1971.

Lee, J. M., *Colonial Development and Good Government*, Clarendon Press, Oxford, 1967.

—*African Armies and Civil Order*, Chatto and Windus, London, 1969.

Legum, Colin, *Pan-Africanism, A Short Political Guide* (Rev. ed.), Pall Mall Press, London, 1965.

Legvold, Robert, *Soviet Policy in West Africa*, Harvard University Press, 1970.

Lemarchand, René, *Political Awakening in the Belgian Congo*, University of California Press, 1964.

—*Rwanda and Burundi*, Pall Mall Press, London, 1970.

Lewis, I. M., *A Modern History of Somalia: Nation and State in the Horn of Africa*, Longman, London, 1980.

—(ed.), *Nationalism and Self-Determination In the Horn of Africa*, Ithaca Press, London, 1983.

Lewis, W. Arthur, *Politics in West Africa*, Allen and Unwin, London, 1965.

Leys, Colin, *European Politics in Southern Rhodesia*, Oxford University Press, 1959.

—*Underdevelopment in Kenya: The Political Economy of Neo-Colonialism*,

Heinemann, London, 1975.
Listowel, Judith, *Amin*, IUP, London, 1973.
Lofchie, Michael, *Zanzibar: Background to Revolution*, Princeton University Press, 1965.
Louis, William Roger, *Imperialism at Bay, 1941–1945: The United States and the decolonisation of the British Empire*, Oxford University Press, 1977.
Luckham, Robin, *The Nigerian Military, A Sociological Analysis of Authority and Revolt, 1960–1967*, Cambridge University Press, 1971.
Lumumba, Patrice, *Le Congo, terre d'avenir,—est-il menacé?*, Office de Publicité SA., Brussels, 1961.
—(*Congo, My Country*, Pall Mall Press with Barrie and Rockliff, London, 1962)
Lusignan, Guy de, *French-Speaking Africa Since Independence*, Pall Mall Press, London, 1969.
MacDonald, Malcolm, *Titans & Others*, Collins, London, 1972.
Mackintosh, John P., et al, *Nigerian Government and Politics*, Northwestern University Press, Evanston, 1966.
Macmillan, Harold, *Pointing the Way*, Macmillan, London, 1972.
—*At the End of the Day*, Macmillan, London, 1973.
Majdalany, Fred, *State of Emergency*, Longman, London, 1962.
Makonnen, Ras, *Pan-Africanism from Within*: edited by Kenneth King, Oxford University Press, Nairobi, 1973.
Marcum, John, *The Angolan Revolution: Vol. 1. The Anatomy of an Explosion (1950–1962). Vol. 2. Exile Politics and Guerrilla Warfare (1962–1976)*, MIT Press, Cambridge.
Markakis, John, *Ethiopia: Anatomy of a Traditional Polity*, Clarendon Press, Oxford, 1974.
Markakis, John, and Ayele, Nega, *Class and Revolution in Ethiopia*, Spokesman, Nottingham, for *Review of African Political Economy, 1978*.
Marnham, Patrick, *Fantastic Invasion*, Cape, London, 1980.
Martin, David, *General Amin*, Faber, London, 1974.
Martin, David, and Johnson, Phyllis, *The Struggle for Zimbabwe: The Chimurenga War*, Faber, London, 1981.
Mason, Philip, *Year of Decision: Rhodesia and Nyasaland in 1960*, Oxford University Press, 1960.
Matthews, Ronald, *African Powder Keg*, Bodley Head, London, 1966.
Mayall, James, *Africa: The Cold War and After*, Elek Books, London, 1971.
Mazrui, Ali, *Soldiers and Kinsmen in Uganda: The Making of a Military Ethnocracy*, Sage Publications, Beverly Hills, 1975.
—*The African Condition*, Heinemann, London, 1980.
Mboya, Tom, *Freedom and After*, Deutsch, London, 1963.
Meredith, Martin, *The Past Is Another Country; Rhodesia: UDI to Zimbabwe*, Pan, London, 1980.
Merriam, Alan, *Congo: Background to Conflict*, Northwestern University Press, 1961.
Miners, N. J., *The Nigerian Army, 1956–1966*, Methuen, London, 1971.
Mitchell, Sir Philip, *African Afterthoughts*, Hutchinson, London, 1954.

Mittleman, James H., *Ideology and Politics in Uganda*, Cornell University Press, 1975.

Mondlane, Eduardo, *The Struggle for Mozambique*, Penguin, London, 1969.

Morgenthau, Ruth Schachter, *Political Parties in French-speaking West Africa*, Clarendon Press, Oxford, 1964.

Morison, David, *The USSR and Africa*, Oxford University Press, 1964.

Morris, James, *Farewell the Trumpets: an Imperial Retreat*, Faber, London, 1978.

Morris-Jones, W. H., and Fischer, G., (eds.), *Decolonisation and After: The British and French Experience*, Cass, London, 1980.

Mortimer, Edward, *France and the Africans, 1944–1960*, Faber, London, 1969.

Munslow, Barry, *Mozambique: The Revolution and its Origins*, Longman, London, 1983.

Murray-Brown, Jeremy, *Kenyatta*, Allen and Unwin, London, 1972.

Mutesa II, the Kabaka of Buganda, *Desecration of my Kingdom*, Constable, London, 1967.

Naipaul, Shiva, *North of South: An African Journey*, Deutsch, London, 1978.

Newitt, Malyn, *Portugal in Africa*, Hurst, London, 1981.

Nkrumah, Kwame, *Ghana: The autobiography of Kwame Nkrumah*, Nelson, London, 1957.

—*I Speak of Freedom: A Statement of African Ideology*, Heinemann, London, 1961.

Nyerere, Julius, *Freedom and Unity*, Oxford University Press, 1967.

O'Brien, Conor Cruise, *To Katanga and Back*, Hutchinson, London, 1962.

Ocran, Maj. Gen. A. K., *A Myth is Broken: An Account of the Ghana Coup d'Etat of 24th February 1966*, Longman, London, 1968.

Odinga, Oginga, *Not yet Uhuru*, Heinemann, London, 1967.

Ogunsanwo, Alaba, *China's Policy in Africa, 1958–1971*, Cambridge University Press, 1974.

Okello, John, *Revolution in Zanzibar*, East African Publishing House, Nairobi, 1967.

Ottley, Roi, *No Green Pastures*, Murray, London, 1952.

Ottoway, Marina, and David, *Ethiopia: Empire in Revolution*, Africana Publishing, New York, 1978.

—*Afrocommunism*, Africana Publishing, New York, 1981.

Ottoway, Marina, *Soviet and American Influence in the Horn of Africa*, Praeger, New York, 1982.

Padmore, George, (ed.), *Colonial and Coloured Unity, a Programme of Action: History of the Pan-African Congress*, Panaf Services, Manchester, 1947; reprinted by Hammersmith Bookshop, London, 1963.

—*Pan-Africanism or Communism*? Dobson, London, 1956.

Pearce, R. D., *The Turning Point in Africa: British Colonial Policy, 1938–1948*, Cass, London, 1982.

Perham, Margery, *The Colonial Reckoning*, Collins, London, 1961.

—*Colonial Sequence, 1930 to 1949*, Methuen, London, 1967.

—*Colonial Sequence, 1949 to 1969*, Methuen, London, 1970.
Pinkey, Robert, *Ghana under Military Rule, 1966–1969*, Methuen, London, 1972.
Pratt, Cranford, *The critical phase in Tanzania, 1945–1968: Nyerere and the Emergence of a Socialist Strategy*, Cambridge University Press, 1976.
Reed, David, *111 Days in Stanleyville*, Collins, London, 1966.
Rivière, Claude, *Guinea: The Mobilisation of a People*, Cornell University Press, 1977.
Robertson, Sir James, *Transition in Africa: From Direct Rule to Independence*, Hurst, London, 1974.
Robinson, Kenneth, *The Dilemmas of Trusteeship*, Oxford University Press, 1965.
Rooney, David, *Sir Charles Arden-Clarke*, Collins, London, 1982.
Rosberg, Carl G., and Nottingham, John, *The Myth of Mau Mau*, Praeger, New York, 1966.
Rosberg, Carl G., and Callaghy, Thomas M., *Socialism in Sub-Saharan Africa*, University of California, 1979.
Rotberg, Robert I., *The rise of Nationalism in Central Africa: The making of Malawi and Zambia, 1873–1964*, Harvard University Press, 1966.
Rotberg, Robert I., and Mazrui, Ali A., (eds.), *Protest and Power in Black Africa*, Oxford University Press, New York, 1970.
Sampson, Anthony, *Macmillan: A Study in Ambiguity*, Allen Lane, London, 1967.
Sanger, Clyde, *Central African Emergency*, Heinemann, London, 1960.
Scott, Ian, *Tumbled House: The Congo at Independence*, Oxford University Press, 1969.
Schwarz, Walter, *Nigeria*, Pall Mall Press, London, 1968.
Selassie, Bereket Habte, *Conflict and Intervention in the Horn of Africa*, Monthly Review Press, New York, 1980.
Shamuyarira, Nathan, *Crisis in Rhodesia*, Deutsch, London, 1965.
Sherman, Richard, *Eritrea: The Unfinished Revolution*, Praeger, New York, 1980.
Short, Philip, *Banda*, Routledge and Kegan Paul, London, 1974.
Slade, Ruth, *The Belgian Congo*, Oxford University Press, 1960.
Slater, Montagu, *The Trial of Jomo Kenyatta*, Secker and Warburg, London, 1955.
Smith, William E., *We Must Run While They Walk: A portrait of Africa's Julius Nyerere*, Random House, New York, 1971.
Stevens, Christopher, *The Soviet Union and Black Africa*, Macmillan, London, 1976.
St. Jorre, John de, *The Nigerian Civil War*, Hodder and Stoughton, London, 1972.
Stockwell, John, *In Search of Enemies: A CIA Story*, Deutsch, London, 1978.
Stremlau, John, *The International Politics of the Nigerian Civil War, 1967–1970*, Princeton University Press, 1977.
Thompson, Virginia, and Adloff, Richard, *French West Africa*, Allen and Unwin, London, 1958.

—*The Emerging States of French Equatorial Africa*, Oxford University Press, 1960.

—*Conflict in Chad*, Hurst, London, 1981.

Thompson, W. Scott, *Ghana's Foreign Policy 1957–1966*, Princeton University Press, 1969.

Timothy, Bankole, *Kwame Nkrumah. From cradle to grave*, Gavin Press, Dorchester, 1981.

Tuinder, Bastiaan A. den, *Ivory Coast: The Challenge of Success*, John Hopkins University Press, 1978.

Urfer, Sylvain, *Une Afrique socialiste: la Tanzanie*, Editions ouvrières, Paris, 1976.

Viard, René, *La Fin de l'Empire Colonial Français*, Maisonneuve et Larose, Paris, 1963.

Vos, Pierre de, *Vie et Mort de Lumumba*, Calmann-Lévy, Paris, 1961.

Wallerstein, Immanuel, *Africa: The Politics of Independence*, Vintage Books, New York, 1961.

Wasserman, Gary, *Politics of Decolonisation: Kenya Europeans and the Land Issue, 1960–1965*, Cambridge University Press, 1976.

Welensky, Roy, *Welensky's 4000 Days: The Life and Death of the Federation of Rhodesia and Nyasaland*, Collins, London, 1964.

Weissman, Stephen R., *American Foreign Policy in the Congo, 1960–1964*, Cornell University Press, 1974.

Wheeler, Douglas L., and Pélissier, René, *Angola*, Pall Mall Press, London, 1971.

Whitaker, Jennifer Seymour, (ed.), *Africa and the United States; Vital Interests*, New York University Press, for the Council on Foreign Relations, 1978.

White, Dorothy Shipley, *Black Africa and de Gaulle: From the French Empire to Independence*, Pennsylvania State University Press, 1979.

Williams, T. David, *Malawi: The Politics of Despair*, Cornell University Press, 1978.

Wilson, Edward, *Russia and Black Africa before World War II*, Holmes and Meier, New York, 1974.

Wilson, Harold, *A Personal Record: The Labour Government, 1964–1970*, Michael Joseph, Weidenfeld and Nicolson, London, 1971.

Wolfers, Michael, and Bergerol, Jane, *Angola in the Frontline*; Zed Press, London, 1976.

Wolfers Michael, and Bergerol, Jane, *Angola in the Frontline*, Zed Press, London, 1983.

World Bank, *An Agenda for Action: Accelerated Development in Sub-Saharan Africa*, Washington, 1981.

Woronoff, Jon, *West African Wager: Houphouet versus Nkrumah*, Scarecrow Press, Metuchen, N.J., 1972.

Young, Crawford, *Politics in the Congo: Decolonisation and Independence*, Princeton University Press, 1965.

—*Ideology and Development in Africa*, Yale University Press, 1982.

Young, Kenneth, *Rhodesia and Independence*, Eyre and Spottiswoode, London, 1967.

Index